CHORUS
OF THE
UNION

CHORUS
OF THE
UNION

HOW ABRAHAM LINCOLN
AND STEPHEN DOUGLAS SET ASIDE
THEIR RIVALRY TO SAVE THE NATION

EDWARD ROBERT
McCLELLAND

PEGASUS BOOKS
NEW YORK LONDON

CHORUS OF THE UNION

Pegasus Books, Ltd.
148 West 37th Street, 13th Floor
New York, NY 10018

First Pegasus Books cloth edition June 2024

Interior design by Maria Fernandez

Library of Congress Cataloging-in-Publication Data is available.

ISBN: 978-1-63936-637-8

10 9 8 7 6 5 4 3 2 1

Printed in the United States of America
Distributed by Simon & Schuster
www.pegasusbooks.com

To my children: Lark, Birch, and Rose

CONTENTS

CHAPTER 1

THE HOMECOMING

Tremont House, Chicago, Illinois, July 9, 1858

S tephen Arnold Douglas liked to make a grand entrance, especially when returning to his hometown after so many months in the capital. Since the U.S. Senate's adjournment on June 14, Douglas had taken nearly four weeks to travel from Washington to Chicago. He stopped first in New York City, to secure a $40,000 loan for his reelection campaign from the city's Democratic mayor, Fernando Wood. Then he spent the Fourth of July with his mother in Clifton Springs, New York, where she lived with her second husband, the man she married after Douglas's father died when his only son was just two months old.

Douglas arrived in Chicago in a style befitting the senior senator from the state of Illinois. Douglas was the best-known politician in America, after only President Buchanan himself, and the most controversial, as the sponsor of the Kansas-Nebraska Act and the leading exponent of popular sovereignty, the right of settlers to decide for themselves whether to allow slavery in the territories.

From Clifton Springs, Douglas rode the New York and Erie Railroad to Buffalo, then the Lake Shore Railway to Cleveland, before finally boarding the Michigan Southern for Chicago. The senator and his party disembarked in La Porte, Indiana, and bounded across the sand dunes in a carriage to meet a party of four hundred followers in Michigan City. Douglas did not want to end his journey at the "shabby" Michigan Southern depot. He wanted to come home to Chicago at Great Central Station, on the corner of South Water Street and Michigan Avenue. Great Central Station was the grandest building in this growing city—an enormous stone structure with a terraced roof and three Romanesque archways to admit the hundred trains arriving daily in Chicago. It was close to the Tremont House, the city's fanciest hotel, where, that night, Douglas planned to make the first speech of his campaign for a third term in the Senate.

This time, he would have a serious opponent: in an unprecedented move, since senators were elected by the legislature, not the populace, the Illinois Republican Party had nominated Abraham Lincoln for U.S. Senate at its June 16 convention in Springfield. Douglas and Lincoln had known each other for nearly a quarter century, since their days as young members of the Illinois legislature—Douglas a Democrat, Lincoln a Whig. While Douglas advanced rapidly in politics, elected to the Senate at age thirty-three, Lincoln served only a single term in the House of Representatives before returning to the obscure life of a railroad lawyer. A lifelong hater of slavery, Lincoln was drawn back into politics by his opposition to the Kansas-Nebraska Act. He made a reputation for himself as the state's leading "anti-Nebraska man"—and therefore its leading anti-Douglas man. At the state Republican convention, Lincoln told the delegates, in what became known as his "House Divided" speech, "I believe this government cannot endure, permanently, half slave and half free. I do not expect the Union to be dissolved—I do not expect the house to fall—but I do expect it will cease to be divided. It will become all one thing or all the other."

Douglas respected Lincoln's oratorical skills and believed he was the toughest opponent the Republicans could have fielded against him.

"I shall have my hands full," Douglas told his friend and ally John W. Forney, a Pennsylvania journalist who would become secretary of the Senate. "He is the strong man of his party—full of wit, facts, dates—and the best stump speaker, with his droll ways and dry jokes, in the West."

When Douglas had first made the journey from New York to Illinois, twenty-five years earlier, as an ambitious young man seeking his fortune in the barely settled West, he traveled by lake steamer and stagecoach. Then, it took twelve days to cover the distance between the Eastern Seaboard and the Northwest. Now, on the nation's newly forged network of railroads, it took two. It was a connection that Douglas, as much as any politician, could claim credit for building.

Great Central Station was a symbol of Douglas's achievements as a rail builder. The station was owned by the Illinois Central Railroad. Created in 1851 by a bill Douglas passed through the Senate, the Illinois Central was the world's longest rail line, stretching from Cairo, at the southern end of the state, to Galena, in its northwest extremity.

Once the special senatorial train rocked to a halt, Douglas emerged and climbed into a carriage, which would become the opulent caboose for a brassy, clamorous parade to the Tremont House. Douglas was a short, stout man, only five feet four inches tall, but he was nicknamed the Little Giant, because his broad chest and oversized head suggested concentrated power—a physical presence magnified by a bass voice powerful enough to reach the ears of the crowd of thousands he was about to address. In an era of dandyish politicians, Douglas dressed the part, wearing a blue frock coat with silver buttons, and hair swept up into a pompadour that may have added an inch or two to his height—always a point of anxiety with the senator, who sometimes tried to conceal his stature by standing behind a table during speeches, hiding his stumpy legs.

Douglas's return to Chicago was heralded by a 150-gun salute in Dearborn Park. Then a procession, led by the German Turnverein Band and two companies of militia, the Emmet Guards and the Montgomery Guards, wended its way through the plank streets, marching beneath banners advertising that Senator Douglas would speak that evening. As the demonstration neared the Tremont House, its many-awninged façade glowing in the light of extra gas burners ignited for the occasion, Douglas's carriage was blocked by the throng of 12,000 crowding the intersection of Lake and Dearborn streets, waiting to hear his address. Whipping and swearing at their horses, knocking down a spectator with the butt end of a quirt, the carriage drivers tried to force their way through the masses. They had almost made it when, from an upper balcony, an enthusiastic Democratic partisan fired off rockets in Douglas's honor. The discharge spooked a dozen horses, including those pulling Douglas's carriage, which "plunged frantically in every direction," according to a newspaper report, bruising several bystanders, and breaking in three places the leg of a man who was "borne fainting into a drug store." Douglas escaped the cab, hurried indoors, and reappeared on the north balcony. Across Lake Street, on the brick wall of a building housing the showroom of Jno. Parmly, Hatter, he was satisfied to see a banner offering, WELCOME TO STEPHEN A. DOUGLAS, THE DEFENDER OF POPULAR SOVEREIGNTY.

The bustling scene beneath that balcony was, in many ways, Douglas's doing. Douglas moved to Chicago in 1847, the year he took his Senate seat. He envisioned the city as the nation's railroad hub, where the manufactured goods of the East would be exchanged for the foodstuffs of Western farmers—a marketplace uniting the commercial interests of the Atlantic Ocean, the Great Lakes, the Gulf of Mexico, and someday soon, he hoped, the Pacific. To Douglas, railroads were not simply a means of transportation, for conveying passengers and products. They bound together the Union, tie by tie, track by track—a Union essential for building Douglas's Young America, a dynamic nation that would fill in all the lands from coast to coast. In the Illinois Central's first five years, the population of Chicago tripled, from 28,260 to 80,028. In the 1850s, the nation's railroad mileage would also triple, from 9,000 to 30,000; 2,500 miles of those tracks were in Illinois, the decade's fastest-growing state, since nearly every line west of Lake Michigan terminated in Chicago. A young Illinois Central executive described the burgeoning city's energy in a letter to his boss, in prose prefiguring Carl Sandburg's poetic tribute:

There were about half a dozen locomotives flying about whis-
tling, screaming, puffing, blowing, backing and going ahead, five
or six hundred teams of every description loading and unloading;
two or three or four . . . buildings going up skyward at the rate
of a loft a day—hammers banging, tin rattling, chisels clinking
and men swarming on what is the handsomest passenger station in the country—immense loads of round hogs coming
over from neighboring depots and not less than fifty cars of
live ones standing here and there on the track; merchandise
of every description scattered around; emigrants crowding
everywhere, passengers running about.

(The Illinois Central had not just been profitable for Chicago, it had
been profitable for Douglas, too: shortly after moving to the city, he began
buying up lakefront property, sixteen acres of which he sold to the new
railroad for $21,320.)

As the railroad overtook the steamboat as the fastest method of transportation through the wilderness, Chicago replaced St. Louis as the Gateway
to the West. Would there be a place, though, for Stephen Douglas in this
new Chicago, and this new Illinois, he had done so much to build? Many
of the city's newcomers were New Yorkers and New Englanders who
followed the Erie Canal and then the Great Lakes westward to their
terminus. Bringing with them the antislavery tendencies of their native
states, they were attracted to the newly formed Republican Party, which
had been organized to oppose another of Douglas's political maneuvers:
the Kansas-Nebraska Act. Spreading slavery to the territories had not been
his motivation for writing the bill. It was, rather, a scheme for overcoming
Southern opposition to a railroad that would follow a northern route to
the Pacific—a route that would embark from Chicago and run through the
Nebraska Territory, which the Missouri Compromise of 1820 had desig-
nated free soil. Eager to boost Chicago as a rail hub, Douglas agreed to
the South's demand that the settlers a railroad would bring to Nebraska be
allowed to decide for themselves whether to open the territory to slavery.

(Despite his assurances to the South that both Kansas and Nebraska would be open to slavery, Douglas believed their climate and soil were unsuited for plantation agriculture.) His bill repealed the Missouri Compromise, but Douglas hoped it would sweep aside the "slavery agitation" standing in the way of a railroad that would bring even more traffic to Chicago, and further bind together his beloved Union. Far from burying the slavery issue, however, the Kansas-Nebraska Act inflamed it. On his first trip back to Chicago after the bill passed, German-Americans burned Douglas in effigy, denouncing him for "an attempt to import Southern aristocracy and Southern contempt of free labor, into the North." When Douglas attempted to give a speech defending the act, at North Market Hall, the crowd booed, heckled, and pelted him with missiles. After he gave up trying to stare and bluster the crowd into silence, the demonstrators followed him to his hotel—the Tremont House—and stood under his window, baying their disapproval.

On this summer evening, from his perch on the balcony of that same hotel, Douglas spotted Lincoln among the masses. At six-foot-four inches tall, dressed always in a somber black three-piece suit, Lincoln was the easiest man to recognize in any crowd. Lincoln, whose most lucrative client was the Illinois Central Railroad, was in Chicago that day to argue a case before the federal court for the Northern District of Illinois. Expecting Douglas to respond to his "House Divided" speech, he had made his way to the Tremont House after court adjourned. Out of respect for his opponent, Douglas invited Lincoln to sit on the balcony while he spoke. Lincoln accepted.

Charles Walker, a local attorney and Douglas supporter, attempted to introduce the senator, but his encomium was cut short by a brawl between the crowd and the cabmen attempting to extricate their horses. A man was clouted in the head with the butt end of a whip. A driver was pulled down from his seat three times in five minutes. After a ten-minute struggle, the horses were finally freed, and Douglas was free to speak. He did indeed intend to answer Lincoln's "House Divided" speech, but before he could do so, he had to address a more pressing political question: the Lecompton Constitution. In the territory of Kansas, which was now applying for statehood, a proslavery legislature had submitted to Congress a constitution declaring the right of property in slaves "inviolable" and banning free Blacks. The slavery clause would be submitted to a popular vote. Should it be rejected, though, existing slave ownership would still be allowed. President Buchanan, eager to appease his Southern supporters in the Democratic Party, favored admitting Kansas to the union under the Lecompton Constitution, since it would restore the balance between free and slave states that had been disrupted by the recent admission of Minnesota. Douglas thought differently. At the previous year's State Agricultural Fair in Springfield, he had taken soundings that convinced him that supporting Lecompton would make his reelection in the free state of Illinois impossible. So he objected to Lecompton, on the grounds that the entire constitution would not be subject to a vote of the people. It wasn't the slavery clause that bothered him, he insisted, it was the violation of popular sovereignty: the right of the settlers to determine their own institutions.

"When I found an effort being made during the recent session of Congress to force a constitution upon the people of Kansas against their will, and to force that state into the Union with a constitution which her people had rejected by more than ten thousand, I felt bound as a man of honor and a representative of Illinois, bound by every consideration of duty, of fidelity and of patriotism, to resist to the utmost of my power the consummation of that fraud," Douglas boomed from the balcony.

Douglas blocked the Lecompton Constitution in the Senate, returning it to Kansas for a full vote. Buchanan took revenge. First, he began dismantling the federal patronage corps on which Douglas had built his political machine in Illinois. He fired the collector of the port of Chicago and the Quincy postmaster, both Douglas appointees, replacing them with administration loyalists. Then, the president encouraged a breakaway faction of Illinois Democrats to walk out of the state convention and nominate its own slate of candidates. That meant Douglas would be facing two challengers for his Senate seat: Lincoln, and his old seatmate Sidney Breese, who had served a term in the Senate from 1843 to 1849.

By defending the principle of popular sovereignty, Douglas told the crowd, he was facing down the radicalism of Free-Soilers and slaveholders, who were both attempting to force their ways of life on the people of the territories, regardless of what those people desired.

"What was my duty, in 1854, when it became necessary to bring forward a bill for the organization of the territories of Kansas and Nebraska?" he asked his 12,000 listeners. "Was it not my duty, in obedience to the Illinois platform, to your standing instructions to your senators, adopted with almost entire unanimity, to incorporate in that bill the great principle of self-government, declaring that it was 'the true intent and meaning of the act not to legislate slavery into any state or territory, or to exclude it therefrom, but to leave the people thereof perfectly free to form and regulate their domestic institutions in their own way, subject only to the Constitution of the United States?' I then defended that principle against assaults from one section of the Union. During the last winter it became my duty to vindicate it against assaults from the other section of the Union."

Stephen Douglas portrayed himself as a moderate on the issue of slavery, standing in the breach between Northern abolitionists and Southern "Ultras." Both were extremists who threatened to break up the Union, the abolitionists by banning slavery, the Ultras by legalizing it nationwide. At the beginning of the decade, Douglas had won national acclaim for shepherding through Congress the Compromise of 1850. That package of bills—including a strengthened Fugitive Slave Law and a ban on the slave trade in the District of Columbia—was intended to defuse the issue for a generation. As the decade neared its end, though, the middle ground on which Douglas had staked his career was disappearing—in no small part because of Douglas's own actions. His Kansas-Nebraska Act helped polarize the nation over slavery, raising Southerners' hopes that they could import their peculiar institution to what had hitherto been free soil, and Northerners' fears that if Congress could no longer prohibit slaveholders from importing their property into the territories, it might not keep slaves out of free states, either.

The Dred Scott decision overturned both the Missouri Compromise and the Kansas-Nebraska Act. The Supreme Court ruled that Congress had no authority over slavery in the territories. This inflamed opinion even further. Douglas, typically, had tried to take both sides. Looking ahead to an 1860 presidential campaign, he knew he would need the support of Southern Democrats to win the nomination, and free Northern states to win the election. He endorsed the substance of the decision, which declared that "the Black man has no rights which the White man is bound to respect." He also insisted that it was not inconsistent with popular sovereignty, since slaveholding would be "a barren and worthless right, unless sustained, protected and enforced by appropriate police regulations and local legislation."

Douglas's both sides–ism had earned him the condemnation of both Abraham Lincoln and Mississippi senator Jefferson Davis—the future leaders of the Union and the Confederacy in the Civil War. In his speech to the Republican convention, less than a month earlier, Lincoln had accused Douglas of belonging to a conspiracy to spread slavery nationwide, along with Chief Justice Roger Taney, President Buchanan, and former president Franklin Pierce: "Stephen and Franklin and Roger and James," he named the cabal. Davis had called popular sovereignty "a thing shadowy and fleeting, changing its color as often as the chameleon"—words that may also have expressed his feelings about his colleague from Illinois, whom he personally despised. Davis demanded that Congress pass a federal slave code to protect slaveholders' right to bring their property into the territories, which would satisfy Douglas's temporizing insistence on "appropriate police regulations."

Three years hence, Douglas would label Davis a traitor for leading the Southern states out of the Union. On this evening, though, his target was Lincoln. Douglas accused his opponent of waging a campaign that would lead the nation toward the twin evils of civil war and Black equality. Douglas believed, fundamentally, that a house divided *could* stand. Moreover, he believed that such division, which he defined as respecting regional differences, was what held the house together. Lincoln wanted to tear down those differences, and with them the entire house.

"Mr. Lincoln asserts, as a fundamental principle of this government, that there must be uniformity in the local laws and domestic institutions of each and all the states of the Union," Douglas declared, "and he therefore invites all the non-slaveholding states to band together, organize as one body, and make war upon slavery in Kentucky, upon slavery in Virginia, upon the

Carolinas, upon slavery in all the slaveholding states in the Union, and to persevere in that war until it shall be exterminated. He then notifies the slaveholding states to stand together as a unit and make an aggressive war upon the free states of this Union. In other words, Mr. Lincoln advocates boldly and clearly a war of sections, a war of the North against the South, of the free states against the slave states—a war of extermination—to be continued relentlessly until one or the other shall be subdued, and all the states shall either become free or become slave."

That, of course, was exactly what happened once Lincoln became president. In 1858, though, only firebrand abolitionists, such as John Brown, believed in going to war to free the slaves. The great majority of Northerners, Lincoln included, were satisfied to recognize the Southern states' right to hold slaves as the price of preserving the Union. At the same time, most Northerners, Douglas included, did not want slavery in their own states. Douglas believed each state and territory ought to regulate its own practices, in accordance with its natural surroundings: "Laws and domestic institutions which would suit the granite hills of New Hampshire would be totally unfit for the rice plantations of South Carolina." Douglas had endorsed the 1848 Illinois Constitution, which banned slavery. He also endorsed the Illinois Black Laws, which mandated fines and imprisonment for Whites who brought slaves into the state, and allowed sheriffs to fine or sell any free Blacks who attempted to settle in their counties. The yeoman farmers of southern Illinois and the Irish laborers of Chicago, two groups strongly supportive of Douglas, had no desire to compete with Black labor, slave or free, and were deeply anxious about the prospect of emancipated slaves flooding the state and undercutting their wages. As historian Elmer Gertz would later observe, "Most people of Illinois hated the sight of a colored person."

Stephen Douglas certainly did. Turning his attention to the Dred Scott decision, he attacked Lincoln for making "warfare" on the Supreme Court, which had ruled that Blacks were not entitled to the same rights as Whites.

"I am opposed to Negro equality," Douglas declaimed. "I repeat that this is a nation of White people—a people composed of European descendants—a people that have established this government for themselves and their posterity, and I am in favor of preserving not only the purity of the blood, but the purity of the government from any mixture or amalgamation with inferior races."

By the time Douglas finished his speech, darkness had fallen over Chicago. The intersection of Lake and Dearborn, crowded for blocks in each direction, was lit only by the lamps strung up for this occasion. As a result of his travels, Douglas had not slept for two nights, so he retreated from the balcony and joined his wife Adele in their room. Douglas owned an estate on the south side of Chicago, but whenever he and Adele came home, they stayed at the Tremont House. With Egyptian marble fireplace mantels, rosewood chairs, linen sheets, and steam heating, it was the most sumptuous lodging the city had to offer.

Tremont House, Chicago, Illinois, July 10, 1858

All Saturday long, bands paraded through the streets of Chicago, accompanied by Republican loyalists distributing handbills advertising a speech by Abraham Lincoln, candidate for United States Senate. Lincoln would speak from the north portico of the Tremont House, the exact spot where Douglas had spoken the night before.

As Lincoln campaigned for the Senate, he planned to do so by shadowing Douglas, taking advantage of the senator's fame and drawing power to guarantee himself an audience. It was, Lincoln wrote a friend, a way to get "a concluding speech on him." It was also a way to force the Democratic Party to foot the bill for the flyers that attracted crowds—an expense that Lincoln, who had lately neglected his law practice in favor of politics, could scarcely afford.

Even with the wholehearted support of the Illinois Republican Party, Lincoln was a lesser draw than Douglas. Despite the marching bands, the handbills, newspaper advertisements, and an expensive fireworks show, the challenger's crowd was smaller than the incumbent's. (The

Chicago Press and Tribune, a Republican newspaper, estimated it at 9,000; the *Chicago Times*, a Democratic paper, at 3,000.) Not even a mid-speech appearance by 400 members of the Seventh Ward German Republican Club could bolster Lincoln's audience to the size of Douglas's.

Lincoln began his speech by mocking Douglas's beloved doctrine of popular sovereignty. Lincoln called it "squatter sovereignty"—"the right of the people to govern themselves, to be sovereign of their own affairs while they were squatted down in a country not their own, while they had squatted on a territory that did not belong to them, in the sense that a state belongs to the people who inhabit it."

Then, Lincoln went after Douglas's claim that he had blocked the Lecompton Constitution in the Senate. The fact was, Lincoln pointed out, far more Republicans than Democrats had voted against Lecompton.

"Who defeated it?" Lincoln asked his listeners.

"Judge Douglas!" they shouted.

"Yes, he furnished the votes himself," Lincoln observed dryly, "and if you suppose he controlled the other Democrats that went with him, he furnished three votes, while the Republicans furnished *twenty*."

The most powerful passage in Lincoln's speech was a rebuttal of Douglas's charge that his "House Divided" speech was an overture to civil war. The Founders, Lincoln insisted, had always intended that slavery would someday pass out of existence, but their designs for its demise had recently been thwarted, first by the Kansas-Nebraska Act, then by the Dred Scott decision. Douglas had created the former and endorsed the latter.

"I have always hated slavery," Lincoln declared, "I think as much as any abolitionist. I have been an Old Line Whig. I have always hated it, but I have been quiet about it until this new era of the Nebraska Bill began. I always believed that everybody was against it, and that it was in the course of ultimate extinction."

If the Founders had intended slavery to expand and flourish, Lincoln asked, why had they banned it in the Northwest Territories? Why had they set 1808 as the end of the African Slave Trade?

Douglas, said Lincoln, looked upon slavery—"this matter of keeping one sixth of the population of the whole nation in a state of oppression and tyranny unequaled in the world"—as a local custom, "only equal to the cranberry laws of Indiana—as something having no moral question to it."

Douglas himself would not have refuted that accusation. Throughout his career, he had addressed slavery as a political and economic issue, believing, as one of his biographers would write, "that its discussion as a moral question would place it on a dangerous level of abstraction."

George Murray McConnel, who was a twenty-one-year-old admirer of Douglas at the time the Kansas-Nebraska Act was passed, later claimed in a memoir that Douglas had told him, "I am not proslavery. I think it is a curse beyond computation, to both White and Black. But we exist as a nation, by virtue only of the Constitution, and under that there is no way to abolish it." Only a war could end slavery, McConnel would recall Douglas saying, and "I am not willing to set fire to the ship in order to smoke out the rats."

On the other hand, Douglas was de facto master of a 2,500-acre cotton plantation in Mississippi, and the one hundred slaves who worked it. Douglas's first wife, Martha Martin, was the daughter of a wealthy North Carolina planter. Colonel Robert Martin offered Douglas the plantation, which was worth $125,000, as a wedding gift. Douglas, who had just joined the Senate, refused. Owning a plantation would have been a liability to a free-state politician, and he did not feel qualified to manage an agricultural operation. The colonel gave it to his daughter instead. When she died, six years into the marriage, Douglas inherited the plantation. Although the property was in his sons' names and was run by a resident overseer, Douglas collected 20 percent of the profits, which he used to advance his political career. So while he was opposed to slavery in his home state, Douglas had no problem profiting from slavery where it was legal and accepted.

Lincoln finished his speech from the Tremont House balcony by criticizing Douglas's stance on the Dred Scott decision. Not only did Douglas support the decision, he insisted that opposition to it amounted to "making war" on the Supreme Court. When the Supreme Court had declared the Bank of the United States constitutional, Andrew Jackson had argued that each branch of government had its own right to interpret the Constitution. Douglas, a "whole hog" Jacksonian, had supported the president. So why now was the Dred Scott decision sacred?

"If I were in Congress, and a vote should come up on a question whether slavery should be prohibited in a new territory, in spite of the Dred Scott decision, I would vote that it should," Lincoln said.

That declaration of the most basic principle of Republicanism drew the loudest applause of the evening, along with shouts of "Good for you!," "We hope to see it!," and "That's right!" The *Press and Tribune*, the city's leading Republican organ, reported that "Mr. Lincoln retired amid a perfect torrent of cheers."

Over two nights in Chicago, Lincoln and Douglas set out the positions they would argue for the rest of the campaign. That Saturday, Lincoln got "a concluding speech" on Douglas. But in speaking from the platform Douglas had occupied a day earlier, and in limiting his remarks to a criticism of Douglas's record, Lincoln made himself look like the junior partner in the rivalry. That is not an unusual position for a challenger, but the relationship between Abraham Lincoln and Stephen Douglas had not always been so unequal. Lincoln had not always been a pesky camp follower, stooping to tug his younger and shorter opponent's coattails. Once, they were simply a pair of ambitious young Springfield politicians, part of the crowd that gathered around the stove in the back room of Joshua Speed's general store after business hours to debate the affairs of the day. Both counted their arrival on the prairie as the beginning of their careers and adult lives. "At twenty-one I came to Illinois," Lincoln later wrote in a campaign biography, linking his new home with his age of maturity. When Douglas was twenty, he left New York State in search of opportunity in the "great west." His five-month journey ended in Jacksonville, a small town thirty-five miles west of Springfield, where he thought expenses would be low and a newcomer welcome. He arrived with five dollars in his pocket. From his new home, Douglas wrote to his brother-in-law that "I have become a *Western* man, have imbibed Western feelings, principles, and interests, and have selected Illinois as my favorite place of adoption, without any desire of returning to the land of my fathers except as a visitor."

Lincoln beat Douglas to the General Assembly by two years, arriving in 1835, just in time to vote against the first of many canny maneuvers that would propel Douglas to the pinnacle of Illinois politics and establish the state's culture of bending the law to suit political self-interest. Barely a year after arriving in Illinois, the twenty-one-year-old Douglas decided he wanted the job of state's attorney, or prosecutor, for the First Judicial District of Illinois, which included Springfield. The post, appointed by the governor, was held by a political rival in the midst of a four-year term. Douglas was a "whole hog" supporter of Andrew Jackson, while the state's attorney was a "milk and cider" Democrat who questioned the president's war on the Bank of the United States. So Douglas helped his local representative, another whole hog Jacksonian, write a bill that shifted the power to name state's attorneys to the legislature. The bill passed, over Lincoln's nay vote, and the legislature installed a new state's attorney for the First Judicial District: Douglas, who had been licensed to practice law for only ten months. Two years later, State's Attorney Douglas was elected to the state House of Representatives, pioneering the Illinois tradition of double dipping: holding multiple offices and collecting multiple government paychecks at once. He soon extended that to triple dipping, when he was appointed registrar of the Springfield Land Office by President Van Buren.

Despite all the titles Douglas piled upon himself, Lincoln was more often the center of attention around Speed's stove, as he amused the gatherings with the frontier yarns that would later lend a rustic tinge to his political persona. Douglas loved a good time—the eligible young bachelor was a popular presence at Springfield's balls and parties—but was never known for his wit, so instead of offering stories of his own, he laughed along at Lincoln's. If anything, Lincoln condescended to his fellow legislator, calling the foot-shorter Douglas "the least man I ever saw" after their first meeting at the State House in Vandalia. (The state capital moved to Springfield in 1839, thanks to the lobbying of Lincoln and his fellow Sangamon County legislators, who were known as the Long Nine, since they all exceeded six feet in height.)

Douglas did, however, throw himself into the political debates that added heat to the stove in Speed's back room. Lincoln and Douglas both planned to stand as presidential electors in the 1840 election—Lincoln for the Whig candidate, William Henry Harrison, Douglas for the Democratic incumbent, Martin Van Buren, Jackson's handpicked successor. One night at Speed's, a year before the election, Lincoln and Douglas became embroiled in such a passionate argument that Douglas proposed they air their differences in a public forum. Lincoln accepted the challenge. On November 19, 1839, the two men debated for the first time, in Springfield. Their main topic of disagreement was the Second United States Bank: Douglas supported pulling its charter, while Lincoln favored extending it. A month later, they were the star attractions in a three-day-long series of debates between Whigs and Democrats that was so successful they decided to take it on the road. (Despite the vivacity of the discussions, Lincoln remained unimpressed with Douglas: "The Democratic giant is here," he wrote sardonically to his friend John T. Stuart, "but he is not now worth talking about.")

In March, the young politicians debated before a thousand people in Jacksonville—half the population of the town. In April, after attending a meeting of the circuit court in Tremont, they stood outside the courthouse and, for the first but by no means the last time, discussed slavery and race relations. Douglas accused Harrison of abolitionism—a dirty word in the central Illinois of 1840. Aware of his home region's anti-Black sentiment and unwilling to allow the Democrats alone to exploit it, Lincoln charged that Van Buren had supported allowing Blacks to vote in New York State. He would repeat that charge in a campaign newspaper, *The Old Soldier*, which he edited with fellow Whigs who supported Harrison. In the July 28, 1840, issue, the Whigs wrote that Van Buren "is in favor of allowing free Negroes and slaves to swear in court against White men!"

Harrison won the election, but Van Buren carried Illinois. From statehood in 1818, until Lincoln's election in 1860, Illinois always voted

Democratic for president. For most of those years, the only dissent from the state's Democratic bent was in the "Whig Belt" that stretched across its midsection. During Lincoln's lone term in Congress, from 1847 to 1849, he was the only Whig in Illinois's seven-member delegation. That helps explain why the political fortunes of Lincoln and Douglas diverged so dramatically beginning in 1840. Douglas, the great collector of political titles, quickly amassed more and bigger offices. Shortly after that year's election, he was appointed secretary of state by Democratic governor Thomas Carlin. He occupied the post less than three months, until the legislature elected him to the Supreme Court of Illinois to fill one of five newly created seats. (Due to Douglas's brief tenure on the court, Lincoln forever after addressed him as "Judge Douglas.") As the state grew, so did Douglas's career. In 1842, he was elected to one of four new congressional seats Illinois had gained in the census. Finally, in 1847, the Democratic legislature elected the thirty-three-year-old Douglas to the U.S. Senate, the body where he would spend the rest of his career. That same year, Lincoln was elected to the House of Representatives. He returned home two years later, after failing to persuade President Zachary Taylor to appoint him commissioner of the U.S. General Land Office, and resumed the itinerant career of a circuit-riding lawyer. Throughout the 1840s and 1850s, Lincoln enviously followed his former colleague's rise to fame and power.

"Douglas had got to be a great man, & [be]strode the earth," Lincoln wrote a friend in 1852. "Time was when I was in his way some; but he had outgrown me & [be]strides the world; & such small men as I am, can hardly be considered worthy of his notice; & I may have to dodge between his legs."

On another occasion, Lincoln expressed his feelings of inferiority toward his onetime peer by writing, "Twenty-two years ago Judge Douglas and I first became acquainted. With me, the race of ambition has been a failure—a flat failure; with him it has been a splendid success. His name fills the nation, and is not unknown, even, in foreign lands."

Lincoln's friend Ward Hill Lamon called him "intensely jealous" of Douglas; Lincoln "longed to pull him down, or outstrip him in the race for popular favor, which they united in considering 'the chief end of man.'"

Now, in 1858, Lincoln finally had a chance to pull down Douglas. It would be a great victory not only for Lincoln, but for the Illinois Republican Party, which was united by two great passions: a loathing for slavery, and a loathing for Douglas. Outside of Illinois, Douglas was more popular with Republicans. New York senator William Seward and *New-York Tribune* editor Horace Greeley so admired his stand against the Lecompton Constitution that they endorsed his campaign. Greeley wrote, "If Illinoisans understood how profoundly obnoxious to Buchanan and the Slavery-extending oligarchy" Douglas had been, "then nothing could prevent his reelection."

Lincoln was aggrieved by Greeley's endorsement of Douglas. "I think Greeley is not doing me right," he complained to his law partner, William Herndon. "His conduct, I believe, savors a little of injustice. I am a true Republican and have been tried already in the hottest part of the antislavery fight, and yet I find him taking up Douglas, a veritable dodger—once a tool of the South, now its enemy—and pushing him to the front. He forgets that when he does that he pulls me down at the same time."

Greeley was far from the only Eastern editor taking an interest in the Illinois senate race. Newspapers in the nation's capital were declaring it the equivalent of a nationwide referendum on slavery and the preservation of the Union.

Illinois, opined the *Washington States*, "is from this time forward, until the Senatorial question shall be decided, the most interesting political battleground in the Union . . . The battle of the Union is to be fought in Illinois. In every respect, then, Illinois becomes as it were, the Union for the time being."

The candidates and their campaigns, who knew Illinois more intimately than a Washington editorialist, understood that the campaign's main battleground would be smaller and more specific than the entire state. The election would be won or lost in central Illinois, the old Whig Belt, a stretch of the American midlands, the region that had always served as a buffer between the extremes of North and South. It was a region whose history made it equally hostile to abolitionism and slavery extension. Douglas headed there next, for a pair of speeches in Bloomington and Springfield. Lincoln followed him.

CHAPTER 2

LINCOLN'S CHALLENGE

McLean County Courthouse, Public Square, Bloomington, Illinois, July 16, 1858

The Douglas Limited departed Great Central Station in the morning, gaily decorated with American flags and banners advertising that STEPHEN A. DOUGLAS, CHAMPION OF POPULAR SOVEREIGNTY was its most prominent passenger. In Bridgeport, the Irish neighborhood at the southern limits of Chicago, laborers stopped work to cheer the senator's train. Douglas was popular with the Irish, because he had repeatedly denounced the nativism of the anti-immigrant, anti-Catholic Know Nothing Party as un-American and unconstitutional. In Joliet, a flatcar bearing a twelve-pound cannon was attached to the caboose, so Douglas could make a thunderous announcement of his arrival at small-town depots farther down the line. As the train left the Great Lakes country, the land flattened, the trees thinned out, and the sky opened up. Heading southwest toward Bloomington, the tracks traced an acute angle across the prairie covering the heart of Illinois.

In Wilmington, a six-pound cannon at the station saluted Douglas's arrival. The twelve-pounder on the flatcar answered. When Douglas emerged onto the train platform to greet men waving hats and women fluttering handkerchiefs, a citizen even older than the century jumped aboard to hug his senator and declare, "Welcome, Judge Douglas, to Illinois!" (It was an appropriate greeting. Although Douglas owned an estate along the Chicago lakefront, Oakenwald, he had rarely been more than a visitor since his election to Congress in 1842. Douglas spent most of his time in Washington, where he had just built an "imposing and showy" mansion with a ballroom, a library, and a drawing room whose most eye-arresting feature was a pair of full-length portraits of the senator and his twenty-two-year-old wife, Adele. That January, the Douglases had opened the mansion with a housewarming party for 2,000 guests. To fully enjoy their new home, though, Douglas would need another term in the Senate.)

Douglas's train paused in the tank towns of Dwight, Odell, Cayuga, Lexington, and Towanda, where he greeted trackside gatherings and invited aboard supporters eager to hear him speak that afternoon. At 3:30, the cannon on the flatcar heralded his arrival in Bloomington. The response was a thirty-two-gun salute—one gun for each state in the Union—from the local militia, the Bloomington Guards. The Guards had marched to the station accompanied by a band that struck up "Hail, Columbia," and "a long line of citizens on horseback, in carriages and on foot."

After the crowds were cleared from the tracks, Douglas and his wife—whose youth and beauty even the Republicans acknowledged were campaign assets—stepped into a carriage for the ride to Landon House. The Bloomington Guards kept a martial pace on either side. It was a greeting worthy of a European prince to a provincial capital, and definitely worthy of Douglas, who loved the pomp that went along with a seat in the United States Senate. At the hotel, draped with pro-Douglas banners, the senator stepped onto the balcony to cheers of "Hurrah for Stephen Douglas, the champion of popular sovereignty!"

In the fading light of half-past-seven, Douglas began speaking in the Public Square, illuminated by rockets fired from Landon House. The speech covered many of the same topics as Chicago's—Lecompton, the mortal danger of Lincoln's "House Divided" platform, the sacredness of the Dred Scott decision—but Douglas added in the accusation that the Danites, the pro-Buchanan Democrats who had bolted the state convention to nominate their own slate, "have formed an alliance with Mr. Lincoln and the Republicans for the purpose of defeating the Democratic Party."

Now that he was in central Illinois, rather than in Chicago, where abolitionist and anti-Nebraska sentiment was strongest in the state, Douglas laid on his White supremacy even thicker. Lincoln, he said, believed that the Declaration of Independence's assertion that "all men are created equal" applied to Blacks. (This was at the heart of Lincoln's antislavery sentiment, because, as he himself put it, a Black woman had as much right as anyone "to eat the bread she earns by her own hands.") That "abolition philosophy" was a falsehood, Douglas insisted. Carried to its logical end, Lincoln's theory of Black equality would lead to Blacks voting, Blacks holding office, Blacks sitting on juries in judgment of Whites, and, the ultimate degradation of pure American blood, Blacks marrying Whites.

"I do not believe that the signers of the Declaration of Independence had any reference to Blacks when they used the expression that all men were created equal, or that they had any reference to Chinese or Coolies, the Indians, the Japanese, or any other inferior race," Douglas thundered. "They were speaking of the White race, the European race on this continent, and their descendants and emigrants who should come here."

As proof that miscegenation sapped the vitality of a nation, Douglas brought up the recent Mexican War. Lincoln had opposed the war, fearing that the captured territory would be opened to slavery, but the conflict had been so popular in central Illinois that the region was spangled with small towns named after its battles: San Jose, Cerro Gordo, Eldorado, Sandoval—all mispronounced by settlers who had only read about those places in newspapers. In Mexico, said Douglas, an all-White American army had defeated a ragtag force of Latin "mongrels": "Ask any of those gallant men of your own country, who went to Mexico to fight the battles of their country, in what friend Lincoln considers and unjust and unholy war, and hear what they will tell you with regard to the amalgamation of races in that country."

Lincoln was in the audience that evening, having made the trip from Springfield to once again shadow Douglas. After the senator finished speaking, a few Bloomington Republicans called on Lincoln to respond. He mounted the speaker's platform but did not give a speech.

"This meeting was called by the friends of Judge Douglas, and it would be improper for me to address it," Lincoln said, before promising to return to Bloomington—which he did, on September 4th.

Like Caesar's Gaul, nineteenth-century Illinois was divided into three parts, each with its own distinct views on the slavery question. The north, settled by New Yorkers and New Englanders, was antislavery, even abolitionist. In the south, the oldest part of the state, the descendants of Kentuckians and Virginians who had crossed the Ohio River early in the century remained in sympathy with the lands of their forebears. The small-time farmers in the land known as Egypt, because the confluence of the Mississippi and Ohio Rivers resembled the Nile Delta, had transferred their political allegiances from Andrew Jackson to Stephen Douglas. In central Illinois, though, Yankees and Southerners mingled, joined by Midlanders who had journeyed westward along the National Road, through Ohio and Indiana, to its terminus at Vandalia. This meeting place of the nation's three dominant cultures, this microcosm of America, turned out to be the perfect crucible for the nation's debate on slavery, and the perfect training ground for the man who would ultimately resolve the issue.

Stephen Douglas, who had held statewide office longer than any politician in Illinois's forty-year history, and knew the state's politics as well as anyone, would charge that Abraham Lincoln's principles "in the North are jet black, in the center they are in color a decent mulatto, and in lower Egypt they are almost white." In fact, Lincoln had spent his career navigating the "mulatto" politics of central Illinois, whose inhabitants were equally appalled by Northern abolitionists and Southerners determined to tear down obstacles to the spread of slavery—seeing both as extremists who attempted to violate the Constitution and threaten the nation's unity.

The first test of central Illinois's attitude toward slavery took place in 1824, when the state held a plebiscite on a constitutional convention. Illinois was nominally a free state, having been paired for admission to the Union with Mississippi, but its constitution allowed the old French settlers along the Mississippi River to keep their slaves, did not cancel existing indentures, and allowed slave labor in the salt mines of the state's southeastern corner. The 1820 Census found 917 slaves and indentured servants living in Illinois. The residents of Egypt, though, wanted to rewrite the state's constitution to lift restrictions on slavery entirely, hoping to attract wealthy planters who were bypassing Illinois—the southernmost free state—for Missouri. Antislavery "non-conventionists" organized meetings and dinners throughout the midsection of Illinois, portraying a convention as a plot to bring the frontier state under the heel of plantation aristocrats, as well as introduce an unsavory Black element to the state.

"[A] poor man in a slave state is not as much respected as in a free one," a polemicist calling himself Spartacus wrote in the *Illinois Intelligencer*, a newspaper published in Vandalia. Spartacus went on to predict that bringing slavery to Illinois would cause "our children to contract bad habits by the vulgar pronunciation or vicious habits of the *negroes*."

The referendum to lift all restrictions on slavery in Illinois failed, by a vote of 6,640 to 4,972. It took a beating in Sangamon County, where Lincoln would eventually settle, losing 722–153. The following census, in 1830—the first since the county's formation in 1821—found 34 free Blacks and 13 slaves in Sangamon. The 1840 Census found 160 free Blacks and 6 slaves. By 1850, there were no slaves. Lincoln's home county validated his belief that if slavery were not allowed to spread, it would eventually dwindle away.

There was a strain of abolitionism in central Illinois, but it was violently—murderously—repressed. In 1829, seven Yale Theological Seminary students resolved to "go out to one of the new western states and there establish an institution of learning." The "Yale Band" founded Illinois College in Jacksonville, recruiting as its president Edward Beecher, pastor of Boston's Congregationalist Park Street Church and brother of *Uncle Tom's Cabin* author Harriet Beecher Stowe. Lincoln's future law partner,

William Herndon, was briefly a student at Illinois College, until his father pulled him out, "believing that the College was too strongly permeated with the virus of abolitionism." In that short time, though, Herndon was converted to his professors' cause: "It was too late. My soul had absorbed too much of what my father considered rank poison."

One of the college's professors was a conductor on the Underground Railroad. When a Louisiana woman brought her Black nurse to Jacksonville, the professor convinced the slave that she was free, as a result of setting foot on Illinois soil. Two students helped her escape, but their party was overtaken, and the slave returned to her mistress in St. Louis. In response to the incident, anti-abolitionist locals gathered at the Morgan County Courthouse to form an "Anti-Negro Stealing Society."

While at Illinois College, Beecher became an intimate of Elijah Lovejoy, the son and grandson of Congregationalist ministers from Maine. Finding the life of a New England schoolmaster unsatisfying, Lovejoy walked 1,200 miles from Boston to St. Louis. He eventually became the editor of a religious newspaper, the *St. Louis Observer*, which he converted to an antislavery organ. After a mob burned to death a free Black who had killed a police officer out of fear that his arrest for public drunkenness would result in sale into slavery, Lovejoy wrote an editorial calling the lynching "savage barbarity." Proslavery vandals stole his composing sticks and destroyed the completed type for his newspaper. Fearing for the safety of his wife and son in a slave state, Lovejoy moved his operations across the river to Alton, Illinois, where he organized the Illinois Anti-Slavery Society. A Missouri mob destroyed another of Lovejoy's presses by throwing it into the river. When Lovejoy's third press arrived, from Cincinnati, it was transported to a warehouse by a dozen armed men. Word spread through the taverns. Vigilantes surrounded the warehouse, throwing stones and firing pistols. Attempting to set the roof on fire, the rioters raised a ladder against the walls. Running outside to push it over, Lovejoy was shot five times. His killers were tried but found not guilty by a Madison County jury.

Lovejoy's murder outraged antislavery Americans. It was the greatest boost to their movement until the publication of *Uncle Tom's Cabin*. But there was barely a word of condemnation in Illinois—except from Lincoln. In a speech to the Young Men's Lyceum of Springfield, Lincoln defended Lovejoy—not for his abolitionist views, which neither he nor the great majority of his neighbors shared, but for his right to express them.

"There is no grievance that is a fit object of redress by mob law," Lincoln told the Lyceum. "In any case that arises, as for instance, the promulgation of abolitionism, one of two positions is necessarily true; that is, the thing is right within itself, and therefore deserves the protection of all law and all good citizens; or, it is wrong, and therefore proper to be prohibited by legal enactment; and in neither case, is the interpretation of mob law, either necessary, justifiable, or excusable."

On a flatboat trip to New Orleans as a young man, Lincoln saw a group of Black men chained together. He had hated slavery ever since. The Lyceum speech was an early example of his ability to couch his opposition to slavery not in abolitionist terms, but as a defense against the tyranny, violence, and intolerance of the "Slave Power." Many Springfieldians considered slave owners and abolitionists equally undesirable, but in his Lyceum speech, Lincoln argued that slavery's defenders were a greater threat to public order than its opponents.

As a legislator, Lincoln was antislavery, but he was also anti-Black—central Illinoisans considered both slaves and emancipated Black people a threat to free White workers and did not want either in their midst. Lincoln voted in favor of an amendment to a voting bill that called for denying Blacks the franchise. It passed, 35–16. He also voted for a resolution asserting that "the elective franchise should be kept pure from contamination by the admission of voters of color." During his first reelection campaign, Lincoln wrote a letter to the *Sangamo Journal*, stating that he favored "admitting all Whites to the right of suffrage who pay taxes or bear arms (by no means excluding females)."

However, during a debate on a resolution against banning slavery in the District of Columbia, Lincoln tried to insert the words "unless the people of the said district petition for same." His motion failed. Lincoln was one of only six representatives to vote no on the resolution, which stated that "we highly disapprove of the formation of abolition societies," and that "the right of property is sacred to the slave-holding states by the Federal Constitution." Lincoln and his Sangamon County colleague Dan Stone filed a protest declaring themselves against both slavery and abolitionism: "They believe that the institution of slavery is founded on both injustice and bad policy; but that the promulgation of abolition doctrines tends to increase rather than abate its evils," the legislators wrote.

This was a middle course that Lincoln would follow right up to his election as president. He never publicly objected to the Illinois Black Laws, which stated that no Black could settle in the state without producing a certificate of freedom, that anyone bringing a slave into Illinois for the purpose of freeing him must produce a $1,000 bond, and that harboring slaves was a felony punishable by thirty lashes and a fine of double the slave's value. When Black abolitionist H. Ford Douglas asked Lincoln to sign a petition in favor of repealing the Black Laws, he declined. As Thomas Ford, who served as governor from 1842 to 1846, wrote in his memoirs, it would have been "dangerous" for an Illinois politician of that era to be seen as pro-Black.

During his years in the Illinois General Assembly, and later in Congress, Lincoln saw slavery as an issue that threatened to cause dissension between Northerners and Southerners, preventing them from cooperating on the Whig platform of a Bank of the United States, high tariffs to protect American industry, and building railroads and canals to develop frontier states such as Illinois. While personally opposed to slavery, he was unwilling to antagonize Southerners by suggesting they give up their slaves.

During his term in Congress, Lincoln consistently voted in favor of the Wilmot Proviso, an unsuccessful bill, sponsored by Representative David Wilmot of Pennsylvania, which would have prohibited slavery in territory conquered from Mexico. Lincoln opposed the Mexican War, which he feared would add slave territory to the nation. To Williamson Durley, an abolitionist in Putnam County, in the northern reaches of his congressional district, Lincoln wrote:

"I think annexation an evil. I hold it to be a paramount duty of us in the free states, due to the Union of the states, and perhaps to liberty itself (paradoxical though it may seem) to let the slavery of the other states alone; while, on the other hand, I hold it to be equally clear, that we should never knowingly lend ourselves directly or indirectly, to prevent that slavery from dying a natural death—to find new places to live, when it can no longer exist in the old."

Given the sentiment against both abolitionists and Blacks in Spring-field, it seems natural that Lincoln would seek a solution to the slavery question that excluded both. He found one in the Colonization Society, a movement to repatriate emancipated slaves to Africa. Lincoln doubted that Whites and free Blacks could live harmoniously together, given one race's history of oppressing the other. Springfield boasted an active colonization movement. The Sangamo Colonization Society was organized in 1833; its members included John T. Stuart, who would become Lincoln's law partner, and John Todd, an uncle to Lincoln's wife, Mary. When the Illinois State Colonization Society established a Springfield chapter in the 1840s, most of its officers were, like Lincoln, Whigs who opposed abolitionism. According to the state society's first annual report, in 1845, it had raised $650 toward purchasing land in West Africa, with the goal of ending the slave trade at its source: "The principle of colonization is the most effectual and economical means of attaining this object." Lincoln addressed the Society's annual meeting in 1853 and 1855 and was elected to its board of managers in 1858.

Despite Lincoln's stands against both abolition and slavery expansion, at the beginning of the 1850s, Douglas was central Illinois's hero on the slavery issue. In 1850, the first-term senator guided through Congress a series of bills that promised to settle the sectional conflict over slavery for at least a generation. The Compromise of 1850 had originally been championed by Henry Clay—Lincoln's political idol—but passed to Douglas's steward-ship as the elder statesman's health failed. The bills included a ban on the slave trade in the District of Columbia; a strengthened Fugitive Slave Law, which required Northern authorities to assist in the capture of runaway slaves; admission of California as a free state; and plebiscites to determine whether to allow slavery in the Utah and New Mexico territories. Presented to Congress as a single package, the Compromise failed, due to opposition from both Southern slaveholders and antislavery Whigs. Douglas, however, realized there was a separate majority for each measure and, in a masterstroke of legislative craftsmanship, passed them each one at a time.

The Compromise of 1850 was wildly popular in central Illinois. Both area congressmen, Democrats Thomas L. Harris and W. A. Richardson, voted for every measure. After their passage, a pro-Compromise rally was held in Springfield, attracting a crowd of prominent Whigs and Democrats, including Democratic governor Augustus C. French. The Sangamon County Whig convention resolved that the proposals contained "the elements of a just and liberal adjustment" and asked for Congress to "sustain Mr. Clay and his worthy co-laborers in their noble efforts to save the country from the evils of the ultraism of the South and the fanaticisms of the North."

When Clay died two years later, Lincoln delivered a eulogy praising the Kentuckian for his moderate course on slavery and taking a swipe at abolitionists: "Cast into life where slavery was already widely spread and deeply seated, he did not perceive, as I think no wise man has perceived, how it could be at once eradicated, without producing a greater evil, even to the course of human liberty itself. His feeling and his judgment, therefore, even led him to oppose both extremes of opinion on the subject. Those who would shiver into fragments the Union of these States; tear to tatters its now venerated constitution; and even burn the last copy of the Bible, rather than slavery should continue a single hour, together with all their more halting sympathizers, have received, and are receiving their just execration; and the name, and opinions, and influence of Mr. Clay, are fully, and, as I trust, effectually and enduringly arrayed against them."

Lyman Trumbull of Alton, then a justice of the Illinois Supreme Court, later a United States senator, would declare in a speech that the Compromise was supported by "all parties, save a few abolitionists, too insignificant to command attention, determined to keep down slavery agitation, and it was kept down—Never was the country freer from abolition and slavery excitement than from 1850 to 1854."

In 1854, of course, Douglas blew up his generation-long comity on slavery—and much of the goodwill it had won for him in central Illinois—by passing the Kansas-Nebraska Act. Less than two weeks after the bill was introduced, the *Illinois State Journal*, Springfield's Whig newspaper, editorialized, "We had hoped to gain a short respite from that old din of 'Slavery Agitation' and 'Slavery Extension' that has been warring in our country so often for the last twenty years, but it seems that it is about to be let in upon as again, more repulsive and disgusting than ever from having been so many times kicked out the door. We can't conceive of a greater piece of mischief than is here set on foot by our senator."

Even moderates were outraged by Douglas's bill, which they regarded as duplicitous and self-serving. David Davis of Bloomington, presiding judge of the state's Eighth Circuit, was contemptuous of abolitionists. But Davis, who would serve as Lincoln's campaign manager at the 1860 Republican National Convention, considered the Kansas-Nebraska Act an even greater threat to sectional harmony.

"There has never been, in my opinion, anything as ill-timed or disastrous to the good feeling of this country as this disturbance of the Missouri Compromise," Davis wrote to his brother-in-law Julius Rockwell, who would soon be appointed senator from Massachusetts.

Into the political fray over the Kansas-Nebraska Act stepped Abraham Lincoln, reviving his old rivalry with Douglas, which had been dormant since the days of Harrison and Van Buren. Lincoln had spent the years after leaving Congress tending to his law practice—years during which his long-held antislavery convictions had little audience in his home region, which was satisfied with the Compromise of 1850, allowing freedom and slavery to coexist in their separate spheres.

Douglas's bill changed Lincoln's political fortunes and set him on a course to the presidency. "I was losing interest in politics," Lincoln would later write in a biographical sketch, "when the repeal of the Missouri

Compromise aroused me again." The repeal horrified antislavery men throughout the North, but as an Illinoisan, Lincoln was in a position to confront its author on his home turf. Sharing a state and a speaking platform with Douglas would transform Lincoln from unknown one-term congressman to the nation's most prominent critic of the Kansas-Nebraska Act. As Douglas's foil, Lincoln built the fame and the political cachet that enabled him to win the 1860 Republican nomination for president, and then the presidency itself. Historians often say that geography is destiny. Had it not been for his struggle with Douglas, Lincoln's name would be no better known to history than that of his successor in Congress, Thomas L. Harris, and less well-known than his predecessor, Edward Baker, who was a senator from Oregon when he was killed at the Civil War battle of Ball's Bluff.

The first step in Lincoln's campaign against Douglas was entirely parochial. In 1854, Lincoln made it his goal to eliminate the pro-Douglas majority in the General Assembly, an important source of the senator's influence over the state. It was a task that required uniting Whigs, anti-Nebraska Democrats, and abolitionists under a baseline principle: opposition to extending slavery into the territories.

The General Assembly had endorsed the Kansas-Nebraska Act, but Lincoln was convinced it was out of loyalty to the state's leading politician, rather than actual support for the bill. Most Illinoisans, he believed, were anti-Nebraska. In a caucus of Democratic legislators, Lincoln wrote to Joshua Speed, "it was thereby discovered that just three, and no more, were in favor of the measure. In a day or two Douglas' order came on to have resolutions passed approving the bill; and they were passed by large majorities!!!"

Lincoln entered the race for state representative from Sangamon County, mainly to aid the reelection of Whig congressman Richard Yates, who now held his old seat in the House of Representatives. In a speech on the House floor, Yates had called Kansas-Nebraska "directly at war with the genius [and] objects of our government."

"[The] question now rises up before us," Yates said, "a present question, not to be avoided, but to be met, whether slavery is to be nationalized;

whether the spread of slavery is to be the chief concern and leading policy of this government; whether it is to be the figurehead of the ship of state, and whether a trade of unequaled barbarity, shocking to the senses of mankind, is to be received under the full sanction of our general government."

Throughout the election season of 1854, Lincoln became Illinois's most prominent "anti-Nebraska man," addressing audiences throughout the state—and finally coming face-to-face with Douglas again. They met in a Bloomington hotel room, on September 12, where the teetotaling Lincoln refused Douglas's offer of a drink, and the impatient Douglas refused Lincoln's offer of a debate. That day in Bloomington, Lincoln began his practice of getting "a concluding speech" on Douglas. Douglas spoke in the afternoon. Lincoln spoke in the evening, arguing that Kansas-Nebraska "was done without the consent of the people, and without their wishes, for if the matter had been put to a vote before the people directly, whether that should be made a slave territory, it should be indignantly voted down." Lincoln appealed to the voters to "fill the lower House with anti-Nebraska members" who would order Douglas to vote for the repeal of his own bill under the "doctrine of instruction," which allowed legislators to dictate the votes of the senators they had sent to Washington.

Lincoln next stalked Douglas in Springfield, where the senator planned to defend popular sovereignty during the State Agricultural Fair. The fair, and the presence of Douglas, would guarantee Lincoln a good-sized audience. On October 3, Douglas spoke for two and a half hours in the State House's Hall of Representatives. The next day, Lincoln bested him—at least for long-windedness—by holding forth for three and a half hours in the same spot. While Lincoln spoke from the speaker's stand, Douglas listened from the clerk's stand, just below him.

"I have not been in public life as Judge Douglas has," Lincoln said in his introduction. "If I should, on that account, misstate any fact, I would be very much obliged to my friend the Judge if he would correct me."

Douglas looked up at Lincoln—at an even greater height than usual—and replied, "It is not always agreeable to a speaker to be interrupted in the course of his remarks. Therefore, if I have anything to say, I will wait until Mr. Lincoln is done."

Douglas was, of course, too headstrong and irascible to abide by that pledge. Knowing his adversary, Lincoln baited him. As Lincoln discussed federal legislation on slavery, he mentioned the Nicholson Letter—an 1847 epistle from Michigan senator Lewis Cass to a supporter, which first articulated the principle of popular sovereignty on slavery in the territories.

"I don't know what my friend the Judge thinks," Lincoln said, looking down at Douglas with the same wry grin that preceded one of his yarns, "but really it seems to me that *that* was the origin of the Nebraska bill."

As laughter and applause swept the chamber, Douglas felt compelled to respond. Rising to his full five-feet-four inches, theatrically shaking his dark mane, Douglas shouted, "No, sir! I will tell you what was the origin of the Nebraska bill. It was this, sir! God created man, and placed before him both good and evil, and left him free to choose for himself. That was the origin of the Nebraska bill."

"Well, then," Lincoln said, still smiling, "I think it is a great honor to Judge Douglas that he was the first man to discover this fact!"

Douglas did not share the crowd's amusement at this remark.

Lincoln went on to argue that the Constitution's three-fifths compromise gave Whites in slave states more power than Whites in free states; because of that, the inhabitants of Kansas and Nebraska should not be allowed to vote themselves excess influence over the nation's affairs. At the same time, Lincoln dismissed doctrines that were "narrow, sectional, and dangerous to the Union" (i.e., abolitionism), promising to respect the Constitutional rights of slaveholders "fully" and "fairly." Douglas then responded to Lincoln for two hours, giving a speech his enemies at the *Illinois State Journal* wrote was "adroit and plausible, but had not the marble of logic in it." The turns at the speaker's stand were the closest the two men had come to debating since 1840.

Lincoln's campaign to elect an anti-Nebraska legislature succeeded; however, Lincoln declined to take his seat, so he could stand in the election to replace Senator James Shields, a Douglas ally who had voted for the Kansas-Nebraska Act, and thus would not be returned to Washington. Lincoln led in the early balloting but came up five votes short of a majority, unable to win the support of anti-Nebraska Democrats, who refused to vote for a Whig. He withdrew and threw his support to Lyman Trumbull, a newly elected Democratic congressman, who would soon turn Republican.

On the same day Lincoln spoke at the State House in response to Douglas, an anti-Nebraska convention met in Springfield. Among the organizers was Owen Lovejoy, brother of Elijah Lovejoy, the abolitionist publisher who had been lynched by a proslavery mob in Alton in 1837, and himself a future Republican congressman. The delegates attended Lincoln's speech and were eager to enlist him in their movement.

Calling their new organization the Republican Party, the convention adopted a resolution maintaining "the right and duty of the General Government to prohibit the extension, establishment or perpetuation of human slavery in any and every Territory of the United States, and in any territory, possession, and country, over which the Union has or may hereafter acquire exclusive jurisdiction."

The Republicans elected Lincoln to the party's central committee and invited him to its first meeting in Chicago. He declined. Their position went further than his own, because it would have prohibited slavery in any future state.

"I have been perplexed some to understand why my name was placed on that committee," Lincoln wrote to Ichabod Codding, the New York–born, Vermont-educated abolitionist who had extended the invitation. Codding had been barnstorming Illinois on an anti-Nebraska speaking tour even more extensive than Lincoln's. "I was not consulted on the subject, nor was I apprised of the appointment until I discovered it two or three weeks afterward. I suppose my opposition to the principle of slavery is as strong as that of any member of the Republican Party; but I had also supposed that the *extent* to which I feel authorized to carry that opposition, practically, was not at all satisfactory to that party."

A member of the American Anti-Slavery Society and the abolitionist Illinois Liberty Party, Codding was considered a radical in central

Illinois—which may explain why Lincoln didn't want to associate with him politically. When Codding spoke alongside Ohio's abolitionist congressman Joshua Giddings, the *Illinois State Journal* called their views "a dangerous extreme. They are in favor of the repeal of the Fugitive Slave Law, and opposed to the admission of any more slave states into the Union on any terms—opinions which, if carried out, would effectually abrogate the compromise measures of 1850." Lincoln would not have argued with that. As he himself put it, in his famous 1854 Peoria speech, "Stand WITH the abolitionist in restoring the Missouri Compromise and stand AGAINST him when he attempts to repeal the Fugitive Slave Law."

The new Republican Party was attempting to fuse Whigs, abolitionists, and anti-Nebraska Democrats into a single antislavery movement. In the winter of 1856, Lincoln finally found a group of antislavery men with whom he was willing to fuse. Paul Selby, editor of the Whig-leaning *Morgan Journal*, organized a convention of like-minded newspapermen to be held on February 22 in Decatur. Conveniently, the meeting coincided with a national Republican convention in Pittsburgh, whose Illinois delegation would include Codding and Lovejoy. Since the abolitionists were out of state, they could not exert their radical influence on any platform the newspaper editors produced.

Lincoln was one of twelve attendees at the Decatur convention, and the only non-journalist. He was not nominated to the Committee on Resolutions but consulted with its members, who produced a manifesto that was strident in its defense of slavery where it existed, but equally determined to prevent it from entering the territories. The entire document was reprinted in the *Peoria Weekly Republican*, under the headline, "Anti-Nebraska Editorial Convention."

"We recognize the legal rights of the Slave States to hold and enjoy their property in slaves under the State laws, and within the jurisdiction of those laws," the resolution stated, "and we further recognize their constitutional right to an enumeration of three-fifths of their slaves in the apportionment of representation, and also their constitutional right to a return of such 'persons owing service under the laws of a State,' as may escape beyond the jurisdiction of those laws under which said service is due."

Having disclaimed any intention of interfering with the Constitutional rights of the slave states, Lincoln and the newspapermen declared their determination to protect the rights of the free states, as well:

> "RESOLVED, That the conditions which are demanded under the plea of 'rights,' as being essential to the security of Slavery throughout its expanded and expanding area, are inconsistent with freedom, and an invasion of our rights, oppressive and unjust, and must be resisted.

> "RESOLVED, That we are in favor of the restoration of the Missouri Compromise, or in other words, that we will strive by all legal means, to restore to Kansas and Nebraska, a legal guarantee against Slavery of which they were deprived at cost of the violation of the plighted faith of the nation."

As the *Weekly Republican* observed, the platform would suit neither the "ultra-abolitionists" nor the "proslavery fanatics," placing it in the middle ground on which Lincoln had been trying to tread.

The moderates had made their move to take control of the Republican movement while the abolitionists were out of town. The next step was the state anti-Nebraska convention in Bloomington. Although he still considered himself a Whig, Lincoln's name appeared on a "Call for a Republican Convention" published in the *Illinois State Journal* on May 10. It was placed there by William Herndon (a delegate to the convention) while Lincoln attended court in Pekin. When Lincoln's fellow Whigs protested, Herndon telegraphed Lincoln for his approval. "All right," Lincoln responded. "Go ahead. Will meet you. Radicals and all." He understood that his presence, and that of other Whigs, was necessary to prevent the convention from producing a "radical" platform.

Lincoln's address to the Bloomington convention is known as his "Lost Speech," because no transcript exists, although it is known that he concluded with this message to the South: "We won't go out of the Union, and you shan't!"

Lovejoy and Codding played prominent roles at the convention, but it was dominated by moderate Whigs and anti-Nebraska Democrats. On two significant points, the 1856 Bloomington anti-Nebraska convention adopted more conservative planks than the 1854 Springfield convention. The 1854 platform called for a ban on slavery in any place it did not presently exist; the 1856 platform simply suggested that Congress's "power should be exerted to prevent the extension of slavery into territories heretofore free." The 1854 convention sought to weaken the Fugitive Slave Law, by allowing free states to grant captured slaves "trial by jury and the writ of *habeas corpus*"; the 1856 convention avoided the issue by promising fidelity to the Constitution "in all its provisions."

That was good enough for Lincoln, who would spend the summer and fall of 1856 campaigning for the Republican presidential ticket of John C. Fremont and William Lewis Dayton. The first Republican campaign was not a success in Lincoln's home region. Reflecting the state's divisions over slavery, Fremont earned 64.3 percent of the vote in northern Illinois, 27.2 percent in central Illinois, and 13 percent in southern Illinois. In Sangamon County, Fremont finished third, behind Buchanan and former president Millard Fillmore. Fillmore was the candidate of the nativist American Party but was seen as "a Unionist alternative to political extremism," because he had signed the Compromise of 1850. The final tally in Sangamon was Buchanan 2,475; Fillmore 1,612; Fremont 1,174. If Lincoln wanted to win a Senate seat, he would have to find a way to unite the anti-Buchanan, anti-Nebraska vote behind the Republican ticket.

Nearly four years after their dueling Kansas-Nebraska addresses at the State House, Douglas and Lincoln returned to Springfield as candidates for the Senate. Much had changed since then, in America and in Illinois.

Edwards's Grove, Springfield, Illinois, July 17, 1858

Douglas's political carnival on rails next made its way the sixty-five miles from Bloomington to the state capital. By the time it arrived, to a fusillade of cannon fire, the train had lengthened to twenty-five cars, to accommodate a welcoming committee whose names filled an entire column of the *Illinois State Register*.

"No man at this day occupies a more conspicuous position before the whole country than Stephen A. Douglas," the *Register* editorialized. "Let us give him here to-day such a welcome as may proclaim that while Illinois appreciates Douglas's personal worth, they do that which is more important to themselves—honor the advocate of popular rights, the champion of the sovereignty of the states, and the right of the majority to rule."

Springfield and its hinterlands gave Douglas that hero's welcome. The Chicago Great Western and the St. Louis, Alton & Chicago railroads chartered excursion trains for farmers who wanted to see the Little Giant in person. At three o'clock, Douglas's locomotive halted at a grove belonging to B. S. Edwards, head of the reception committee. Douglas was met by Springfield's own Capital Guards and their accompanying band, who escorted him to the speaker's platform. Lincoln, who had hitched a ride on Douglas's train, slipped anonymously out of his berth and headed home to plan his own speech at the State House that evening.

Speaking to a crowd standing in mud frothed up by the rain shower that had coincided with his arrival, Douglas began, as usual, by defending his stance on Lecompton. Then, however, he anticipated the Thirteenth Amendment by predicting that Lincoln would attempt to abolish slavery not by war, but by constitutional means.

"What is his remedy for this imaginary wrong which he supposes to exist?" Douglas asked. "The Constitution of the United States provides that it may be amended by Congress passing an amendment by a two-thirds majority of each house, which shall be ratified by three-fourths of the states, and the inference is that Mr. Lincoln intends to carry this slavery agitation into Congress with the view of amending the Constitution so that slavery can be abolished in all the states of the Union."

This was a less harrowing route to abolitionism than the sectional war Douglas had accused Lincoln of fomenting. Still, he said, banning slavery nationwide "would be a uniformity not of liberty, but of despotism." It would violate the nation's founding principles, which guaranteed the (White) residents of every state the right to choose their own institutions—"the right to have slavery or not have it; to have Negroes or not have them."

Fear of an all-powerful federal government was a bedrock of the nineteenth-century Democratic platform. It was why the Democrats had differed from the Whigs on a national bank, and funding for internal improvements: if Washington wielded such power over the nation's purse, it could certainly wield that power over slavery. (Douglas, as a Northern Democrat representing an industrial state, did not mind the federal government investing in railroads, but as a presidential aspirant, he had to take into account the sentiments of the party's Southern wing.)

"Mr. Lincoln and myself differ radically and totally on the principles of this government," Douglas said. "He goes for consolidation, for uniformity in our local institutions, for blotting out state rights and state sovereignty, and consolidating all the power of the federal government."

This was another prescient statement, another example of Douglas forecasting Lincoln's presidency. The Civil War, and the constitutional amendments it produced, would begin America's transformation from a collection of "sovereign" states to a nation governed by a strong central government. Douglas was, quite accurately, laying out two competing visions of governance and inviting Illinoisans to choose.

Douglas ended the speech with this backhanded compliment to his opponent: "Mr. Lincoln is a kind-hearted, amiable, good-natured gentleman, with whom no man has a right to pick a quarrel, even if he wanted one. He is a worthy gentleman. I have known him for twenty-five years, and there is no finer citizen, and no kinder-hearted man. He is a fine lawyer, possesses high ability, and there is no objection to him, except the monstrous revolutionary doctrines with which he is identified, and which he conscientiously entertains, and is determined to carry out if he gets the power."

Douglas at least made it clear that his differences with Lincoln were political, not personal. Throughout the campaign, he was much more likely to compliment Lincoln, both on the stump and in person, than vice versa. Lincoln told friends that not speaking of Douglas was "the best mode of treating so small a matter." Then, unable to help himself, he groused that Douglas "will tell a lie to ten thousand people one day, even though he knows he may have to deny it to five thousand the next." Douglas, Lincoln said, had "bamboozled thousands into believing him." Some of these vituperative opinions may have originated in Lincoln's envy of Douglas, which had been eating away at him for twenty years. However much he joked about Douglas's height, the senator was no small matter in Lincoln's mind, or the mind of any Illinois Republican. Republicans' hatred of Douglas and slavery were inseparable, because they saw the one as enabling the other. Also, Lincoln was a moralist, while Douglas was a practical politician, less likely to ascribe differences in policy to defects of character. Douglas, who threw enormous parties and drank enormous quantities of liquor, was far more sociable and fonder of bonhomie than the gloomy, solitary, abstemious Lincoln.

As Lincoln prepared to speak at the State House that evening, he had every reason to believe that his antislavery message would be more enthusiastically received than it had been eight, or even four, years ago. In 1854, Douglas had predicted that "in less than five years, you would need a search warrant to find an anti-Nebraska man." Less than five years later, he retracted that prediction, confessing that "I did not claim the powers of a prophet." The Kansas-Nebraska Act was just the first of many events that had turned public opinion in Springfield against the bullying of the Slave Power. Unlike Chicago and Boston, which rioted when federal officials attempted to return escaped slaves to their masters, Springfield was not aroused to action when Lincoln's law partner, William Herndon, defended a runaway slave before the United States commissioner. Herndon lost the case, and the slave was returned to Kentucky without protest from the spectators, who did not see the Fugitive Slave Law as compelling the

North to participate in the practice of slavery, but as means of enforcing a right guaranteed to slaveholders by the Constitution—adherence to which was the glue holding the Union together.

"However many of them may have expressed their dissatisfaction at the oppression of some of the provisions of the Fugitive Slave Law, so long as it remained on the Statute Book, they exhibited a perfect willingness to see the law take its course," the *Illinois State Journal* wrote of the spectators. "Upon the announcement of the Commissioner's decision, the crowd quietly dispersed, and the negro was delivered up to the claimant."

The Fugitive Slave Law protected slavery where it already existed. Only an abolitionist could object to that. The Dred Scott decision, however, evoked a stronger reaction in central Illinois. The *Quincy Daily Whig* ran an article quoting an "Old Line Whig" who called the decision so "tyrannical" and "outrageous" it turned him Republican: "There is a point beyond which the slave power cannot lead man."

Even before Dred Scott, Northern outrage over the aggressiveness and intolerance of the proslavery movement had been growing. On May 21, 1856, a proslavery militia attacked Lawrence, Kansas, which had been founded by Massachusetts abolitionists, killing a settler and destroying a printing press used to publish an abolitionist newspaper. The next day, in Washington, South Carolina representative Preston Brooks walked onto the Senate floor and delivered a savage caning to Massachusetts senator Charles Sumner, in retaliation for a speech decrying the violence in "Bleeding Kansas" and calling for its admission as a free state. Both incidents were reported in the *Illinois State Journal*, which denounced the "bloody deeds" of the "border ruffians" in Kansas, and the "cowardly assault" by Brooks, who was identified as "a member of the Douglas faction."

In *The Origins of the Republican Party, 1852–1856*, historian William E. Gienapp argues that the Sack of Lawrence and the caning of Sumner converted "thousands" of Northerners to Republicanism.

"The symbols of Bleeding Sumner and Bleeding Kansas allowed Republicans to attack the South without attacking slavery directly," Gienapp wrote. "By appropriating the great abolitionist symbol of the Slave Power and linking it to Northern rights, Republicans made a more powerful appeal to Northern sensibilities than they could otherwise have done."

Attacking the Slave Power without attacking slavery directly was, of course, the needle Lincoln had been trying to thread for his entire political career. Now that message had a more receptive audience in the heart of Illinois. In his State House speech, hours after Douglas's rally in Edwards's Grove, Lincoln brought up both Kansas and Brooks—and again attempted to tie Douglas to the conspiracy to nationalize slavery.

Lincoln began, though, with a self-deprecating comparison between himself and Douglas: "Senator Douglas is of world-wide renown. All the anxious politicians of his party have been looking on him as certainly, at no distant day, the President of the United States. They have seen in his round, jolly, fruitful face, post offices, land offices, marshalships and cabinet appointments, bursting and sprouting out in wonderful exuberance, ready to be laid hold of by their greedy hands. On the contrary, nobody has ever expected me to be president. In my poor, lean, lank face, nobody had ever seen that any cabbages were sprouting out." Lincoln was posing as the underdog to win over his audience; they responded to his juxtaposition of well-fed Douglas and scarecrow Lincoln with cheers and laughter. It was true that in the summer of 1858, no one thought of Lincoln as a potential president. By the end of the Senate campaign, though, he would join the list of contenders for the Republican nomination, while Douglas's near-certain prospects of winning the Democratic nomination would be in peril.

Lincoln pointed out that Douglas's endorsement of the Dred Scott decision was a violation of his beloved popular sovereignty, because it forbade settlers from excluding slavery: "the Judge is not sustaining popular sovereignty, but absolutely opposing it," Lincoln said to cheers. "He sustains the decision which declares that the popular will of the territories has no constitutional power to exclude slavery during their territorial existence."

Preston Brooks's caning of Sumner, Lincoln argued, represented a shift in Southern attitudes toward slavery, which had followed the invention of the cotton gin. The Virginia founders had set up a system that anticipated slavery's demise, but their descendants were finding it too profitable to abandon. The governor of South Carolina was even talking about reviving the African slave trade to fill the new territory *Dred Scott* had opened to slavery—another cause for alarm in the North.

"Mr. Brooks, in one of his speeches, when they were presenting him with canes, silver plate, gold pitchers, and the like, for assaulting Senator Sumner, distinctly affirmed his opinion that when this Constitution was formed, it was the belief of no man that slavery would last to this day," Lincoln said, taking care to link Southern violence with slavery expansion. "But he went on to say that the men of the present age, by their experience, have become wiser than the framers of the Constitution, and the invention of the cotton gin had made the perpetuating of slavery a necessity."

And who was collaborating with the South to perpetuate slavery, by helping it acquire new slave territory, so the institution could thrive and grow? Douglas, of course.

"Judge Douglas is *for* Supreme Court decisions when he likes them, and against them when he does not like them," Lincoln said. "He is for the Dred Scott decision because it tends to nationalize slavery—because it is part of the original combination for that object. It so happens, singularly enough, that I never stood opposed to a decision of the Supreme Court until this. On the contrary, I have no recollection that he was ever particularly in favor of one until this. He was never in favor of any, nor opposed to any, till the present one, which helps to nationalize slavery."

Douglas did not attend Lincoln's speech. That night, he met with the state Democratic committee to plan the schedule for his Senate campaign through the end of August.

"Do not spend too much time in the North," Representative Thomas Harris had written to Douglas. "The entire South as well as the Military Tract"—in western Illinois—"is regarded by all as safe beyond question."

Harris, who represented Springfield in Congress, may have been motivated by political self-interest: his reelection prospects would benefit from appearances by Senator Douglas in central Illinois. The Douglas campaign took his advice, though, scheduling summer rallies in small towns spanning the midsection of the state: Clinton, Monticello, Paris, Hillsboro,

Greenville, Edwardsville, Winchester, Pittsfield, Beardstown, Havana, Lewistown, Peoria, Lacon, and Ottawa.

Lincoln was making the same calculations. In an "1858 Campaign Strategy" memorandum, he scribbled out a list of central Illinois districts where the combined vote for Republican nominee John C. Fremont and Know Nothing nominee Millard Fillmore had been close to, or exceeded, the vote for Buchanan in 1856—these were districts the Republicans could win. "Struggle for the following," he wrote. By Lincoln's calculations, 19 districts with 22 representatives were "Democrats certain," 19 districts with 27 representatives were "Republicans certain," while 20 districts with 26 representatives—almost all in central Illinois—were "Questionable." Douglas would be campaigning in the Questionables. So, of course, would Lincoln. Wherever Douglas went, he went, too.

St. Louis, Alton & Chicago Railway, July 18, 1858

Douglas's journey downstate had been pompous and overweening, noisome with brass bands and cannon fire. His return home, on the rails of the St. Louis, Alton & Chicago, was sentimental. As the train sped through the night, Irish workingmen in trackside cottages interrupted evening smokes to lift their pipes in salute. Crowds gathered at rural depots, ordinarily empty at that hour, to celebrate Douglas's progress with the discharge of "pocket pistols." The train paused in Wilmington, so Douglas could again greet the elderly supporter who had embraced him on the platform during his trip down. In Bridgeport, on the outskirts of Chicago, G. Whillikins, the *Chicago Times* newspaper poet, hoped to deliver "a node to popular sovereignty" to Douglas, but the local switchmen set the train on a course to Great Central Station, forcing Mr. Whillikins to save it for the following Sunday's edition. As the train passed the slaughterhouses, though, it was greeted with a row of animal carcasses hung "by some persons unknown . . . to be indicative of the Douglas party at the close of the campaign." Douglas ignored the insult. The throngs he had addressed, in Chicago, Bloomington, and Springfield, were bigger than any audiences Lincoln could attract. The Democrats were going to win the Questionables and reelect Douglas to the Senate.

Law Office of Norman B. Judd, Chicago, Illinois, July 22, 1858

A few days after Douglas returned home, Lincoln traveled to Chicago himself—not on a chartered train, but using a free pass issued by the Illinois Central Railroad in appreciation of his legal counsel. Lincoln had been summoned to Chicago for a strategy session with the Republican State Committee, which had decided that his practice of attaching himself like a camp follower to the Douglas campaign was making him look ridiculous. The Democratic press mocked Lincoln as a candidate desperate for a crowd. The *Chicago Times* addressed this suggestion to Republican state chairman Norman Judd: "There are two very good circuses and menageries traveling through the State; these exhibitions always draw good crowds at country towns. Mr. Judd, on behalf of his candidate, at a reasonable expense, might make arrangements with the managers of these exhibitions to include a speech from Lincoln in their performances. In this way Lincoln could get good audiences, and his friends be relieved from the mortification they feel at his present humiliating position."

The committee came up with a proposal more dignified than a circus: a series of debates. Horace Greeley, whose *New-York Tribune* was taking an obsessive interest in the Illinois Senate race, expressed the hope that "Messrs. Lincoln and Douglas will speak together at some fifteen or twenty of the most important and widely accessible points throughout the state"—thus providing plenty of newspaper copy. The *Chicago Press and Tribune* also suggested the candidates "canvass the State together, in the usual western style."

When the committee presented Lincoln with the proposal, in Judd's law office, he was reluctant to debate Douglas. Douglas was the most popular politician in Illinois and had spent years honing his rhetorical skills in the Senate. This would no longer be two callow strivers arguing in front of a few curiosity seekers in a courthouse square. Douglas would pack the crowds with his followers, who would hoot their disapproval of Lincoln's inferior arguments. Despite these objections, Judd finally prevailed upon Lincoln to write a letter to Douglas, challenging him to debate. Lincoln drafted the brief note in Judd's office.

My Dear Sir,

Will it be agreeable for you to make an arrangement for you and myself to address the same audiences during the present canvass? Mr. Judd, who will hand you this, is authorized to receive your answer; and, if agreeable to you, to enter into the terms of such agreement.

Your obedient servant,

A. LINCOLN

Judd promised to track Douglas down in Chicago and deliver the letter to him personally.

Chicago, Illinois, July 24, 1858

Norman Judd spent three days looking for Stephen Douglas. When Judd finally located the senator, Douglas reacted indignantly to the letter he was bearing.

"What do you come to me with such a thing as this for?" Douglas blustered.

Douglas knew the newspapers were demanding debates between the candidates but could see no advantage in allowing Lincoln to share a platform with him.

"Between you and me, I do not feel that I want to go into this debate," Douglas told intimates. "The whole country knows me and has me measured. Lincoln, as regards myself, is comparatively unknown, and if he gets the best of this debate—and I want to say he is the ablest man the Republicans have got—I shall lose everything. Should I win, I shall gain but little."

Douglas had already scheduled a slate of campaign appearances and was unwilling to allow Lincoln to piggyback on any of those. He was also unwilling to allow Sidney Breese, the Buchanan-backed candidate, to horn in on any debates. On the other hand, Douglas relished a challenge and was sensitive to accusations that he was afraid to take on Lincoln. As the *Chicago Press and Tribune* wrote, debates were "the usual, almost universal western style of conducting a political campaign, and it has been justly held that the candidate who refused to speak in that way had no better reason than cowardice for declining the challenge."

And so, the same day he received Lincoln's letter from Judd, Douglas dictated a reply. He would not cancel any existing engagements. He would not debate Breese. He was surprised that Lincoln had not made the proposal earlier—in Chicago or Bloomington. Nonetheless, Douglas wrote, "I will, in order to accommodate you as far as it is in my power to do so, take the responsibility of making an arrangement with you for a discussion between us at one prominent point in each Congressional District in the state, except the second and sixth districts, where we have both spoken,* and in each of which cases you had the concluding speech. If agreeable to you, I will indicate the following places as those most suitable in the several Congressional Districts at which we should speak, to wit: Freeport, Ottawa, Galesburg, Quincy, Alton, Jonesboro, and Charleston."

Douglas had laid out the itinerary for what would become the most famous congressional election in American history. He had also written the letter that would, ultimately, make Abraham Lincoln president of the United States.

On the road between Bement and Monticello, Piatt County, Illinois, July 29, 1858

Douglas continued his campaign to win central Illinois with a Tuesday afternoon speech to a crowd of 6,000 in Clinton, the seat of DeWitt

---

* Chicago was in the second district, Springfield in the sixth.

County. With Lincoln and Judge David Davis seated on the platform beside him, Douglas defended himself against Lincoln's charge that he was part of a conspiracy to nationalize slavery, along with "Franklin and Roger and James." Lincoln's concluding speech, delivered by candlelight in the courthouse that evening, was less well attended.

"There are but few present," Lincoln said to the two or three dozen in the courtroom when he began speaking, "but as I made the announcement that I would speak, and as you have probably stayed or come for the express purpose of hearing me, I felt it due to you that I should fulfill my promise. I will go on and reply to Douglas in full—notwithstanding the smallness of the meeting."

Eventually, a Republican procession arrived at the courthouse, filling the room and kindling Lincoln's enthusiasm for his oration.

On Thursday the 29th, Douglas spoke in Monticello. As the senator and his party were leaving town, on their way to Bement, a railway stop seven miles to the south where Douglas planned to catch a train to Paris, they encountered Lincoln, who was headed for Monticello. Both carriages came to a halt. Lincoln jumped out to shake Douglas's hand.

"Come to, Lincoln, return to Bement," Douglas said, assuming Lincoln was planning his usual follow-up speech. "You see we have only a mile or two of people here. I will promise you a much larger meeting there than you will have at Monticello."

"No, Judge," Lincoln replied, "I can't. The fact is I did not come over here to make a speech. I don't intend to follow you anymore; I don't call this following you. I have come down here from Springfield to see you and give you my reply to your letter. I have it in my pocket, but I have not compared it with the copy yet. We can compare the two now, can't we?"

"You had better compare the two at Monticello," Douglas said. "When you have your answer ready, send it to me at Bement, where I intend to remain until the one o'clock P.M. to the east."

Lincoln agreed to do so. Then he again shook hands with Douglas and assured the senator he had given up following him. When Lincoln got to Monticello, though, he gave a thirty-minute speech in the same grove where Douglas had just spoken. As long as he was there, in the wake of Douglas, he might as well campaign, too. After that, though, Lincoln kept his word, returning to Springfield on the midnight train, rather than trailing Douglas to Paris. From Springfield, Lincoln went on to Chicago, where he would work out his own schedule of appointments with the Republican State Committee.

The letter Lincoln dispatched to Douglas in Bement was somewhat querulous. He had not proposed a series of debates during their appearances in Chicago and Bloomington, he wrote, because "I did not know but that such proposal would come from you; I waited, respectfully, to see." Lincoln also disputed Douglas's contention that he had always gotten the last word: "At Chicago, July 9th, you made a carefully prepared conclusion on my speech of June 16th. Twenty-four hours after, I made a hasty conclusion on yours of the 9th. In the meantime, you had made another conclusion on me at Springfield, which I did not hear, and of the contents of which I knew nothing when I spoke; so that your speech made in daylight, and mine at night, on the 17th, were both made in perfect independence of each other."

Lincoln ended the letter with this postscript: "As matters now stand, I shall be at no more of your exclusive meetings; and for about a week from today a letter from you will reach me at Springfield."

When Douglas's letter reached Lincoln, he was not entirely happy with its contents. Douglas proposed that the candidates alternate openings, with himself going first at Ottawa, on August 21. That would give Douglas four openings to Lincoln's three. Lincoln was the challenger, though; he needed the publicity from these debates more than Douglas did. "I accede," he responded, "and thus close the arrangement."

The 1858 Illinois Senate debates were set. They were, at the time, the Douglas-Lincoln debates. The contestants' later fortunes would cause history to remember them the other way around.

CHAPTER 3

"ALL PRAIRIEDOM HAS BROKEN LOOSE"

Washington Square, Ottawa, Illinois, August 21, 1858

In Ottawa, the site of his first debate with Stephen Douglas, Abraham Lincoln made the grand entrance. On this hot high summer Saturday, 15,000 spectators crowded the wooden sidewalks of Ottawa, converging on the village by canal boat, horseback, wagon, carriage, and foot, doubling its population in an afternoon.

"The crowd had a holiday air," a woman remembered half a century later. "It seemed out of place to me, for those were serious questions that Mr. Lincoln and Mr. Douglas were debating. The people paid for the gayety of that day in the horrors of the Civil War."

Lincoln would not have the first word—as the incumbent, Douglas got the initial opening speech—but he would have the crowd. Ottawa lay in the Third Congressional District, represented by the abolitionist Owen Lovejoy.

By the time Lincoln arrived at the Rock Island Railroad depot on the noon train from Chicago, thousands of Republicans had gathered outside. He was greeted with three cheers, then hustled into a carriage decorated with evergreen boughs and antislavery slogans. Slowly, the carriage rolled toward the mansion of Mayor J. O. Glover, preceded by a marching band and a bunting-draped float on which stood thirty-two waving girls, one for each state in the Union. Lincoln was being borne toward his destiny, for it was on this day, in this place, that he would become a national figure, whose arguments against the spread of slavery were published in newspapers across the nation, adding his name to the list of Republican presidential contenders two years hence. Ottawa was an appropriate setting for this sudden swelling of Lincoln's fame: there the Fox River, a tertiary stream, flows into the Illinois River, which grows in power until it meets the Mississippi.

Douglas received a more rustic greeting. He arrived by carriage from Peru, seventeen miles downriver. At Buffalo Rock, a bluff overlooking the Illinois, the senator was met by farm wagons, buggies, and a band. The procession, which straggled out for nearly a mile, guided him to Geiger House, Ottawa's leading hotel, where he delivered a pre-debate speech. The Republican and Democratic bands arrived simultaneously in the town square. Trapped by the crowds, they expressed their partisan rivalry by playing as loudly as possible, trying to drown each other out. There was so much competition for space near the speakers' platform, which had been erected beneath the square's few trees, that spectators climbed onto pine planks. After a few boys caused part of the platform's roof to collapse on the heads of the reception committee, marshals shooed the crowd back onto the baking grass.

The debate was scheduled for two o'clock, but it took Lincoln and Douglas so long to work their way through thousands of bodies that the speaking did not commence until half past. Lincoln jovially patted boys on the head, joking to one's mother, "Here comes Douglas; a little man in some respects but a mighty one in others." Once he reached the stand, he handed his heavy black frock coat to Ottawa's Republican state senator, Burton C. Cook. "Hold it while I stone Douglas," Lincoln told Cook.

The first stone belonged to Douglas, though, and he used it to attack Lincoln with what even he later admitted was a falsehood. Douglas began his opening speech by hearkening to the days when there had been two national parties, the Whigs and the Democrats, both equally devoted to the principle of allowing the states and the territories to decide for themselves the slavery question, both able to proclaim their doctrines "in Louisiana and Massachusetts alike." Douglas attempted to defend the Kansas-Nebraska Act as consistent with the doctrines of both parties, but ended up admitting that he himself had shattered the nation's comity on slavery: "Up to 1854, when the Kansas and Nebraska Bill was brought to Congress for the purpose of carrying out the principles which both parties had up to that time endorsed and approved, there had been no division in this country in regard to that principle except the opposition of the Abolitionists."

Thus, anyone who opposed Kansas-Nebraska must be an abolitionist. After President Pierce signed the act into law, Lincoln, a Whig, and Illinois's current junior senator, Lyman Trumbull, an anti-Nebraska Democrat, "entered into an arrangement, one with the other, and each with his respective friends, to dissolve the old Whig party on the one hand, and to dissolve the old Democratic party on the other, and to connect the members of both into an Abolition party under the name and disguise of a Republican party."

Ottawa was in Yankee northern Illinois, but the crowd was nonetheless peopled with Democrats, who here cried "Hurrah for Douglas"—music to the ears of Lincoln, who welcomed the chance to win them over.

From a pocket of his jacket, Douglas pulled a clipping from the *Illinois State Register*, a Springfield newspaper published by his friend and political ally Charles Lanphier. It was a report on a Republican meeting held in Springfield in October 1854—a meeting to which Lincoln had been invited by the New York–born, Vermont-educated abolitionist Ichabod Codding, but refused to attend.

Yet Douglas proceeded as though Lincoln had organized the meeting and drafted its platform, which dedicated the Republican Party to repealing the Fugitive Slave Law, prohibiting the admission of new slave states, abolishing slavery in the District of Columbia, and excluding slavery from the territories. In fact, Lincoln endorsed only the last measure.

"My object in reading these resolutions," Douglas declared, "was to put the question to Abraham Lincoln this day, whether he now stands and will stand by each article in that creed and carry it out"—just as he had (supposedly) intended in 1854.

"I ask Abraham Lincoln to answer these questions in order that when I trot him down to Lower Egypt I may put the same questions. I desire to know whether Mr. Lincoln's principles will bear transplanting from Ottawa to Jonesboro?"—the site of the third debate, scheduled for September 15, in proslavery southern Illinois.

After interrogating Lincoln, though, Douglas became sentimental toward his opponent, reflecting on their long acquaintance, which went back twenty-five years, to the days when "I was a school-teacher in the town of Winchester, and he a flourishing grocery-keeper in the town of Salem." (This was a dig at the teetotaling Lincoln, since a "grocery" was an establishment that sold liquor.) When Douglas and Lincoln met as young legislators in Vandalia, in 1836, Douglas "had a sympathy with him, because of the uphill struggle we both had in life. He was then just as good at telling an anecdote as now. He could beat any of the boys wrestling, or running a fast race, in pitching quoits or tossing a copper, could ruin more liquor than all the boys of the town together, and the dignity and impartiality with which he presided at a horse race or fist fight excited the admiration and won the praise of everyone."

Douglas never insulted Lincoln personally, but he used his opening speech to put Lincoln on the defensive over the issue of Black equality. Douglas, who had held statewide office longer than any other Illinois politician, knew his constituents did not want slavery in their midst, but did not want emancipation, either, and for the same reason: both would force Whites to compete with Black labor. This anxiety was especially acute among the Irish ditchdiggers and southern Illinois dirt farmers who made up Douglas's base—more so than among the educated Yankee professionals who had gravitated toward the Republican Party.

"Do you desire to strike out of our state constitution that clause which keeps slaves and free Negroes out of the state, and allow the free Negroes to flow in, and cover your prairies with Black settlements?" Douglas asked, to cries of "No, no!" and "Never!" from the Democrats. "Do you desire to turn this beautiful state into a free Negro colony, in order that when Missouri abolishes slavery she can send 100,000 emancipated slaves into Illinois, to become citizens and voters, on an equality with yourselves? If you desire Negro citizenship, if you desire to allow them to come into the state and settle with the White man, if you desire them to vote on equality with yourselves, and to make them eligible for office, to serve on juries, and to adjudge your rights, then support Mr. Lincoln and the Black Republican Party, who are in favor of citizenship of the Negro."

Douglas sat down, and a coatless Lincoln stood to reply. One reason the 1858 Illinois senate debates are such a picturesque event in American history is the physical difference between the candidates. Two years hence, the spindly Lincoln would become, at six-foot-four, the tallest man ever to win the presidency. Douglas, five-foot-four, with a massive head atop a swelling torso, like a pair of stacked cannonballs, would have been the shortest. Charles Dickey, the sixteen-year-old son of T. Lyle Dickey, a Douglas supporter who later served on the Illinois Supreme Court, noted the distinction not just between their physiques, but in their speaking styles: "Douglas had a deep bass voice which could be heard in the distance, but his enunciation was not distinct and only the crowd within a hundred feet could understand what he said. Lincoln on the other hand, had a high tenor voice and very distinct enunciation, so he could be heard and understood out to the extreme edge of the crowd."

Douglas had thrown the Black citizenship accusation in Lincoln's lap, giving him no choice but to reassure the crowd that he, too, believed in White supremacy. Throughout the campaign, Lincoln emphasized that he supported economic equality for Blacks, but not social or political equality—a distinction unlikely to win over Whites who felt threatened by cheap Black labor, be it slave or free.

Lincoln began his reply by quoting from an 1854 speech in Peoria. He had favored freeing all the slaves and deporting them to Liberia but realized "its sudden execution is impossible. If they were all landed there in a day, they would all perish in the next ten days."

Africans had been enslaved in North America for 239 years. For the moment, the country was stuck with the practice of slavery—but not forever, Lincoln hoped. The country would be stuck with the Africans forever, but it should not follow that emancipation would put them on an equal footing with their former masters.

"I have no purpose directly or indirectly to interfere with the institution of slavery in the states where it exists," Lincoln said, refuting Douglas's charge that he was an abolitionist. "I believe I have no lawful right to do so, and I have no inclination to do so. I have no purpose to introduce political and social equality between the White and Black races. There is a physical difference between the two, which in my judgment will probably forever forbid their living together upon the footing of perfect equality, and inasmuch as it becomes a necessity that there must be a difference, I, as well as Judge Douglas, am in favor of the race to which I belong, having the superior position. I have never said anything to the contrary, but I hold that notwithstanding all this. There is no reason in the world why the Negro is not entitled to all the natural rights enumerated in the Declaration of Independence, the right to life, liberty, and the pursuit of happiness. I hold that he is as much entitled to those as the White man. I agree with Judge Douglas he is not my equal in many respects—certainly not in color, perhaps not in moral or intellectual endowment. But in the right to eat the bread, without leave of anybody else, which his own hand earns, he is my equal and the equal of Judge Douglas, and the equal of every living man."

(Lincoln referred to his opponent as "Judge Douglas" because he had spent two years on the Illinois Supreme Court. The title was both less impressive, and more pejorative, than "Senator.")

Lincoln cleared up Douglas's description of him as a "grocery keeper"—"Lincoln never kept a grocery in the world," he said, although "it is true that Lincoln did work the latter part of one winter in a small still house, up at the head of a hollow." Then he moved on to a more significant point of contention between himself and the judge: whose position on slavery was most consistent with the Founders' intentions. As Douglas saw it, the United States was created as a union of free and slave states, with protections for slavery written into the Constitution (although the word "slavery" appeared nowhere therein). There was no reason it could not continue that way in perpetuity. A house divided against itself had stood for eighty-four years and could continue standing. Lincoln believed the Founders had shared his antislavery convictions—even though most signers of the Declaration of Independence and nearly half the delegates to the Constitutional Convention were slaveholders. Lincoln looked past that to the fact that they had banned the African slave trade and prohibited slavery in the Northwest Territories. That was proof they opposed slavery's expansion and favored setting it "in the course of ultimate extinction." The cotton gin changed that course by making slavery too profitable for the South to abandon, but the Founders' designs were clear.

"But lately I think—and in this I charge nothing on the Judge's motives—lately I think that he, and those acting with him, have placed that institution on a new basis, which looks to the perpetuity and nationalization of slavery. And while it is placed upon this new basis, I say and I have said, that I believe we shall not have peace upon the question until the opponents of slavery arrest the further spread of it, and place it where the public mind shall rest in the belief that it is in the course of ultimate extinction; or, on the other hand, that its advocates will push it forward until it shall become alike lawful in the states, old as well as new, North as well as South. Now, I believe if we would arrest the spread, and place it where Washington and Jefferson and Madison placed it, it would be in the course of ultimate extinction, and the public mind would, as for eighty years past, believe it was in the course of ultimate extinction. The crisis would be past and the institution might be let alone for a hundred years, if it should live so long, in the states where it exists, yet it should be going out of existence in the way best for both the Black and White races."

Of course, Lincoln *did* charge Douglas's motives on the expansion of slavery. Douglas's endorsement of the Dred Scott decision, he asserted, was part of the senator's campaign to prepare the public for the next Dred Scott decision, one that would prohibit the states themselves from excluding slavery: "This being true and this being the way as I think that slavery is to be made national, let us consider what Judge Douglas is doing every day to that end," Lincoln said. "This man sticks to a decision which forbids the people of a territory, and he does not because he says it is right in itself—he does not give any opinion on that—but because it has been decided by the Court, and being decided by the Court, he is, and you are bound to take it in your political action as law—not that he judges at all of its merits, but because a decision of the Court is to him a 'Thus saith the Lord.'"

When the speaking was over, both candidates were borne off the platform on the shoulders of their supporters. Douglas accepted a ride back to Geiger House, from which he quickly caught a train home to Chicago. After a few blocks, Lincoln ordered his bearers "Now, boys, let me down, please" and walked the rest of the way to Mayor Glover's house, where he shook hands with supporters. In the evening, Lincoln accompanied Lovejoy to the LaSalle County Courthouse, to hear the congressman speak from the steps. Then he was guided back to his lodgings by a torchlight parade.

"Douglas and I, for the first time this canvass, crossed swords here yesterday," Lincoln wrote to his friend J. O. Cunningham the next day; "The fire flew some, and I am glad to know I am yet alive. There was a vast concourse of people—more than could [get] near enough to hear."

Those who had not been able to hear would be able to read. After the candidates, the most important figures on the speakers' platform were a pair of stenographers, one representing the Republican *Chicago Press and Tribune*, the other the Democratic *Chicago Times*. The *Press and Tribune*'s reporter, Robert Hitt, known as "the only representative of the shorthand art in the Northwest," had perfected his skill taking college lecture notes, and made a living as a court reporter in Chicago. Mid-debate, Hitt handed his notes to a runner, who boarded a train to Chicago and transcribed them during the ride. After the debate ended, Hitt headed to Chicago himself to complete the job. The *Press and Tribune* published the debate in full. Lincoln would call Hitt "about the only man I had ever known in my life connected with newspapers in whose honesty I fully believed." He was less pleased with the *Times*'s stenographer, James B. Sheridan, employed by the Douglas campaign to ensure that pro-administration Democratic newspapers reported his speeches accurately. Republicans accused the *Times* of botching Lincoln's speeches so badly they were incomprehensible. The *Times* responded that "the Republicans have a candidate for Senate of whose bad rhetoric and horrible jargon they are ashamed."

Within the week, debate transcripts had reached New York, where they were published in full in Horace Greeley's *New-York Tribune*, the city's largest newspaper, with a circulation of 200,000, and the nation's most influential organ of Republicanism.

"Perhaps no local contest in this country ever excited so general or so profound an interest as that now raging in Illinois, with Senator Douglas, the Federal Administration, and the Republican Party headed by Messrs. Lincoln and Trumbull as the combatants," the *Tribune* reported. "As our readers are already aware, one of the features of this remarkable contest is a series of public meetings in different parts of the State, where Mr. Douglas and Mr. Lincoln successively address the people. The first of these meetings was held at Ottawa on Saturday, the 21st, inst. Of the two, all partiality being left out of the question, we think Mr. Lincoln has decidedly the advantage."

According to the most influential newspaper editor in America, Illinois was the state to watch in 1858, and Lincoln was the Republican to watch.

Passenger House, Mendota, Illinois, August 27, 1858

Norman Judd finally located Lincoln at two in the morning on the day of the second debate. Judd had heard reports that Lincoln was devoting his campaign speeches to denying he wanted to free the slaves and allow them to vote and marry Whites—as he had done during the Ottawa debate—and was irked by his candidate's defensive posture. At a congressional nominating convention in Augusta, Lincoln addressed an audience of Clay Whigs, most of them migrants from slave states. According to a later report in the *Chicago Press and Tribune*, he devoted the first hour of his speech to "an examination of Clay's principles on the slavery question, and to repelling the charges, made against the speaker, that he was an 'Abolitionist' in favor of 'negro equality' and 'amalgamation.'" Lincoln would have the first hour in Freeport. He planned to use his time to answer, point by point, the "interrogatories" Douglas had set on his plate in Ottawa, regarding his alleged support of abolitionist measures. Judd wanted Lincoln to attack.

Lincoln agreed to meet with Judd before the Freeport debate, but first Judd had to find him. Lincoln had telegraphed that they should meet him in Freeport on Thursday night, but when Judd and fellow Republican State Committee member Ebenezer Peck arrived there, they learned that Lincoln had traveled to Mendota, a small town sixty miles to the south, where passengers changed trains from Chicago to St. Louis, so he could make a ceremonial entrance to Freeport on debate day. At two in the morning, they found Lincoln at a trackside inn, had him woken up, and talked strategy while the candidate "looked very comical sitting there on the side of the bed in his short night shirt."

Earlier that day, Judd and Peck had consulted with *Chicago Press and Tribune* publisher Joseph Medill, who drafted a letter he hoped would reach Lincoln before the debate, outlining a line of attack:

Put a few ugly questions at Douglas, as—
- Do you care whether slavery be voted up or down.
- Will you stand by the adjustment of the Kansas question on the basis of the English bill compromise.
- Having given your acquiescence and sanction to the Dred Scott decision that destroys popular sovereignty in the

Territories will you acquiesce in the other half of that decision when it comes to be applied to the states, by the same court?

- What becomes of your reunited popular sovereignty in Territories since the Dred Scott decision?

Lincoln rehearsed his replies to Douglas with Judd and Peck. But when Judd suggested "a slight change of the phraseology" to satisfy the antislavery Republicans of Freeport, Lincoln refused to alter his language. Douglas was already accusing him of showing one face to northern Illinois and another to Egypt.

"Now gentlemen, that is all," Lincoln replied. "I wouldn't tomorrow mislead any gentleman in that audience to be made president of the United States."

Judd left the room worried that Lincoln "wouldn't budge an inch from his well-studied formulas." The next morning, though, as Lincoln rode the train to Freeport with Judd and Peck, he composed four pointed questions for Douglas. The second question, a more polished version of Medill's "What becomes of your vaunted popular sovereignty?" challenge, would produce the most significant moment of the seven debates. Douglas's response would divide the Democratic Party, cost him his chairmanship of the Committee on Territories, and make his election as president two years hence impossible. If Lincoln's path to the presidency had opened the previous Saturday in Ottawa, Douglas's would close that Friday in Freeport.

Freeport, Illinois, August 27, 1858

Lincoln arrived at 10:00 A.M. on an Illinois Central special, to the grand reception promised by the welcoming committee: 2,000 Republicans crowded around the depot, though the day was gray and damp. Freeport was the northernmost of the seven debate sites, which inclined the crowd toward Lincoln, and the railroads were offering discounted excursion fares from Chicago: $4.35 for a round trip.

"All prairiedom has broken loose," the *New York Evening Post* reported of the throngs. "The streets are fairly black with people. It was astonishing how deep interest in politics this people take. Over many miles . . . eager participants come—on foot, on horseback, in wagons drawn by horses or mules, men, women and children, old and young; the half sick, just out of the last 'shake'; children in arms, infants at the maternal font, pushing on."

The crowd followed Lincoln to Brewster House. He made a short speech at the hotel then went to his room to wash off the dust of his journey. Lincoln's attempts to rest before the debate were interrupted by Republicans demanding he show himself at the balcony. Douglas, who had spent the night at Brewster House, shook hands in the lobby. Out in the streets, Lincoln fans from nearby Winnebago County trotted about in a wagon, chopping a log with axes.

Learning that the grandiloquent Douglas planned to arrive at the speaker's stand in a carriage drawn by four gray horses provided by the local postmaster, a Douglas appointee, local Republicans determined to outdo him in grandeur. They sent to next-door Carroll County for a Conestoga wagon, pulled by six sturdy farm horses. Lincoln reluctantly climbed into the wagon, his long legs dangling from the box, for a ride a Democratic paper said made him resemble "the skeleton of some greyhound."

Realizing his planned entrance had been outshone, Douglas simply walked the two blocks from Brewster House to the debate site. Douglas at least surpassed Lincoln in personal finery. He was "dressed like a cavalier—ruffled shirt, dark blue coat, light trousers and shiny shoes." Lincoln's "coarse, faced coat" was too short in the sleeves, and his trousers bagged at the knees.

"Douglas is no beauty, but he certainly has the advantage of Lincoln in looks," wrote the *New-York Tribune*'s correspondent. "Very tall and awkward, with a face of grotesque ugliness, he presents the strongest possible contrast to the thickset, burly bust and short legs of the judge."

Before the debate could begin, at two o'clock, Lincoln's favorite stenographer had to be called to the stand.

"Hold on Lincoln, you can't speak yet!" *Chicago Press and Tribune* editor William Bross shouted as Lincoln rose to make his opening statement. "Hitt isn't here, and there is not use your speaking unless the *Tribune* has a report."

"Hitt ain't here?" Lincoln asked anxiously. "Where is he?"

"If Hitt is in the crowd he will please come forward!" Bross shouted. "Is Hitt in the crowd? If he is, tell him Mr. Bross of the *Chicago Tribune* wants him to come here on the stand and make a verbatim report for the only people in the Northwest that has enterprise enough to publish speeches in the full!"

From far away, Hitt responded that he was on hand but couldn't squeeze through the crowd. So the spectators passed him overhead to the stand. Once Hitt was settled, with his pen and notebook, Lincoln began.

As Lincoln had promised Judd and Peck—to their dismay—he began on the defensive, answering the questions Douglas had posed to him six days earlier, in Ottawa.

Question 1: I desire to know whether Lincoln today stands as he did in 1854, in favor of the unconditional repeal of the Fugitive Slave Law?
Answer: I do not now, nor ever did, stand in favor of the unconditional repeal of the fugitive slave law.

Question 2: I desire him to answer whether he stands pledged today as he did in 1854, against the admission of any more slave states into the Union, even if the people want them?
Answer: I do not now, nor ever did, stand pledged against the admission of any slave states into the union.

Question 3: I want to know whether he stands pledged against the admission of a new state into the Union with such a constitution as the people of that state may see fit to make.

Answer: I do not stand pledged against the admission of a new state into the Union with such a constitution as the people of that state may see fit to make.

Question 4: I want to know whether he stands pledged to the abolition of slavery in the District of Columbia?
Answer: I do not stand today pledged to the abolition of slavery in the District of Columbia.

Question 5: I desire him to answer whether he stands pledged to the prohibition of the slave trade between the different states?
Answer: I do not stand pledged to the prohibition of the slave trade between the different states.

Question 6: I desire to know whether he stands pledged to prohibit slavery in all the territories of the United States, north as well as south of the Missouri Compromise line.
Answer: I am impliedly, if not expressly, pledged to a belief in the right and duty of Congress to prohibit slavery in all the United States territories.

Question 7: I desire him to answer whether he is opposed to the acquisition of any new territory unless slavery is first prohibited therein.
Answer: I am not generally opposed to honest acquisition of territory, and, in any given case, I would or would not oppose such acquisition, accordingly as I might think such acquisition would or would not aggravate the slavery question among ourselves.

Many of Douglas's questions were based on a false premise. As Robert Hitt discovered during a search through the *Press and Tribune* archives after the Ottawa debate, the resolutions Douglas had tried to pin on Lincoln were not even from the Springfield convention (which Lincoln had not attended), but from a county meeting of northern Illinois abolitionists in Aurora. Douglas had heard about the resolutions in a speech delivered by Thomas Harris, a Democratic candidate for Congress in the Springfield district. Before the Ottawa debate, he wrote to Lanphier asking for "the time and place at which that convention was held, whether it was a mass meeting or a delegate Convention, whether Lincoln was present and made a speech and such other facts concerning the matter as you may be able to give."

Lanphier sent Douglas a copy of Harris's speech, in which he read the Aurora resolutions and claimed they had been adopted by the state convention. That was good enough for Douglas to connect them with Lincoln—and every other Republican in Illinois. After Hitt uncovered the error, the *Tribune* published an article, two days after Ottawa debate, declaring, THE RESOLUTIONS WERE FRAUDS AND FORGERIES FROM FIRST TO LAST and charging that Douglas "basely, maliciously and willfully LIED." The newspaper printed the actual Springfield resolutions, which did not call for repealing the Fugitive Slave Law, nor abolishing slavery in the District of Columbia.

By the day of the Freeport debate, both candidates were aware that Douglas had tried to associate Lincoln with a set of resolutions from "a one-horse meeting in Aurora." Nonetheless, Lincoln responded. A quarter century of experience in Springfield politics had taught Lincoln the importance of separating himself from the radical notions of Yankee abolitionists, especially if he wanted to win over Fillmore voters in his home Whig Belt. The Aurora resolutions were so far outside the Illinois mainstream that they contained only one policy difference between Lincoln and Douglas: prohibiting slavery in the territories. That was the basic principle of Republicanism, the issue that had brought the party into existence. The error committed by Harris and Lamphier, and repeated by Douglas, had turned out to Lincoln's advantage; it allowed him to look moderate, by distinguishing his positions from those of

Joshua Giddings, Owen Lovejoy, Salmon P. Chase, and Frederick Douglass—the "Black Republican" abolitionists Douglas accused him of being in bed with.

Having dispensed with Douglas's questions, to the cheers of the Republican audience, Lincoln went on the offensive with four questions of his own:

> Question 1. If the people of Kansas shall by means entirely unobjectionable in other respects, adopt a state constitution and ask admission into the Union under it, before they have the requisite number of inhabitants according to the English Bill—some ninety-three thousand—will you vote to admit them?

> Question 2. Can the people of a United States territory, in any law against the wishes of a citizen of the United States, exclude slavery from its limits prior to the formation of a state constitution?

> Question 3. If the Supreme Court of the United States shall decide that states cannot exclude slavery from their limits, are you in favor of acquiescing in, adopting, and following such decisions as a rule of political action?

> Question 4. Are you in favor of acquiring additional territory, in disregard of how such acquisition may affect the nation on the slavery question?

"Good, good!" cried the throng.

Douglas had always believed that territories had the power to exclude slavery: if they didn't, there was no such thing as popular sovereignty. Now, though, he had to find a way to square his signature doctrine with the Dred Scott decision, the Supreme Court's ruling that slaveholders had a right to bring their lawful property into the territories. If Douglas agreed that the territories could not restrict slavery, he would open himself to charges that he was attempting to "Africanize" the continent, as the Republican *Chicago Press and Tribune* had put it; if he disagreed, he would outrage Southern Fire-Eaters, who were agitating for a federal slave code that would protect the right to slavery in the territories. Douglas was running for reelection to the Senate in the free state of Illinois, so he chose the latter course.

"I answer emphatically, as Mr. Lincoln has heard me answer a hundred times from every stump in Illinois, that in my opinion the people of a territory can by lawful means, exclude slavery from their limits prior to the formation of a state constitution," Douglas answered in response to Question 2. "It matters not what way the Supreme Court may hereafter decide as to the abstract question whether slavery may or may not go into a territory under the Constitution, the people have the lawful means to introduce it or exclude it as they please, for the reason that slavery cannot exist a day or an hour anywhere, unless it is supported by local police regulations."

"Right, right!" called the Democrats.

"Those police regulations can only be established by the local legislature, and if the people are opposed to slavery they will elect representatives to that body who will by unfriendly legislation effectively prevent the introduction of it in their midst. If, on the contrary, they are for it, their legislation will favor its extension. Hence, no matter what the decision of the Supreme Court may be on that abstract question, still the right of the people to make a slave territory or a free territory is perfect and complete under the Nebraska Bill."

This became known as Douglas's Freeport Doctrine. As he pointed out, he had made the same argument to other Illinois audiences, including at his Chicago homecoming speech two and a half months earlier. Those speeches, however, had not been published in newspapers throughout the nation. Southerners would respond by labeling Douglas a traitor to the rights of slaveholders, to the Democratic Party, and to the Constitution.

"Judge Douglas avowed the doctrine in his speech at Freeport, that the people of a territory, while in their territorial condition, have a right to establish or prohibit slavery," editorialized the *Nashville Patriot*. "This is the quintessence of squatter sovereignty, which has been repudiated by all parties in the South, with a few insignificant exceptions. The Washington *Union* regards it as placing Douglas irrevocably beyond the pale of the great Democratic party."

Coming after his opposition to the Lecompton Constitution, Douglas's Freeport Doctrine made him look, to the defenders of slavery, even worse than a Republican. Lincoln was at least up front about his opposition to slavery's spread; Douglas had pretended his Kansas-Nebraska Act would make its spread possible, but now Southerners were beginning to believe that his "popular sovereignty" was as much an obstacle to their institution's expansion as the Wilmot Proviso would have been. One of Douglas's chief arguments against Lincoln was that Lincoln was a sectional, Northern politician, while he was a national politician whose views on slavery could attract votes from both Northerners and Southerners. Douglas had risen to fame as the architect of the Compromise of 1850, but much had changed in eight years, and much of that change had been the result of the Kansas-Nebraska Act, which had created the Republican Party and the candidacy of the man challenging him for Senate. Douglas was now attempting to straddle a gap that was growing too broad for any politician to cover. The Northern abolitionists and the Southern Fire-Eaters Douglas had attempted to marginalize with his moderation were growing stronger in their respective sections. North and South were united only in their growing distrust of Douglas, who was seen as talking out of both sides of his mouth to placate all parties.

Douglas was never moderate in his support of White supremacy, though. He left the Freeport audience with an anecdote about "Fred Douglass" consorting with White women—which was where Lincoln's racial equality nonsense would lead the country.

"The last time I came here to make a speech, while talking from the stand as I to you people of Freeport, as I am doing today. I saw a carriage and a magnificent one it was, drive up and take a position on the outside of the crowd; a beautiful young lady was sitting on the box seat, whilst Fred Douglass and her mother reclined inside, and the owner of the carriage acted as driver. All I have to say on that subject is that those of you who believe that the Negro is your equal and ought to be on an equality with you socially, politically, and legally, have a right to entertain those opinions, and of course will vote for Mr. Lincoln."

There were cries of "Down with the Negro," but that November, the people of Stephenson County voted for Mr. Lincoln.

Union County Fairgrounds, Jonesboro, Illinois, September 15, 1858

In Ottawa, Douglas had promised to trot Lincoln down to Egypt, to see if he would dare repeat his antislavery doctrines there. He was speaking of Jonesboro, the seat of Union County, in deepest southern Illinois. (Egypt was the common nickname for the region. One Egyptian held that it was so called because the land around the confluence of the Ohio and Mississippi resembled the Nile Delta—indeed the city where they met was named Cairo, pronounced CARE-oh. According to another theory, Egypt got its name after a hard frost in 1831 forced northern Illinois farmers to travel south to buy feed for their livestock. Like the sons of Jacob in the Bible, they were said to be "going down to Egypt for corn.")

The longest-settled section of Illinois, Egypt had been populated by migrants from Kentucky and Tennessee and remained in sympathy with the South, culturally and politically. There was even a slave living in Jonesboro in 1858, a sixty-eight-year-old woman who had moved there with her mistress from Fleming County, Kentucky.

With nearly three weeks between the debates in Freeport and Jonesboro, and the necessity of traversing the length of the state, both candidates had the time and opportunity to campaign in the central Illinois Whig Belt, the swing region that would be far more important to their fortunes than the northernmost and southernmost debate sites. Lincoln spoke at the Tazewell County Republican Convention in Tremont, at Morton's Grove in Clinton, and in Carlinville, Bloomington, Monticello, Mattoon, Paris,

Hillsboro, Edwardsville, Highland, and Greenville. His theme was, generally, what is all this fuss that is being made about Blacks? He also had an answer to his opponent's Frederick Douglass anecdote: slavery, not freedom, led to race mixing. "Douglas pretends to be horrified at amalgamation, yet had he not opened the way for slavery in Kansas, could there have been any amalgamation there? Is not slavery the great source of it? You know that Virginia has more mulattoes than all the northern states!"

Of course, those "mulattoes" were the product of forced relations between slave masters and enslaved women, which produced less anxiety among Whites than the thought of Frederick Douglass sharing a carriage with their women.

As Douglas wended his way downstate, he gave two- and three-hour-long speeches in Joliet, Pontiac, Lincoln (named after his opponent, for lending his legal expertise to its incorporation in 1853), Jacksonville, Carlinville, and Belleville. In Pontiac, Douglas took questions after his speech. "They say you have turned your coat half a dozen times," a man said, commenting on Douglas's reputation for double talk. Douglas replied that he had drawn Northern ire for Kansas-Nebraska, and Southern ire for his opposition to the Lecompton Constitution, thus proving that "I stand by my principles and follow them to their logical conclusion, and I will not depart from them either to the right or the left to flatter one section or another." What Douglas saw as his consistency was earning him enemies on both sides of the slavery debate.

Two days before the debate, Douglas boarded the steamboat *James H. Lucas* in Chester, for the trip down the Mississippi to Cairo. He was accompanied by his wife and a party of dignitaries including Usher F. "For God's Sake" Linder, who'd been given that nickname after Douglas wrote him a letter entreating him to attend the Freeport debate: "For God's sake, Linder, come up into the Northern part of the State and help me. Every *dog* in the State is let loose after me."

Douglas's reception in Cairo was not as enthusiastic as he might have hoped for in Yellow Dog Democratic Egypt. The local Democrats were divided between Douglas's candidacy and the administration, or National, wing of the party, which had united with Buchanan to punish Douglas for his opposition to the Lecompton Constitution. Nicknamed Buchaneers, or Danites (after the Biblical shrine at Dan that rivaled Bethel in Israel), they held a competing state convention in April in Springfield, nominating a slate of statewide candidates, including former senator Sidney Breese for Douglas's seat. (Breese, who was known as "Father of the Illinois Central," for his early railroad lobbying in the Senate, felt slighted that Douglas claimed credit for the project.) Buchanan did his part by firing Douglas appointees from federal patronage jobs and replacing them with his own men—he had fired the Cairo postmaster, who was waiting on the Ohio River levee for the steamboat's arrival. An agitated Douglas felt he was fighting a campaign on two fronts—against Republicans and Danites. During his Belleville stop, he had lashed out at the publishers of a Danite newspaper as "a poor, weak, palsied man, tottering on the verge of the grave, with hardly strength enough to utter the blasphemy his tongue frames, and the other an arrant knave, who has cheated everybody in Belleville, and is despised by every one who knows him."

Douglas's supporters greeted the steamboat's landing by firing a cannon imported from Mound City, seven miles up the Ohio River. The cannon in Cairo was "a Buchanan cannon" and "would certainly have bursted on such an occasion" mocked the Danite *Cairo Weekly Times and Delta*.

"How d'ye do Mr. Douglas?" the chairman of the welcoming committee asked the senator, who was dressed plantation style in a white hat and coat.

"I am tolerable," Douglas responded.

Douglas led a small procession—including the twelve-piece Jonesboro Sax-Horn Band, led by an Austrian immigrant who had studied music in Vienna and performed for Emperor Maximilian—to the Taylor House. A ball in his honor was scheduled at the hotel that night. Douglas delivered a speech to a crowd of six hundred or so while Adele spent the afternoon in the kitchen, helping bake pies for the evening's guests. (To build enthusiasm for Douglas, Cairo's mayor chartered a steamer to offer free rides from Mound City. Only twenty people took him up on it.) Douglas left the ball early, to rest up for the next day's debate, but his vivacious young wife danced until midnight with the local notables.

The Wednesday afternoon crowd at Jonesboro was by far the smallest of the seven debates. Only about 1,400 traveled by railroad and ox cart to the shaded hill just outside of town where a rough-hewn platform had been erected against a walnut tree. Lying within the Shawnee Hills, Union County was rockier, hillier, and more forested than the rest of Illinois—and more sparsely populated, too, since its unsuitability for agriculture meant settlers had bypassed it for the more fruitful prairies. Douglas rode a carriage to the debate site, once again behind the Jonesboro Sax-Horn Band and an anti-Danite banner reading: MY SON, IF BOLTERS ENTICE THEE, CONSENT THOU NOT. Lincoln walked up the hill from the county courthouse with his friend Dale Phillips of Anna. Lincoln, who expected no reception in Union County, and received none, had spent the previous night at Phillips's house, with Horace White and Robert Hitt of the *Press and Tribune*. They were watching Donati's Comet, one of the brightest of the nineteenth-century. (As Lincoln mounted the hill, Professor Terpinitz, the leader of the Sax-Horn Band, asked "Who is that strange-looking man?"

"Why, that is Lincoln from Springfield who is going to debate Douglas," one of his musicians told him.)

In Jonesboro, Douglas again had the first word. Douglas had promised to force Lincoln to declare his antislavery principles before a crowd of Southern sympathizers. ("I will bring him to his milk," Douglas boasted before the debate.) The Republicans, he charged, ran on an abolition platform in the northern counties—prohibiting new slave states, repealing the Fugitive Slave Law—but changed their complexions once they left Chicago, from Black to "mulatto" to White.

"A little further south they became bleached and grew paler just in proportion as public sentiment moderated and changed in this direction," Douglas said. "They were Republicans or Abolitionists in the North, anti-Nebraska men down about Springfield, and in this neighborhood they contented themselves with talking about the inexpediency of the repeal of the Missouri Compromise."

Up North, "you find that all the conventions are called in the name of the Black Republican party; at Springfield, they dare not call a Republican convention, but invite all the enemies of the democracy to unite, and when they get down into Egypt, Trumbull issues notices calling upon the 'free democracy' to assemble and hear him speak."

Before the Democrats of Jonesboro, Lincoln not only asserted his opposition to the spread of slavery, he attacked the legal foundations of Douglas's Freeport Doctrine and asked Douglas whether he would support federal legislation to protect slaveholders' rights in the territories. That pried at another wedge between Douglas and the South.

The Freeport Doctrine's "proposition that slavery cannot enter a new country without police regulations is historically false," Lincoln argued. Dred Scott's master had kept him captive in Minnesota, not only without police regulations, but in defiance of the law prohibiting slavery in the Northwest Territories.

"This shows that there is vigor enough in slavery to plant itself in a new country even against unfriendly legislation," Lincoln said. "It takes not only law but the enforcement of law to keep it out."

Southerners believed it took not only law but the enforcement of law to bring it in. As Mississippi senator Jefferson Davis argued, Douglas's popular sovereignty was a threat to slaveholders because it created a vehicle for abrogating their property rights. Congress, Davis believed, had an obligation to pass a federal slave code—a law requiring territorial governments to provide police regulations for the protection of slavery. Lincoln asked Douglas whether he agreed with that demand: "If the slaveholding citizens of a United States territory should need and demand congressional legislation for the protection of their slave property in such territory, would you, as a member of Congress, vote for or against such legislation?"

In his rejoinder, Douglas responded that he would vote against it: "It is a fundamental article in the Democratic creed that there should be non-interference and non-intervention by Congress with slavery in the states, nor territories," he said to cheers as loud as 1,400 Egyptians could muster.

"Mr. Lincoln could have found an answer to his question in the Cincinnati platform, if he had desired it. The Democratic Party have always stood by that great principle of non-interference and non-intervention by Congress in the territories, and I stand on that question now."

Douglas had borrowed a cannon from a local militia company, the Sill House Grays. It was fired at dramatic moments in the oratory while a young man shouted "Bully for you!" and "Hit him again!"

A young Lincoln supporter named John McLean was so eager to see his hero that he rode twenty-five miles to Du Quoin, where he caught an Illinois Central train to Jonesboro. He was disappointed by the sight and the sound of his hero, but not by his oratory.

"As much as I admired Lincoln and the things for which he stood, his personal appearance was very disappointing," McLean would recall many years later. "He was a very tall man, standing about six feet six inches in his boots. While Douglas was speaking, Lincoln sat in a chair that was rather low, and as his feet were drawn in well toward the chair his knees were elevated to such a height and at such a sharp angle that it gave him a ludicrous appearance; and as he sat there he had a sad, far-away look in his eyes that gave me the impression that he was grieving about something and paying no attention whatever to the argument and eloquence of Judge Douglas. When the judge finished and Lincoln was introduced, he began to rise out of his chair, it seemed to me, one section at a time, until finally he stood head and shoulders above those around him. If I had been disappointed at his appearance, I certainly was at his delivery, for he began his address in a high-pitched, treble voice, all out of proportion to his massive head and frame, and accompanied it with rather an awkward carriage and gesture; but as he warmed into his subject, I became unconscious of his appearance and his voice, in the realization that I was listening to a wonderful message from a great soul, as with unerring accuracy, he recalled every point Douglas had made and demolished it with unerring accuracy."

Twenty-five-year-old Tillman Manus, a Tennessee native and lifelong Democrat, was won over to the Republican cause because he agreed with

Lincoln's plan to deport the Blacks to Africa. Manus would enlist in the Union Army during the Civil War, causing his father to disinherit him, since his uncles were Confederates.

Douglas did not win over any Danites. After the debate, Colonel John Dougherty, leader of Egypt's Buchanan faction and candidate for state treasurer, climbed onto the platform to make a speech "denouncing Douglas in the strongest possible terms." Not even Douglas's cannon could drown out Dougherty's condemnation. (Dougherty was an ally of Lincoln's. They had met that July in Springfield, where Dougherty had promised the Danites would run a statewide slate of candidates. "If you do this, the thing is settled—the battle is fought," Lincoln told him.)

The next day, both candidates traveled by train to Centralia, where the state fair was in session. The Danites organized an evening rally, headlined by former governor John Reynolds, their candidate for superintendent of public instruction. Reynolds asserted that "Stephen A. Douglas had deserted the Democracy and gone over to Black Republicanism." The Douglas men countered this with a speech from Linder, standing on a platform car across the fairgrounds from Reynolds. (Linder was a former Whig. Lincoln worried his support for Douglas would hurt the Republican ticket among conservative central Illinois Whigs—the election's most important swing voters.)

Douglas's appearance in Jonesboro did not win over the local newspaper, the *Jonesboro Gazette*, which published an editorial headlined REASONS FOR OPPOSING DOUGLAS. One reason: as an advocate of states' rights, Douglas had no problem with New York allowing Blacks to vote. If Blacks could vote in New York, they could run for Congress and make laws governing Whites: "Now we say New York has no such right, as the Dred Scott decision has declared that a negro can in no manner become a citizen of the United States; and consequently Senator Douglas opposes the Dred Scott decision."

No matter how many times Douglas fulminated against Negro equality from the stump, he was still not racist enough for Egypt. Douglas's popular sovereignty would always offend those who believed God had made Blacks fit only to serve Whites, and that no legislature, anywhere, should be allowed to rule otherwise.

Coles County Fairgrounds, Charleston, Illinois, September 18, 1858

Charleston was a town of just 847 people, with two hotels, a courthouse, and a railroad depot, but throughout the course of the debates, it was not outdone for pageantry. Both candidates spent the night in Mattoon, Douglas at the Essex House, Lincoln at the Pennsylvania. (Douglas had enjoyed a much more comfortable journey on the Illinois Central from Centralia to Mattoon than Lincoln. He was accompanied, in a luxurious car, by railroad vice president George B. McClellan, a future Union general and, like Douglas, a future Democratic presidential opponent of Lincoln's. Lincoln boarded a crowded train at midnight. Finding no empty seats, he sneaked into a saloon car to sleep.) In the morning, the candidates paraded the ten miles to Charleston, the Republicans on the south road, the Democrats on the north, to prevent a partisan traffic jam. Lincoln rode in a carriage drawn by a team of cream-colored horses and was heralded by the "Bowling Green" band from Terre Haute, Indiana. In Douglas's procession were sixteen young men in frock coats and bow ties, and sixteen young women in billowing dresses, mounted on horseback, each carrying an American flag mounted on an ash pole or a hickory stick. Ash represented the Whigs, hickory the Democrats—the two "national" parties whose adherents would unite to reelect Douglas. The Republicans outdid that display with a flower-covered float on which stood thirty-two women, carrying banners with the name of each state, wearing blue velvet caps encompassed with wreaths of green and emblazoned with silver stars. The float was trimmed with cedar and hung with bunting and local prairie flowers. On one side was a banner proclaiming, WESTWARD THE STAR OF EMPIRE MAKES ITS WAY, OUR GIRLS LINK-ON TO LINCOLN, THEIR MOTHERS WERE FOR CLAY. On the other side, the names of the candidates on the Republican ticket: Lincoln, Richard Oglesby for Congress, Thomas Marshall for state senate, W. W. Craddock for state house. Trotting in front of the float was local beauty Eliza Marshall aboard "Old Whitey," a horse representing Kansas, the prospective thirty-third state. Old Whitey's blanket read I WILL BE FREE. As if that weren't overwhelming enough, the Republicans had stretched an eighty-foot banner from a corner of the Coles County Courthouse to a building on the west side of the town square (which was, like every other building on the square, red, white, and blue with flags and bunting). On the banner was painted a teenaged Lincoln, standing in a Kentucky wagon pulled by three oxen. The words beneath: OLD ABE THIRTY YEARS AGO—two years before his arrival in Illinois.

Debate day was sunny and mellow, a Saturday three days before the end of summer. From the surrounding prairie hamlets—Dogtown, Bloody Hutton, Greasy Creek, Paradise, Muddy Point, Farmington, Goose Lake Prairie—12,000 spectators thronged into the tiny county seat, carrying signs proclaiming EDGAR COUNTY GOOD FOR 500 MAJORITY FOR THE LITTLE GIANT, THIS GOVERNMENT MADE FOR WHITE MEN—DOUGLAS FOR LIFE, ABE THE GIANT KILLER, and SUPPORT ABRAHAM LINCOLN, THE DEFENDER OF HENRY CLAY."

The site of the first debate in the all-important Whig Belt, Charleston was familiar territory to Lincoln. His father had farmed in Coles County, and his beloved stepmother, Sarah Bush Lincoln, still lived on the Lincoln homestead. (According to local lore, Sarah was in attendance that day. When Lincoln spotted her during the procession to the fairgrounds, he stepped out of his carriage to kiss her.) Lincoln had also practiced law in Charleston. Although Charleston was part of the Fourth Judicial Circuit, it was on the road between Shelbyville and Paris, two Eighth Circuit county seats. Lincoln often stopped there to drum up cases and visit his cousin, Dennis Hanks, who lived on the town square. (Seven years earlier, though, Lincoln had refused to visit his father's deathbed, writing to stepbrother John Johnston, "Say to him that if we could meet now, it is doubtful whether it would be more painful than pleasant." Neither did Lincoln attend the funeral or provide a headstone for his illiterate father, who would have preferred his strapping son stick to farming rather than pursue law and politics.)

Once the candidates reached the fairgrounds, Douglas having ridden there in a carriage with his wife, Republicans unfurled a banner portraying Lincoln holding a club over a prostrate Douglas, labeled LINCOLN WORRYING DOUGLAS AT FREEPORT. Outraged Democrats demanded it be carried off. Lincoln agreed, saying, "Let us have nothing offensive to any man here today." Just before Lincoln rose for his opening remarks, though, Democrats approached the speakers' platform with their own offensive banner: NEGRO EQUALITY, a caricature of Lincoln and a Black woman. Two of Lincoln's supporters jumped off the platform and tore it down.

By the time of the Senate campaign, Lincoln had practiced politics in central Illinois for a quarter century. He knew its voters' prejudices, and he knew that to win, he had to convince them that he shared those prejudices. That, perhaps, motivated his opening speech, which can be hard to reconcile with the later Lincoln, who met with Frederick Douglass at the White House, signed the Emancipation Proclamation, and lobbied for the passage of the Thirteenth Amendment.

"While I was at the hotel today an elderly gentleman called upon me to know whether I was really in favor of producing a perfect equality between Negroes and White people," Lincoln began, to general laughter at such a ludicrous notion. "I will say then that I am not, nor have ever been in favor of bringing about in any way the social and political equality of the White and Black races, that I am not nor have ever been in favor of making voters or jurors of Negroes, nor of qualifying them to hold office, nor to intermarry with White people; And I will say in addition to this that there is a physical difference between the White and Black races which will forever forbid the two races living together on terms of social and political equality. And inasmuch as they cannot so live, while they do remain together there must be the position of superior and inferior, and I as much as any other man am in favor of having the superior position assigned to the White race. I say upon this occasion I do not perceive that because I do not want a Negro woman for a slave I must want her as a wife. My understanding is that I can just let her alone. I am now in my fiftieth year, and I certainly never have had a Black woman for either a slave or a wife. So it seems to me quite possible for us to get along without making either slaves or wives of Negroes."

Lincoln's witty parsing of the differences between economic and social equality drew cheers and laughter from the crowd. Once he was finished establishing that he was as devoted to White supremacy as any central Illinois farmer—or Senator Douglas, for that matter—Lincoln turned to an attack on his opponent's Senate record. In 1856, the Senate had passed a bill, sponsored by Senator Robert Toombs of Georgia, establishing a procedure for Kansas to pass a constitution, the first step toward joining the Union. (The bill died in the Republican-controlled House, which feared it could allow Kansas to enter as a slave state.)

Just before the debates, Lyman Trumbull was persuaded to return to Illinois to campaign for Lincoln (or at least against Douglas). During his first speech, in Chicago, Trumbull accused Douglas, as chairman of the Committee on Territories, of conspiring with Southern senators to strip out a provision from the Toombs bill requiring that Kansas's constitution be ratified by a vote of the people. That proved that Douglas's guiding principle was not popular sovereignty but appeasing Southern slaveholders. It was certainly a different tune than Douglas sang during his protests against the Lecompton Constitution. Trumbull, who had witnessed his seatmate's machinations, charged that "there was a preconceived arrangement and plot entered into by the very men who now claim credit for opposing a constitution not submitted by the people to have a constitution formed without giving the people the opportunity to pass upon it . . . it is the most damnable effrontery that man ever put on to conceal a scheme to defraud and cheat a people out of their rights, and then claim credit for it."

According to Trumbull, Toombs's original bill stated that a constitution must be "accepted by the convention, and ratified by the people at the election for the adoption of the Constitution." The bill that emerged from Douglas's committee simply required that a constitution must be "accepted by the convention." Trumbull repeated his charges in a speech at Alton. An outraged Douglas privately called Trumbull a "miserable, craven-hearted wretch," who "would sooner have both his ears cut off than make the charge to my face." In a speech at Jacksonville, Douglas said he would not refute Trumbull, but that Lincoln, having "endorsed the character of Trumbull's veracity," should "hold him responsible for the slanders."

Lincoln picked up the "slanders" in Charleston. In their three previous meetings, Lincoln and Douglas had argued about freedom, slavery, the racial caste system, and the meaning of the Declaration of Independence. They spent most of their afternoon in Charleston haggling over a clause in an obscure piece of legislation that never made it into law.

"The point upon Judge Douglas is this," Lincoln charged. "The bill that went into his hands had the provision in it for a submission of the constitution to the people; and I say its language amounts to an express provision for a submission, and that he took the provision out. He says it was known that the bill was silent in this particular; but I say, Judge Douglas, it was not silent when you got it. It was vocal with the declaration when you got it, for a submission of the constitution to the people. And now, my direct question to Judge Douglas is, to answer why, if he deemed the bill silent on this point, he found it necessary to strike out those particular words."

Douglas thought that Lincoln had wasted his hour: "He has devoted his entire time to an issue between Mr. Trumbull and myself, and has not uttered a word about the politics of the day."

Nonetheless, Douglas was obliged to defend himself against Lincoln and Trumbull. He considered their charges irrelevant. He had never been a proponent of the Toombs bill, which would have allowed Kansas to join the Union with a population of 25,000, rather than the 93,420 required for a representative in Congress. His committee, however, adopted the bill. In any case, a clause requiring a referendum was irrelevant, because no statehood bill had ever included one: "The general rule made the law silent on the subject, taking it for granted that the people would demand and compel a popular vote on the ratification of their constitution." Douglas accused Trumbull of "falsehood and slander," of "trump[ing] up a system of charges" to distract from Douglas's success at "showing up Lincoln's Abolitionism and Negro equality doctrines."

Focusing as it did on the minutiae of committee votes and congressional amendments, Charleston was the least enlightening of the seven debates. Lincoln might just as well have left the topic of the Toombs bill to Trumbull, because his own retelling of the charges left him little time for more substantive arguments.

During his rejoinder, Lincoln enlisted the support of Orlando Ficklin, a former congressman and Douglas supporter who was sitting behind his candidate on the platform. Lincoln and Ficklin both represented Illinois during Lincoln's lone term in Congress—Lincoln as a Whig, Ficklin as a Democrat. As he answered Douglas's accusation that he had refused to vote for appropriations for the troops during the Mexican War, Lincoln asked Ficklin to step forward.

"I do not mean to do anything with Mr. Ficklin except to present his face and tell you that he personally knows it is a lie! He was a member of Congress at the only time I was in Congress, and he knows that whenever there was an attempt to procure a vote of mine which would indicate the origin and justice of the war, I refused to give such endorsement, and voted against it; but I never voted against supplies for the army, and he knows, as well as Judge Douglas, that whenever a dollar was asked by way of compensation or otherwise, for the benefit of the soldiers, I gave all the votes that Ficklin or Douglas did, and perhaps more."

Uncomfortably, Ficklin allowed that he was a friend of both Lincoln and Douglas. Lincoln, he recalled, had voted for a resolution put forward by Representative George Ashmun, a Massachusetts Whig, denouncing the war as unconstitutional. Ficklin did not deny Douglas's charges, but neither did he endorse them. That was the best a Democrat could do for Lincoln.

Lincoln got off his most stinging line on Douglas after the debate. Speaking to a group of supporters at the hotel, he said "I flatter myself that thus far my wife has not found it necessary to follow me around from place to place to keep me from getting drunk." (Adele Douglas was a devoted political wife, accompanying her husband to every debate and making sure he dressed well. After Douglas's first wife died, his wardrobe went to seed, but he put on a dapper appearance during the debates.)

Douglas had indeed been fueling his campaign with brandy. During the rejoinder, Lincoln said that unless Douglas came up with a better reason for deleting popular sovereignty from the Toombs Bill, "it will not avail him at all that he swells himself up, takes on dignity, and calls people liars." Douglas responded with a string of curses so loud that stenographer Robert Hitt could not hear Lincoln speak. Some blamed the outburst on alcohol. Lincoln's law partner, William Herndon, would later say that during this stage of the campaign, Douglas was as "bloated as I ever saw him; he drinks very hard indeed; his look is awful to me, when I compare him as he now looks with what he was in February 1858."

The campaign was wearing on Lincoln as well. Two days after the Charleston debate, he again tried to "get the last word" in on Douglas, at Freeland Grove in Sullivan. Learning that Douglas would speak at one o'clock, Lincoln wrote to him, "I will postpone to 3 o'clock." Nonetheless, Republicans arrived at the grove before Douglas finished speaking and brawled with the senator's supporters. Douglas blamed the donnybrook on Lincoln, whose supporters had arrived half an hour earlier than the time promised in the note: "It was a deliberate attempt on the part of his friends to break up a Democratic meeting . . . in order to prevent me from expressing his alliance with the Abolitionists, and repelling the false charges he made against me at Charleston, and to which I had no opportunity to reply at that place." In the weeks to come, Lincoln crisscrossed the Whig Belt, speaking in Danville, Urbana, Springfield, Jacksonville, Winchester, Pittsfield, Metamora, Peoria, Pekin, and Knoxville. During his frenetic travels, Lincoln ran into Julian Sturtevant, president of Illinois College, at the Jacksonville train station.

"Mr. Lincoln, you must be having a weary time," Sturtevant said as they walked together toward the hotel.

"I am," Lincoln replied, "and if it were not for one thing I would retire from the contest. I know that if Mr. Douglas's doctrine prevails it will not be fifteen years before Illinois itself will be a slave state."

The morning after his Jacksonville speech, Lincoln was late in getting up and had to borrow a horse to catch up with the party escorting him to Winchester. By the time he overtook his escorts, the horse was "white with sweat" and Lincoln "black with dust." Lincoln spent two nights in Winchester—at the Haggard Hotel.

Old Main, Knox College, Galesburg, Illinois, October 7, 1858

Galesburg was nicknamed "Abolition City." The northwestern Illinois town was home to Knox College, founded in 1837 by George Washington Gale, an antislavery Presbyterian minister from upstate New York. Knox's founding document, "The Circular and Plan," condemned slavery, and its trustees opened their homes to runaway slaves, making Galesburg an important stop on the Underground Railroad. Progressive for its day, Knox educated women and Blacks, including Hiram Revels, who would serve as a Republican senator from Mississippi during Reconstruction. Douglas had visited Galesburg in 1854, to debate the Kansas-Nebraska Act with the college's second president, Jonathan Blanchard. Knox had an active antislavery society: its students passed an anti-Nebraska resolution declaring that Douglas had failed "entirely to represent our views and wishes." The school held a Great Anti-Nebraska Convention with speeches from Ichabod Codding and Joshua Giddings, two of the abolitionists Douglas was always trying to associate with Lincoln. Blanchard called Douglas "a Northern doughface . . . like a hired overseer cracking the whip for his Southern masters." Douglas argued that Blanchard's abolitionism demonstrated the anti-Nebraska movement's radical character.

The debate took place on the Knox campus, outside Old Main, adorned for the occasion with a KNOX COLLEGE FOR LINCOLN banner. The Monmouth Glee Club paraded anti-Douglas banners through the streets: Douglas erasing the popular referendum clause from the Toombs bill; DUG AT FREEPORT, with the Dred Scott platform collapsing beneath the senator; "Coming from Egypt," Lincoln striking Douglas with a cane; Douglas sent sprawling as he tried to straddle donkeys named Popular Sovereignty and Dred Scott; a locomotive labeled FREEDOM about to collide with Douglas's ox cart, as his terrified Black driver exclaimed, "For God, Massa, I bleves we's in danger!"

This beacon of Yankeedom was the perfect site for Lincoln to expound on the fundamental difference between Republicans and Democrats. Prohibiting slavery in the territories was the difference in policy, but that sprang from a conviction that slavery was immoral—a conviction Douglas did not share with Lincoln.

To avoid fighting their way through the 10,000 spectators thronging the campus, the candidates reached the speakers' platform by climbing through a window, later commemorated as the Lincoln-Douglas Window. Lincoln, who had less than two years of formal schooling, cracked that he had "finally gone through college."

Perhaps because Lincoln had impugned Douglas's popular sovereignty credentials in Charleston, the incumbent began his opening speech with a criticism of the English Bill. The bill, sponsored by Democratic representative William Hayden English of Indiana and supported by President Buchanan, offered Kansans nearly 4 million acres of public land and admission to the Union with its current population of 35,000—if it accepted the Lecompton Constitution. If Kansas rejected Lecompton, the territory would have to wait for statehood until it had enough people to form a congressional district: 93,420. The English Bill was unpopular in the Northwest—where Douglas was running for reelection, and would have to win in 1860—because it offered an inducement for Kansas to enter as a slave state. So Douglas, ever the practical politician, opposed the bill, arguing in the Senate that the land grant amounted to congressional interference with Kansans' popular sovereignty. That April, the bill passed the Senate, 31–22, and the House, 112–103, supported by the Southerners, who by that point were in favor of anything Douglas opposed and opposed to anything he favored. Douglas, however, suspected that Kansans would reject the offer. On August 2, they did, by a vote of 11,300 to 1,788. That was a good outcome for Douglas: it ratified his position on popular sovereignty, and it delayed statehood for Kansas, meaning the likely Republican state would not have a vote in the 1860 presidential election.

Douglas told the Galesburg crowd that he had not supported the English Bill because "if the people of Kansas had only agreed to become a slave-holding state under the Lecompton constitution, they could have done so with 35,000 people, but if they had insisted on being a free state, as they had a right to do so, then they were to be punished by being kept out of the Union until they had nearly three times that population. I then said in my place in the Senate, as I say to you now, that whenever Kansas has population enough for a slave state she has population enough for a free state."

Douglas again distinguished himself from the Southern Fire-Eaters—and appealed to the constituency he was courting—by asserting that just because Blacks were inferior to Whites, it did not follow that they must be slaves. The most proslavery Southerners believed the institution was an "incalculable blessing" to Blacks because it had transported them from "primitive" Africa to "civilized" America. They also believed it was the natural lot of Blacks to liberate Whites from the most onerous labor necessary for survival. As Jefferson Davis once declared, "Negro slavery . . . is necessary for the quality of the White race." Without it, the poorest Whites would be forced to demean themselves by picking cotton.

"While I hold that under our constitution and political system the Negro is not a citizen, cannot be a citizen, and ought not to be a citizen, it does not follow by any means he should be a slave," Douglas said. "On the contrary, it does follow that the Negro, as an inferior race, ought to possess every right, every privilege, every immunity which he can safely exercise consistent with the safety of the society in which he lives. Humanity requires, and Christianity commands that you shall extend to every inferior being, and every dependent being, all the privileges, immunities, and advantages which can be granted to them consistent with the safety of society. If you ask me the nature and extent of these privileges, I answer that is a question the people of each state must decide for themselves. Illinois has decided that question for herself. We have said that in this state the Negro shall not be a slave, nor shall he be a citizen."

That, of course, was what Illinoisans wanted to hear. For the Galesburg crowd, it was as antislavery as Douglas could get while remaining faithful to popular sovereignty. Southerners would hear it as another heresy, along with the Freeport Doctrine and Douglas's opposition to Lecompton.

"It will be remembered," recalled B. F. Arnold, a future Galesburg mayor who attended the debate, "that Douglas's replies to many of Lincoln's questions were far more pleasing to the Illinois Democrats than they were to the southern wing of the party. I believe this cost him the presidency."

As often happened in the years leading up to the Civil War, Douglas found himself occupying a position between Jefferson Davis and Abraham Lincoln. Saying that Blacks didn't have to be slaves offended Davis; saying that they could be slaves offended Lincoln. Lincoln used his reply to assert that slavery was "evil"—an opinion he knew Galesburg shared.

"If you will take the Judge's speeches, and select the short and pointed sentences expressed by him—as his declaration that 'he don't care whether slavery is voted up or down'—you will see at once that this is perfectly logical, if you do not admit slavery is wrong. Judge Douglas cannot logically say that he don't care whether a wrong is voted up or down. Judge Douglas declares that if any community want slavery they have a right to have it. He can say that logically, if he says that there is no wrong in slavery; but if you admit that there is a wrong in it, he cannot logically say that anybody has a right to do wrong. And from the difference of sentiment arises the real difference between Judge Douglas and his friends, on the one hand, and the Republicans on the other. Now I confess myself as belonging to that class in the country who contemplate slavery as a moral, social, and political evil, and looks hopefully to the time when as a wrong it may come to an end."

As Lincoln spoke, Douglas glared at him from a seat on the platform, chewing anxiously on the butt of an unlit cigar. More than any other moment in the debates, Lincoln's reply at Galesburg was a crystalliza-tion of the nation's dispute over slavery, raising it from a mere political issue—where Douglas would have preferred it to remain—to a question of the nation's soul. If slavery was not wrong, it could go anywhere—and would. If Douglas's belief that there was no moral difference between slavery and any other property triumphed, that would prepare the way for a second Dred Scott decision, allowing slaveholders to settle with their property in any state from Maine to California.

In Galesburg, Lincoln was addressing people who had been as electrified by the Kansas-Nebraska Act as he had, who also saw it as a Trojan horse for allowing America's greatest sin to break out of the states where it was now confined and cover every inch of the nation.

"Judge Douglas, and whoever like him teaches that the Negro has no share, humble though he may be, in the Declaration of Independence, is going back to the era of our liberty and independence, and so far as in him lies, muzzling the cannon that thunders annual joyous return," Lincoln said; "that he is blowing out the moral lights around us, when he contends that whoever wants slaves has the right to hold them; that he is penetrating, so far as lies in his power, the human soul, and eradicating the light of reason and the love of liberty, when he is in every possible way preparing the public mind, by his vast influence, for making the institution of slavery perpetual and national."

It was Lincoln's most eloquent language of the campaign—so eloquent it would later be inscribed on a plaque affixed to Old Main—and it drew the loudest applause, along with cheers of "Hurrah for Lincoln!" and "That's the true doctrine!" This was a far stronger assertion of Republican ideals than Lincoln's endorsement of White supremacy in Charleston—a fact noted by Douglas, who once again accused Lincoln of tailoring his message to the section where he was speaking. Nonetheless, some Republicans still did not think Lincoln had been aggressive enough. The last two debates would take place in the Mississippi River towns of Quincy and Alton. On his way to Quincy, Lincoln crossed the river to give a speech in Burlington, Iowa, where he stayed at the home of former governor James W. Grimes.

"I had read his debates with Mr. Douglass [sic] up to that time and we frankly discussed and criticized the points made by each of the disputants," Grimes would write to William Herndon in 1866. "I insisted that he suffered Mr. Douglas to put him too much on the defensive—that he should assume the aggressive and attack his adversary in turn—that it was useless to defend himself against Mr. Douglas's charges, for as one could be refuted another would be trumped up."

After listening to this advice, Lincoln asked for writing materials then went up to his room and spent an hour and a half outlining his remarks in Quincy, which would be his last chance to deliver an opening speech. He returned to Grimes's parlor "with half a sheet of paper in his hand upon which he had noted down the leads of the speech he intended to make at that place and which upon reading his speech made there I was satisfied was the same prepared in my house."

Washington Park, Quincy, Illinois, October 13, 1858

The Quincy debate was a homecoming for Stephen Douglas. The ambitious Douglas never remained long in one place, but he lived in Quincy from 1841 to 1847, taking bachelor lodgings at the Quincy House, serving as a justice of the Illinois Supreme Court and a congressman. Douglas landed in Quincy as a result of one of his early political machinations. In 1839, Douglas, whose Democrats were popular with Irish immigrants, argued before the state supreme court that aliens should be allowed to vote in Illinois as long as they had lived in the state six months. The Whig-majority court was not sympathetic to his pleas. When the Democrats took control of the legislature the following year, they concocted a scheme to win the alien case and take control of the judiciary by adding to the court five justices, who would be appointed by the legislature. Douglas, then secretary of state, was one of the five new justices. Each justice was assigned to preside over a judicial circuit. Douglas got the Fifth, which covered the Military Tract of western Illinois, moving to Quincy to take up his duties. The Fifth Judicial District included the Mormon settlement of Nauvoo. Douglas won the esteem of the Mormons when he ruled that their leader, Joseph Smith, could not be extradited to Missouri to face a treason charge: Whig newspapers accused him of trying to win over Mormon voters.

Douglas was always looking for votes. After the 1840 census, fast-growing Illinois gained four seats in Congress. Douglas ran in the new Fifth Congressional District, defeating his Whig opponent, future Lincoln confidant Orville Hickman Browning, by 461 votes. After Douglas was elected to the Senate in 1847, he moved to Chicago with his new wife. Quincy was the state's busiest Mississippi River port, with wharves and factories lining Quincy Bay, at the terminus of the Chicago and Quincy Railroad. Still, it was only the second city of Illinois. Douglas saw that a metropolis would rise where the rails met the Great Lakes, not the river.

Still, Quincy welcomed back its temporary son. Arriving by train from Augusta the night before the debate, he was escorted to the Quincy House by a torchlight procession. The Wednesday morning of the debate, Douglas watched from his hotel window as a parade said to be two miles long made its way toward Washington Park, with a portrait of Douglas, wrapped in a wreath, carried by the vanguard. He then spent half an hour in the carpet store of his old friend John Bert, finally excusing himself to get a shave and lunch before the debate. Lincoln was on a morning train with future Missouri senator and interior secretary Carl Schurz, who was on his way from Chicago to Quincy to campaign for the Republicans among the German community. When Lincoln boarded the train at Monmouth, Schurz "observed a great commotion," as the passengers jumped out of their seats to greet the candidate.

"How are you, Joe? Glad to see you, Dick!" Lincoln greeted them back jovially.

Schurz, seeing Lincoln in person for the first time, was "somewhat startled by his appearance." Lincoln was several inches taller than anyone else on the train. His clean-shaven face "looked even more haggard and careworn than later when it was framed by whiskers." He wore a "battered" stove-pipe hat. "His lank, ungainly body was clad in a rusty black dress coat with sleeves that should have been longer; but his arms appeared so long that the sleeves of a 'store' coat could hardly be expected to cover them all the way down to the wrists." In his left hand, Lincoln held a cotton umbrella and "a black satchel that bore the marks of long and hard usage," leaving his right hand free to shake the hand of every man in the car.

"I had seen, in Washington and in the West, several public men of rough appearance," Schurz would write in his memoirs, "but none whose looks seemed quite so uncouth, not to say grotesque, as Lincoln's."

The antislavery German-Americans were an important Republican voting bloc. Lincoln sat down with Schurz, and "in a somewhat high-pitched but pleasant voice," chatted with him about the arguments he planned to make in the upcoming debate.

At the depot, Lincoln was presented with a floral bouquet arranged by Quincy's Republican women and serenaded by a choir singing "Columbia, the Gem of the Ocean." Although he expressed a desire to "foot it to Browning's," he was conveyed there in a carriage for a pre-debate meeting with his mutual Douglas opponent. (Browning would end up occupying the Senate seat that Lincoln and Douglas were contesting, appointed by Governor Richard Yates after Douglas's death. He would also precede Schurz as interior secretary.)

Lincoln had only visited Quincy once before, in 1854, to campaign for Archibald Williams, who was running unsuccessfully for Congress on an anti-Nebraska platform. As the candidates and the dignitaries assembled on the wooden speaker's stand, facing Fifth Street, a boy jumped up to peddle cigars. Douglas purchased two; Lincoln abstained. Just before the debate began, a bench set up on the platform for the ladies collapsed. Several women were taken across the street to Dr. Watson's office, more startled than injured.

In his opening speech, Lincoln attacked Douglas, as Governor Grimes had urged. More precisely, Lincoln attacked Douglas's attacks on him. Douglas had called Lincoln's rhetoric Black in the North, "mulatto" in the central part of the state, and White in the South. Lincoln quoted from a debate in which he'd declared he had "no purpose to introduce political and social equality between the White and Black." He had said that in Ottawa, "in the Lovejoy district—in the personal presence of Lovejoy." Lincoln again challenged Douglas on whether he would support a Supreme Court decision allowing slaveholders to take their property into free states: "Judge Douglas had the privilege of replying to me at Galesburg, and again he gave me no direct answer as to whether he would or would not sustain such a decision if made." Lincoln then made his most pointed retort to Douglas's attempt, at Ottawa, to tie him to the Aurora abolition resolutions. He called the resolutions a forgery then turned around, faced his seated opponent, and repeated, "Yes, Judge, I did dare to say forgery."

In Galesburg, Lincoln had identified the morality of slavery as the most significant difference between the Republicans and the Democrats. In Quincy, he identified Douglas as the author of his party's moral stance. Slavery was a "disturbing" and "dangerous" element, but Douglas, almost alone among American politicians, proposed to leave it in its current state.

"I will say now that there is a sentiment in the country contrary to me—a sentiment which holds that slavery is not wrong, and therefore it goes for policy that does not propose dealing with it as a wrong," Lincoln declared near the end of his hour. "That policy is the Democratic policy, and that sentiment is the Democratic sentiment. If there be a doubt in the mind of any one of this vast audience that this is really the central idea of the Democratic Party, in relation to this subject, I ask him to bear with me while I state a few things tending, as I think to prove that proposition. In the first place, the leading man—I think I may do my friend Judge Douglas the honor of calling him such—advocating the present Democratic policy, never himself says it is wrong. He has the high distinction, so far as I know, of never having said slavery is either right or wrong. Almost everybody else says one or the other, but the Judge."

The Republicans in the crowd laughed. Lincoln had a way of putting things plainly and humorously. Douglas looked Lincoln up and down and muttered, "How long, oh Lord, how long?"

The Douglas who rose to respond was not the same Douglas who had stepped triumphantly off the Michigan Central in Chicago, or even the same Douglas who had begun the debates in Ottawa by asserting that the Democrats were the only national party. Douglas's powerful voice had withered to a whisper. Schurz thought that Douglas looked rather natty and well-groomed in "excellently fitting broadcloth and shining linen," but also that "his face seemed a little puffy, and it was said that he had been drinking hard with some boon companions either on his journey or after his arrival." Douglas's visage was "dark and scowling," his voice "hoarse and rough . . . like a barking sound," his tone "angry, dictatorial, and insolent." Douglas had campaigned even harder than Lincoln, traveling 5,000 miles in one hundred days, by stagecoach, riverboat, raft, horseback, and private rail car, delivering 130 speeches. His constitution was weaker than Lincoln's, and he dissipated his vigor by fueling his travels with alcohol. Nonetheless, the Little Giant was strong enough to produce ninety minutes of "Sophisms" and "appeals to prejudice," as Schurz would put it.

Lincoln's aggressive opener had put Douglas on the defensive. He acknowledged that the "Springfield resolutions," as he called them, had not actually been adopted in Springfield. That was only a "quibble," though, because they had been adopted in Aurora, Bloomington, Rockford, "and by nearly all the Republican conventions in northern Illinois where his party is in a majority." Anyone who would "charge a forgery" on *Illinois Register* publisher Charles Lamphier or Congressman Thomas L. Harris, who had provided Douglas with the resolutions, "only proclaims himself a slanderer."

Quincy has gone down in history as the ugliest of the seven debates. By mid-October, less than a month before the election, Lincoln and Douglas were fully on each other's nerves. Douglas defended his refusal to say whether slavery was right or wrong on the grounds that the Constitution was silent on the issue, leaving it up to each state "to do as it pleases on the subject of slavery."

"I do not choose to occupy the time allotted to me in discussing a question that we have no right to act upon," he said. "I thought that you desired to hear us answer questions within our constitutional power of action."

Douglas then tried to turn the morality question around on Lincoln by arguing that limiting the spread of slavery violated the tenets of Christendom, since confining the slaves to the seventeen states where they now lived would result not just in the institution's extinction, but the extinction of the Blacks themselves. Lincoln "would prohibit slavery everywhere in the territories," Douglas said. "He would thus confine slavery within its present limits. When he thus gets it confined, and surrounded, so that it cannot spread, the natural laws of increase will go on until the Negroes will be so plenty that they cannot live on the soil. He will hem them in until starvation seizes them, and by starving them to death, he will put slavery in the course of ultimate extinction. If he is not going to interfere with slavery in the states, but intends to interfere and prohibit it in the territories, and thus smother slavery out, it naturally follows, that he can extinguish it only by extinguishing the Negro race, for his policy would drive them to starvation. This is the humane and Christian remedy that he proposes for the great crime of slavery."

Whenever Douglas accused Lincoln of abolitionism, Lincoln responded that he did not want to free all the slaves right away, he merely wanted to confine slavery to its current sphere, so it would eventually wither away, at some date far beyond this election. Now, Douglas was portraying the anti-slavery position as *worse* than abolitionism. Freeing the slaves would allow them to scratch out a living anywhere in this abundant nation. Lincoln's plan was a recipe for genocide.

In his rejoinder, Lincoln again argued that his antislavery convictions were no different than those of the Virginia founders, who had placed slavery "in the course of ultimate extinction." Sensible Southerners agreed "until the invention of the cotton gin made slavery too profitable to abandon."

"Judge Douglas could not let it stand upon the basis upon which our fathers placed it, but removed it and put it upon the cotton gin basis," Lincoln said.

Lincoln then attempted to undermine Douglas's Freeport Doctrine. Members of territorial legislatures took oaths to uphold the Constitution. Refusing to protect the rights of slaveholders would violate their constitutional rights, as set out by the Dred Scott decision.

"If you withhold that necessary legislation for the support of the Constitution and constitutional rights, do you not commit perjury?" Lincoln asked. "Judge Douglas has sung paeans to his 'popular sovereignty' doctrine until his Supreme Court cooperating with him has squatted his squatter sovereignty out." He went on, to big laughs from the Republicans. "He has at last invented this sort of do-nothing sovereignty—that the people may exclude slavery by a sort of 'sovereignty' that is exercised by doing nothing at all. Is not that running his popular sovereignty down awfully? Has it not got down as thin as the homeopathic soup that was made by boiling the shadow of a pigeon that had starved to death?"

Only the expiration of three hours ended the mudslinging. As he stepped off the platform, Lincoln complained that he was "very dry" after speaking for ninety minutes. Looking at Ernest Schierenberg, editor of the *Quincy Tribune*, he remarked that "as there's a Dutch editor present, he might lead the way to an oasis." Schierenberg led the way to the No. 9 saloon, catty-corner from Washington Park. The normally abstemious Lincoln drained three glasses of beer, refusing the offer of a fourth with "I have had all I cared for."

Back at his room in Quincy House, Lincoln sat down for an interview with David R. Locke, a correspondent with the *Sandusky Commercial-Register*. Before they talked, Lincoln pulled off his boots "to give my feet a chance to breathe." Then he removed his coat vest, necktie, and collar, and allowed one suspender to drop off his shoulder. He leaned back in a chair, propping one stockinged foot atop the other, and predicted the Republicans would win the most votes in the upcoming election, but that Douglas would be reelected to the Senate, because the legislature was apportioned in favor of the Democrats.

"You can't overturn a pyramid, but you can undermine it," Lincoln told Locke, "that's what I have been trying to do."

As always, Lincoln enjoyed showing off his wit. When Locke mentioned a recently deceased Illinois politician known for his vanity, Lincoln joked about the man's well-attended funeral: "If General —— had known how big a funeral he would have had, he would have died years ago."

On November 6—four days after the election turned out exactly as Lincoln had foreseen—this item appeared in Locke's newspaper, under the headline LINCOLN FOR PRESIDENT—perhaps the first time those words had ever been published:

"We are indebted to a friend at Mansfield for the following special dispatch: 'Editor *Sandusky Register*: An enthusiastic meeting is in progress here tonight in favor of Lincoln for the new Republican Candidate for President.'"

The meeting, however, probably never took place. Locke, who would later become famous by writing the letters of Petroleum V. Nasby (a satire of a Copperhead Democrat), loved practical jokes and might have invented the item to build up the name of a politician who had impressed him. The *Mansfield Herald* hadn't heard of it: "we are inclined to think that a large and enthusiastic political meeting would be likely to come to our knowledge . . . The truth is, the *Register* has been hoaxed."

Nonetheless, the story was picked up by Eastern newspapers and was said to have caught the attention of the New Yorkers who invited Lincoln to speak at Cooper Union. If so, Quincy may have contributed as much as any debate to Lincoln's rise to the presidency.

City Hall, Alton, Illinois, October 15, 1858

With only two days between the final debates, Lincoln and Douglas traveled from Quincy to Alton on the steam packet *City of Louisiana*. They arrived at Alton before dawn on debate day. Lincoln made his headquarters at the Franklin House, Douglas at the grander Alton House, where he and Adele shared breakfast with Lincoln.

For the first time, Lincoln's family joined him at a debate. That morning, Mary and Robert rode the eighty miles from Springfield on the Chicago & Alton, which was offering half-price tickets for debate goers. Fifteen-year-old Robert wore the gold-trimmed blue jacket and white pants of the Springfield Cadets. As soon as the train arrived, at 10:30, the Cadets set off marching through the streets of Alton, behind Merritt's Cornet Band. Mary, meanwhile, made her way alone to Franklin House to meet her husband. The Lincoln banners in the streets outnumbered

the Douglas banners. LINCOLN NOT YET TROTTED OUT, read one, a refer-
ence to Douglas's vow to trot Lincoln down to Egypt. TOO LATE FOR THE
MILKING, read another. And the largest: FREE TERRITORIES AND FREE MEN/
FREE PULPITS AND FREE PREACHERS/FREE SCHOOLS AND FREE TEACHERS.
Douglas's men, reported the Republican *Alton Daily Courier,* "concentrated
their whole energies in one grand, magnificent, superb, right-royal banner,
which was suspended over Third Street, between the store of Mr. Henry
Lee and the Bank building. The words 'Popular Sovereignty'—'National
Union'—'S.A. Douglas, the People's choice,' were surmounted by a very
buzzard-like bird, ready poised to swoop down upon his prey, and surrounded by five stars, intended as we suppose, to represent the four States of
Pennsylvania, Ohio, Indiana, and Iowa, which have already put their knives
to the throat of Mr. Douglas, and Illinois, which will do so in November,
after which he will be ready politically for the buzzard."

Nonetheless, Alton was Democratic turf—Lovejoy had been lynched
there. On her walk from the depot to Franklin House, Mary heard far more
shouts for "the Little Giant" and "Popularity" than for "Old Abe" or "Free
Territories and Free Men." A thousand Douglas supporters had arrived on
a boat from St. Louis, greeted by the firing of cannons and the blaring of
military music. As soon as Mary made it to Franklin House, she repaired
to her room with a splitting headache.

Lincoln was in the hotel sitting room with Senator Lyman Trumbull,
who lived in Alton, when former lieutenant governor Gustave Koerner
joined them.

"Let us go up and see Mary," Lincoln suggested to Koerner, who had
last seen Mary more than twenty years earlier, when she was a Kentucky
belle and he a law student at Transylvania University in Lexington. When
they were reunited, Lincoln told Koerner, "Now tell Mary what you think
of our chances! She is rather dispirited."

Koerner told Mary that the Republicans were certain to carry the state
and "tolerably certain" of winning a majority in the legislature. That assess-
ment was, as even Lincoln would have admitted, optimistic. It was what
Mary needed to hear that morning, though.

When the debate began, at 2:00 P.M., beside the not-yet-completed City Hall overlooking the river, Douglas's voice had been further weakened by the strain of speaking in Quincy. Koerner thought he looked "bloated" and "haggard."

"In conversation he merely whispered. In addressing his audience he made himself understood only by an immense strain, and then only to a very small circle immediately near him." The *Daily Courier* called Douglas's voice "completely shattered and his articulation so very much impeded that very few of the large crowd he addressed could understand an entire sentence."

Douglas may have been unintelligible, but he was as agitated as he'd ever been during a debate. He devoted a large portion of his opening speech to portraying himself as the defender of true Democratic principles against the Danites and the Buchanan administration. With the election only two and a half weeks away, and with the Danites running candidates in enough districts to swing the results to the Republicans, Douglas's Senate seat depended on persuading the voters that he and his followers were the real Democrats.

Douglas had voted against the Lecompton Constitution because "it was not the act and deed of the people of Kansas, and did not embody their will." He had voted against the English Bill because "it is a violation of the fundamental principles of this government to throw the weight of Federal power into the scale in favor of the slaveholding than the free states." His fidelity to the Democratic principle of popular sovereignty made him a heretic to President Buchanan, who was wielding the power of federal patronage to defeat him. The executive branch bullying the legislative branch violated the constitution's separation of powers. It also put Buchanan in the league with the abolitionists.

"In this state, every postmaster, every route agent, every collector of the ports, and every federal office holder, forfeits his head the moment he expresses a preference for the Democratic candidate against Lincoln and his Abolition associates," the embattled Douglas raged hoarsely. "A Democratic administration which we helped to bring into power, deemed it consistent with its fidelity to principle and its regard to duty, to wield power in this state in behalf of the Republican Abolition candidates in every county and in every congressional district against the Democratic Party."

Aware that a boatload of Missourians was on hand, Douglas made a play for their support, which he would need in the presidential election two years hence. Lincoln wanted an all-powerful federal government. Douglas favored states' rights—an eternal argument in American politics.

"We in Illinois tried slavery, kept it up for twelve years, and finding it was not profitable we abolished it for that reason, and became a free state," he said. "You in Missouri must judge for yourselves whether it is a wise policy for you. If you choose to follow our example, very good; if you reject it, still well, it is your business, not ours. If the people of all the states will act on the great principle, and each state mind its own business, attend to its own affairs, take care of its own Negroes and not meddle with its neighbors, then there will be peace between the North and the South, the East and the West, throughout the whole Union."

Lincoln's reply was his closing argument of the campaign and contained his most powerful moral language yet. To support his contention that the Declaration of Independence applied to Blacks, he quoted Henry Clay, his political idol, a Whig whose legacy both parties were trying to claim: "As an abstract principle," Clay had said, "there is no doubt of the truth of that declaration." Until three years ago, no one had disputed Clay. Then Chief Justice Taney did so in the Dred Scott decision, and Douglas followed his lead. It was "an evil tendency, if not an evil design; I combat it as having a tendency to dehumanize the Negro—to take away from him the right of ever striving to be a man. I combat it as being one of the thousand things constantly done in these days to make property, and nothing but property of the Negro in all the states of the union."

One by one, Lincoln kicked in every leg of the stool from which Douglas was proclaiming his slavery policy. The Dred Scott decision would destroy popular sovereignty, by making slavery universal in the territories and the states. Allowing slavery into the territories would not preserve the Union but destroy it. Slavery had split in two the Methodist Church, the Presbyterian Church, the Unitarian Church, and would divide the nation next: "How many times have we had danger from this question? Go back to the day of the Missouri Compromise. Go back to the Nullification question at the bottom of which lay this same slavery question. Go back to the troubles that led to the Compromise of 1850. You will find that every time, with the single exception of the Nullification question, they sprung from an endeavor to spread this institution."

Allowing the spread of slavery did not increase White freedom, but threatened it. Where could an immigrant attempting to escape European peasantry find a place to build a free and prosperous life? Nowhere, if he had to compete with slavery. The Democrats had a large immigrant following, but if Douglas's policies were carried to their conclusion, America would no longer be "an outlet for free White people everywhere, the world over—in which Hans and Baptiste and Patrick, and all other men from all the world, may find new homes and better their conditions in life."

During Douglas's rejoinder, he made a statement that summed up his views on Blacks, slavery, and the Union more bluntly than the tens of thousands of words he had spoken during this canvass.

"I care more for the great principle of self-government, the right of the people to rule, than I do for all the Negroes in Christendom," he declared. "I would not endanger the perpetuity of the Union. I would not blot out the inalienable rights of the White men for all the Negroes that ever existed."

"The people" meant "White people," for America was a White man's country, in which the "inferior" Blacks had no claim on citizenship. Douglas believed in Manifest Destiny, in a nation covered with White settlements from the Atlantic to the Pacific, knit together by a network of railroads converging on his hometown of Chicago. None of that would be possible without a strong Union. Stephen Douglas would not allow the weeping sentiments of bleeding-heart abolitionists to destroy it.

Meredosia, Illinois, October 18, 1858

The campaign continued after Alton. When Lincoln stepped off a train in Naples, an Illinois River town in Scott County, he saw "about fifteen Celtic gentlemen, with black carpet sacks in their hands." Later that day at Meredosia, he told the crowd he suspected they were Irishmen imported to that Whig Belt district to vote for Douglas. For this, the *Jacksonville Sentinel* castigated him as anti-immigrant: "Doubtless Mr. Lincoln entertains a holy horror of all Irishmen and other adopted citizens who have sufficient self respect to believe themselves superior to the Negro. What right have adopted citizens to vote Mr. Lincoln and his Negro equality doctrines down. He would doubtless disenfranchise every one of them if he had the power."

There was an anti-immigrant Know Nothing element in the Republican Party. The Democrats tried to associate Lincoln with it. Lincoln never publicly condemned nativism in strong terms, because he needed the votes of nativists, but at Meredosia, he denied being one of their number, repeating that denial in a letter to Edward Lusk, a local farmer: "I am not, nor have ever been connected with the party called the Know Nothing party, or the party calling themselves the American party." (In a private letter to his friend Joshua Speed, three years earlier, Lincoln had been much more critical of the Know Nothings: "How can anyone who abhors oppression of negroes be in favor of degrading classes of white people?")

Decatur, Illinois, October 19, 1858

At a Douglas rally, before a crowd of 6,000, Theophilus Lyle Dickey read a letter. It was a letter Abraham Lincoln had begged its author not to write. John J. Crittenden, a senator from Kentucky, holder of Henry Clay's old seat and the most prominent living embodiment of Clay's Whig principles, was endorsing Stephen Douglas for the U.S. Senate. Lincoln and

Crittenden had once been allies: during Lincoln's term in Congress, both had opposed the Mexican War. As a conservative Southern Whig, and a slaveholder, Crittenden refused to join the Republican Party. He disagreed with Lincoln's antislavery doctrines and admired Douglas for standing up to the administration on the Lecompton Constitution.

T. Lyle Dickey had also been an ally of Lincoln's: "I love you & want you to be a U.S. Senator from Illinois," he wrote Lincoln in 1854, even though the Kentucky native believed that slavery was protected by the Constitution and could coexist with freedom. After Lincoln's "House Divided" speech, Dickey concluded that Lincoln had "gone over completely to the abolitionists." He joined the Douglas campaign, causing a rare angry outburst in Lincoln, who told Henry C. Whitney that "he did not know any of his friends he felt so badly about losing as Dickey." As an old Kentuckian, Dickey knew Crittenden and wrote him a letter asking his permission to make public "the substance of a conversation between us in relation to Judge Douglas."

Crittenden's endorsement held a lot of sway among old Whigs in Central Illinois. Lincoln was so worried it would go to Douglas that he wrote to Crittenden on July 7, expressing the hope that he would remain neutral: "I am prompted . . . by a story being whispered about here that you are anxious for the reelection of Mr. Douglas to the United States Senate, and also of Harris, of our district, for the House of Representatives, and that you are pledged to write letters to that effect to your friends here in Illinois, if requested. I do not believe that story, but it gives me some uneasiness."

Crittenden replied that, although he and Douglas "have always belonged to different parties, opposed, in principle, to each other . . . we concurred & acted together in opposing the enforcement of the Lecompton Constitution upon the people of Kansas . . . The position taken by [Douglas], was full of sacrifice, & full of hazard, yet he took it, and he defended it, like a Man."

Crittenden did not feel "a single particle of personal unkindness or opposition" to Lincoln, but he had on his desk several letters from Illinoisans, including one asking him to say "whether I did not, at Washington, have a certain conversation with the writer concerning Mr. Douglas. To those letters I must answer in a proper manner—As to the future, Sir, I cannot undertake to promise or to impose any restrictions on my conduct."

The letter to which Crittenden referred was Dickey's. Crittenden not only gave Dickey permission to relate their conversation, he provided him with a letter stating that "the people of Illinois little knew how much they really owed" their senator, who should be reelected "as a rebuke to the Administration and a vindication of the great cause of popular rights & public justice."

Dickey waited to release the letter until two weeks before the election, when it would have maximum effect on the voters. After he read it aloud in Decatur, it was published in the Democratic *Chicago Times* and *Illinois State Register*. Crittenden's letter was a tremendous blow to Lincoln. As Representative Thomas Harris wrote to Douglas, Crittenden would "control 20,000 American or old line Whig votes in center & south"—enough, perhaps, to swing a close election.

Springfield, Illinois, October 30, 1858

Three days before the election, 5,000 Lincoln supporters held a torchlight rally for their hometown candidate in Springfield. The demonstration was so boisterous that Lincoln was unable to deliver a full speech, but he did get these words out: "My friends, today closes the discussion of this canvass. The planting and the culture are over; and there remains but the preparation, and the harvest. I stand here surrounded by friends—some political, all personal friends, I trust. I have borne a laborious, and in some respects to myself, a painful part in the contest. Through all, I have never assailed, or wrestled with, any part of the constitution. In resisting the spread of slavery to new territory, and with that, what appears to me to be a tendency to subvert the first principle of free government, my whole effort has consisted, to the best of my judgment, I have labored for, not against, the Union."

That same day, the *Chicago Press and Tribune* attempted to spring its own October Surprise on Douglas: an accusation that he earned $15,000 a year by renting out the slaves on his late wife's Mississippi plantation to fellow planters "who make themselves whole by whipping out of the chattels an unusual amount of labor." The source of this intelligence was said to be Senator John Slidell of Louisiana, who also reported that the slaves were "badly fed, badly clothed, and excessively overworked!"

Slidell had spent two days in Chicago that July. An ally of President Buchanan, Slidell intended to remove Douglas-appointed officeholders from federal posts and distribute funds to Danite candidates. Allegedly, he also spread rumors about the Douglas family plantation to Dr. Daniel Brainard, a local surgeon who held a federal post at the Marine hospital. Brainard repeated the accusations to the *Press and Tribune*, attributing them to Slidell. After the election, Slidell would deny making any such statements to Brainard, and Brainard would deny ever retelling them to the Republican press. Of Douglas's overseer, Slidell would write, "a more honorable man or better master cannot be found in Louisiana."

If Slidell actually did try to portray Douglas as the Simon Legree of Illinois, his whispering campaign would have no influence on the outcome of the election.

Election Day, November 2, 1858

When Illinois voted, on a gloomy, rainy autumn Tuesday, the Democrats won 40 of the 75 seats in the state House of Representatives; they also maintained their majority in the state senate, 14–11. The results guaranteed Douglas a third term in the United States Senate, but they were also a victory for Lincoln. As he had predicted to David R. Locke, the Republicans carried the popular vote. The representatives who would vote for Lincoln won 125,111 votes, compared to 95,311 for Douglas. The Democrats won five of the nine congressional races, despite being outpolled 125,668 to 122,186. In the race for state treasurer, Republican James Miller defeated William B. Fondey, 127,609 to 125,430; for superintendent of public instruction, Republican Newton Bateman defeated former governor Augustus C. French, 124,556 to 122,413.

The Democrats were so successful in the down-ballot races because the legislature had last been reapportioned in 1854 and thus did not reflect migration into northern Illinois, the fastest-growing section of what was, in the 1850s, the fastest-growing state in the Union. During that decade, the population of Chicago increased 224 percent, from 29,963 to 112,172. How skewed in Egypt's favor was the legislature? A district that made up half of Cook County sent two representatives to Springfield, with 6,241 and 6,223 votes. A Republican from Rock Island County went to the legislature with 5,213 votes; a Democrat from Monroe County, in southwestern Illinois, did so with 1,283.

Lincoln's prospects were also hurt by his failure to carry his home territory, the much-contested Whig Belt of central Illinois. The Republicans lost both seats in Lincoln's home of Sangamon County, by about 300 votes apiece. They lost the seats in Morgan and Scott counties, where Lincoln had complained of espying Irish carpetbaggers. They won seats in Coles and Edgar counties, near Charleston, but lost both districts in Adams and Fulton counties, by 300 or 400 votes. The Republicans ran up the popular vote with big victories in heavily populated northeastern Illinois.

"An apportionment law ridiculously adopted to the existing facts has secured Mr. Douglas a substantial but undeserved triumph," editorialized *Chicago Press and Tribune*. "Now who's cheated?"

The newspaper's publisher, Joseph Medill, calculated that a fair apportionment would have elected forty-one Republican representatives and fourteen senators, sending Lincoln to Washington. Republican districts required an average of 19,685 inhabitants to elect a representative and 58,900 for a senator, while Democratic districts required 15,675 and 47,100. Douglas "was elected for the reason that 740 voters in 'Egypt' are an offset to 1,000 in 'Canaan.'"

David Davis blamed Crittenden's letter for the loss of "the Pharisaical old Whigs in the Central counties." The embittered Davis also blamed the carpetbagging "Irish colonization" of central Illinois for Lincoln's defeat.

Lincoln's loss had a thousand fathers—the apportionment, the Crittenden letter, the Irish vote—but its consequences fell on only one man.

As he studied returns in his law office on election night, Lincoln saw that he was beaten. Walking home in the rain, he later told his secretary, John Hay, "My foot slipped out from under me, knocking the other one out of the way, but I recovered myself and lit square: and I said to myself, 'He's a slip and not a fall.'"

Of course, Lincoln was recalling his loss from the pinnacle of the presidency. At the time his mood was much gloomier, in keeping with the season, and his nature. Two days after the election, he wrote to Crittenden, "The emotions of defeat, at the close of a struggle in which I felt more than merely selfish interest, and to which defeat the use of your name contributed, are fresh upon me; but, even in this mood, I can not for a moment suspect you of anything dishonorable."

The Senate election set up both Lincoln and Douglas for their presidential confrontation two years later. Lincoln had demonstrated he could carry a state that was essential to the Republican Party's chances in 1860. In a one-on-one contest with Douglas, unmediated by the legislature, Lincoln would have won. Within days, Republicans in other states were calling on him to run for president. Israel Green, a druggist from Findlay, Ohio, who helped found his state's party, wrote to the *Cincinnati Gazette* on November 6, proposing a ticket of Lincoln for president and John Pendleton Kennedy of Maryland as vice president. When the *Chicago Democrat* proposed a national candidacy, newspapers across the country reported that "Wentworth's Chicago paper suggests Lincoln for President or Vice President."

Douglas received letters from admirers across the country, congratulating him on his victory and assuring him their support should he run for president in 1860. Most were from Northern states, but James B. Ficklin of Fredericksburg, Virginia, wrote "that I can assure you as a Democrat of Eastern Virginia that it is to you and you only that the great body as the people of this state look to as 'the Man of the Hour.'"

It was not to be. To run for president, Douglas had to keep his Illinois Senate seat, but to keep his Illinois Senate seat, he had been forced to adopt positions that were poison to Southern voters, who were indispensable to a Democratic candidate's success: his Freeport Doctrine, his opposition to the Lecompton Constitution. Douglas had beaten Lincoln by arguing that only his principles could be proclaimed in the North and the South, but he refused to see that the dispute between the sections had become irreconcilable. Douglas looked like the victor, but at the end of 1858, the Little Giant's political prospects were in decline, while Lincoln's were ascending.

CHAPTER 4

THE OHIO CAMPAIGN

State House, Columbus, Ohio, September 7, 1859

The invitation to barnstorm Ohio was extended by George Manypenny, chairman of the Ohio Democratic State Central Committee and editor of Columbus's *Ohio Statesman*. The state was electing a new governor, to replace the abolitionist Republican Salmon P. Chase, who hoped the legislature chosen that fall would send him to the Senate. A Democratic victory in those campaigns would be a bell-wether in 1860, not just for Ohio, but the entire Northwest, the region essential to both parties' presidential chances. Who better to plead the Democratic cause than the North's most prominent Democrat, the likely nominee at Charleston, the man who had just vanquished Lincoln?

"I have the honor to invite you to our state during the canvass which will be opened only in August," Manypenny wrote Douglas, "to address the people at a few prominent points of access to large bodies of our fellow citizens. If it be in your power to give us eight or ten days of your time, say between the middle of September and first of October (or such other period as would best suit you), we would esteem it a great favor."

Douglas agreed to speak in Ohio in early September, on his way home to Chicago for the United States Agricultural Society's fair, where he would appear with John J. Crittenden, whose letter of endorsement the year before had done so much to undermine Lincoln's support among Old Whigs. Ohio would choose delegates to the Charleston convention in January, and Douglas was anxious to win their support.

The Northern states had taken on added importance to Douglas's presidential hopes because his difficulties with the South had multiplied since the debates with Lincoln—specifically because of his assertion, at Freeport, that slavery could not exist in the territories without friendly legislation. The previous November, almost immediately after his Democrats won control of the Illinois legislature, Douglas and his wife boarded the *City of Memphis* for a post-campaign vacation, a voyage that would ultimately take them to Havana and New York City. On its trip down the Mississippi River, the steamer stopped in St. Louis, Memphis, and New Orleans, where Douglas delivered speeches in defense of popular sovereignty—and the Freeport Doctrine.

Douglas told a crowd of thousands in New Orleans that he accepted the Dred Scott decision, but that territorial legislatures might disagree with it: "The owner of slaves, the same as the owner of any other species of property, has a right to remove to the territory and carry his property with him. It is true that a question may arise after his arrival in the territory, how and to what extent his property is to be protected and encouraged? This is a question for the people of the territory to determine through their legislature. Congress has never yet passed laws for the protection of any kind of property in any of the organized territories of the United States."

If the Freeport Doctrine itself was hairsplitting, this was splitting the hair even more finely, to appeal to a Southern audience. Douglas did not dispute the right of slaveholders to bring slaves into a territory, but he would not stand up for their right to keep slaves in a territory: "Non-action on the part of the legislature, an omission to pass a slave code or to furnish remedies and provide penalties for the violation of the rights of property, would practically exclude it from the territory as effectually as a constitutional provision against its introduction," he argued.

Douglas's southern sojourn meant he was absent from Washington when the Senate Democratic Caucus assembled on December 9 to determine committee assignments for the following session. The caucus voted 17–9 to remove Douglas as chairman of the Committee on Territories. Douglas's ouster was engineered by the Buchanan Administration, which had never forgiven his Lecompton heresy. The leading voices against Douglas were his nemeses Jefferson Davis of Mississippi and John Slidell of Louisiana. Douglas's speeches to their constituents had done nothing to win them over. Later that year, Senator William Gwin of California explained that "the doctrines he had avowed in this Freeport speech had been condemned in the Senate by his removal from the Chairmanship of Territorial Committee of that body." (Douglas's circuitous journey to the capital lasted more than a month. On January 5, the day he was reelected to the Senate by the Illinois legislature, Douglas was in Philadelphia, where he received a congratulatory telegram from Charles Lanphier: "Glory to God and the Sucker Democracy. Douglas 54, Lincoln 41. Announcement followed by shouts of immense crowd present. Town wild with excitement. Democrats firing salute. Guns, music and whisky rampant.")

In his New Orleans speech, Douglas pointed out that Congress had passed no legislation protecting slavery in the territories. The South's demand for a federal slave code became the subject of a confrontation on the Senate floor between Douglas and Albert Gallatin Brown of Mississippi, as fiery a Fire-Eater as stalked the upper chamber. On February 23, Brown rose in favor of "a bill asking protection for our slave property in the territories." Dissenting from the doctrines of "the Senator from Illinois," Brown asked his fellow senators, "If the Territorial Legislature refuses to act, will you act? If it pass unfriendly acts, will you pass friendly? We have a right of protection for our slave property in the Territories. The Constitution, as expounded by the Supreme Court, awards it. We demand it, and we mean to have it."

The South believed slavery must expand or die. That meant into the Territories, into Cuba, and into more of Mexico (which Douglas, a believer in Manifest Destiny, was willing to annex). The drive to acquire more slave territory was not merely about property rights or economics. Southern politicians feared living among an excess slave population, for the safety of their families, and the honor of their women. Blacks already outnumbered Whites in Mississippi, an imbalance likely to increase, since European immigrants were not attracted to states where they would have to compete with slave labor. Master and servant was the only proper relationship between Whites and Blacks, ordained by God, and beneficial to both races. So deeply was this need to dominate an "inferior" race ingrained in Southern identity that Brown declared, "if we do not get our constitutional rights, we will dissolve the Union. True manhood requires it." Then he added, "I do not want to stumble into the presidential contest of 1860 without knowing where we stand."

This was a direct threat to Douglas: endorse a federal slave code or lose the South's support at Charleston. Douglas knew, though, that paying such a price for the nomination would make it worthless: running on the platform of a federal slave code would cost him the electoral votes of every Northern state.

"I never would vote for a slave code in the Territories in Congress," he responded to Brown on the Senate floor, "and I have yet to learn that there is a man in a free state of the Union, of any party, who would."

Douglas amplified that answer in a letter to J. B. Dorr, a Des Moines newspaper editor: if "the Convention shall interpolate into the creed of the party such new issues as the revival of the African slave trade, or a Congressional slave code for the territories, or the doctrine that the Constitution of the United States either establishes or prohibits slavery in the Territories beyond the power of the people legally to control it as other property—it is due to candor to say that, in such an event, I could not accept the nomination if tendered to me."

With the election of 1860 a year away—an election that might be his last chance to win the presidency he had coveted for most of his career—Douglas was already fighting a three-front campaign: against the antislavery Republicans, the proslavery Southerners, and the Doughface Buchanan Administration. To bring his case to the public, Douglas took a step unprecedented in American politics: he published a nineteen-page essay in *Harper's New Monthly Magazine*—titled "The Dividing Line Between Federal and Local Authority: Popular Sovereignty"—a historical justification for Douglas's signature political doctrine. *Harper's* was the nation's leading literary magazine, with more than 50,000 readers. Douglas, who had met the magazine's founder and editor, Fletcher Harper, at a New York City dinner party, may have been the only politician prominent enough to command so much space in its pages.

For all his cachet as a senator, though, Douglas was no intellectual. He enlisted the aid of historian George Bancroft, author of the six-volume *History of the United States: From the Discovery of the American Continent*. For the first time in an active life, he settled at his desk to read deeply, spending the summer of 1859 buried in law and history books borrowed from the Library of Congress. Nonetheless, even Douglas's future biographer would call the essay "long and tedious, written in dull, turgid style that lacked completely the vibrancy of his utterances from the speaking platform. It was repetitious to the point of annoyance, and actually contained little that was new. The arguments were often contrived and involved, and the tone suggested the arc of a man pushed to desperation by the attacks of his critics."

Douglas read history backward, claiming that popular sovereignty had its origins in the American colonies' disputes with the British Crown over slavery. He began the essay by dividing the Democratic Party into three schools of thought on slavery: those who believed the Constitution "neither establishes nor prohibits slavery in the States or Territories beyond the power of the people legally to control it; those who demanded a federal slave code; and those who believed it the Supreme Court's duty to protect slavery in the territories."

Douglas, of course, belonged to the first category. Ever the hairsplitter, he justified his belief in popular sovereignty by arguing that there were certain powers Congress could "confer but can not exercise, such as relate to the domestic affairs and internal policy of the Territory."

During the Senate debates, Douglas and Lincoln had both claimed their views on slavery were in the tradition of the Founding Fathers. At a time when the Founders were still part of living memory—Jefferson and Adams had been dead only thirty-three years—their imprimatur was essential. Attempting to gain it, Douglas insisted that the American Revolution had broken out because the British refused to allow their colonies to regulate slavery. When Virginia tried to regulate slave shipments by imposing a tax on slaves, the Crown canceled it. The war was "not for Independence in the first instance, but for the inestimable right of local Self-government under the British Constitution."

This was torturing the historical record to suit Douglas's convictions on the current crisis. According to Douglas, the Declaration of Independence was written and the Revolution fought to defend popular sovereignty, "the specific claim on the part of the Colonies—denied by the King and Parliament—to the exclusive right of legislation touching all local and internal concerns, slavery included."

Thus, the territories of the 1850s stood in the same position as the colonies of the 1770s, and those who would impose a slave code, or prohibit slavery, stood in the same position as King George III, the villain of the Declaration of Independence.

Douglas shifted from shaky historical ground to shaky Constitutional ground by insisting that, in the right to regulate their internal affairs, there was no difference between states and territories. The constitution stipulated that "Congress shall have the power to dispose of and make all needful rules and regulations respecting the territory or other property belonging to the United States." But "territory" applied to land, not to "a political community or government of any kind."

The Supreme Court disagreed. In the 1828 case *The American Insurance Company et. al. v. Canter*, Chief Justice John Marshall ruled that after Florida was acquired by the United States, it did not "participate in political power" or "share in the government" until it became a state. Congress disagreed as well: the Northwest Ordinance and the Missouri Compromise banned slavery in certain territories.

Douglas argued that the distinction between federal and local authority on slavery had been established by the Constitution's fugitive slave clause, which identified a slave as "a person held to service or labor in one state, under the laws thereof." The slave states ought to appreciate that slavery was under the control of individual states—and, by extension, territories—because they "would never consent for a moment that their domestic relations—and especially their right of property in slaves—should be dependent on federal authority."

The *Harper's* essay was a continuation of Douglas's Senate debate with Albert Gallatin Brown. It was conducted in a Northeastern journal that would never have devoted so much space to an essay defending the rights of slaveholders. The alliance between Douglas and *Harper's* was an early—perhaps the earliest—example of the symbiotic relationship between political celebrity and the popular press, which would fully develop in the twentieth-century. As Harper brothers Joseph Wesley and Fletcher later wrote, when Douglas "proposed to furnish us with a paper on 'Popular Sovereignty' we took the whole matter into careful consideration, and decided that, without reference to party politics, the subject was of such paramount interest that our readers would be glad to have, in permanent and accessible form, the carefully elaborated views of a statesman whose public experience had necessarily familiarized him with territorial jurisprudence."

The essay certainly attracted nationwide attention. It was reprinted in the *Chicago Times* and the *New York Times*, and the *Harper's* office was flooded with letters from big thinkers, eager to write a response. However, it did Douglas no favors in the South. Brown wrote to Douglas, with senatorial courtesy, that he had "made the best of a bad case." But Georgia's Senator Alfred Iverson wrote "I cannot believe that the Southern Democracy will commit so suicidal an act as to adopt either Judge Douglas as their candidate for the Presidency, or his dangerous political heresies." The proslavery *Louisville Courier* declared Douglas's offering his crowning insult to the

South: "His anti-Lecomptonism was bad, his Freeport essay was worse, but his 'copy-righted' Squatter Sovereignty essay was worst of all."

The day before Douglas spoke in Columbus, the *New York Times* predicted that his address would open the presidential campaign in the West, providing the ideal public forum for defending his *Harper's* essay: "He could find no more appropriate locality for a full and frank exposition of a comprehensive and decisive national policy than at Columbus, in the very heart of the Congressional district which has shown itself more rebellious against such a policy than any other in the whole range of the great Northwestern states." (Columbus was represented in Congress by Samuel S. Cox, who opposed Buchanan and the Lecompton Constitution and supported Douglas and Popular Sovereignty.)

On the morning of the 7th, Douglas arrived in Columbus on a train from Pittsburgh, where he had spoken to a crowd outside the St. Charles Hotel. He debarked to a thirteen-gun salute from Capt. Ijams's Gun Squad "and paraded behind a military company to his lodgings at the American House," where "calls from the yeomanry" prevented him from catching up on the rest he'd lost during the journey from Washington. Five thousand people were waiting to hear Douglas at the State House, jamming the steps and the rotunda, peering out the windows of the east portico, where the speaking stand had been erected, and cramming onto a 250-by-80-foot elevated platform. Gamely, the travel-weary Douglas departed after dinner for the capitol, where he was serenaded by Maier's Band and introduced by George Manypenny.

Washington McLean, editor of the Democratic *Cincinnati Daily Enquirer*, advised Douglas not to attack the Republicans, since "tens of thousands" were potential Douglas voters, nor to make the territorial question the theme of his speech. Douglas was in Ohio to support the Democratic candidate for governor, Rufus Ranney, a former justice of the state supreme court.

"Give a history of the Democratic party and show what it has accomplished for the country," McLean wrote Douglas. "Make one of your lofty and national speeches."

Douglas was not one to back down from a fight, even when fighting didn't benefit him politically. His pugnacity had led him to accept Lincoln's challenge. Their debates had created a new rival for the presidency and damaged his own presidential prospects in the South. Feeling embattled by both Republicans and Southern Democrats, Douglas devoted his Columbus speech to denouncing their views on the territorial question.

The Republicans intended to "excite, agitate and divide the country until slavery shall be abolished or established throughout the country," Douglas shouted. At their 1856 Philadelphia convention, which nominated Fremont, the party platform declared "that Congress possesses sovereign power over all the Territories of the Union and that it is both their right and duty to exercise that power for the abolishment and prohibition of African slavery."

As the *New York Times* had predicted, Douglas repeated several points from his *Harper's* essay: disputes between the Crown and the colonies over slavery caused the Revolution; Jefferson wanted a prohibition on slavery in the Northwest Territories, but Congress struck it out, "recognizing these Territories as states and the right of the people inhabiting them to decide the slavery question to suit themselves"; the Republicans were behaving like the British Parliament, willing to grant the people self-government "in all cases excepting the Negro." So were the Southerners, who didn't "trust local laws to protect their slaves." The Republican platform "has a Negro under every plank," Douglas declared. "There is not a White plank in their entire platform. It is all armed against the South, and if you go South among the Fire-Eaters of Louisiana you will find their petitions aimed as directly against the North."

The Republicans and the Southerners "presented to us two cases for Congressional intervention—one from the North and the other from the South—one against slavery and the other for slavery—one to compel the people not to have slavery when they want it, and the other to compel the people to have slavery where they do not want it."

It was entirely a presidential campaign speech. Not once did Douglas mention Rufus Ranney, or even the outgoing governor, Chase, whose abolitionism would have made him an obvious target for Douglas's criticism of the Republican Party's Black fixation. By sticking to national issues, Douglas again created a pioneering moment in the relationship between politics and journalism. His 7,100-word speech was telegraphed to New York City at a cost of $497 and published in its entirety on the front page of the next morning's *Times*. No politician had ever commanded such interest from a newspaper. Technology, Douglas's celebrity, and the sense that the 1860 election would be the most important in the nation's history had produced an innovation in popular media.

"The telegraph gives the speaker in the furthest East or West an audience as wide as the Union," wrote *Times* editor Henry Raymond. Douglas "is talking to all America . . . the importance of the issues involved in the approaching Presidential election gives a special value to this new feature of journalism at the time."

Court Street Marketplace, Cincinnati, Ohio, September 9, 1859

Handbills posted throughout Cincinnati announced that Douglas would speak at Court Street on the 8th; however, he was forced to delay his speech a day due to illness, lingering in Dayton until 4:00 P.M. on the 9th, when he caught a train to Cincinnati. Douglas hoped the midland region of a Northwestern state would embrace his message of checking sectional extremism in the interest of national unity. He avoided the Western Reserve, the New England–settled corner of northeastern Ohio represented in Congress by the abolitionist Joshua Giddings. Ohio's settlement patterns were similar to Illinois's, with a Yankee north, a Midland midsection, and an Appalachian south, making it a swing state that could be won by Douglas or Lincoln. As in Illinois, elections were won or lost in the middle of the state. (In 1856, Ohio was the southernmost state won by Fremont, who carried it by 17,000 votes.)

Cincinnati, although it lay along the Ohio River, was a cosmopolitan Northern city, more populous than Chicago, with a large number of

German immigrants—no guarantee for Douglas, who would lose Hamilton County to Lincoln by 751 votes in the next year's presidential election.

Met at the Cincinnati, Hamilton, and Dayton depot by 4,000 supporters, Douglas begged off giving a speech, saving his strength for the evening: "He was not well," reported the *Enquirer,* "suffering from a cold. The reception address was omitted, and he was escorted to a carriage and drawn by four horses to Burnet House."

Few politicians spoke longer or more often than Douglas, but few were less constituted to endure the strain of a hard campaign. At Court Street Marketplace, bonfires blazed on street corners. Rockets illuminated the night. An American flag was spread across the street, with an attached canvas bearing a welcome to Douglas. Twenty thousand Cincinnatians thronged the marketplace. Fainting spectators had to be extracted from the crowd. So intense was excitement to see Douglas that window seats overlooking the viewing platform were auctioned off for five dollars.

In Cincinnati, Douglas made another presidential campaign speech, calling out the radicalism of his most likely Republican opponents: Chase, Seward . . . and Lincoln, the Springfield lawyer.

"Mr. Seward, Governor Chase, Mr. Sumner, and the leaders of the Republican Party united with the Southern Fire-Eaters in resisting the Compromise Measures of 1850 because they asserted the doctrine of non-intervention and popular sovereignty," Douglas told the crowd, projecting his voice as deeply into the marketplace as he could after his illness. Yet Congress, led by Henry Clay, who came out of retirement to spend his last days in service to the Union, "adopted the principles of non-intervention and popular sovereignty over the heads of Northern abolitionists and Southern interventionists. This great principle must be met and must be decided in the presidential election of 1860."

Did any Republican dissent from Lincoln's "House Divided" speech? Or from Seward's Rochester speech, which declared freedom and slavery an "irrepressible conflict"? Or from Chase's abolitionism? Cincinnati was a border city. Uniquely among the great growing metropolises of the North, only a river separated it from slave territory. How, asked Douglas, could

Cincinnati live in harmony with Covington, Kentucky, its sister city across the Ohio, "if you wait until the states become all free or all slave?"

"When they change their politics!" a voice from the crowd shouted.

"A Republican in the crowd says he expects that harmony when freedom triumphs. There you find an endorsement of the position of Seward and Lincoln that the states must all be free in order to have harmony."

Mentioning Lincoln alongside Seward and Chase, the presumed frontrunners for the 1860 Republican nomination, meant that Douglas continued to take his fellow Illinoisan seriously; the Senate race had not ended their dispute. Perhaps he took Lincoln more seriously than Lincoln took himself. In the late summer of 1859, Lincoln could barely imagine himself as president.

Wooster, Ohio, September 16, 1859

The day after Douglas's Cincinnati speech, there appeared in the *Washington Constitution* a lengthy rebuttal to his *Harper's* article, titled "Observations on Senator Douglas's Views of Popular Sovereignty, as Expressed in Harper's Magazine for September, 1859." It was unsigned but known to be the work of President Buchanan's attorney general (and fellow Pennsylvanian), Jeremiah Black. This was another salvo from an administration bent on Douglas's political destruction. Black took issue with every point of Douglas's essay, writing mockingly that "never before has any public man in America so completely revolutionized his political opinions in the course of eighteen months," pointing out that Douglas had told a crowd in New Orleans that he accepted the Dred Scott decision (although not pointing out that he defended the Freeport Doctrine in the same speech). The *Harper's* essay, wrote Black, "shows no sign of the eloquent Senator; it is even without the logic of the great debater. Many portions of it are very obscure. It seems to be an unsuccessful effort at legal precision; like the writing of a judge, who is trying in vain to give good reasons for a wrong decision on a question of law which he has not yet mastered."

Black defended the Dred Scott decision: it was a slaveholder's constitutional right to take his property anywhere that property was not prohibited by local law. This refuted Douglas's weakest argument: that a territory could, by denying police protections, prohibit slavery as thoroughly as any state. Black pointed out, correctly, that "the Supreme Court has decided that a Territorial Legislature has not the power which he claims for it." Black then quoted Douglas's own words from 1856, when as chairman of the Committee on Territories, he blocked Kansas's antislavery Topeka Constitution: "The sovereignty of a Territory remains in abeyance, suspended in the United States, in trust for the people until they shall be admitted to the Union as a state."

Black was not the first politician to accuse Douglas of changing his views for political expediency. The attorney general's rebuttal was republished in a pamphlet, which Douglas read aboard a train on his way to deliver a speech in Wooster. That left Douglas no time to recover from his outrage. Nor could he forget that Black had written to federal officeholders during the previous year's Senate race, urging them to vote for Republicans rather than Douglas Democrats. To Black, there was no difference between Douglas and an abolitionist, "except such a man, elected by democratic votes, would do more injury to the democratic cause than an abolitionist."

Freshly wounded, his grudge against Black intensified, Douglas delivered the most vituperative speech of his career. Douglas rarely took political differences personally; if he did, he did not express those grievances publicly. On Black, though, he exhausted his entire vocabulary of invective. Douglas did not normally pay notice to political attacks, he told the Wooster crowd, but he had to respond to Black, out of respect for the high office he held.

First of all, it was "an infamous falsehood" to suggest that he did not accept the Dred Scott decision.

"What can be thought of the man who will prostitute a high government office by writing deliberate falsehoods to mislead the American people?" Douglas exclaimed bitterly. "No wonder he made it anonymous."

Black, said Douglas, was "a calumniator and knew that what he was writing was a tissue of falsehoods from beginning to end . . . I never said a territory was a sovereign power. I never uttered such a piece of nonsense . . . while the territories are not sovereign, they have the inalienable right to self government."

Black responded to Douglas's outburst in Wooster by penning an appendix to his essay; it was another helping of scorn on Douglas's insistence that territories possessed the same powers as states, as well as on Douglas's literary skills. ("The article in *Harper's* is extremely difficult to understand. Its unjointed thoughts, loose expression, and illogical reasoning, have covered it with shadows, clouds and darkness.") Douglas wrote a twenty-three-page pamphlet in response to Black's response. Black again answered. Their rhetorical duel finally ended in November, and only due to health problems in the Douglas family. Douglas's wife took ill after giving birth to a daughter. Douglas tended her faithfully, but once she recovered, he became so "feeble" he could not finish his final rejoinder and gave his secretary permission to publish an unfinished draft.

"Here let the controversy close for the present, and perhaps forever," he wrote.

Husband and wife recovered their health, but their daughter, Ellen, would die at the age of eight months, in the midst of her father's presidential campaign.

State House, Columbus, Ohio, September 16, 1859

News of Douglas's Ohio tour had appeared September 1 in the *Ohio Statesman*. The Democrats were bringing in their biggest name to argue the party's case for the fall election, so the Republicans needed a speaker who could put Douglas in his place. They immediately thought of Lincoln, who had put Douglas on the spot over popular sovereignty during the Illinois Senate debates and could now demolish his *Harper's* essay. Ohio was home to politicians more prominent than Lincoln, but Chase and Senator Benjamin

Wade were seen as too radical on abolition to appeal to Cincinnati moderates, while congressman and former governor Tom Corwin was too much of an Ohio Valley conservative for the Western Reserve.

"It was smart quarterbacking," Ohio historian Earl W. Wiley would write. "It implied, incidentally, that the Ohio leadership looked upon Lincoln as a progressive conservative in 1859—progressive enough for central Ohio and conservative enough for southern Ohio . . . The intangibles of the situation that would ultimately send him to Washington were quietly beginning to assert themselves."

Lincoln had been refusing out-of-state speaking engagements all year, pleading the need to rebuild his legal practice after the expense and distraction of the Senate campaign. However, the Ohio Republican State Central Committee offered Lincoln an invitation in terms he found impossible to refuse: "Now, we desire to head off the little gentleman, and in behalf of the Republican State Central Committee, I invite you to visit our State to make a few speeches. Say 3 or 4, at such prominent points as we may select . . . We want to make our victory complete this year," Secretary William T. Bascom wrote Lincoln.

Presented another opportunity to get in the last word on "the little gentleman," Lincoln wrote back, "I shall try to speak at Columbus and Cincinnati; but cannot do more." Lincoln followed Ohio Republican politics, which that year were consumed with the Oberlin-Wellington Rescue Case. A slave named John Price escaped from his master in Kentucky and took refuge in Oberlin, Ohio, whose namesake college had been founded by religiously motivated abolitionists from western New York. After two years, Price was discovered and captured by slave catchers. To avoid local outrage, federal marshals spirited Price to the Wadsworth House in Wellington, nine miles south of Oberlin. But word got out. Six hundred Oberlin residents walked to Wellington and surrounded the hotel. They helped Price climb out a window then hid him at the home of James H. Fairchild, a future president of Oberlin College. Price made his way to Canada and freedom, but thirty-seven of his rescuers were arrested for violating the Fugitive Slave Law. Two were convicted in federal court and jailed. The men appealed their convictions to the Ohio Supreme Court, whose chief justice, Joseph R. Swan, was an antislavery man who had been elected in 1854 on a wave of revulsion toward the Kansas-Nebraska Act. Despite his personal opposition to the Fugitive Slave Law, Swan ruled that the state court had no standing to overrule a federal court: "I am now compelled to say, under the solemn duties of a judge, bound by my official oath to sustain the supremacy of the Constitution and the law, the prisoner must be remanded."

For obeying federal law and the Constitution, Swan was denied renomination at the June 2nd Republican State Convention, which was dominated by the abolitionist triumvirate of Chase, Wade, and Giddings. The convention also adopted a resolution calling for the "repeal of the Fugitive Slave Act of 1850 as subversive of both the rights of the state and the liberties of the people, and as contrary to the plainest duties of humanity and justice, and as abhorrent to the moral sense of the civilized world." For governor, the party nominated William Dennison Jr., an ex-Whig from Cincinnati.

Lincoln read about these developments in Springfield and was not pleased by what he saw as the Ohio Republicans' creeping radicalism, especially as the presidential campaign approached. Lincoln's friend Samuel Galloway, who represented Columbus in Congress for one term before his defeat by Douglas's ally Samuel Cox, wrote Lincoln that Swan had been "sacrificed to propiate the fanatics." His rejection was "a stain upon our Republicanism," which would result in the party's defeat that fall in Ohio, and nationwide in 1860. "You are my choice," Galloway told Lincoln. "Your program and principles as set forth in your discussions with Judge Douglas will suit all Republicans, especially those of the old Whig stamp."

"Two things done by the Ohio Republican convention—the repudiation of Judge Swan, and the 'plank' for a repeal of the Fugitive Slave Law—I very much regretted," Lincoln wrote back. "These two things are of a piece; and they are viewed by many good men, sincerely opposed to slavery, as a struggle against, and in disregard of, the constitution itself. And it is the very thing that will greatly endanger our course, if it not be kept out of our national convention."

Lincoln agreed that Chase "may not be the most suitable as a candidate for the presidency," but he also told Galloway, "I must say I do not think myself fit for the Presidency."

Although Lincoln's attitudes differed from the state party's platform, his moderation was exactly what the central committee was looking for. After Douglas spoke in Columbus, Bascom sent Lincoln this update: "There is no man in the Union who under the circumstances can do so much good in central and southern Ohio as you can, and more especially to follow Douglas . . . Douglas had a large meeting here. His speech was his magazine article over again, and produced no results."

Lincoln's meeting in Columbus was not nearly as large. He also spoke from the east portico of the State House, but to a smaller, less enthusiastic crowd. For one thing, his appearance had been scheduled at the same time as the Franklin County Agricultural Fair, a popular local event. The Young Men's Republican Club, charged with promoting the event, took out advertisements announcing the speaker as the "Hon. ABRAHAM C. LINCOLN, of Illinois." (Lincoln had no middle name.) Finally, Chase's supporters took no interest in Lincoln—nor did Chase himself, who had been in Columbus earlier that week, but left for northern Ohio before Lincoln arrived. It was a familiar situation for Lincoln. He'd experienced it when he followed Douglas at the Tremont House, and at Springfield. The people only turned out to hear Lincoln when he debated the Little Giant. Lincoln was so little regarded in Ohio that no one from the central committee met him at the train depot, only catching up with him at his hotel before the 3:00 P.M. speech.

Lincoln had several aims that day. One, of course, was to poke holes in Douglas's *Harper's* essay. But he also wanted to make sure Republicans were not seduced by Douglas's opposition to a federal slave code. As he wrote in a series of notes for his Ohio speeches, Douglas's stand was purely opportunistic. If Douglas truly endorsed Dred Scott, he must also endorse a slave code, but "Douglas never lets the logic of principle, displace the logic of success . . . It will then be a question whether the Republican party of the nation shall make him President, in magnanimous gratitude for having opposed a Slave code." Lincoln meant to convince Republicans that Douglas's position, "whether for or against a slave code for or against Lecompton, leads inevitably to the nationalizing and perpetuity of slavery, and the Republican cause cannot live by it."

Even before Lincoln arrived in Columbus, the *Ohio Statesman*, the local Douglas organ, attached his name to the "fanatics of Oberlin" who were trying to force Black equality, Black suffrage, and race mixing on White Ohioans.

"In pursuance of their base design to fasten negro-equality upon this State the Republicans have sent abroad for champions of that amalgamation principle," the *Statesman* editorialized. "On Friday next one of them, Abe Lincoln of Illinois, is to address them at this city. In debating with Senator Douglas during the memorable contest of last fall, Mr. Lincoln declared in favor of negro suffrage, and attempted to defend that vile conception against the Little Giant."

At three o'clock that afternoon, a man a young woman would remember as "tall, sad, earnest, grave" stepped in front of an audience the *Statesman* would ridicule as a "beggarly account of empty boxes."

Lincoln first refuted the *Statesman*'s accusation that he favored Black suffrage. He quoted the newspaper, then he quoted himself, from the debates in Ottawa and Charleston, disclaiming any belief in the political or social equality of Whites and Blacks. Once Lincoln had assured his listeners that he was not an "Oberlin fanatic," he could get down to the business of his speech: attacking Douglas, particularly his recent foray into journalism.

"I will occupy a good portion of your time here in drawing your attention to certain points" in the *Harper's* essay—another example of Douglas treating slaves as a species of portable property, no different than cattle, tobacco, onions, or potatoes.

"I suppose the institution of slavery really looks small to him," Lincoln said. "He is so put up by nature that a lash upon his back would hurt him, but a lash upon anybody else's back does not hurt him."

Lincoln attacked Douglas's most specious arguments: that territories were equal to states, and that the Revolution had been fought over popular sovereignty. Lincoln was not yet Douglas's equal as a political operator, but the debates had proven he was Douglas's intellectual superior. Lincoln was better read, for one thing. Not only had he read more widely than Douglas, he knew *how* to read. When Douglas studied history—as he had done for the first time while researching the *Harper's* essay—he sought only to validate his own beliefs. Lincoln could apply the lessons of history to the present crisis, and find, from the time of the Founders to his own day, a consistent opposition to the spread of slavery. Douglas's historical ignorance provided Lincoln with an easy target. Lincoln didn't have to set up a straw man because the *Harper's* essay *was* a straw man.

Perhaps equating states and territories was "necessary for this squatter sovereignty, but is it true?" Lincoln asked. "If there is no difference between them why not make the territories states at once? What is the reason that Kansas was not fit to come into the Union when it was organized into a territory, in Douglas's view?"

Douglas's doctrine that Congress had no right to interfere in a polity's internal affairs was circular logic. It was up to Congress to decide when a settlement became a territory. So if the Southerners could prevent Congress from organizing new lands into territories, they could prevent "popular sovereignty" from keeping their slaves out: "In a word, the whole thing, at the dash of a pen, is at last put in the power of Congress; for if they do not have this popular sovereignty until Congress organizes them, I ask if it at last does not come from Congress."

The two main objects of the *Harper's* essay were to show that the Founders favored popular sovereignty, and that Dred Scott had not stamped it out. To prove the first, Douglas ignored the Northwest Ordinance of 1787, passed by the Congress of the Confederation and reaffirmed by Congress under the new constitution, which prohibited slavery in territories north of the Ohio River—including Ohio.

"Now he asks the community to believe that the men of the Revolution were in favor of his great principle, when we have the naked history that they themselves dealt with this very subject matter of his principle, and utterly repudiated his principle, acting upon a precisely contrary ground,"

Lincoln said incredulously. "It is as impudent and absurd as if a prosecuting attorney should stand up before a jury and ask them to convict A as the murderer of B, while B was walking alive before them."

The Founders had prohibited slavery in the territories. Dred Scott made it a right. Douglas was so invested in popular sovereignty as a fundamental principle of American democracy that he tied logic into knots to prove it had been endorsed by both the Founding Fathers and the Taney Court. In fact, argued Lincoln, it had been repudiated by both. Douglas's attempt to reconcile popular sovereignty with Dred Scott "was a bare absurdity—no less than that a thing may be lawfully driven away from where it has a right to be."

Lincoln spoke again that evening, to an even smaller audience at the Young Men's Republican Club at City Hall. He did not make much of an impression on Columbus, but he did get the *Ohio Statesman* to concede that he did not favor Black suffrage, and that he belonged to the "Corwin wing" of the Republican Party—followers of former senator and current representative Tom Corwin, a moderate ex-Whig—and not the "real Republicanism" of "Chase, Giddings and Co." The newspaper could not let that go without expressing a Douglas-style suspicion that Lincoln had bleached his politics for central Ohio: "We apprehend that if Mr. Lincoln had made a speech at Oberlin, he would not have gone to much trouble to correct the charge made by us that he was in favor of negro voting."

Montgomery County Courthouse, Dayton, Ohio, September 17, 1859

Stopping in Dayton to change trains for Cincinnati, Lincoln stood on a box in front of the courthouse, where he delivered a two-hour speech to what the *Dayton Daily Empire* described as "a meager crowd, numbering scarce 200 . . . they were half Democrats, who attended from mere curiosity."

There was no stenographer on hand to record Lincoln's every word, but the local reporters got down the gist of the talk, which was a repetition of what he'd said in Columbus the day before. It was also a preview of what he would say in Cincinnati that night: the Northwest Ordinance had established Congress's right to prohibit slavery in the territories; it was also the reason Ohio was a free state and Kentucky a slave state, even though the climates were identical on both sides of the river.

"Mr. Lincoln closed with an eloquent defense of the rights of free labor," reported the *Weekly Dayton Journal*, friendlier to Lincoln than the Democratic *Daily Empire*. "The free White man had a right to claim that the new territories into which they and their children might go to seek a livelihood should be preserved free and clear of the incumbrance of slavery, and that no laboring White man should be placed in a position where, by the introduction of slavery into the territories, he would be compelled to toil by the side of a slave."

(Jefferson Davis argued that slavery protected the dignity of White labor, by sparing Whites from the most backbreaking jobs. Lincoln took the opposite stance: slavery degraded White labor, because poor White farmers could not compete in a plantation economy. That was one reason his father had moved the family from Kentucky to Indiana. Little Pigeon Creek, Indiana, was also in the Ohio River Valley, so perhaps he felt that biographical detail would resonate in Dayton.)

Among that meager gathering of two hundred was at least one important figure: former and future congressman Robert C. Schenck, who had served in Washington alongside Lincoln, and also opposed the Mexican War because it expanded the territory available for slavery. That evening, Schenck delivered a political speech of his own in Dayton. When the subject of the next president came up, Schenck suggested that "if an honest, sensible man was wanted, it would be well to nominate the distinguished gentleman from Illinois who had addressed them that day." That, Lincoln said, was the first time his name had been proposed for the presidency in a public forum. Schenck was a Lincoln delegate at the 1860 Republican National Convention, and his loyalty was rewarded during the Civil War, with a commission as a brigadier general.

Fifth Street Market, Cincinnati, Ohio,
September 17, 1859

Moncure Daniel Conway was the twenty-seven-year-old pastor of Cincinnati's First Unitarian Church. Born into a slaveholding First Family in Virginia, Conway went north to study at Pennsylvania's Dickinson College, where he took on Yankee ways. Not just any Yankees, but the most scandalously radical: abolitionist New England transcendentalists and pacifist Quakers. While studying at Harvard Divinity School, Conway befriended Ralph Waldo Emerson and was radicalized by the case of Anthony Burns, a slave who escaped from Virginia to Boston. Burns's owner, Charles Suttle, an acquaintance of Conway's family, went to court to reclaim his property under the Fugitive Slave Law. An abolitionist mob stormed the federal courthouse in an attempt to free Burns. The mob killed a deputy but failed to rescue the fugitive. A month later, at a Fourth of July rally sponsored by the Massachusetts Anti-Slavery Society, Conway spoke from the same platform as William Lloyd Garrison and Henry David Thoreau. Alarmed by the violence of both slaveholders and abolitionists, he delivered "a plea for the peaceful separation of North and South after the manner of Abraham and Lot." Leaving Boston, Conway took up a pulpit as pastor of the First Unitarian Church of Washington, D.C. Fired for his antislavery sermons, he went west to Cincinnati, where he had already lost a third of his congregation by denying the divinity of Christ.

As an easterner, Conway had never heard of Abraham Lincoln when he decided to take a stroll through the marketplace on the evening of the 17th. Lincoln began speaking at eight o'clock, an hour after his train arrived at the Cincinnati, Hamilton, and Dayton depot to a far larger and more boisterous crowd than he'd faced in Columbus. He was greeted at the station by a welcoming committee, then conveyed to the marketplace in an open carriage, escorted by a German band, torch bearers, and a booming cannon. He now stood in a balcony on the north side of the square, bonfires illuminating his face for 4,000 listeners.

Conway only intended to linger a few moments on the fringes of this unexpected gathering, but "something about the speaker, and some words that reached me, led me to press nearer." Asking the speaker's name, he was told "Abraham Lincoln."

As he edged closer to the balcony, to see the face belonging to the name, Conway was reminded of poet Robert Browning's description of a German professor: "Three parts sublime to one grotesque." Lincoln's face was "battered and bronzed, without being hard," his nose prominent, buttressing "a high and strong forehead," his eyes sad, his mouth and chin "too close together" between hollow cheeks.

"On the whole Lincoln's appearance was not attractive until one heard his voice, which possessed variety of expression, earnestness, and shrewdness in every tone," Conway would write in his autobiography. "The charm of his manner was that he had no manner: he was simple, direct, humorous. He pleasantly repeated a mannerism of his opponent—'This is what Douglas calls his gur-reat principle'; but the next words I remember were these: 'Slavery is wrong!'"

In Cincinnati, Lincoln delivered the cleverest, most effective speech of his many campaigns against Douglas. The crowd was full of Kentuckians who had crossed the river to boo the Black Republican. They murmured and hissed when he declared, "Slavery is wrong." Lincoln pretended to address them, offering an endorsement of Douglas as the presidential candidate who could best serve the interests of Southern slaveholders. In fact, he was aiming to convince Ohioans that Douglas was a quisling for the South.

Acknowledging the Kentuckians in his audience, who no doubt believed slavery was "a good thing," Lincoln proposed "to try to show you that you ought to nominate for the next presidency, at Charleston, my distinguished friend, Judge Douglas. In all that there is a difference between you and him, I understand he is sincerely for you, and more wisely for you, than you are for yourselves."

The South needed a Yankee president to maintain support for slavery in the free states. This was a longstanding Democratic strategy. The party's last three nominees had been Northerners: Lewis Cass of Michigan, Franklin

Pierce of New Hampshire, James Buchanan of Pennsylvania. Douglas expected that tradition to hold at Charleston.

Lincoln had always believed Douglas was a proslavery mole in the North, the definition of a doughface. Douglas sometimes offended Southerners, as with his Freeport Doctrine. Without such sops to the free states, though, "he would lose his hold upon the North, and, by consequence, would lose his capacity to serve you."

During his Mississippi riverboat tour the previous December, Douglas described to a Memphis crowd "a line drawn by the Almighty across this continent, on the one side of which must always be cultivated by slaves." If God had ordained slavery for the South, who could say it was wrong for the North?

"Whenever you can get these Northern audiences to adopt the opinion that slavery is right on the other side of the Ohio, whenever you can get them, in pursuance of Douglas's views, to adopt that sentiment, they will very readily make the other argument, which is perfectly logical, that that which is right on that side of the Ohio, cannot be wrong on this, and that if you have that property on that side of the Ohio, under the seal and stamp of the Almighty, when by any means it escapes over here, it is wrong to have constitution and laws to 'devil' you about it . . . In this matter Judge Douglas is preparing the public mind for you of Kentucky, to make perpetual that good thing in your estimation, about which you and I differ."

"Speak to Ohio men, and not to Kentuckians," shouted a man too dense to get the drift of Lincoln's rhetoric.

"I beg permission to speak as I please," replied Lincoln, who went on to tell "Kentuckians" that popular sovereignty would lead to "the revival of the slave trade, whenever you want it." If a man had a sacred right to bring slaves into a territory, then who could tell him not to buy slaves in Africa? Douglas opposed repealing laws against importing African slaves. That might offend Kentuckians. It shouldn't, because "if he said less than that, he would lose the power of 'lugging' the Northern states to your support."

Lincoln's Cincinnati speech, Ohio historian Daniel J. Ryan would write, "contributed more to the Republican victory in 1860 than any single speech ever made. Not that it converted Whigs, Democrats, or Americans, but because it served to divide the Democrats of the South from the Democrats of the North on Douglas's candidacy for the presidency."

One American party member, Cincinnati solicitor Rutherford B. Hayes, wrote to Ohio secretary of state Addison Peale Russell, expressing a hope that Lincoln not offend nativists by giving "a too strictly partisan cast to his address . . . injury might be done if party names and party doctrines were used by Mr. Lincoln in a way to displease the American element of our organization." Hayes must have been displeased with what he heard that night.

Once Lincoln was done offering advice to "Kentuckians," he offered some to Republicans. The party must not interfere with slavery where it existed, nor oppose a fugitive slave law. To do otherwise would violate the Constitution. Lincoln was again allying himself with the Corwin wing of the Ohio Republican Party, dominant in the southern part of the state. (Lincoln had not been asked to speak in Cleveland, where such views would have been unpopular, and which was safe Republican territory, anyway.) On the other hand, Republicans could not nominate a candidate "who declares himself against us in regard to the prevention of slavery." The slave states were lost to the Republicans, but a man who "declares himself inimical to our purpose" would lose all the free states, too—every state except, perhaps, Maryland.

Lincoln speculated that there were "plenty of men in the slave states" who agreed with these principles and were worthy of a spot on the next Republican ticket. In fact, there was only one man in any state: Abraham Lincoln of Illinois.

Moncure Conway left the Fifth Street Market a Lincoln man. The next year, he reprinted Lincoln's speeches in *The Dial*, a transcendentalist literary magazine he founded, and voted for him in November, "the only vote I ever did cast for a president, having in Washington had no vote and in later years no faith in any of the candidates or in the office."

Election Day, October 11, 1859

The October elections were a triumph for Ohio Republicans—and Lincoln. Dennison defeated Ranney for the governorship, 184,557 to 171,226. Republicans picked up twelve seats in the state senate and fourteen in the House, gaining control of both chambers and guaranteeing Chase's election to the Senate.

Two days after the vote, Bascom wrote to Lincoln that the returns "dispose of all the hopes of Douglas in Ohio. Squatter sovereignty is dead here. We feel that some credit of this result is due to you, and on behalf of our Republican friends I again return you our most grateful thanks." Galloway wrote that "your visit to Ohio has excited an interest in your favor."

Lincoln had brought to Ohio a scrapbook containing the *Chicago Press and Tribune*'s clippings of his Senate debate remarks, and the *Chicago Times*'s of Douglas's. He had also saved copies of their speeches in Chicago, Bloomington, and Springfield. Lincoln was hoping to interest a publisher but inadvertently left the book in his room at the Neil House in Columbus. (Lincoln had already tried and failed to persuade two Springfield publishers to bring out a debate volume.) Discovering the book missing, Lincoln wrote the hotel's management, who forwarded it to Springfield.

Thanks to Lincoln's role in the Republican victory, there was interest in publishing the debates. In early December, the party's central committee wrote to Lincoln thanking him for "the prompt and efficient aid rendered us in the late campaign" and requesting "for publication in permanent form, authentic copies of those debates, together with your two Ohio speeches, as a document that will be of essential service to the cause in the approaching presidential campaign."

After Galloway promised to raise funds to publish a book, Lincoln enlisted a young German American journalist named John G. Nicolay to deliver his scrapbook to Columbus. Lincoln had met Nicolay during visits to the State Library office of his employer, Secretary of State Ozias M. Hatch, which was "practically the Republican campaign headquarters for both city and State." With the support of the state central committee, the debate volume was published by Follett, Foster & Co., although not without "difficulties interposed by the fears, suspicions and envying of some sensitive friends of a certain aspirant for the Presidency," Galloway wrote Lincoln. (That would have been Chase, who also omitted his name from the letter requesting copies of the debates.) Published in March 1860, the book sold 50,000 copies, at 50 cents apiece, advancing Lincoln's candidacy for the nomination at the upcoming Republican convention. It might not have been published at all if he hadn't accepted the invitation to speak in Ohio.

As for the Democrats, they tried to put the best face on the defeat, for the party and for Douglas. The *Cincinnati Enquirer* noted that the Democratic vote had increased in the three counties where Douglas had spoken: Franklin (Columbus), Hamilton (Cincinnati), and Wayne (Wooster), and that Dennison's margin over Ranney was smaller than Ohio's combined vote of Fremont and Fillmore over Buchanan in 1856. Douglas had not been the problem; the problem had been not enough Douglas.

"Those facts lead us to believe that if Senator Douglas could have delivered ten or fifteen speeches in different parts of the State, the Democracy would have been aroused to an extent that would have led to the complete redemption of Ohio from Republican misrule," the *Enquirer* opined. If Douglas were nominated in Charleston, he would carry Ohio "by a large majority," and sweep the Northwest on a popular sovereignty platform.

Douglas received letters of encouragement from Ohio Democrats who assured him that the 1859 results meant nothing for 1860. Abner Backus, a member of the Ohio Democratic State Central Committee, informed Douglas that the party had set January 5 for its convention to nominate delegates for Charleston. He was confident of carrying a majority of senatorial districts for Douglas, passing a resolution authorizing the delegates to vote as a unit, and delivering Ohio's twenty-three electoral votes—the third largest prize, after New York and Pennsylvania—to Douglas. This must have been welcome news, since Douglas had campaigned in Ohio with hopes of securing its convention delegates.

"I fear you may think Ohio will go against you next fall but this is a great mistake," supporter James M. Cox wrote Douglas from Mansfield.

"In case you are our candidate next fall she will give you 30 to 40 thousand majority. Wherever you have been in Ohio she has gone right. In Wayne Co. Our whole ticket is elected by about 500 maj. And old Hamilton too has gone Democratic and elected every candidate on our ticket."

Cox's assurances did not come true. Douglas would lose Ohio to Lincoln in 1860. The results of 1859 were a sign that his chance at the presidency—his last chance—was slipping away, while Lincoln's prospects were growing. The Ohio Campaign was the first time in their twenty-year rivalry that Lincoln had bested Douglas in the race of ambition, both in votes and offices won. Douglas may have been the most prominent, influential politician of the 1850s, but Lincoln was going to play that role in the 1860s.

Just five days after Ohio voted, an event occurred that further damaged Douglas's fading political fortunes: in Harpers Ferry, Virginia, a messianic abolitionist named John Brown led a raid on the federal arsenal, hoping to inspire a slave rebellion that would consume the South.

CHAPTER 5

CHARLESTON: PRELUDE TO DISUNION

Institute Hall, Charleston, South Carolina, April 23, 1860

I n early spring, Charleston was blooming. Inside the walled-in gardens of homes on the city's cobblestone streets, the jessamine, the wisteria, the Cherokee rose, and the azalea were in blossom, attracting the lazy buzz of hummingbird wings. Along the Battery, the wharfside promenade, semitropical Atlantic breezes stirred the stiff leaves of palmetto trees. Beyond, on the water, the starched white sails of pleasure boats gleamed in the sunshine.

A port city of 40,000, Charleston was similar to Boston, Philadelphia, and Savannah in the narrowness of its streets, the insularity of its people and institutions, and the length of its settlement in this young republic: nearly two centuries by the time the Democratic delegates began arriving, many from states that had belonged to France or Spain when Charleston was a

British colony. There could not have been a more beautiful, more exotic setting for a convention than Charleston. The Wisconsin delegation snow-shoed to the depot in Madison. When they debarked in Charleston, its members plucked roses from the city's bushes. There could not have been a more inconvenient setting either: Charleston was huddled around a harbor, so reaching it by train required six transfers just from Washington. Delegations from the Atlantic states recognized that Charleston looked to the sea and arrived at the convention on pleasure cruises. The *S.R. Spaulding* brought the Massachusetts delegates, along with the thirty-member Brass Band of Boston, which blared "Yankee Doodle," a tune certainly not pleasing to the ears of Charlestonians. From Philadelphia sailed the steamer *Keystone State*, loaded with five hundred barrels of hard liquor and three hundred kegs of beer, enough booze to slake the Pennsylvanians' thirst through what they expected to be a long, bitterly contested convention. The New Yorkers brought the ultimate entertainment: female passengers who were not listed on the manifest by name, but only as "friends" of the delegates.

There could not have been a convention site worse for Stephen Douglas's chance at the nomination, either. Charleston had been chosen as a consolation prize to the South after the 1856 convention at Cincinnati nominated yet another Northerner, James Buchanan. The first Southern city to host a convention, Charleston was a quarter the size of Cincinnati, and not prepared to accommodate thousands of visitors. In January, as the Illinois Democratic Party appointed its twenty-two delegates, Douglas wrote to Charles Lanphier, expressing his hope that "the convention might appoint as many assisting or consulting delegates as it chooses . . . it is important that all our leading men in the State should be at Charleston." This proved impossible due to the logistics of transportation and lodgings. Like small-town hustlers fleecing city slickers, Charleston innkeepers were taking advantage of the conventioneers' demand by charging the inflated price of five dollars a day for room and board. The Douglas campaign set up its headquarters in the two-story Hibernian Hall, a square and a half from the convention site. On the first floor were work rooms with writing tables and stacks of *Chicago Times* publisher James W. Sheahan's *The Life of Stephen A. Douglas*, which was flattering enough to the senator to serve as a campaign biography. On the second floor were hundreds of white-sheeted cots—a makeshift dormitory for the Northwestern delegations, who were all expected to vote for Douglas. (Douglas remained in Washington, following the tradition that presidential candidates did not appear at conventions to badger delegates for votes.)

It was not simply logistics that made Charleston inhospitable to Douglas. Charleston was the cultural hearth of the Cotton South. Among its first settlers were Barbadian planters, who brought with them their plantation help, and a legal code that set out rules for whipping, branding, and mutilating slaves who offended "any Christian." South Carolina had been represented in the Senate by John C. Calhoun, who believed slavery was beneficial to Blacks, and whose insistence that his state had a right to nullify federal tariffs was an early stirring of the secessionist movement. The city's most influential newspaper was the *Charleston Mercury*, edited by Robert Barnwell Rhett Jr., a fiery defender of White Southern honor whose editorials were hostile to abolitionists, to Yankees, and to Douglas in particular. (Rhett's father, a former senator and congressman, had been preaching since the 1830s that secession was preferable to federal control of slavery.)

"We are now on the eve of events which will shortly either remodel the political organization of the country, or shake the Union to its centre," Rhett wrote on the day the convention opened. "We are about to embark in the election that may end in the inauguration of a Black Republican or a Freesoil Democrat, differing from the former only in being less openly but more treacherously hostile." After quoting a Calhoun speech that accused both parties of courting abolitionists, he concluded that the North was "willing to sacrifice the Union at the altar of abolition." Rhett had told his friend and fellow secessionist Representative William Porcher Miles that the "demolition of the party" was the first step toward breaking up the Union.

Southerners insisted they were only defending their constitutional right to take their legal property into the territories, which the Supreme

Court had endorsed in the Dred Scott decision. On this principle, the slave states had been preparing all year to break up the convention. When Alabama Democrats met in January to choose delegates to Charleston, they passed a resolution that "it is the duty of the General Government, by all proper legislation, to secure an entry into those territories to all the citizens of the United States, together with their property of every description, and that the same shall remain protected by the United States while the Territories are under its authority." If the full convention disagreed, Alabama's delegates were "positively instructed" to withdraw.

The Alabama Platform, as it was called, was adopted by a convention under the sway of former congressman William Lowndes Yancey, founder of the proto-secessionist League of United Southerners. Yancey, who would be dubbed "Prince of the Fire-Eaters" at Charleston, had walked out of the 1848 Democratic National Convention when Lewis Cass was nominated on a popular sovereignty platform. Only one delegate followed. Yancey spoke out against the Compromise of 1850, believing that any compromise—such as banning the slave trade in the District of Columbia—was a step on the slippery slope to abolition. The Compromise passed Congress, with Southern votes. By 1860, Southern opinion had finally caught up with Yancey. John Brown's raid on Harpers Ferry raised on every plantation fears of a race war if the slaves were freed, or if they were confined to their current limits and outbred their masters. Increasingly, secession was seen as a matter of survival. Yancey, whose powerful pleas for disunion had earned him the nickname "Orator of Secession," told the Alabama convention that the South must secede if the country elected a Black Republican, or even a Democrat who refused to provide constitutional protections for slavery—a platform Douglas had vowed not to run on.

"I am now, as I have ever been, ready to seize upon the Constitution in which these rights are guaranteed" to "form a new Union" of Southern states, he said. To defend it, Southerners must be prepared to "tread a pathway in blood."

Yancey's rhetoric was aimed at Douglas, whom he labeled the South's "greatest and most dangerous" enemy because of his Freeport heresy.

"The disruptionists came here in defiant and hectoring spirit and your enemies are bitter to the bitter end," *Mobile Register* editor John Forsyth wrote Douglas from the convention, where he was a member of the Alabama delegation. Then he added, "the convention admitted me and my side by 295 to 155—a clear majority of 140 votes—a pretty strong endorsement that a man might be a Douglas man & not cease to be a Democrat."

A week and a half before the Charleston convention, Douglas received a letter from "several gentlemen" in Montgomery, warning him that "Mr. Yancey will go into the convention strongly prepared to attack your principles; and an ardent desire to defeat you for the nomination of the party for the presidency."

In response to Harpers Ferry, Douglas had submitted a resolution asking the Senate Judiciary Committee for a bill suppressing conspiracies "to invade, assail, or molest the government, inhabitants, property, or institutions of any other state or Territory of the Union"—whether those conspirators were the Emigrant Aid companies of New England or the Blue Lodges of Missouri, which had done battle in Bleeding Kansas. He then declared that Harpers Ferry was "the natural, logical, inevitable result of the doctrines and teachings of the Republican Party." If Douglas had been trying to assuage Southern terror of another John Brown, he failed. The South—correctly—saw Douglas's resolution as an expansion of federal power that could be used to suppress secession.

As went Alabama, so went Mississippi. On February 2, Jefferson Davis rose in the Senate to propose six resolutions protecting the rights of slaveholders in the territories. The most important, and most offensive to the North, was number four, which declared that neither Congress nor a territorial legislature had the power to violate a slaveholder's constitutional right to take his property into a territory, and that "if experience should at any time prove that the judiciary does not possess power to insure adequate protection, it will then become the duty of Congress to supply such deficiency."

This was an attack on the Freeport Doctrine, and a demand for a federal slave code. Davis did not expect the Senate to pass his resolutions; he just wanted to put senators on record, in advance of the convention. The resolutions were endorsed by the Democratic caucus, except, of course, for Douglas, who complained that "the integrity of the Democratic party [was] to be threatened by abstract resolutions." They were also endorsed by Buchanan, who told California senator Milton S. Latham that he favored Senator Joseph Lane of Oregon as the nominee. During that meeting, Latham "thought I observed a deadly hostility to Mr. Douglas."

Northwesterners reacted with alarm to the South's demands. Adopting a federal slave code would guarantee the election of a Republican. (Which would have suited the secessionists' plans.) From Cleveland, delegate Henry B. Payne wrote to Douglas: "If the cabal of the senate can control the convention and establish their Lecompton Slave Code—proslavery creed . . . In Ohio the election would go by default. Such a candidate as Breckinridge on such a platform would be beat by 50,000."

Payne proposed walking out of the convention if it produced a slave code platform—the same tactic the Southerners were proposing if it didn't. On the eve of the convention in Charleston, each delegation prepared for the upcoming clash in its own separate lodgings. Oregon and California pitched tents on the Battery. Maine and Rhode Island stayed four or five to a room at Mills House. Massachusetts roomed in a boarding house next door to the *Mercury* offices. The fieriest Southern delegations—Alabama, Mississippi, Texas, Virginia, and North Carolina—checked into the Greek Revival Charleston Hotel, the city's fanciest, at ten dollars a night. Expecting to gross $280,000 from the largest gathering in the city's history, the hotel had ordered 300 quilts and hair pillows, 1000 palm leaf mattresses, 500 maple bedsteads, and 100 toothbrushes with matching combs. Other Southern delegates were welcomed into the lavish homes of the local gentry.

"Northerners became conscious of that subtle ability which Charlestonians possessed of making others conscious of the fact that they were outsiders," a historian would write. Leery of the city's secessionist sympathies, and fearing "personal violence" from Charlestonians, some Douglas allies had lobbied the Democratic National Committee to move the proceedings to Baltimore or New Orleans.

In a private parlor at the Charleston Hotel, William Lowndes Yancey held court with his fellow Southerners, plotting even before the convention began to bring it to an end. The Southern states could not agree on a candidate of their own, but the night before the opening gavel, Georgia, Alabama, Mississippi, Louisiana, Florida, Arkansas, and Texas all agreed to walk out if Douglas was nominated. It was rumored that some delegates from North Carolina, Virginia, Kentucky, and Missouri would follow them.

Before the convention opened, Southerners taunted Murray McConnel, an Illinois delegate, telling him to go back where he came from and join the Republicans.

"I am surprised at the bitterness of some of our Southern opponents," McConnel reported. "They go so far as to call us all abolitionists and say we had better stay at home and attend the Chicago convention where we ultimately belong."

Under the bylaws of the Democratic Party, the nominee would require a two-thirds majority. Of the 606 delegates, 230 were from slave states. Even if Douglas won every Free-Soil vote, he would still come up short.

"My opinion still is that the chances are against the nomination of Douglas," wrote Cincinnati journalist Murat Halstead. "I can see how he can get a majority vote, but I cannot figure out a two-thirds vote for him."

Institute Hall, where the delegates assembled at noon that Monday, was the one Charleston establishment large enough to accommodate the convention. A six-year-old Italianate brick edifice, with a terracotta roof and high, rounded windows, the hall seated 3,000: 2,000 in the galleries and 1,000 on the floor, where workmen had been bolting wooden chairs to pine planks by the half dozen. In an expression of state pride, the wall behind the stage was painted with symbols of South Carolina produce and industry, as well as a scantily attired woman pointing a dagger at a globe. The hall's only drawback was that it was too close to the street: conventioneers demanded the city sprinkle sawdust on the pavement to muffle the squeaking and grinding of carriage wheels.

The Douglas forces were led by the candidate's home-state ally William Richardson, described by Halstead as "a large, coarse, powerful man, with a harsh but distinct voice that is heard above the clamor of a Convention like a fire-bell over the clatter of engines in the street." Richardson "was stalking up and down among the Douglas delegations, his forehead furrowed with heavy wrinkles, his face glowing, his shirt collar wilted down, his coat-cuffs rolled halfway up to his elbows, a palm leaf fan in his hand which he used spasmodically, and as he moved about, he pulled wires here and there, encouraging this man to pitch in and that one to subside."

Before Richardson could go to work, though, the Illinois delegation had to win a credentials fight against a rival slate headed by Isaac Cook, Buchanan's appointee as Chicago postmaster. Richardson won. So, too, New York's pro-Douglas delegation was also seated, defeating a challenge from New York City's "doughface" mayor, Fernando Wood. The Little Giant had his first victories of the convention.

Institute Hall, Charleston, South Carolina, April 24, 1860

Caleb Cushing of Massachusetts, who served as attorney general under Franklin Pierce, was not a Douglas man. The Douglas forces were unhappy with his election as president of the convention. Once he took the rostrum to accept the position, though, he made a speech that could have been lifted from Douglas's debates with Lincoln. After asserting to loud and long applause that the Democratic Party stood for states' rights and the Constitution, he declared that the party's opponents "are those who labor to overthrow the Constitution, under the false and insidious pretense of supporting it; those who are aiming to produce in this country a permanent sectional conspiracy of one half the states of the Union against the other half; those who impelled by the stupid and half insane spirit of faction and fanaticism, would worry our land on to revolution and to civil war."

The Douglas men won another victory when they passed a resolution allowing delegates from uninstructed states to vote as they pleased. This would enable Douglas to win votes from New York, New Jersey, and Pennsylvania, which had sent divided delegations to the convention. Douglas was not as strong in the mid-Atlantic states as he was in New England and the Northwest. After that triumph, though, Douglas's supporters made a mistake that would cost their candidate the nomination at Charleston and his chance at the presidency and perhaps contribute to the breakup of the Union. They agreed to adopt a platform before nominating a candidate. The Southern states had already decided to bolt unless that platform included a federal slave code. Nearly a year before, Douglas had written a letter to an Iowa newspaper editor, asserting that he would never run on such a platform. The two positions were irreconcilable. Douglas's supporters, devoted as they were to the Union, may have underestimated the South's secessionist impulses—as Northerners would repeatedly do during the coming crisis. Robert Barnwell Rhett Sr. confronted Richardson, outside Institute Hall, to deliver the South's demands.

"Give me an endorsement of the decision of the Supreme Court of the United States in the Dred Scott case, and we will give you the whole South for Mr. Douglas," the South Carolinian told the Illinoisan, "but fail to do this, and the South leaves you—the Democratic Party will be divided—and Mr. Douglas defeated."

As Rhett recalled, Richardson simply smiled, believing the South would "divide and succumb," as it had in all sectional controversies dating back to the Missouri Compromise.

The critical fight, then, would not be over the nomination, but the platform. As the *New York Herald* reported, the Northern states had enough votes to adopt the same platform as the 1856 Cincinnati convention, which endorsed "non-interference by Congress with slavery in state or territory." That platform, though, had been approved before the Dred Scott Decision, as well as the Lecompton Controversy, the Lincoln-Douglas debates, and John Brown's raid. If the North used its majority to do so, the *Herald* predicted, "the South, after unitedly opposing the doctrine of squatter sovereignty, would secede and elect a slave code platform, and nominate upon it some such man as Jefferson Davis. The prevailing opinion is that the Convention will break up in a row, growing out of disputes relative to the construction of a platform."

Institute Hall, Charleston, South Carolina,
April 25, 1860

Although the Northerners made up a majority of the delegates, they did not have a majority on the Resolutions Committee, which was tasked with drawing up a platform. That committee consisted of one member per state. Fifteen of the thirty-two states permitted slavery; they found allies in the California and Oregon delegations, which were made up of Lecompton Democrats hostile to Douglas. As the committee deliberated, a rumor swept the convention that Richardson had the authority to withdraw Douglas's name from consideration if the platform insisted on protecting slavery in the territories.

Douglas's supporters lost a vote on a resolution to limit speakers to ten minutes, which would have put a cork in Fire-Eaters such as Yancey; the Orator of Secession was famous for his hour-long speeches.

While the convention awaited the platform reports, the doors of Institute Hall were thrown open to the Charleston public—including, for the first time, ladies. They showered petals on the head of New York's John Cochrane, who had made the motion to admit them.

"The gentleman forgets to tell the ladies that he is a bachelor," Thomas Craig of Missouri ribbed Cochrane. The proceedings broke up for several minutes, as the entire hall burst into laughter. "I was about to inform the ladies," Cochrane said, attempting to defend himself. Craig had another riposte ready. "Oh, no matter! There is no need to volunteer the announcement, for the looks of the gentleman are a sufficient guarantee that he has not been, and never can become a married man."

That was one of the few lighthearted moments on an anxious day for the convention—a day many delegates feared was the last for a united Democratic Party.

"There is an irreconcilable difference in the doctrines respecting slavery in the Territories between the Northern and Southern wings of the Democratic party," reported Murat Halstead. "The platform must be drawn with elaborate ambiguity, and capable of two constructions, or the party must be divided . . . Tomorrow is understood to be the crisis of the Convention. We hear hourly that a crisis involving the fate of the country is at hand."

Institute Hall, Charleston, South Carolina,
April 26, 1860

There was nothing ambiguous about the platform resolutions offered by Southern delegates. LeRoy Pope Walker of Alabama proposed that "it is the duty of the Federal Government, in all its departments, within their constitutional sphere, to afford adequate protection and equal advantage to all descriptions of property recognized as such by the laws of any of the States, as well within the Territories as upon the high seas, and every piece subject to its exclusive power of legislation."

This was not only a demand for a slave code, but, in its insistence that the federal government protect property "upon the high seas," for a reopening of the Atlantic slave trade. Yancey himself had argued that banning the importation of slaves was unconstitutional, "unjust and an insult to the South."

A Rhode Island delegate offered a compromise—the Cincinnati Platform, with this caveat: "To preserve the Union, the equality of the States must be maintained, the decisions of the Courts enforced, and that every branch of the Federal government shall exercise all its constitutional powers in the protection of persons and property, both in the States and Territories."

That was too ambiguous for the Alabamians, who prevailed upon the Rhode Islander to postpone consideration of his resolution until the platform committees had completed their work; they knew the majority report would be more to the South's liking.

"I appeal to my friend from Rhode Island not to push this question," pleaded Alabama delegate R. G. Scott. "It will be a fatal blow to the harmony that ought to prevail here."

Institute Hall, Charleston, South Carolina,
April 27, 1860

On the day the members of the platform committee submitted their reports, harmony did not prevail. First up, at 11:30 in the morning, was William Waightstill Avery of North Carolina, with the majority report, endorsed by the fifteen slave states plus California and Oregon. The report was all that Alabama could have hoped for. The first resolution was an attack on popular sovereignty: neither Congress nor a territorial legislature had the power to abolish or prohibit slavery in the territories. The third resolution proclaimed, "the duty of the Federal Government to protect, when necessary, the rights of persons and property on the high seas, in the Territories, or wherever else its constitutional authority extends."

Then came the minority report, presented by Benjamin M. Samuels of Iowa, on behalf of fifteen free states. On the question of slavery, it resolved that "all questions in regard to the rights of property in States or Territories arising under the Constitution of the United States are judicial in their character, and the Democratic party is pledged to abide by and faithfully carry out such determination of these questions as has been made by the Supreme Court of the United States." This could be read as an endorsement of the Dred Scott decision, but also a repudiation of the South's demand for congressional protection of slavery in the territories.

What Samuels delivered was a minority report in name only: the fifteen undersigned states represented a majority of the convention's delegates and would adopt their platform when it came to a floor vote. History records that the Civil War began in Charleston on April 12, 1861, when South Carolina militia bombarded Fort Sumter. One could just as well call the platform fight at the 1860 Democratic National Convention the first battle of the war. The South's justifications for secession and rebellion were spelled out on the floor of Institute Hall, as Southern delegates expressed their fears of Northern domination, Black uprisings, and the extinction of the White race—all inevitable consequences of confining slavery to its current boundaries. Such would be the results of popular sovereignty.

A federal law protecting slavery in the territories was a matter of "life and death" for the South, Avery argued. If the natural increase of the slave population was provided no room for emigration, the slaves must either be freed or rise up against their masters. If they were freed, competition between White and Black laborers would lead to "the expulsion of the Blacks in bloodshed beyond the borders of the state." The South was attempting to expand slavery by democratic means, but if expanding slavery required a war, it was willing to wage a war, and call it a struggle for survival.

The majority platform, Avery pointed out, had been endorsed by "the banner states of the Union—127 electoral votes, every one of which will be Democratic." The states endorsing the minority platform "cannot be depended on to cast a single Democratic electoral vote!"

Which was why the Northern states wanted that platform. Northern Democrats were experiencing their own existential crisis: ever since the passage of the Kansas-Nebraska Act, they had been losing ground to the Republicans. In 1854, Ohio had been represented by twelve Democrats in the House of Representatives; it was now represented by six. Ohio senator George Pugh, who would lose his seat to Salmon P. Chase as a result of the 1859 elections, objected to the majority report because "I will not arm the federal government with such a power . . . it tramples the people of the Territories into dust."

Benjamin Samuels offered a more practical objection: if Northern Democrats ran on a slave code platform, they would be annihilated by the Republicans—who would use their power to annihilate the Southern way of life.

"The Democracy of the North would stand as a shield against fanaticism, and interpose our breasts as a shield when John Browns array themselves against the South," Samuels promised.

The speaker awaited by all the convention—and all of Charleston—was Yancey. When he rose to speak during the afternoon session, the galleries rang with applause for several minutes. To accommodate the stem-winder he planned to deliver, Yancey asked the convention to grant him an extra half hour, atop the one-hour time limit. He used his time to promise an apocalypse if the South didn't get its way. Southerners were anxious about the 1860 census, which would augment the North's power in Congress, since immigrants were attracted almost exclusively to free labor states. As a threatened minority, the South was demanding Constitutional protections.

"We hold the Constitution up against our orgies of passion—against your loose notions of the rights of the minority," Yancey howled. "Ours is the property invaded—ours the interests at stake. The honor of our children—the honor of our females—the lives of our men all rest upon you. You would make a great seething cauldron of passion and crime if you were able to consummate your measures. Bear with us, then, if, as we stand on what is but a sleeping volcano, we say to you, to you we will not yield our position."

The South had been led to believe it would benefit from the Kansas-Nebraska Act, which granted slaveowners the right to settle in territories closed thirty years earlier by the Missouri Compromise. Yet "this delightful fruit that was to be so sweet to the lip, after having been deprived of it for so many years—has been made, like the Dead Sea fruit, to turn to ashes on Southern lips." In Kansas, the proslavery Lecompton Constitution had been quashed by Douglas, "the brilliant statesman who is the boasted leader of the column of the Northwest."

Yancey had spent part of his childhood in Troy, New York. His widowed mother married a Presbyterian minister who took a parsonage there and became involved with the abolitionist movement. In those days, he recalled, "abolitionists were pelted with rotten eggs." Now, abolitionism was so respectable it had divided into three wings: abolitionists, Free-Soilers, and "squatter sovereignty men." Douglas fell into the third category.

Yancey's followers so mistrusted the North that they had adopted "the widespread, deep-seated conviction that the South, with her institutions, is unsafe in the Union." If the South compromised with the Douglas delegates by accepting squatter sovereignty, "she establishes the fact that the government cannot be maintained."

Yancey's incitement to secession was interrupted repeatedly by applause, shouting, and stamping on the wooden floor. An even wilder scene ensued when Connecticut's W. D. Bishop moved to adopt the majority report. Delegates climbed atop chairs, "screaming like panthers, and gesticulating like monkeys." Inaudible in the chaotic din were the president's gavel and the shrieking voice of a Missouri delegate, pleading to adjourn before the convention collapsed in violence. Bishop was surrounded by threatening delegates. Senator William Bigler of Pennsylvania told him, "If the majority press their point now, there is a minority that will resist at all hazards."

Finally, President Cushing managed to gavel the convention to adjournment. The North's intentions were clear. So was the South's determination to resist them. Senator Robert Toombs and Representative Lucius Gartrell of Georgia telegraphed their delegates: if Alabama walks out, you must follow.

The dominoes were set to fall.

Institute Hall, Charleston, South Carolina, April 30, 1860

The Democratic Party shattered on a Monday, the seventh day of the convention, along the same lines the nation would shatter that winter, and in the same place, too. That December, South Carolina's Secession Conference would assemble in Institute Hall, where it voted 169–0 to leave the Union. The building became known as Secession Hall until it burned down a year later.

Benjamin Butler of Massachusetts, a future Union general, moved to lay the platform vote on the table and proceed directly to nominating a candidate. Butler had previously tried to paper over the differences between North and South by proposing to simply readopt the 1856 Cincinnati Platform. That motion had been rejected. So was this one. Both sides were ready for the confrontation. When the president called for a vote on the minority platform, it was adopted, 165–138. New York voted for it 35–0,

Ohio 23–0. Against the great cities of the North, the seven votes of rural Mississippi and Louisiana's six could hardly prevail.

William Shepperd Ashe of North Carolina appealed to the Northern delegates to "pause before consummating this action. It can but lead to a division and ruin for as a representative of North Carolina, I cannot remain in this convention if this platform is adopted."

The North's mind was made up, though. William Richardson asked for the floor, to cries of "Hear Richardson!" There was some hope that he would break the impasse by offering to withdraw Douglas's name, thus allowing the convention to adopt a platform the South could stomach. Instead, he simply declared that Illinois and the Northwest would be content with the Cincinnati platform. Former senator Charles Stuart of Michigan—who lost his seat after Republicans swept the legislature in the wake of Kansas-Nebraska—delivered a belligerent speech in defense of Northern honor, which probably ended all hopes of keeping the South in the convention. Stuart addressed Yancey directly: "That gentleman had asked if the Democracy of the North and Northwest had anything to lose by agreeing to his request, and the request of his state. I would answer, in property, in dollars and cents, nothing. But when I am asked to yield up a principle of honor, then I would say never, never, never. Four years ago it was unanimously agreed in the Convention at Cincinnati upon the request of Alabama—I will give no harsher term—upon the doctrines of the Cincinnati platform unanimously. For ten years they have been before the North, and have pledged their sacred honor to stand by these self-same principles."

Yancey took this as an attack on himself, his state, the South, and its rights. He had never disputed that the Cincinnati Platform protected the South, but argued that the platform "as construed by Douglas and his friends is hostile to our construction of it. After having told the South that it embraces the doctrine of squatter sovereignty, they offer us that platform; therefore, they refuse the South protection of their property in the territories, and not only that, they can be driven out of the territories."

That ended the debate between North and South. After Stuart and Yancey spoke, the walkout began. Alabama went first, of course. Tall, thin, bearded LeRoy Pope Walker, future Confederate secretary of war, approached the clerk's desk to read the Resolutions of Alabama's Democratic State Convention. The delegates and the galleries listened in silence as he recited his state's position—"that the Congress of the United States has no power to abolish slavery in the Territories, or to prohibit its introduction into any of them"—and his instructions if such a platform was not adopted: "It becomes our duty to withdraw from this convention." Mississippi went next, with chairman David C. Glenn mounting a chair and telling the Ohio delegation, "It is right that we part. Go your way, and we will go ours." Then went Louisiana, South Carolina, Florida, Texas, and Arkansas. Georgia and Virginia asked to retire and consider their course of action. The seceding delegates departed Institute Hall, marched down Meeting Street, took a right on Broad, and reassembled in the Greek revival St. Andrew's Hall, site of upper-class Charleston's most lavish social affairs, the Jockey Club and St. Cecilia's Society ball. In the main hall, the Southerners declared their dispute with the "Rump Convention" they had just bolted to be a dispute over one man: Douglas. If the convention refused to nominate a candidate "whose opinions are a direct concurrence with ours," the bolters had to take responsibility into their own hands.

Charleston celebrated the walkout as though it were the birth of a new nation, which, in a way, it was, although that nation would be short-lived. Yancey, the new idol of secession, addressed the breakaway convention to cries of "Three Cheers for Yancey!" After the bolters adjourned, the Charleston Brass Band led the crowd to the *Mercury* offices, where it serenaded Robert Barnell Rhett Jr. Thousands gathered in front of City Hall to listen to speeches by Yancey and Mississippi's Lucius Lamar. The "Constitutional Democratic Convention," as Yancey called the bolters, would vindicate the South's constitutional rights, while the "Rump Convention" would be a meeting of a sectional party, representing a minor faction of Free-Soil Northerners. "Perhaps even now," Yancey said, "the pen of the historian was nibbed to write the story of the new revolution."

"Three cheers for the Independent Southern Republic!" came a cry from the crowd. The cheers were offered mightily.

Murat Halstead, who stood in the City Hall crowd, noted the "Fourth of July feeling in Charleston—a jubilee. There was no mistaking the public sentiment of the city. It was overwhelmingly and enthusiastically in favor of the seceders. In all her history Charleston had never enjoyed herself so hugely."

Rhett's newspaper was even more contemptuous of the Douglas delegates than Yancey, labeling their gathering "The Squatter Sovereignty Convention." In the next morning's edition, Rhett didn't miss the Independence Day comparison, either: "The events of yesterday will probably be the most important that have taken place since the Revolution of 1776," he wrote. "The last party pretending to be a National party, is broken up; and the antagonism of the two sections of the Union has nothing to arrest its fierce collisions."

Institute Hall, Charleston, South Carolina, May 1, 1860

Surrounded by a hostile city, the remaining delegates now had the task of choosing a presidential candidate. The convention was in its eighth day—longer than anyone had expected to spend in Charleston. The Ohio delegation had run out of Kentucky whiskey, having brought a barrel large enough to last only a week. The weather was intolerable, the temperature rising to a sodden one hundred degrees, then plunging as a weekend rainstorm softened the dusty streets to mud. Beyond their physical discomforts, many of the delegates had become convinced that the entire convention was futile, now that the Southern states, which provided the majority of electoral votes for Democratic candidates, had walked out. "The president will be nominated in Chicago," they mumbled to one another, all assuming it would be Seward.

Nonetheless, the delegates had a job to do. They could not hand the country over to Seward and the Black Republicans without putting up a fight. The morning session began with the Georgia delegation announcing that "after mature deliberation," they had "felt it to be their duty, under existing circumstances, not to participate further in the deliberations of the Convention." At that, twenty-six of the thirty-four Georgians rose from their seats and walked out of the room, to join their fellow Southerners at St. Andrew's Hall. Among those who remained was Solomon Cohen, who, in so many words, told the convention that the only way to reunite the party was by nominating someone other than Douglas.

"I will stay here until the last feather be placed upon the back of the camel," Cohen promised, no doubt meaning Douglas's nomination. "I will stay until crushed and broken in spirit, humiliated by feeling and knowing that I have no longer a voice in the counsels of the Democracy of the Union—feeling that the Southern States are a mere cipher in your estimation—that all her rights are trampled under foot; and I say here that I shall then be found shoulder to shoulder with him who is foremost in this contest."

If Douglas was such a divisive figure in his own party, what hope did he have of uniting the nation behind his candidacy? The Northwesterners had come to Charleston to nominate Douglas, and they weren't going to be bullied out of their choice by a faction that abandoned the convention rather than respecting the will of its majority. John R. Howard of Tennessee rose to propose two resolutions, both of which would be fatal to Douglas's nomination. Tennessee "and her sister state of Kentucky, which stood between the two extremes of the country," had written what they considered a compromise platform: all citizens had a right to bring their property into the territories, and "neither their rights of person nor property can be destroyed or impaired by Congressional or Territorial legislation."

That was a repudiation of popular sovereignty. Richardson told Howard that "my honor and manhood forbid me from retreating from my position. There will be no surrender on the Douglas side." If the South wouldn't compromise, neither would the Northwest.

Howard's second resolution was that the nominee must receive two-thirds of all votes the convention was eligible to cast—including those of the Southerners who had walked out. That meant Douglas would need

202 of the 253 votes still on the floor. Howard's resolution passed, 141–112; Ohio, Indiana, and Illinois all voted no, but the New Yorkers cast a decisive 35 votes in favor, hoping that if Douglas failed to find 202 votes—as he surely would—they could substitute their ex-governor Horatio Seymour as a compromise candidate acceptable to the South.

When the first ballot was cast that evening, Douglas received 145½ votes—not even half the total of eligible delegates. Senator R.M.T. Hunter of Virginia was second with 42, followed by former treasury secretary James Guthrie of Kentucky with 35½, and Senator Andrew Johnson of Tennessee with 12. Senator Joseph Lane of Oregon, the administration's choice, received 6 votes. The convention cast 12 ballots that day, with scarcely any movement to Douglas. By the time Richardson motioned for adjournment, Douglas's total stood at 150½.

Charleston Theatre, Charleston, South Carolina, May 2, 1860

On Wednesday morning, the *Charleston Courier* carried an ad for a "Meeting of the Constitutional Democratic Convention": "The delegates who have withdrawn from the Convention, at Institute Hall, will assemble at the CHARLESTON THEATRE, at 10 o'clock A.M., this day, pursuant to the adjournment. Seats are reserved for the ladies. All other portions of the building, not reserved for Delegates, are open to the public."

The Constitutional Democratic Convention was attended by 118 delegates from 11 states (including the 41 members of Fernando Wood's rejected New York delegation). The *Courier* celebrated the gathering as the glorious demonstration "that 'Southern rights' and 'Southern Interests' are not to be considered footballs for politicians and Janus-faced carpenters of ambiguous platforms." Senator James Bayard of Delaware, who had joined the bolters in hopes of providing some border state moderation to the proceedings, was elected chairman and made clear the convention's anti-Douglas intentions. If the Democrats "nominated on the ambiguous platform, a candidate who is the known expounder of doctrines contrary to the states of the union, they maintain the principles of squatter sovereignty," he stated. In that case, "we may take the nomination into our own hands."

Yancey submitted the majority platform to the new convention's Committee on Platform, which endorsed it unanimously. He argued that the convention should not claim the name "Democratic Party," from which it had withdrawn, or be branded as "Secession Democracy." It should be known as the "Constitutional Democracy," since it was simply defending the principles of that document. Then the man who had preached secession for a decade denied that he had ever intended to break up the party, or the nation.

"We may be called Disunion Democrats," Yancey said. "We are not disunionists. We have put nothing on the record to justify this assertion; yet it will be easy to attach to the name the weight of the disunion movement. We do not as yet know how our action will be received by our constituents, but if our action be valid, in support of the constitutional rights of the South, let us leave the result to God."

Institute Hall, Charleston, South Carolina, May 2, 1860

There was, by this point, no chance of nominating a candidate in Charleston, no matter how many ballots were cast. The city had lost interest in seeing delegates vote the same way over and over again. Those who still wanted to sit in the sparsely populated galleries were no longer even asked to present tickets at the door. Vainly did the convention await a telegram from Douglas in Washington, withdrawing his name, so the delegates could draft a compromise platform and select a compromise candidate, which might lure the seceders back to Institute Hall. In Cincinnati, Douglas had sacrificed his candidacy for Buchanan in exchange for a one-term promise. Buchanan had repaid Douglas by doing everything possible to undermine his chances in Charleston: on the first ballot, the Pennsylvania delegation, over which the president held sway, divided its votes between Douglas and his rivals.

Why reward administration meddling by allowing Buchanan a say over the next nominee? The Douglas forces had a strategy beyond Charleston: they would adjourn the deadlocked convention for six weeks and reconvene with pro-Union Southern delegations in place of the seceders. After the fifty-seventh ballot—the twenty-first in a row on which Douglas received 151½ votes—William S. Gittings of Maryland moved to adjourn until the third Monday in June. (Gittings may have had a parochial motivation, since the convention would meet again in his hometown of Baltimore.) Douglas had stood firm against the South, which hoped by its withdrawal to force him off the ticket. Yet even Douglas's supporters believed the nomination they had preserved for him was worthless.

"The friends of Douglas now concede that he is beaten," the *New York Herald* reported the next day. "Some of the anti-Lecompton men have been freely canvassing the prospects at Chicago, and expressing the hope that a prudent nomination would be made."

If it turned out to be Seward, as everyone expected, well, the South would be getting what she deserved—and, perhaps, what she wanted.

Institute Hall, Charleston, South Carolina, May 3, 1860

The Charleston convention lasted twice as long as its predecessor in Cincinnati. The last session was brief, since the delegates couldn't wait to get out of town. They had already agreed to meet again on June 18 in Baltimore. There was nothing left to do but vote for it. There were motions to substitute New York and Philadelphia as convention cities. Neither was considered friendly to Douglas—New York hoped to nominate its own ex-governor, and Philadelphia was controlled by Buchanan—so the motions failed. Cushing sent the remaining delegates away with the hope that the collapse of this convention was not a prelude to the collapse of the Union itself.

"I will not believe that the noble work of our fathers is to be shattered into fragments," the chairman said, "this great Republic to be but a name, a history of a mighty people once existing, but existing no more as a shadowy memory, or as a monumental ruin by the side of the pathway of time! I fondly trust that we shall continue to march on forever—the hope of nations, as well in the Old World as in the New—like the bright orbs of the firmament, which roll on without rest, because bound for eternity; without haste, because predestined for eternity, so it may be with this glorious Confederation of states."

After that flowery bit of oratory, the delegates raced to their lodgings to shove their clothes into carpet bags, valises, and trunks, pay their bills, and down one last drink, "as though life and fortune depended upon their reaching the depots in time for the first trains out," the *Courier* reported. The night train pulled away from Charleston with a Southern languor, bearing the bedraggled delegates toward the first of six transfers between the convention city and Washington. Only the faro bank men left town looking happy: their gambles had paid off far more handsomely than those of the politicians.

Charleston Theatre, Charleston, South Carolina, May 3, 1860

When news of the adjournment reached the so-called Constitutional Democrats, they were stunned that there was no longer a convention to which they could return. The Douglas men had called their bluff. Their walkout had failed to scuttle Douglas's candidacy, so they were now forced to proceed as an independent, Southern party. H. R. Jackson of Georgia moved to nominate candidates for president and vice president. N. B. Burrows of Arkansas proposed the convention prepare an address to the nation, outlining the rights claimed by the South. Burrows spoke of those rights in biblical terms: "We have, Mr. President, in our possession the Ark of the Covenant, the platform of the Democratic Party, made by seventeen states of the union in accordance with the usages and customs of the Democratic Party. We have rescued it from the ruins of the failing Democracy, have bound it to a place of safety, and established a bodyguard around it. Ours is the holy task and the holy charge."

The American people would acknowledge that the majority platform was based on sound constitutional principles, Yancey believed: "There is a hope that the people will get their rights in the Union, as guaranteed by the Constitution."

Senator Bayard wasn't buying that. Every proposal he'd heard that day signaled another step toward secession. When Jackson proposed that the Constitutional Democrats reassemble in Washington on the second Monday in June—a week before the Baltimore convention—Bayard announced he wouldn't be there. He had endorsed the majority platform. He had walked out of the convention because he could not bind himself to supporting Douglas as the nominee. But he could not "take part in any purpose of organizing a Southern convention." Perhaps he could if he were from Alabama or Mississippi, but some of his fellow Delawareans had remained in Institute Hall. Bayard pleaded with the Southerners to wait until after the Baltimore convention before taking any actions "which you cannot with honor retrace," or which would shatter the Democratic Party.

"If you destroy nationality of feeling in a nation such as this, you must necessarily plunge this nation into internecine war," he said. "There is no telling by what immediate cause it will be brought about, whether by quarrels as to border lines or the rights of states, but come it must."

The Southerners dismissed this as the handwringing of a temporizing border state ninny. The Northerners had irredeemably offended their honor by refusing to abandon squatter sovereignty and Douglas. Never would Alabama send delegates to Baltimore, declared Judge A. B. Meek. At the state convention, the vote to elect this delegation had been 499–12: "That was the strength of the Douglas Squatter Sovereignty Doctrine in Alabama."

Jackson moved that Democrats who favored the majority platform be invited to send delegates to Richmond—a real Southern city. There were now, officially, two Democratic parties.

Washington, D.C., May 4, 1860

The day after the Charleston conventions broke up, Senator Milton
S. Latham of California encountered Douglas in Washington. Douglas had
been drinking and was in a combative mood. He upbraided Latham over
an April 16 speech that scolded Northerners for interfering with slavery
and endorsed the South's claims of its constitutional rights. California had
not taken Douglas's side at the convention. It had voted for the majority
platform, and its four delegates had supported former New York senator
Daniel Dickinson on the first ballot. The state's large military presence and
population of federal employees put it in Buchanan's pocket.

With a look of anger conquering his face, Douglas called his enemies
"blood hounds after my life. This controversy has but commenced."

"There is too much fire in your eye for a great man," Latham told his
colleague. "You show too much passion. Keep cool. It will come all right."

"You will feel when they get after me," Douglas said.

"I have had them after me, but they couldn't bite, so long as I preserved
my own temper," responded Latham, still trying to calm Douglas.

"Your speech is quoted everywhere against me," Douglas told Latham.
"I won't read it for fear I might get angry at you."

"Read it. You will be undeceived. It was not regarded by your true friends
as an attack."

Douglas, who was seeing enemies everywhere, agreed to do so. The
controversy which so angered him was scheduled to recommence in June.
By then, the Republicans would have a nominee.

CHAPTER 6

CHICAGO: EVERYBODY'S SECOND CHOICE

The Wigwam, Chicago, Illinois, May 16, 1860

A braham Lincoln turned out to be the perfect leader to guide the nation through the Civil War, and toward the abolition of slavery. He was not, however, an indispensable man, nor was his presidency inevitable. In the spring of 1860, Lincoln was simply the right man from the right place. He won the Republican nomination both because of who he wasn't—William Seward, the New York abolitionist considered too radical by Lower North Republicans—and where he was from: Central Illinois, the swing region of a swing state. Illinois had voted for Buchanan in 1856. The Republicans needed to flip the "Sucker State" to win in 1860, along with New Jersey, Pennsylvania, and Indiana. All four states contained significant populations of conservative Whigs who had voted for Fillmore because they were not yet comfortable with the antislavery, anti-Nebraska Republicans. Fillmore received 24 percent of the vote in New Jersey, 17 percent in Pennsylvania, 9 percent in Indiana, and 15 percent in Illinois. Bringing those voters into the Republican Party was the key to victory. Seward was the party's presumptive nominee—the Democrats in Charleston all thought they were choosing a candidate to oppose him—but his talk of an "irrepressible conflict" between freedom and slavery was alarming to Republicans whose states bordered on slave territory and contained Southern-sympathizing populations. Andrew G. Curtin and Henry S. Lane, the Republican candidates for governor in Pennsylvania and Indiana, insisted they would lose with Seward at the top of the ticket. Lane threatened not to run if Seward was nominated. In his home state, Seward had the opposition of *New-York Tribune* editor Horace Greeley, the nation's most influential Republican journalist. Greeley, who served three months in Congress at the same time as Lincoln, was disgruntled that Seward and his patron, New York party boss Thurlow Weed, had not supported his ambition to become governor. The *Tribune* was backing Missouri's Edward Bates, a former slaveholder and the most conservative contender for the nomination.

Long before the convention, Lincoln's Illinois allies recognized that his political career in half-Yankee, half-Southern Springfield, where he had been required to find a middle ground between abolitionists and slavery sympathizers, would make him the perfect compromise candidate for the presidency. Jesse Fell, a friend from Bloomington who helped conceive the Lincoln-Douglas Debates, explained to Lincoln that his moderate reputation would enable him to defeat Seward, Chase, and Bates for the Republican nomination. Lincoln was skeptical.

"Oh, Fell, what's the use of talking of me for the presidency, whilst we have such men as Seward and Chase and others who are so much better known to the people, and whose names are so intimately associated with the Republican Party?" Lincoln bemoaned to his friend.

"The men you allude to, occupying more prominent positions, have undoubtedly rendered a larger service in the Republican cause than you here; but the truth is, they have rendered too much service to be available candidates," Fell reassured Lincoln. "Seward and Chase have both made long records on the slavery question, and have said some very radical things which, however just and true in themselves, and however much these men may challenge our admiration for their courage and devotion to unpopular truths, would seriously damage them in the contest, if nominated. We must bear in mind, Lincoln, that we are yet in a minority; we are struggling against fearful odds for supremacy. We were defeated on the same issue in 1856, and we will be again in 1860, unless we get a great many new votes from what might be called the old conservative parties. These will be repelled by the radical utterances and votes of such men as Seward and Chase. What the Republican Party wants, to ensure success in 1860, is a man of popular origin, of acknowledged ability, committed against slavery aggressions, who has no record to defend and no radicalism of an offensive character to repel votes from parties hitherto adverse."

Like Fell, Lincoln recognized that the Republicans needed to chart a middle course. He warned political allies of the dangers of bending too far to pursue Southern votes or to accommodate abolitionists. To Mark Delahay, a Kansas Senate hopeful, Lincoln wrote that "lower[ing] the Republican standard in deference to Douglasism" or "the Southern opposition element . . . would surrender the object of the Republican organization—the preventing the spread and nationalization of slavery," thus losing the party more votes than it would gain. He wrote to Schuyler Colfax, a congressman from Indiana, to discuss "hedg[ing] against divisions in the Republican ranks generally, and particularly in the contest of 1860." He continued: "The point of danger is the temptation in different locations to 'platform' for something which will be popular just there, but which, nevertheless, will be a firebrand elsewhere, especially in a National convention. As instances: the movement against foreigners in Massachusetts; in New Hampshire, to make obedience to the Fugitive Slave Law punishable as a crime; in Ohio, to repeal the Fugitive Slave Act; and squatter sovereignty to Kansas. In those things there is enough explosive matter to blow up half a dozen conventions."

Seward was from Auburn, New York, in the heart of the state's Burned-Over District, a crucible of religiously motivated crusades. One of the most fervently antislavery regions in the nation, it was an outpost of the moralistic political culture that had spread west from New England, and that believed the role of government was to build a perfect society. Central Illinois was defined by an individualistic political culture, a less idealistic system in which political factions competed for spoils and patronage, and government was expected to stay out of moral issues—beliefs it shared with New Jersey, Pennsylvania, and Indiana. As politicians, Seward and Lincoln came of age in these contrasting cultures and learned to appeal to their constituents' beliefs and prejudices. In 1848, Seward delivered a speech in Cleveland against Ohio's Black Codes, which prohibited Blacks from voting, sitting on juries, or holding office: "We in New York are guilty of slavery still, by withholding the right of suffrage from the race we have emancipated." In Springfield, Lincoln refused to sign a petition calling for the repeal of Illinois's Black Laws. During the Charleston debate, he denied that he favored Black suffrage. Seward's maiden speech in the Senate had condemned two planks of the Compromise of 1850: he opposed the Fugitive Slave Law, and he wanted to go beyond abolishing the slave trade in the District of Columbia by abolishing slavery itself. "[A] higher law than the Constitution demanded resistance to slavery," he said. Lincoln believed the Fugitive Slave Law was a constitutional promise to the South and professed no intention to interfere with slavery where it existed.

John Brown's raid on the federal arsenal at Harpers Ferry made even Republicans more skeptical of Seward: the party's opponents, especially in Illinois and Pennsylvania, argued that Seward's antislavery rhetoric had incited Brown's insurrection. Lincoln's old friend Josiah Lucas, who was postmaster of the House of Representatives, wrote him from Washington that Seward "would not be the nominee . . . Late developments have certainly damaged him . . . Our friends regard him as a dead weight and in doubtful districts he would lose instead of gaining us votes."

On December 3, 1859, the day after Brown was hanged, Lincoln delivered a speech in Leavenworth, Kansas, disassociating himself from the rebel's actions, while associating them with Southern threats of secession—again situating himself in the middle ground between radical extremes on the slavery question.

"Old John Brown has just been executed for treason against a state," Lincoln said. "We cannot object, even though he agreed with us in thinking slavery wrong. That cannot excuse violence, bloodshed, and treason. It could avail him nothing that he might think himself right. So, if constitutionally we elect a president, and therefore you undertake to destroy the Union, it will be our duty to deal with you as old John Brown has been dealt with."

If Seward was not to be the Republican nominee, was there any reason to believe, as the presidential election year opened, that it would be Lincoln? Whatever his interest in the office, Lincoln knew he was a dark horse and had not presumed to declare himself a candidate. However, his friends were maneuvering to improve his chances. When the Republican National Committee met at New York's Astor House on December 21, 1859, to choose a convention site, Norman Judd suggested Chicago as "good neutral ground where everyone would have an even chance." Moreso than Buffalo, in Seward's home state; Cleveland, in Chase's; St. Louis, in Bates's; or Harrisburg, in Pennsylvania senator Simon Cameron's. In this, Judd had Lincoln's collusion; Lincoln wrote him a week before the meeting that "some of our friends here, attach more consequence to getting the National convention into our State that I did, or do. Some of them made me promise to say so to you." The committee did not take Lincoln seriously enough to consider that Chicago might help his chances, so Illinois's largest city prevailed over St. Louis by a single vote—a vote that may have delivered the nomination, and the presidency, to Lincoln.

Lincoln humored Jesse Fell by providing him with a short autobiography for a flattering profile in Pennsylvania's *Chester County Times*. Lincoln described himself as a child of the wilderness, unschooled and "raised to farm work." "At twenty-one I came to Illinois," he wrote, was elected to the legislature and Congress, but "was losing interest in politics, when the repeal of the Missouri Compromise aroused me again."

Fell told Lincoln that on his trips to New York and New England, he was often asked, "Who is this man Lincoln, of your State, now canvassing in opposition to Senator Douglas?" Lincoln may not have believed he was nationally renowned, but in October 1859 he was invited to New York City to speak before the Young Men's Republican Central Union of New York. Prominent New Yorkers, including Greeley, William Cullen Bryant, Hamilton Fish, and David Dudley Field, were auditioning moderate Western candidates who might have a better chance of carrying the swing states than Seward. Lincoln's address would follow speeches by Frank Blair of Missouri and Cassius Clay, the Kentucky abolitionist. (Chase declined an invitation.) The speech was scheduled to be delivered at Henry Ward Beecher's Plymouth Church in Brooklyn, but because of intense public interest in Lincoln, it was moved to the new Cooper Union in Manhattan. More than 1,500 Republicans turned out to hear Lincoln on the night of February 27. As in his Ohio speeches, Lincoln presented his antislavery positions as consistent with the Constitution and the intentions of the Founders. As he had done during his campaign against Douglas, he argued that expanding slavery would expand the social ills that accompanied the institution. Lincoln pointed out that the law forbidding slavery in the Northwest Territories had been passed by a Congress consisting of sixteen of thirty-nine framers of the Constitution. The law had been signed by George Washington, a slaveholder who nonetheless wrote a letter to the Marquis de Lafayette opposing the spread of slavery and expressing hope for a confederation of free states. The Constitution, Lincoln argued, was "literally silent" on the right to bring slaves into the territories. Not only that, it was silent on the right to hold slaves.

"An inspection of the Constitution will show that the right of property in a slave is not distinctly and expressly affirmed in it," Lincoln told the crowd, who had all paid a quarter to hear him speak. "Neither the word 'slave' nor 'slavery' is to be found in the Constitution, nor the word 'property' even, in any connection with language alluding to the thing slave, or slavery, and that whenever in that instrument the slave is alluded to, he is called 'a person'—and wherever his master's legal right in relation to him is alluded to, it is spoken of as 'service or labor which may be done'—as a debt payable in service or labor. Also, it would be open to show, by contemporaneous history, that this mode of alluding to slaves and slavery, instead of speaking of them, was employed on purpose to exclude from the Constitution the idea that there could be property in man."

The Cooper Union speech was such a hit that Lincoln was offered a flood of invitations to speak in New England. Over the next two weeks, he delivered ten speeches, in New Hampshire, Rhode Island, and Connecticut—all states presumed safe for Seward at the convention. After a speech in Concord, New Hampshire, the state's Republican chairman, Edward H. Rollins, predicted that Lincoln could carry the Granite State by 10,000 votes; in nearby Manchester, Mayor Frederick Smyth introduced Lincoln as "the next president."

"No! No! That is impossible," Lincoln protested. "Mr. Seward should and will receive the nomination. I do not believe that three States will vote for me in the convention."

Despite that protestation, the presidential bug had bitten Lincoln. After returning to Springfield, he wrote to Lyman Trumbull that "the taste is in my mouth a little" and predicted that neither Seward nor Bates could beat Douglas in Illinois. With Seward at the top of the ticket, the Republicans might not even carry the legislature: "Suppose he should gain us a thousand votes in Winnebago [County], it would not compensate for the loss of fifty in Edgar."

Other Illinois Republicans felt the same way—and thought Lincoln was the solution.

"Lincoln . . . is the most available candidate for unadulterated Republicanism—Presidential, I mean," Nathan M. Knapp of Winchester wrote to Illinois secretary of state Ozias Hatch. Commenting on Seward, Knapp continued, "I am not for him under any circumstances. If the Republican Party is bent on him it will be because of their unfitness for self government . . . with Seward, Hale, Chase, or Giddings, we are gone up. I am a Lincoln man first last and all the time. Douglas will be the nominee.

Lincoln deserves it against him, and it would be a shame not to give it to him. He can beat him by 10,000 votes in Illinois."

The 645 delegates who assembled in Decatur for the Illinois State Republican convention on May 9 felt the same about Lincoln. They intended to nominate him as a favorite son who would receive Illinois's twenty-two votes for president at the Chicago convention a week hence—at least on the first ballot. Although candidates did not customarily appear at nominating conventions, Lincoln was so eager for his home state's support that he arrived in Decatur on May 8, spending an "uncomfortable night," sharing a bed too short for his long legs with Nathan Knapp.

Jesse Fell had told Lincoln he could win the nomination because he was "a man of popular origin." Richard Oglesby, the future governor and senator who was in charge of organizing the Decatur convention, seized on that and cast about for a gimmick that would represent Lincoln's log cabin background. A few days before the convention, Oglesby asked Lincoln's cousin, John Hanks, what sort of work Lincoln did on the family homestead in Macon County.

"Not much of any kind but dreaming," Hanks allowed, "but he did help me split a lot of rails when we made a clearing twelve miles west of here."

The next day, Oglesby and Hanks took a buggy to the site of the old farm on the Sangamon River. Hanks identified two rails the cousins split from black walnut and honey locust trees. Oglesby attached the rails to the underside of his buggy and drove them back to Decatur, where he stored them in his barn.

Between delegates and spectators, Decatur was expecting 3,000 visitors—almost as many as the prairie city's population. To accommodate them, Oglesby ordered the construction of a "Wigwam," as temporary political structures were then known. He spent $253 on lumber for seating, a platform, and roof supports, then rented a circus tent to cover the crowd. Reflecting his ambivalence at attending the convention, Lincoln lingered near one of the entrances. His height and his significance to the proceedings made it impossible for him to blend into the masses, though. During the first day's afternoon session, Oglesby rose and told the chairman, "I am informed that a distinguished citizen of Illinois, and one who Illinois will ever delight to honor, is present, and I wish to move that this body invite him to a seat on the stand—Abraham Lincoln."

The cheering crowd was packed too tightly for Lincoln to walk through, so his lanky body was passed overhead to the dais. A bit later, during the ballot counting for governor, Oglesby brought out the rails.

"An old Democrat of Macon County desires to make a contribution to the convention," he declared. As the crowd cried "Receive it!" Hanks and Isaac Jennings walked into the Wigwam, each carrying a rail labeled ABRAHAM LINCOLN, THE RAIL CANDIDATE FOR PRESIDENT IN 1860. TWO RAILS FROM A LOT OF THREE THOUSAND MADE IN 1830 BY JOHN HANKS AND ABE LINCOLN."

It was not a bombshell. A few days earlier, the *Illinois State Journal* had promoted the convention by promising "a lot of rails . . . still sound and firm, like the men who made them. Shall we not elect the Rail Mauler President?" Lincoln, though, was a good enough sport to act surprised.

"Well, gentlemen, I must confess I do not understand this," he said, looking amused. "I don't think I know any more about it than you do. I helped build a log cabin and split some rails near Decatur, but I can't say that these are the identical rails. I'm sure I split some better than these!"

On the second day of the convention, John M. Palmer, who had run unsuccessfully for Lincoln's old seat in Congress the year before, offered a resolution that Lincoln was the convention's choice for president, and that all Illinois delegates be instructed to vote for him. Without his home state united behind him, Lincoln could not hope to advance beyond the first ballot. Illinois's regional divisions mirrored the Republican Party's, so binding the delegates was essential to prevent defections.

"I am not in a position where it would hurt much for me to not be nominated on the national ticket," Lincoln had written to Judd in February: "but I am when it would hurt some for me to not get the Illinois delegates . . . Your discomfited assailants are most bitter against me: and they will, for revenge upon me, lay to the Bates egg in the South, and the Seward egg in the North, and go far toward squeezing me out in the middle with nothing."

The motion carried unanimously, although, as Lincoln had surmised, some of the delegates preferred other candidates. Orville Hickman Browning of Quincy believed that Bates "would strengthen our organization in the South, and remove apprehension in the South of any hostile purpose on the part of Republicans to the institutions of the South," as well as "bring to our support the old whigs in the free states, who have not yet fraternized with us, and to give some check to the ultra tendencies of the Republican party."

When Browning got to Chicago, though, he followed the convention's instructions and voted for Lincoln.

The 1860 Republican National Convention was the first held in Chicago, the city that would go on to hold more political gatherings than any other. It was the first convention held in any Western city. Chicago's population had more than tripled over the past decade, to 109,260, raising its rank to ninth in the nation. The burgeoning metropolis was determined to use this event to demonstrate that it was now one of America's great cities. Chicago built its own wood-and-canvas Wigwam at the corner of Lake and Market streets, overlooking its sluggish river. Vastly larger and more ornate than Decatur's rustic structure, Chicago's Wigwam was described by the *Press and Tribune* as "the largest audience room in the United States," illuminated by gaslight and adorned with the coat of arms of each state, separated by wreaths of evergreen.

"The pillars supporting the roof, which form a contiguous row along the front of the platform, bear, on the side of the audience, busts of distinguished men, supported by figures of Atlas," the *Press and Tribune* wrote. "Over the center of the stage is suspended a large gilt eagle."

Chicago was expecting 25,000 visitors for the convention. As trains from Buffalo and Niagara Falls steamed into Michigan Central Station bearing Eastern delegates, they were greeted by a city illuminated in welcome, the lights of homes along Michigan Avenue reflected in the glittering lake. Thousands gathered at the station to cheer the arrival of "New England" or "Old Massachusetts," and debarking delegates were paraded to their lodging by "Wide Awakes," young Republican cadets dressed in glazed caps and capes and bearing torches.

Lincoln remained in Springfield, but David Davis, his campaign manager, arrived in Chicago on May 12, four days before the convention opened. He set up his headquarters in two rooms at the Tremont House, where he was soon joined by a dozen of Lincoln's Illinois allies. Davis intended to use Illinois's home-state advantage to benefit his candidate. The nomination would be decided in the Tremont House, not the Wigwam. Horace Greeley also checked into the hotel, in his capacity as a delegate for Oregon, a young state he had never visited.

"There are now at least a thousand men packed together in the halls of the Tremont House, crushing each other's ribs, tramping each other's toes, and titillating each other with the gossip of the day," wrote Murat Halstead, who was covering the Republican convention in Chicago as thoroughly as he covered the Democrats in Charleston, "and the probability is, not one is possessed of a single political fact not known to the whole which is of the slightest consequence to any human being. The current of the universal twaddle this morning is that 'old Abe' will be the nominee . . . the question on which everything turns is whether Seward can be nominated. His individuality is the pivot here, just as that of Douglas was at Charleston."

When the convention opened, on Wednesday morning, Pennsylvania's David Wilmot, author of the Proviso, was named chairman and presented with a gavel carved of oak from the USS *Lawrence*, the flagship of Commodore Oliver Hazard Perry, whose most famous sayings were "Don't give up the ship" and "We have met the enemy and, he is ours." In his opening remarks, Wilmot declared, "Slavery is sectional, liberty national." Yet unlike the Democrats, the Republicans had not attracted delegates from every state. After the convention named a permanent organizing committee consisting of one member from every state and territory represented, a Kentucky delegate asked the chair to recite the names of the missing states.

"Tennessee," Wilmot began. "Arkansas, Mississippi." The delegates laughed at the name of Jefferson Davis's state. "Louisiana, Alabama." They laughed and hissed at William Lowndes Yancey's. "Georgia, South Carolina." More laughter at the state where Southern delegates had walked out of the Democratic convention. "North Carolina, Florida. I believe that includes the names of all the states."

The slave states of Kentucky, Virginia, Maryland, and Texas had all sent delegations to Chicago. When the question of allowing them full representation came up, Wilmot objected: "Can it be possible that those gentlemen who come here from states in which there is no organized party are to come here and by their votes control the action of the convention?"

John Hoge Ewing of Pennsylvania rose to defend the slave state Republicans as more courageous than their free-state brethren. Chauncey Fitch Cleveland, the former governor of Connecticut, argued that acknowledging the South would refute "the lie" that the Republicans were a sectional party.

"We are not a sectional party!" Cleveland shouted. "We want the slave states to come here and be represented."

"Gentlemen of the convention, I cannot believe that you are prepared to stifle the voice of Texas, because the Republican Party is in its infancy," declared Texas delegate M. S. C. Crawford, "for though it is its infancy, it is a hopeful child. Gentlemen, the foreign population—the Germans—are with us."

The delegates cheered madly at this profession of slave state devotion. Texas was granted six votes, Maryland eight, Virginia fifteen, and Kentucky twelve.

Davis assigned each of his Illinois lieutenants a doubtful delegation; in the nights leading up to, and during, the convention, they canvassed the hotels, trying to win votes for Lincoln. The next-door state of Indiana was the first to pledge itself to Lincoln. The delegation's chairman, former congressman Caleb B. Smith, came to Chicago as a Bates man. The Hoosiers heard a vigorous pitch from Maryland's Frank Blair, who argued that only Bates could win the border states of Maryland and Missouri. Gustave

Koerner countered that Bates couldn't win Illinois. If Bates were nominated, his support for Millard Fillmore's Know Nothing candidacy at the 1856 Whig convention would cause the Germans to abandon the party. (Before the convention opened, the Germans met at Chicago's Deutsch Haus and threatened to do just that.) Orville Hickman Browning, a former Bates supporter, testified that Lincoln was an enemy of nativism.

The Hoosiers were more interested in stopping Seward than nominating Bates; Koerner and Browning convinced them that Lincoln was their only chance to do so. What finally brought Indiana into the fold, though, was Davis's suggestion that Smith would be granted a cabinet post in a Lincoln administration.

"We are going to have Old Abe for sure," Davis told *Chicago Press and Tribune* editor Joseph Medill. "We promised them everything they asked. We promised to see Smith put in the cabinet."

Davis did not have Lincoln's permission to make such promises. In the midst of the convention, Lincoln would telegraph Edward Baker that his agents should "make no contracts that bind me." But patronage was the coin of nineteenth century politics. From his home in Springfield, Lincoln could pretend to be above political horse trading, but unless Davis could imply the promise of government jobs, he had nothing to offer in exchange for Lincoln votes.

Even Kansas's tiny six-man territorial delegation got the hard sell from the convention's most prominent figures. Thurlow Weed visited the Kansans at Briggs House to argue that Seward was the only man with the "executive ability" and "statesman-like qualities" to lead the nation through the coming crisis. Weed was followed by Horace Greeley, who threw his felt hat on the hotel room table and insisted, "to name Seward is to invite defeat. He cannot carry New Jersey, Pennsylvania, Indiana, or Iowa." To bolster his case, Greeley brought in the governor of each state. Andrew Curtin of Pennsylvania insisted, "I could not win with Mr. Seward as our candidate."

The time to stop Seward was running short, though. On Thursday, the convention was expected to adopt a platform then vote on a nominee.

The Wigwam, Chicago, Illinois, May 17, 1860

The morning of the convention's second day began with a parade for Seward. Setting out from their lodgings at Richmond House, the New York delegation marched four abreast behind a band uniformed in epaulets and scarlet caps, imported to blare the praises of the candidate. Behind the delegates straggled a few thousand locals, conscripted and paid by Weed. The Seward men wore badges and stepped to the tune of "O, Isn't He a Darling?" As they passed the Tremont House, they shouted three cheers for Seward, loud enough for Lincoln men to hear them.

The Lincoln men, though, were determined not to be outmarched, out-shouted, or outnumbered in their own state. Once the nomination came up for a vote, they would have to match the Sewardites roar for roar inside the Wigwam. Norman Judd dispatched telegrams to every little prairie town with a rail depot, offering special train fares that he hoped would entice Lincoln's supporters to converge on Chicago. To ensure Lincoln men would gain admission to the Wigwam once they arrived, Ward Hill Lamon visited a print shop, where he ordered counterfeit tickets, on which he forged the signatures of convention officials.

The Sewardites' confidence increased even more when the convention decided that the nominee would need only a majority of votes from the delegates present—233. The Committee on Credentials had issued a report suggesting a majority of the Electoral College—304 votes—to avoid the appearance of a sectional nominee. That figure, however, was uncomfortably close to the two-thirds majority demanded by the Democrats—and most Republicans did not want to repeat the stalemate in Charleston. As with Douglas in Charleston, there was enough hard-core anti-Seward sentiment in Chicago to prevent him from reaching two-thirds. As A. B. James of New York pointed out, "I was not aware that [the Democrats] ever adopted that rule until 1836, and again in 1844, when it became necessary for the interest and purposes of slavery that the minority would rule the majority."

The New Yorkers, who had seventy votes themselves, were confident that their candidate would amass a commanding lead on the first ballot, providing him the momentum to win a majority once the favorite-son candidates dropped out.

When the Platform Committee presented its report, during the afternoon session, Ohio abolitionist Joshua Giddings rose to propose that the convention write the promises of the Declaration of Independence into the party's Statement of Principles. Lincoln had repeatedly cited the Declaration during his debates with Douglas, as a guarantee of freedom for all Americans, Black or White. The convention, though, voted down Giddings's amendment. Defeated, the sixty-four-year-old firebrand shuffled toward the exit, the fire inside him gone cold. Delegates begged him to remain. The New Yorkers promised to bring the Declaration to a second vote. Inconsolable, Giddings left the Wigwam.

The Declaration did come up for a second vote. This time, George Conway of New York asked the delegates whether they were "prepared to go upon the record and before the country as voting down the words of the Declaration of Independence?" The delegates shouted "no!" and voted yes. As adopted, the platform endorsed the principles promulgated in the Declaration of Independence and embodied in the Federal Constitution: "That all men are created equal, that they are endowed by their Creator with certain inalienable rights; that among these are life, liberty, and the pursuit of happiness."

That was a plank on which Lincoln could run. So was Section 8, the purest expression of Republicanism: "That the normal condition of all the Territory of the United States is freedom . . . and we deny the authority of Congress, of a Territorial legislature, or of any individuals to give legal existence to slavery in any Territory of the United States." The convention also added a clause opposing "any change in our Naturalization Laws or any State legislation by which the rights of citizenship hitherto accorded to immigrants from foreign lands shall be abridged or impaired." The so-called Dutch plank, because it was written to secure German votes, was a rebuke to the Know Nothings, and to a Massachusetts law requiring immigrants to be citizens for two years before they could vote.

The platform was adopted before the adjournment hour of five o'clock, so Seward's forces called for a vote on the nominee, confident they could win on the first ballot. They may have been right. At that moment, the streets of Chicago and the floor of the Wigwam were dominated by voices demanding Seward. The clerks, though, had not expected the convention to proceed so swiftly and smoothly and thus had not prepared tally sheets for voting. The little matter of tally sheets turned out to be an unexpected hinge of history. Over the objection of the Sewardites, the convention adjourned for the day, postponing a vote on the nomination until Friday, by which time tally sheets could be printed. That gave the wily Davis an extra seventeen hours to build support for Lincoln. It was all the time he needed.

Despite the delay in balloting, the New Yorkers were so confident Seward would win they returned to Richmond House to throw a champagne supper, at which they were said to have consumed three hundred bottles. Davis, meanwhile, returned to the Tremont House, where three delegates each from Indiana, Illinois, New Jersey, and Pennsylvania formed a Committee of Twelve to settle on a candidate who could beat Seward. The week before the Republican convention, the Constitutional Union Party met in Baltimore to nominate former senator John Bell of Tennessee for president. This raised even more concerns about Seward's ability to carry the swing states. The Constitutional Unionists were old Whigs from the Upper South—including Kentucky's John J. Crittenden—and might attract conservative voters in the Lower North.

The Committee of Twelve convened at 6:00 P.M. in David Wilmot's room, but as the clock passed midnight—balloting day—still had not settled on a candidate. Dropping in on the deadlocked deliberations, Greeley was convinced that Seward's opponents would not be able to unite against him. The New Yorker's nomination seemed assured.

"The friends of Seward are firm, and claim ninety votes for him on the first ballot," he cabled to his newspaper in New York. "Opposition to Seward not fixed on any man. Lincoln is the strongest, and may have altogether forty votes. The various delegations are still caucusing."

At 11:40 P.M. on Thursday, Halstead cabled the *Cincinnati Commercial* his conclusion that "the opposition to Gov. Seward cannot concentrate on any candidate, and that he will be nominated."

In the wee hours, the committee took a straw vote. Since Lincoln had the support of Illinois and Indiana, he was the leading candidate. Thomas H. Dudley of New Jersey offered that his state would give up its favorite son candidate, Senator William L. Dayton, if Pennsylvania would give up Cameron. But Pennsylvania—the largest swing state, with twenty-seven votes, and the second-largest delegation, overall, after New York—needed more persuading. Governor Curtin dreaded running on a ticket with Seward, but his state was committed to voting for Cameron on the first ballot. Cameron was not a serious contender for the nomination, so Davis needed to give the Pennsylvanians a reason to vote for Lincoln on the second.

On Thursday afternoon, Davis had asked Jesse K. Dubois to telegraph Lincoln that Pennsylvania could be won over if Cameron were promised secretary of the treasury.

"I authorize no bargains and will be bound by none," Lincoln wired back.

"Damn Lincoln!" Dubois expectorated when he read the telegram. The Illinoisans, who were wheeling and dealing so hard for Lincoln that they hadn't slept more than two hours a night, were unanimous in their disgust for the candidate's impractical rectitude.

"I am very sure if Lincoln was aware of the necessities—" Leonard Swett purred.

Davis finished his sentence.

"Lincoln ain't here," he said. "And don't know what we have to meet, so we will go ahead, as if we hadn't heard from him, and he must ratify it."

Early that Friday morning, Davis and Swett negotiated with Cameron's lieutenants. Whatever promises they made were enough to bring Pennsylvania into the Lincoln column.

"My assurance to them," Swett wrote Lincoln apologetically, the week after the convention, was that "they should be placed upon the same footing as if they had originally been your friends . . . I only write to suggest the very delicate situation I am placed towards them so that you might cultivate them as much as possible."

Lincoln, who recognized a political debt when one was forced upon him, ended up appointing Cameron to Treasury.

All week, Lincoln's friends wrote him encouraging letters from Chicago. On Monday, Dubois and Herndon informed Lincoln that "Indiana is all right, Ohio is prepared to do a good part after Chase has had his compliments paid him, New Hampshire and N Jersey are talking out for you . . . Some of the Penna delegates have said to me that they will be quite as well satisfied with you as with Cameron." On Wednesday, Kansas's Mark Delahay wrote, "Unless Seward has strength sufficient early in the Balloting to give him the nomination, you I think will be nominated." And that Thursday, Davis telegraphed, "Am very hopeful don't be Excited nearly dead with fatigue."

Even as the Committee of Twelve haggled, members of its delegations were canvassing Chicago's hotels, raising doubts about Seward and promoting Lincoln as a substitute. Henry S. Lane personally lobbied Vermont and Virginia, hoping to undermine Seward in New England and the South.

"I am governor of Indiana," Lane said. "I know my people well. In the south half of my state a good proportion of my people . . . have come from slave states of the South. They were poor people, forced to work for a living, and they did not want to bring up their families to labor in competition with the slaves, so they have moved to Indiana to get away from the influence. They will not tolerate slavery in Indiana or on our free territories but they will not oppose it where it is, if only it will stay there. These people want a man of the Lincoln type as their president. They are afraid Seward would be influenced by the abolition element of the East and make war on slavery where it is. This they do not want, so they believe Lincoln understands this as one of their kind would be acceptable, and would probably get the support of the entire element. If at any time the South should undertake in the interest of slavery to destroy the Union we can depend on everyone of this class to shoulder his musket and go to the front in defense of a United Nation even at the cost of slavery itself."

Virginia would support Lincoln on the first ballot, Vermont on the second, after a courtesy vote for its own Senator Jacob Collamer. By the time the sun rose over Lake Michigan on Friday morning, Seward was finished.

The Wigwam, Chicago, Illinois, May 18, 1860

The Seward men were out at dawn. Effervescent from a night of champagne, confident of a day of victory, they marched out of Richmond House, behind a band attired like Central European soldiery. Their demonstration was so long, and so loud, that not all the marchers were able to cram into the Wigwam, which was already crowded with early arriving Lincoln supporters who had answered Judd's summons and bore Lamon's counterfeit tickets.

When the time came for balloting, William M. Evarts of New York was the first to rise and nominate Seward. There were enough Sewardites in the hall to raise what Swett would recall as "a deafening shout." Weed had paid Tom Hyer, the former heavyweight champion from New York, to canvass the streets for leather-lunged locals. The noise "appalled us a little," Swett confessed, but Lincoln's supporters were more numerous, better organized—and louder. Women were ordered to wave handkerchiefs, men American flags. The crowd in the street awaited a signal that Lincoln's name had been placed in nomination. This was done by Norman Judd, who rose second, after Evarts. It was by then obvious to all inside the Wigwam that Seward and Lincoln were the main contenders.

"I desire," Judd declared, "to put in nomination as a candidate for President of the United States, Abraham Lincoln of Illinois."

The resulting clamor was so deafening that the Seward men determined to outshout it, to prove that their man was the convention's man, too. When Michigan's Austin Blair seconded Seward's nomination, "the shouting was absolutely frantic, shrill and wild," Halstead reported. "No Comanches, no panthers ever stuck a higher note, or gave screams of more infernal intensity."

The men on the floor flung their black hats across the room, and the women in the galleries fluttered their handkerchiefs. The crowds were carrying on as though the Republican nomination would be decided by a shouting match. Ohio's Columbus Delano offered a second for "the man who can split rails and maul Democrats." The pride of "Hoosiers and

Suckers" was at stake, in the words of Swett: "Five thousand people at once leaped to their seats, women not wanting in the number, and the wild yell made soft vesper breathings of all that had preceded. A thousand steam whistles, ten acres of hotel gongs, a tribe of Comanches, headed by a choice vanguard from pandemonium, might have mingled in the scene unnoticed."

(Halstead described the outcry for Lincoln as sounding like "all the hogs in Cincinnati giving their death squeals together.")

Governor Lane was so aroused he danced on a table, swinging his hat and cane.

"Abe Lincoln has it by the sound now," a voice called from the floor; "Let us ballot."

Once the din subsided, the balloting began. The New England states were called first. Geographically and ideologically, they should have gone for Seward, a fellow Yankee reformer. Maine split its votes, 10 for Seward, 6 for Lincoln. New Hampshire, where Lincoln had been declared the next president after his Cooper Union speech, went for him 7–1. Massachusetts was solidly for Seward, 21–4, but Rhode Island and Connecticut scattered their ballots among minor contenders. Seward won the biggest prize, when Evarts declared, "The state of New York casts her seventy votes for William H. Seward." That was expected, though; less expected was Virginia giving a majority of its votes to Lincoln, and Indiana giving him all its votes. Those results were both due to Lane's persuasiveness. The governor's eyes gleamed as the roll was called, while the Seward men traded anxious looks.

After the first ballot, Seward led Lincoln, 173½ to 102, but 40 percent of his votes had been cast by New York. Cameron, Bates, and Chase all received support from their home states, but little elsewhere. Lincoln's support was spread among twelve delegations, in all parts of the country. A majority of delegates wanted to defeat Seward—"Stop Seward" was now the convention's motivating sentiment. Lincoln was the only candidate who could stop him, the only remaining alternative to Old Irrepressible. Davis's strategy of making Lincoln everybody's second choice, and the validity of the deals he'd cut the night before, would be tested on the second ballot, when states abandoned their favorite sons in favor of a winner.

The first domino to fall was Vermont. A subject of Lane's lobbying, the Green Mountain State switched its 10 votes from Collamer to Lincoln. The New Yorkers, wrote Halstead, "started as if an Orsini bomb had exploded." Pennsylvania, though, was the turning point. When Pennsylvania cast 48 votes for Lincoln, to 2½ for Seward, New York understood it was beaten. After the balloting was completed, Seward still led, 184½ to 181. The weight of the convention was shifting toward Lincoln, though. Seward had reached the limit of his support, but there were votes for Bates, Chase, and Dayton that could swing Lincoln's way.

On the third ballot, New Jersey gave up Dayton for Lincoln, as it had proposed to do during the Committee of Twelve conclave. Ohio moved 15 votes from Chase to Lincoln. The final tally stood at 231½ for Lincoln—1½ votes short of a majority. Ohio's David Cartter leapt atop his chair and, in his stammer, told the chair, "I rise to announce the change of four votes of Ohio from Mr. Chase to Mr. Lincoln."

Standing atop the Wigwam was a man whose job was to relay the results to the crowd in the streets. Hearing immense cheers for the new nominee, he gestured through the skylight at the secretaries, demanding to know what had just happened.

"Fire the salute!" a secretary cried. "Abe Lincoln is nominated!"

Like a wave, as the cheering within the Wigwam abated, it expanded outside. Then the noise in the streets inspired a renewed celebration on the convention floor, so loud that the delegates could not hear the cannon boom, and knew it had been fired only by the sight and smell of smoke drifting through the seams in the canvas. A delegate pulled a photograph of Lincoln off the wall of an anteroom and paraded it through the screaming crowd. On the floor, delegates tore the pasteboard signs with the names of their states off their staffs and waved them aloft. Only the New Yorkers refused to join in this celebration, but Evarts was gracious enough to move that Lincoln's nomination be made unanimous. John Andrew of Massachusetts, another pro-Seward state, seconded the motion. Republican unity was national unity, writ small.

"The Republican Party is today, gentlemen, the only united national party in America," Andrew proclaimed to his fellow delegates. "It is the cause of liberty. By universal concession, it is the cause of the Union, and it is the only party in the nation which stands by the Union and holds no secessionist in its ranks."

At the beginning of the day, Lincoln had not been enthusiastic about his chances. "Well, I guess I'll go back to practicing law," he told his friend James C. Conkling, just returned from Chicago. Conkling assured him that "the tendency was to drop Seward." Still, Lincoln awaited news of the convention's deliberations in the *State Journal* offices. After seeing the results of the second ballot, though, Lincoln began to believe he could win. He killed the anxious hours between ballots by shooting pool, playing town ball, and telling his favorite yarns. As marching bands paraded through the streets of Chicago, heralding Lincoln's victory, a messenger boy burst into the newsroom, handing Lincoln this cable: "Mr. Lincoln, you are nominated on the third ballot." Lincoln shook hands with the crowd that had been waiting out the balloting with him, declared, "I reckon there's a little short woman down at our house that would like to hear the news," and headed home.

Thrilled that their small town was most likely the home of the next president of the United States, Springfieldians fired off a cannon, tolled church bells, and marched by torchlight to Lincoln's house at Eighth and Jackson. Lincoln stepped outside, apologizing that his home was too small to invite all his neighbors inside.

"We will give you a larger house on the fourth of March next," a member of the crowd cried.

Stephen Douglas, who had more interest in news of Lincoln than anyone else in Washington, learned the identity of the Republican nominee before anyone else in Washington, in a message from Representative John B. Haskin of New York. The Republicans in Congress were far more excited than the Democrats, who had been hoping to run against Seward.

"I do not think there were a dozen out of our 112 who did not join in the rejoicing, and all was hilarity, confidence, and enthusiasm on one side," Schuyler Colfax wrote to Lincoln. "The Democrats on the contrary looked depressed and disappointed; and the Dem. Members from Ills. Said frankly that, even with Douglas, they were not confident of saving their state."

Douglas appeared in the House chamber and, to Colfax's surprise, offered praise for his once and future opponent. One of Douglas's supporters assured him the presidential election would have the same result as the Senate race: "You have beaten him once and will beat him again."

Douglas knew Lincoln better than anyone in the capital, and knew he was in for a fight—a stronger fight than Seward would have put up.

"I've often met my fellow senators in debate, but none of them have ever proved so hard a match as Lincoln," he told Colfax and a score of congressmen. "No stronger nomination than Lincoln's could have been made by the Republicans in all America. His selection will kindle a glow of enthusiasm that no one else could have effected. No man can get as many votes by the thousands in the Northwest as Lincoln."

Douglas, who expected to be nominated when the Democrats reconvened in Baltimore, did not go so far as to say he couldn't beat Lincoln. Lyman Trumbull thought that was the case, though. In a letter to Lincoln, congratulating him on winning the Republican nomination, he had this to say about Douglas: "I think it finishes his prospects."

CHAPTER 7

"YOU WILL HAVE TO GO TO ILLINOIS FOR YOUR NEXT PRESIDENT"

Front Street Theatre, Baltimore, Maryland, June 18, 1860

When the Democrats reassembled in Baltimore, for a second attempt at nominating Douglas for president, most of the delegates from the shattered Charleston convention returned. William Lowndes Yancey, who led the Southern walkout over the convention's refusal to adopt a federal slave code, was back again to defend Alabama's constitutional rights. Yancey and his Fire-Eating compatriots were not the only Alabama delegation, though. In the view of Douglas and his allies, the delegates who bolted at Charleston had forfeited their seats. To prevent the bolters from deadlocking and disrupting the Baltimore convention, Douglas's men encouraged pro-Union Democrats in Alabama, Georgia, and Louisiana to elect their own slates. These would be recognized by the

Northern states, which controlled a majority of votes. The tactic was likely to outrage the rest of the Southern states, but it was the only way to keep Yancey out of the hall—and ensure enough votes to nominate Douglas.

In Alabama, John Forsyth, Douglas's newspaper editor friend from Mobile, organized a meeting in Selma for choosing delegates to nominate a candidate "who may be able to save the Government from the hands of those who will not regard our Constitutional rights, and be the means of securing the Constitution and the Union."

At the same time, a "Yanceyite Disunionist convention" in Montgomery was selecting its own slate for Baltimore and for a meeting of Southern Democrats that would assemble in Richmond, the week before the regular Democratic convention. One of the attendees, the editor and publisher of the *Montgomery Advertiser*, denounced Douglas as "a demagogue, a broken-down politician who has acted so dishonestly that he was obliged to have the presidency to save his fortunes."

"We repudiate the late Montgomery Convention, its delegates, its acts," Forsyth wrote to Douglas. "We have just begun the fight and mean yet to drive the Yanceyites to the wall."

Another correspondent assured Douglas he would carry Alabama by a 10,000 majority in November, because the pro-Union northern part of the state would outvote "the great slave interest" of the South.

In Louisiana, Douglas's former Senate colleague Pierre Soulé led a convention in New Orleans "for the purpose of supplying the vacancies caused by the withdrawal of the Louisiana convention from Charleston."

In Georgia, Douglas had the support of former congressman and future Confederate vice president Alexander Stephens, who wrote a letter in favor of sending delegates to Baltimore, but against repeating the demands Georgia had made in Charleston: Southerners could still take their slaves "wherever the people want it," Stephens wrote. "If we have not enough of the right sort of population to compete longer with the North in the colonization of New Territories and States, this deficiency can never be supplied by any such act of Congress as that now asked for." Stephens pleaded the case for popular sovereignty at a statewide meeting in Milledgeville, but a coalition of Treasury Secretary Howell Cobb and pro-secession Democrats elected a slate that would once again insist on a slave code.

"All of us who will not endorse the Charleston seceders and Congressional Intervention for Protection are pointed at as 'Douglas men' and thereby seen to be regarded as heretics to the South and her interests," John W. Duncan wrote Douglas from Atlanta. "When the Baltimore convention assembles the seceders at Charleston will present themselves again clamoring for admission . . . If admitted the same ultimatum will be demanded and the convention must either refuse it or stultify themselves."

While Douglas's Southern supporters maneuvered to take the places of seceding delegates, Southern politicians vented their hard feelings over Charleston on the Senate floor. Jefferson Davis reintroduced a set of resolutions endorsing federal protection of slavery in the territories. If this was an attempt to bait Douglas, it succeeded. Over the course of two days, May 15 and 16, the gentleman from Illinois delivered a speech defending popular sovereignty, congressional nonintervention, and the unity of the Democratic Party. Douglas reminded his Southern colleagues that they had endorsed nonintervention at the Cincinnati convention in 1856, and that Buchanan had won the election on that platform. But even he must have realized the Dred Scott decision had changed the South's attitude toward bringing slaves into the territories: Southerners now regarded it as a constitutional right, granted by the Supreme Court, and were becoming increasingly aggressive in defending that right. They had broken up the Democratic Party over it in Charleston, and some of them, like Yancey and Rhett, were prepared to break up the Union if the North didn't give them what they wanted. Douglas was pleading to hold not only his party together, but his country. He predicted a civil war if the South got its way.

"I believe that the principle involved in this discussion involves the fate of the American Union," he told the Senate. "Whenever you incorporate intervention by Congress into the Democratic creed, as it has become the cardinal principle of the Republican creed, you will make two sectional parties, hostile to each other, divided by the line that separates the free from the slaveholding States, and present a conflict that will be irrepressible, and will never cease until the one shall subdue the other, or they shall divide in order that they may live in peace."

That day and the next, Davis delivered his rejoinder, defending his state's right to withdraw from a party that refused to endorse its principles. For attempting to force the minority platform on the South, Davis accused Douglas of arrogance exceeding the Sun King's.

"Does the Senator consider it a modest thing in him to announce to the Democratic convention on what terms he will accept the nomination; but presumptuous of a State to proclaim the principle on which she will give him her vote? It is an advance on Louis Quatorze."

Next to attack Douglas was Judah P. Benjamin of Louisiana, less than a year away from joining the Confederate cabinet, first as attorney general, then secretary of war. Benjamin also accused Douglas of believing he was entitled to the Democratic nomination. Louis XIV's motto was "*L'etat c'est moi.*" In the view of the Charleston bolters, Douglas's was "*Le parti c'est moi.*"

"The proposition of the honorable senator from Illinois was that he was the embodiment of the Democratic Party, and that all who dissented from this modest proposition were rebels," Benjamin said.

As at Charleston, Douglas would again be the central figure in Baltimore, with the delegates divided between those who thought he was the party's only hope of defeating Lincoln, and those who considered him a traitor to the Constitution. The first group was mostly from the free states of the Northwest.

"The Old Line Whigs who did not vote for Buchanan are holding their breath, as indeed are we all until June 18," H. W. Starr of Burlington, Iowa, wrote to Douglas. "Hundreds here say they will vote for no man but you. [Your] nomination [is necessary] if the Northwest is to be carried. I believe the Iowa delegation are with you to the death."

After Charleston, the Douglas Democrats were in no mood to compromise with the South or allow Fire-Eaters to disrupt a reconstituted convention. August Belmont, Douglas's most loyal supporter in the New York delegation, was not in favor of readmitting delegates who had walked out at

Charleston "unless regularly accredited by newly convened state conventions and not participants of the Richmond." Belmont was particularly determined to keep Yancey out of the hall. Since New York would cast the decisive vote on delegate credentials, this was good news for Douglas. The New Yorkers were not as devoted to Douglas as the Northwesterners, though; many would have been happy to throw him over in favor of Horatio Seymour.

A week before the Baltimore convention opened, delegates from the states that led the Charleston walkout met in Richmond's Metropolitan Hall for a "Constitutional Democratic Convention." Alabama, Mississippi, Louisiana, South Carolina, Georgia, Texas, and Florida were all represented, by many of the same delegates who represented them in April. The convention took no action, though. The Southerners decided to proceed to Baltimore, where they would give the North one last chance to respect their rights by adopting a slave code platform. The convention issued this statement:

> At Charleston, we exerted ourselves assiduously, earnestly, for days and weeks, hoping that we might agree—that we might concur with the majority of that body—that they would concede to us what seemed to our apprehension, to clearly belong to us. But, governed by objects of self—of personal aggrandisment—they sternly refused . . . we shall make one more attempt at reconciliation.

The convention agreed to reassemble in Richmond on the 25th. For what purpose was left unstated, but the *New York Herald* predicted the Southerners would nominate their own candidate for president if the Baltimore convention took any of the following actions: refuse to admit seceding delegates; refuse to modify the minority platform; or abolish the two-thirds rule, which would allow Douglas to win the nomination without Southern support. After two days of inaction, the Southerners continued on to Baltimore, except for the South Carolina delegation, which had been ordered not to participate in another Yankee farce. The Floridians went, but only as observers. The Richmond convention did not choose a candidate, or endorse a platform, but it demonstrated that the cotton states would again put up a united front in Baltimore.

When the Baltimore convention was gaveled to order at ten o'clock on the morning of the 18th, chairman Caleb Cushing ruled that "only those states be called which were present at the adjournment."

That left out all the delegations recently arrived from Richmond. A New Yorker proposed submitting the question of their admission to a Committee on Credentials. There was a wrinkle, though. Alabama, Georgia, and Louisiana had all sent competing sets of delegates: one composed of Fire-Eating seceders, the other of Douglas men elected by conventions of "conservative" pro-Union Democrats organized after the crack-up in Charleston. The Committee on Credentials—made up mainly of Northern delegates, already admitted—would have to choose between the two.

Many delegates were hostile to the Southerners' desire to return. "What did they do at Richmond?" asked Pennsylvania's H. B. Wright. "They adjourned that convention, and today hold it in terrorism over us if we do not come to their terms." Another Pennsylvanian demanded a pledge "that they will not countenance a seceders' convention, in another place." But Andrew Ewing of Tennessee warned that barring the Southern states in June would cost the party their electoral votes in November. That was the committee's dilemma: loyalty to Douglas, or party unity. Those had been impossible to reconcile in Charleston. They would be in Baltimore, too.

Front Street Theatre, Baltimore, Maryland, June 21, 1860

On the fourth day of the convention, the Committee on Credentials issued its report. So great was the clamor to hear the result that spectators crowded onto the convention floor. The overpopulated boards collapsed, causing delegates to race for the windows and doors.

"Everyone was 'scratching' for the door," wrote a correspondent, "but soon the ladies recovered from the fright and declared 'they would not leave until Douglas was nominated.'"

The majority report was everything Douglas could have wished for: it readmitted delegates from Texas, Florida, and Mississippi, but also proposed granting credentials to new delegations from Alabama and Louisiana, those led by Forsyth and Soulé. Georgia and Arkansas would be divided between seceders and Douglas men; if the seceders decided to walk out again, "the other portion of said delegates . . . shall be entitled to cast the entire votes of said state."

Two Arkansans came to blows during the committee's debate over their state's delegation. Representative Thomas C. Hindman, one of the Charleston seceders, insisted that only 150 men had attended the pro-Douglas nominating convention in Madison—and that not all were from Arkansas. William M. Hooper, a delegate elected by that convention, declared the charge "false—unqualifiedly false" and jabbed a finger three times in Hindman's direction. Hindman responded to the provocation by drawing a pistol and striking Hooper in the face.

"A duel between the parties is expected as a matter of course, but it will probably be delayed until the Convention adjourns," the *New York Herald* reported. In the hot-blooded Democratic politics of 1860, that amounted to a restoration of order.

The minority report favored readmitting all the seceders. The question occupying Baltimore was which way New York would vote—with the majority, for a convention that was guaranteed to nominate Douglas; or with the minority for a deadlocked convention that might turn to Seymour as a compromise candidate. The convention adjourned at 4:30 P.M., to give the New Yorkers time to deliberate. The liberated delegates filled the streets surrounding Monument Square, holding competing rallies. Baltimore was no Charleston, but there was secessionist sympathy in the city. Every night, crowds gathered outside Gilmore House (where the Illinois and the Alabama delegations were both, uncomfortably, lodged) calling for Yancey. He appeared twice.

"I am neither for the Union, per se, nor against it, per se," Yancey told his admirers. "I am for the Constitution."

The friends of Douglas, he said, "are small men, with selfish aims—corrupt and abolitionized. They are ostrich-like—their head is in the sand of squatter sovereignty, and they do not know their great, ugly, ragged abolition body is exposed."

(Gilmore House was Yancey's only public forum in Baltimore. He was refused a ticket to the Front Street Theatre by a functionary who wrote, "I am of the opinion that Mr. Yancey had ought not to be admitted to the floor of the convention nor none of his crew.")

Meanwhile, R. A. Hunter, leader of the Louisiana seceders, offered to bet Douglas's supporters a million dollars that their candidate would not carry a single Cotton State. The Douglas men responded that if he lost, the South would have to live under "an abolition president."

"What office has Buchanan given you?" the Douglasites taunted the seceders.

"What office has Douglas promised you?" the seceders shot back.

Late that evening, Douglas received a telegram in Washington: "Vote in New York delegation for new delegates Louisiana and Alabama forty two to twenty seven."

Douglas was going to be the nominee—but of how many Democrats?

Front Street Theatre, Baltimore, Maryland, June 22, 1860

Before the convention was called to order that morning, Douglas sent a telegram to Dean Richmond, chairman of the New York delegation, thanking him for his state's support, and offering to withdraw his name, if that would prevent another Southern walkout: "If my enemies are determined to divide and destroy the Democratic party, and, perhaps, the country, rather than see me elected, and if the unity of the party can be preserved, and its ascendency perpetuated by dropping my name and uniting upon some other reliable Non-intervention and Union-loving Democrat, I beseech you, in consultation with our friends, to pursue that course which will save the party and the country, without regard to any individual interests."

Douglas had sent a similar letter to William Richardson, who suppressed it, not willing to sacrifice Illinois's favorite son on the altar of Southern intransigence. Richmond did the same, not out of devotion to Douglas, but because New York could not meet the South's demands.

The convention voted on the credentials of each seceding state, one by one. When Alabama was called, New York voted for the Forsyth delegation. When Louisiana was called, New York voted for the Soulé delegation. Every free state voted likewise. The slaveholding states—Virginia, North Carolina, Tennessee, Kentucky, Maryland—voted to welcome the seceders back. As the clock inched toward 5:00, though, the chair proposed a roll call on tabling the credential committee's minority report, thus shutting out the seceders for good. New York switched sides and voted "no," along with the South.

During the recess, rumors consumed the convention hall. Was New York trying to make a last-minute deal to replace Douglas? Had Douglas offered to withdraw? Richardson denied it. New York was willing to admit the Louisiana bolters, but Alabama and Yancey were out of the question. That wasn't good enough for the Richmond contingent: either all the seceders came back, or none came back. So, after the recess, when the vote to table the minority report came up again, New York cast its decisive thirty-five votes for "aye." That, wrote Murat Halstead, "settled this as all other contested questions . . . Upon those motions being carried the action in each case was final and irrevocable."

New York was not willing to compromise on Yancey, but it was willing to compromise on a platform. John Howard of Tennessee proposed a slave code plank he hoped would be acceptable to both: that "the citizens of the United States have an equal right to settle with their property in the territories; and that, under the decision of the Supreme Court, which we recognize as the correct exposition of the Constitution, neither the right of persons nor property can be destroyed or impaired by Congressional or Territorial legislation." Howard's resolution endorsed both the Dred Scott decision and the principle of nonintervention. It rejected Douglas's Freeport Doctrine, but even so, Richardson declared it acceptable to Illinois.

The convention tried to move on to nominating Douglas, but Charles Wells Russell of Virginia demanded the floor. Virginia had remained in the Charleston convention, but now, nervously, solemnly, Russell withdrew it from Baltimore.

"I understand that the action of this Convention upon the various questions arising out of the reports from the Committee on Credentials has become final, complete, and irrevocable," he said. "And it has become my duty now, by direction of a large majority of the delegation from Virginia, respectfully to inform this body that is inconsistent with their convictions of duty to participate longer in its deliberations."

Only one Virginian had walked out at Charleston; this time, most of its delegates rose to leave, shaking hands and bidding farewells as they departed the theater—farewells that would last five years. North Carolina went next, followed by eight of the ten Tennesseans. (Harvey Watterson, one of the "gallant spirits from the land of Jackson" who remained, declared his hope that the convention would nominate a candidate who endorsed the Cincinnati platform.) Oregon withdrew, objecting that "gentlemen as much entitled to seats as ourselves, in our opinion, are excluded from the floor." So did California, and half of Maryland. Kentucky asked for time to consult; so did Missouri, although one Missourian, N. C. Claiborne, insisted the convention proceed to balloting at that late hour, and nominate Douglas.

Claiborne was a Southern man, "born and raised beneath the sunny sky of the South," without "a drop of Yankee blood, with 300 years of Southern ancestors buried in the same soil that sheltered Washington's bones," yet he was called a traitor to his section because he had voted for Douglas in Charleston. When the Virginians rose to depart, Claiborne was shocked to see "the mother of States starting madly from a National Convention"; however, "the Democratic Party has passed through ordeals before," and he was certain it would emerge from this one united, harmonious, "and victorious over every foe," with Douglas carrying Missouri by 25,000 votes. (Claiborne was the only Douglas man to correctly call his state. Douglas would win Missouri, by 429 votes, over Bell—the only state he won.)

When Claiborne sat down, the delegates cried, "Question, question!" It was a call for balloting, but at 10:30, the night was well advanced. A motion to adjourn passed instead. The remaining delegates would have to wait another day to nominate Douglas.

Front Street Theatre, Baltimore, Maryland, June 23, 1860

Before the balloting could begin, the convention had to hear Kentucky's decision. The Bluegrass State was split right down the middle—ten withdrew, nine remained. One of the remainers, W. B. Reed, was not about to abandon the party just because it wouldn't nominate his state's favorite son, James Guthrie.

"We, of Kentucky, stand here opposing secession and sectionalism North and South," Reed shouted to loud applause. "We stand with you as a wall of fire in opposing both extremes."

The Democratic Party in Baltimore was a sail shot through with holes, unable to gather enough wind to propel its bark forward. The free and slave states were divided. The border states were divided among themselves. Cushing stepped down as chair, unwilling to preside over a convention in which most states were not fully represented. Governor David Tod of Ohio took his place. Even the slave states were divided among themselves. Only twenty-five of the thirty-three states remained to cast a ballot for president. Virginia, North Carolina, Arkansas, Tennessee, and Georgia were partial delegations. Alabama and Louisiana were disputed. As the roll was called, the chairmen of the substitute delegations all rose to declare their devotion to the Union.

"We come here prepared to see the most desperate efforts to break up the Democratic Party," said L. E. Parsons of Alabama. "Shall that be done?"

"No, no!" cried the delegates.

"Shall it be said," Parsons continued, "that in 1860, here in Baltimore, the grave of this Union was dug? The Star-Spangled Banner still waves over us—shall it continue to wave?"

"Yes, yes!" shouted the applauding delegates.

Alabama cast its nine votes for Douglas. Soulé cast Louisiana's six votes for Douglas. Since every delegate who opposed Douglas's nonintervention principles had either been refused admission or walked out, he was the convention's nearly unanimous choice, receiving 173½ of the 190½ votes cast. Guthrie received the votes of the few loyal Kentuckians, Vice President Breckinridge five votes, and Seymour one from Pennsylvania. After Pennsylvania voted, a New York delegate read a letter from Seymour, stating that "I cannot under any circumstances be a candidate for President or Vice president." After the disruption and deadlock in Charleston, Douglas's allies had engineered a convention guaranteed to nominate their candidate. They had just one technical problem: 173½ votes was not two-thirds of the 303 votes all the states were entitled to cast. There were not 202 votes in the entire theater. To get around this technicality, New York offered a resolution:

> That Stephen A. Douglas, of the State of Illinois, having now received two-thirds of all the votes given in this Convention, he is hereby declared, in accordance with the rules governing this body and in accordance with the uniform custom and rules of the former Democratic National Conventions, the regular nominee of the Democratic party of the United States for the office of President.

That was the original rule. The New Yorkers insisted the "full convention" rule had been adopted after the Charleston walkout, to thwart Douglas.

"If we had adopted this resolution at Charleston, as we ought to have done, we would have concluded long since," said a Virginian.

Maryland objected, though, so the convention took a second ballot. Douglas received 181½ votes, with 7½ for Breckinridge and 5½ for Guthrie. (Even Kentuckians voted for Douglas this time.) When New York's resolution was resubmitted, Kentucky proposed that, instead of changing the rules, the convention simply declare Douglas its unanimous nominee.

"Is there any objection to withdrawing the resolution and declaring the nomination by a big, old-fashioned Democratic yell?" asked a Missourian.

There wasn't. A full-throated "aye" nominated Douglas, followed by another full-throated cheer when Governor Tod declared Douglas "the nominee of the Democratic Party of the United States. And may God, in his infinite mercy protect him, and with him this Union."

The Keystone Club unfurled a banner—DOUGLAS, THE NEXT PRESIDENT OF THE UNITED STATES. PENNSYLVANIA GOOD FOR 40,000 FOR DOUGLAS." The band struck up "Hail to the Chief." A delegate proposed "three cheers for Douglas." The Democrats finally had a candidate. Meanwhile, a few blocks away, in the 8,000-capacity Maryland Institute Hall, another group of Democrats was nominating another candidate. The delegates who abandoned the Douglas coronation at Front Street Theater joined with the Southerners who were never admitted for what they called a "National Democratic Convention," and the newspapers called a "Seceders Convention." It was, for the most part, a reunion of the Richmond crowd, but the 162 delegates included representatives from California, Oregon, Pennsylvania, Maryland, and Cushing's Massachusetts. The Southerners had originally planned to reassemble in Richmond if the Yankees didn't surrender to their demands for a slave code, but they decided not to wait. If the South nominated its candidate in the same place, and on the same day, as the Douglasites, it would be reported in the newspapers at the same time and look equally representative of the will of the Democratic Party.

"The Convention assembled elsewhere, and from which you have withdrawn, has lost all title to the designation of national," declared Virginia's Charles Russell, the temporary chairman. "It can no longer continue to perform the functions of a National Democratic Convention, and everyone believes that all true Democrats will unite to declare it unsound in national relations. You and those who you represent are a majority of the people of the Democracy and the Democratic states."

(One of the South's objections to the Charleston minority platform and the Douglas nomination was that both had been favored by states that would vote Republican in November. When Davis brought that up in the Senate debate, Douglas pointed out that Illinois had voted Democratic for president in every election since becoming a state, while Mississippi voted Whig in 1840.)

The delegates applauded when Russell named them the real Democrats, but there was another speaker they wanted to hear from, a speaker who had not been heard from at the Front Street Theatre, because he been refused admission. As the afternoon session came to a close, the seceders' convention clamored for Yancey.

In the evening, Cushing was named chairman of the breakaway convention. The delegates waved handkerchiefs and hats as he advanced to the rostrum, his brass-buttoned blue coat recognizable to all. Since Cushing was from Massachusetts, his presence allowed the seceders to claim that their movement was not merely sectional, *and* that it represented the real Democracy. Cushing, said Russell, was merely resuming his role as chairman of the National Democratic Party.

The convention's first order of business was to adopt the majority platform from Charleston. Its second was to nominate candidates for president and vice president. Dr. George B. Loring of Massachusetts proposed Vice President John C. Breckinridge, one of the "statesmen of Kentucky" who had brought "the sectionalism of the North at their feet by their gallantry."

The tumult at the announcement of Breckinridge's name was so intense that balloting was unnecessary—he was clearly the convention's choice. Protocol demanded a vote, though, so the roll of states was called. The result was eighty-one for Breckinridge, twenty-four for Daniel Dickinson of New York. Senator Joseph Lane of Oregon was nominated for vice president.

Now that the South had its own presidential ticket, the calls arose again for Yancey. The breakaway convention's other big winner finally answered them with a speech.

"The storm clouds of faction have drifted away, and the sunlight of principle, under the Constitution, shines brightly upon the National Democracy," Yancey declared in his piercing clarion voice, leaning toward the edge of the platform on his toes and extending his right arm, projecting his whole voice and body toward the listeners. "The Democracy, the Constitution, and through them the Union, are yet safe. I am, however, no worshipper of the shrine of the Union. I am neither for the Union nor against the Union—neither for disunion nor against disunion. I urge or oppose measures upon the ground of their constitutionality and wisdom or the reverse."

Douglas and his disciples believed disunion was unconstitutional; Yancey believed disunion could be a remedy for preserving the Constitution. He ended his speech with scorn for the Douglas convention, for popular sovereignty, and implicitly, for Unionism: "I will let Mr. Douglas rest where his friends here placed him, contending, however, that they have buried him today beneath the grave of squatter sovereignty. The nomination that was made (I speak it prophetically), was made to be defeated and it is bound to be defeated."

National Hotel, Washington, D.C., June 25, 1860

No man in America had more wealthy friends than August Belmont, a Wall Street banker. When the Democratic National Committee met two days after the conventions, its members chose Belmont as their chairman, hoping he could "smite the Manhattan rock and cause campaign funds to flow."

Not even a moneybags like Belmont could raise funds for a candidate as beleaguered as Douglas, who was seen as a certain loser now that the Democratic Party had split apart beneath his feet, stranding him as the leader of a faction with no strong base of support in any of the nation's bickering sections. As was customary in presidential elections, Belmont began his fundraising drive by asking for $100 from the Democratic Party in each of the 237 congressional districts. Then he went after the big money, depositing $1,000 from his own bank account in a Douglas national campaign fund, and asking wealthy New York Democrats to do the same. A month passed. Neither effort raised a cent. Belmont made "a most *urgent personal*

appeal" to steamship magnate George Law, who had supported Douglas
for the nomination. Law refused to donate to Douglas's presidential campaign. The New York pashas were reluctant to contribute for two reasons.
First, they believed that the competing candidacies of Douglas, Bell, and
Breckinridge guaranteed Lincoln would carry their state. Second, New
York had strong commercial ties to the South, so its merchants were
afraid of alienating Southern customers. Ephraim Smart, the Democratic
candidate for governor in Maine, begged Belmont for money. Henry
H. Sibley, the Democratic national committeeman from Minnesota, told
the chairman that $10,000 could deliver the state's four electoral votes to
Douglas. Belmont informed them that the party's cupboard was bare. It
could not raise $10,000 for the entire nation, he told Sibley.

In late July, Belmont wrote a desperate letter to Douglas, detailing his
financial failures. Unless the party could demonstrate "some assurance of
success" to businessmen and politicians, "I fear that it will be impossible to
raise the necessary funds for our campaign." To win New York, Belmont
suggested a tactic never before employed in presidential politics: a speaking
tour of the state. On the advice of his handlers, Lincoln was sitting idly
in Springfield, going nowhere, saying nothing. Throughout the republic's
eighty-two-year history, that was how presidential candidates had always
conducted themselves. Actively campaigning for the presidency, as Lincoln
and Douglas had done for the Senate two years earlier, was considered
beneath the dignity of the nation's highest office. No candidate, though,
had ever found himself in Douglas's situation: bereft of money, and facing a
possible fourth-place finish in the Electoral College, which would eliminate
him from a contingent election in the House of Representatives should any
candidate fail to win a majority.

"I know that my suggestion for you to stump our state is not in accordance with what has hitherto been considered customary in Presidential
campaigns, but the reckless conduct of the Administration and of your
enemies renders exceptional exertions on our side necessary," Belmont
wrote to Douglas on July 28.

By the time Douglas received Belmont's letter, he had come to the same conclusion himself. After his nomination in Baltimore, Douglas promised to make no political speeches—"If my political opinions are not known to the people of the United States now, it is not worthwhile for me to attempt to explain them," he said, noting that the presidential campaign would be "the first time in my life that I have been placed in a position where I had to look on and see a fight and not take a hand in it."

Douglas, though, could no more refrain from explaining his political opinions to the people or taking a hand in a fight than he could have refused Lincoln's challenge to seven debates. After a series of meetings with political allies in New York made clear his desperate situation, he decided to embark on the first modern presidential campaign, a cross-country speaking tour with stops in the Northeast, the Northwest, and even the South. Douglas still hoped he could carry enough Southern and Northwestern states to prevail in the Electoral College, but almost as important as winning the presidency was rescuing the Democratic Party from the Fire-Eaters. Douglas discouraged fusion tickets of his candidacy and Breckinridge's in Pennsylvania and Rhode Island, believing they would "disgust the people and give every Northern state to Lincoln."

"We must make the war boldly against the Northern abolitionists and the Southern disunionists, and give no quarter to either," he wrote Charles Lanphier. "We should treat the Bell and Everett men friendly and cultivate good relations with them, for they are Union men . . . We can have no partnership with the Bolters."

Douglas began his campaign in New England, the land of his birth and childhood. His loyal lieutenant, William Richardson, had canvassed the region and thought a vigorous campaign could win over Maine, New Hampshire, Rhode Island, and Connecticut. Most politicians thought Douglas had little chance of defeating Lincoln in New England, where abolition sentiment was stronger than anywhere else in the country.

United States Hotel, Hartford, Connecticut, July 16, 1860

Mindful that he was undertaking an unprecedented—and, in the minds of many, undignified—journey, Douglas tried to pretend that there was nothing political about his travels. He was heading up to Boston to see his brother-in-law, James Madison Cutts, graduate from Harvard. That would be followed by a sentimental call at his boyhood home in Brandon, Vermont. Finally, he would visit his mother in Clifton Springs, New York. They had not seen each other in two years. If, along the way, the crowds that greeted his train insisted on a few words concerning the issues of the day, he would try to gratify them. To the thousands who gathered outside his hotel in Hartford, Douglas explained, "I was expecting to pass through this city on my way to visit a relative in a neighboring state, and had no expectation of meeting such a concourse of my fellow citizens. It is true I am a 'Yankee boy,' born among the Green Mountains of Vermont, but proud as I am of the wide prairie of the West, I have never ceased to feel a pride also on the growth, prosperity, and happiness of New England."

The pandering to his regional roots out of the way, Douglas gave a speech condemning both the Republicans and the Southern Democrats for "agitating the country in furtherance of the views of their particular sections." Only his wing of the Democratic Party stood for nonintervention by Congress, just as the Democrats had in 1856, and the Whigs in 1852, Douglas said, trying as ever to ignore the changes wrought by his own Kansas-Nebraska Act and the Dred Scott decision.

"I am afraid I have been betrayed into making a political speech," Douglas apologized after fifteen minutes, before withdrawing to his rooms. "I only meant to express my gratitude at this reception."

Harvard University, Cambridge, Massachusetts, July 18, 1860

On his way to Harvard's commencement, Douglas stopped to deliver an eight-minute speech in Worcester, where a salute was fired in his honor.

Then he addressed a crowd of 10,000 in Boston's Bowdoin Square—from the balcony of Revere House, from which he noted "your God-like Webster had defended the principle of nonintervention in Territories, after voting for the Compromise of 1850."

"The history of Massachusetts is the history of constitutional liberty," Douglas declared, ever the politician flattering a home crowd. "The battles of the Revolution were all fought in defense of the right of people, of colonies, and provinces and territories, to manage their own affairs."

During Harvard's commencement exercises, Douglas sat on the platform with Massachusetts's most prominent politicians—Governor Nathaniel P. Banks and Senator Charles Sumner. Also present was Edward Everett, former Harvard president and John Bell's running mate. Everett was a unionist, at least, so Douglas could tolerate his company. At the post-commencement banquet, Harvard president Cornelius Felton introduced Douglas as a founder of the University of Chicago.

"I wish I had been a son of Harvard," Douglas responded, "but if I am not her son, I might now at least claim to call myself a friend of the family."

Douglas had no prospect of carrying Massachusetts, one of the most antislavery states in the nation. Massachusetts had a different conception of liberty than Douglas, who believed it was for Whites only. The commonwealth's governor and both its senators were Free-Soilers or outright abolitionists. Boston was the home of William Lloyd Garrison, publisher of the *Liberator* and founder of the American Anti-Slavery Society, to whose radicalism Douglas had so often tried to tie Lincoln during their debates. In 1854, after the arrest and trial of escaped slave Anthony Burns caused a riot that killed a prison guard, President Pierce sent federal troops to Boston to ensure Burns was returned to his master in Virginia. Massachusetts then tried to undermine the Fugitive Slave Law with a "liberty law" guaranteeing slaves a trial by jury. This was the "sectional prejudice" Douglas had claimed to deplore during his speech at Revere House, but Massachusetts was rich in historic monuments, and Douglas wanted to claim them all as birthplaces of popular sovereignty. At the Lexington battlefield, he donated $160 to the Lexington Monument Fund. In Charlestown, where he had been invited by the mayor to view the seventeen-year-old Bunker Hill Monument, he declared in the shadow of the obelisk that "the men who fought against British tyranny at Lexington and Bunker's Hill, had contended for the same right—the inalienable right of self-government—which I am contending for now. Remain true to the great principle which your forefathers established at such cost, and cherish the policy of nonintervention in the domestic affairs of different states and territories as the bond of mutual peace and prosperity."

Then Douglas headed north to Vermont, to his hometown of Brandon. He would receive a cordial homecoming for a returning son, but a few months hence, he would lose Vermont to Lincoln by the largest margin of any free state.

Brandon House, Brandon, Vermont, July 28, 1860

WELCOME OF HON. STEPHEN A. DOUGLAS TO HIS NATIVE TOWN!! read the placards posted around Brandon, a village of 3,000 built along the falls of the Neshoba River, in the Green Mountains of western Vermont. "This distinguished gentleman, with his estimable lady, are expected to visit Brandon, the town of his birth, on Saturday 28th inst., arriving at 4 o'clock P.M. when he will be received by a Committee of Citizens, with a band of music and military escort, and conducted to Brandon House, where suitable addresses may be expected."

When Douglas arrived, at four thirty in the afternoon, the band struck up "Hail, Columbia!" and "Hail to the Chief." The Allen Grays formed a square around the senator's carriage, which halted for a few moments before his birthplace, a white frame house beside the Baptist Church. There, Douglas's father had fallen dead of a heart attack before the fire, while holding his two-month-old son in his arms.

Brandon welcomed Douglas with all the pageantry a little mill town could muster for the return of its most famous native, and the visit of a presidential candidate. Its enthusiasm for Douglas the Vermonter, however, did not extend to Douglas the politician. Since Douglas had left, in the 1830s, abolitionism had gone from a fringe belief espoused by a few heaven-on-Earth idealists to the mainstream of Brandon politics. Motivated by the revivalism of the Second Great Awakening, Brandon's Baptist Church condemned slavery as a sin and opened its doors to meetings of the local Anti-Slavery Society. The state's Baptist newspaper, the abolitionist *Vermont Telegraph*, was published in Brandon, and its state representative, a member of the Liberty Party, passed a bill guaranteeing freedom to any escaped slave who reached Vermont, in defiance of the Fugitive Slave Law.

Years before, while receiving an honorary degree from Middlebury College, Douglas had remarked that Vermont was an excellent place to be born, provided one emigrated early. Even before he reached Brandon, he received a letter from a local woman asking, "Was it not rather an afterthought to perpetuate such a joke at the expense of your native state?"

During his speech in front of Brandon House, with the forest-clad mountains to his left and the cascading river to his right, Douglas tried to explain himself. In unconquerable Vermont, which resisted not only the British crown, but annexation by New York, he had learned to love liberty and self-government.

"I once remarked, perhaps half in jest, that Vermont was a good state to be born in provided you emigrate when young," Douglas said. "So I say now, Vermont is a glorious place to be born in—to educate and train your children. Here, you inculcate virtue, you train them in the habits of industry—you teach them the necessity of labor."

Emigration, though, was what cemented the Union. In Illinois, Douglas had mingled with the "best bloods" of New England, New York, Kentucky, Virginia, and South Carolina, whose features were "all blended in a single generation."

"One thing is certain," he asserted. "You will have to go to Illinois for your next president. Illinois is rich in corn, in commercial wealth, and rich in candidates for the presidency."

Brandon would go to Lincoln for its next president. In November, Brandon voted Republican, 403–102. As the *Brandon Gazette* noted,

Douglas may have hurt his cause by "appearing to assume that the Republicans by whom he was surrounded had evil intentions against the union. We assure him there could be no greater mistake. That nefarious game is played only by southern Democrats and their Northern abettors."

Despite those disagreements, Brandon's Republicans treated Douglas to a fireworks show and a concert by two cornet bands, even though some worried that such a friendly greeting to Douglas would help him win Vermont, or at least demonstrate that popular sovereignty had a following in New England. The next morning, Douglas and Adele left Brandon on the 7:00 train, bound for Burlington, Montpelier, Concord, Manchester, Nashua, Lowell, and Providence—all in states he would lose to Lincoln.

State House, Concord, New Hampshire, July 31, 1860

"The New Hampshire boy who removes west is as capable of governing himself as his brother who stays at home. Look around your own neighborhood. A gentleman has two sons. One is a restless, energetic, and daring fellow; the other has a good nature, good disposition, and is a quiet fellow. Which one went west, and which one stayed at home and lived with daddy and mamma?"

"Not the lazy one!"

"The bold and ambitious young fellow went to the prairie or the wilderness; carved out his own fortune, made his own farm, put up his own fences, and perhaps split his own rails! I reckon the wild boy had sown his wild oats pretty well, and was as capable of self-government as the brother who remained at home with daddy and mamma!

"The Republicans want the federal government to wield its power against slavery everywhere; and the Disunionists want it wielded for slavery everywhere. Thus you find an 'irrepressible conflict' between them. The one is the antipodes of the other, but each is necessary to the existence of the other. The Republicans of the North and the Disunionists of the South occupy precisely the same relation to each other as the two blades of a pair of scissors; they both turn on the same point and cut the opposite directions. Intervention by Congress in the territories is the point on which both turn.

"I presume that many of you have business before Congress of some kind or other. If so, ask your Representative, when he comes home, what became of the bill. He will tell you he did the best he could, but it was lost for the want of time."

"That's so!"

"Congress lost the whole session in discussion of the slavery question, and there was no time for the regular business of the session. One might be interested in the Pacific Railroad bill; another in the French Spoliation Bill. And when you ask for them, you were told they were lost for want of time. Slavery occupied the whole time. The Negro question takes up all the time and there is no time left to attend to the material needs of the county."

"The interests of White folks!"

"Yes, the interests of White folks. In my opinion, this government is the White man's government. It was made by White men for the benefit of White men. And I think White men have a right to a small portion of the time, at least, to attend to their business. Now, you will never have appropriate legislation on these questions—and I am not discussing what that legislation should be—until you banish the Negro question from the halls of Congress."

Rocky Point, Warwick, Rhode Island, August 2, 1860

At the last stop on his New England tour, Douglas was the guest of honor at the largest clambake in Rhode Island's history. ("Arrangements all made," H. B. Sayles of Providence wired Douglas. "You arrive here Wednesday Clam bake Thursday next week. No failure must occur.") He had drawn a crowd of 10,000 in Providence, but he drew an even bigger crowd to Rocky Point, a promontory that thrust itself into Narragansett Bay. From morning to early afternoon, steamers arrived from Providence, crowded with supporters of Lincoln who nonetheless wanted "to see and hear a statesman of Mr. Douglas's acknowledged ability and pluck." And, of course, to eat clams, their state's favorite delicacy.

Douglas had never been to a clambake, but he was eager to experience "one of the peculiar institutions" of Rhode Island. Every state had its own peculiar institution, Douglas told the masses, and "ought to respect the others."

"There is a charm about this beautiful day, a life in this sea air, and something in that peculiar institution that makes me think you can afford to bargain with our Southern friends that if they will let you alone you will let them alone," Douglas said. "I have more fondness for your clams than I have for their Negroes; still, every man to his taste, and if they prefer them, we must respect them."

Douglas ended his New England journey with twelve days in Newport, dancing at balls with Adele, swimming in the sea, and attending lectures at the annual meeting of the American Association for the Advancement of Science. No one was fooled by the recreational crescendo to his sojourn, just as no one had been fooled by his protestations that he was simply attending to personal business in New England. There was no distinction between Douglas the man and Douglas the politician: his character was so defined by ambition that he was incapable of any action that would not bring him closer to consummating his desire for the presidency.

"No other man in the Union would have the audacity to stump the country as a candidate for the presidency," a newspaper editorialized. "In any other equally prominent politician, such a course would excite general disgust, but it is so thoroughly in keeping with his character and political habits that no one thinks it worth while even to affect surprise."

Douglas's campaign was "not a seemly or a welcome sight" wrote the *New York Times*, because the presidency was "too high to be reached by a mere stump-speaker, and too dignified to be canvassed for like a County Clerkship or a seat in Congress." Henry C. Whitney, a friend of Lincoln's, felt that Douglas's "forlorn" campaign of making speeches to anyone he thought might vote for him "was a very humiliating and for that time unique spectacle."

Douglas was mocked for declaring that his destination was his seventy-one-year-old mother's house in upstate New York, but never getting around to visiting her, even though his campaign took him to Troy and Albany. A political cartoon depicted Douglas toting a rucksack, walking in the opposite direction of a signpost pointing toward Clifton Springs, where Sarah Fiske lived with her second husband, Gehazi Granger. (Both Douglas's mother and stepfather would outlive him by eight years.) "This is a very crooked road," the caption read, "but I keep right along. I think I'll find Clifton Springs, where my Mother lives, soon after the Election." A reporter for the *Troy Whig* located Sarah, who told him she was hoping to see her Stephen on every arriving train, because "he never writes when we may expect him." Douglas's enemies found the fact that Douglas's mother couldn't locate her son so amusing they published a broadside titled 'BOY' LOST, with this description of Douglas: "He is about five feet nothing in height, and about the same in diameter the other way. He has a red face, short legs, and a large belly. Answers to the name of 'Little Giant.' Talks a great deal, and always about himself. He has an idea that he is a candidate for the presidency. Had on, when he left, drab pants, a white vest, and blue coat with brass buttons; the tail is very near the ground. Any information concerning him will be gratefully received by his afflicted mother."

State Fairgrounds, Springfield, Illinois, August 8, 1860

While Douglas scurried around the country, futilely insisting that he was the only man who could save the Union, Lincoln remained at home in Springfield, awaiting the duties of a presidency that seemed more inevitable each day. As the nominee of a united Republican Party, contending with a Democracy divided three ways, Lincoln was advised that his most prudent course of action was to do nothing and say nothing, right up until Election Day. William Cullen Bryant, editor of the *New York Evening Post*, wrote Lincoln that candidates who offered no opinions stood the best chance of success: "I am sure that I but express the wish of the vast majority of your friends when I say that they want you to make no speeches, write no letters as a candidate, enter into no pledges, make no promises, nor even give any of those kind words which men are apt to interpret into promises."

After winning the nomination, Lincoln engaged John Nicolay to handle his mail. Nicolay's chief function was repelling correspondents who expressed curiosity about Lincoln's life or principles. At Lincoln's instruction, he drafted a pair of form letters to "Applicants for Biographical Data" and "Requests for Political Opinions." The latter informed letter-writers that Lincoln's "positions were well-known when he was nominated, and . . . he must not now embarrass the canvass by undertaking to shift or modify them." Lincoln did consent to draft an autobiographical sketch for journalist John L. Scripps, who was writing a campaign biography that would be published by the *Chicago Press and Tribune*. ("He regrets his want of education, and does what he can to supply the want.") He also responded to a letter from Abraham Jonas, who informed him that Democrats were collecting affidavits from Irishmen who claimed to have seen Lincoln leaving a Know Nothing Lodge in Quincy in 1854—a charge that could damage Lincoln with immigrant voters. Lincoln wrote back that he had never entered a Know Nothing lodge "at Quincy, or elsewhere."

Throughout the summer, Lincoln received increasingly optimistic letters from his allies, assuring him of success in the swing states in November. After the Democratic convention shattered a second time, Schuyler Colfax wrote from Indiana that "no ticket could have been nominated by the seceders better calculated to divide the Inda. Dem'y and assume the State to you than Breckenridge [*sic*] and Lane." Pennsylvania's Alexander McClure told Lincoln, "This State is confessedly ours," and Lyman Trumbull predicted Douglas would not win a single electoral vote. Even Thurlow Weed believed New York was "abundantly safe," despite his and his fellow Republicans' disappointment over Seward's defeat in Chicago. To cultivate Weed's support, Lincoln had entertained him in Springfield in the days after the convention.

Though confined to Springfield, Lincoln still tried to involve himself in the campaign. Richard W. Thompson, a leader of the Constitutional Union

Party in Indiana, wrote that he was inclined to support Lincoln rather than Bell, and might be further inclined if the two men could get together and discuss the campaign. Lincoln dispatched Congressman Henry Winter Davis of Maryland—David Davis's cousin—to meet with Thompson in Washington. Then he sent Nicolay to see Thompson in Terre Haute with the instructions, "Tell him my motto is 'fairness to all,' But commit me to nothing." Thompson ended up supporting Lincoln to prevent Douglas from winning the state. Lincoln broke his practice of not discussing his record to reassure James E. Harvey of Pennsylvania that he was in favor of tariffs—an issue more important than slavery in that state—providing past examples of his support.

Only once, though, did Lincoln appear in public during the 1860 presidential campaign: at a Republican rally in Springfield, on August 8. He could hardly have avoided it, since the entire Republican movement in the Midwest was, essentially, coming to him. Among the featured speakers were Gustave Koerner, Senator James Rood Doolittle of Wisconsin, and Lyman Trumbull. Wide Awake companies from Illinois, Missouri, and Wisconsin converged on Springfield, riding on half-fare excursions. Beginning at nine o'clock, the companies, whose members numbered in the thousands, marched past Lincoln's house on their way to the fairgrounds. The ten-mile-long procession lasted two and a half hours. Lincoln emerged to greet them, wearing a white suit for the hot day.

By midafternoon, the fairgrounds were packed with Republicans on a summer Wednesday. It was a thrilling sight and a thrilling day, because the Republicans knew they were going to win the presidency: Douglas and his demoralized Democrats could not attract such crowds, even in the great cities of the East. The *Chicago Press and Tribune* called "the Republican demonstration . . . the largest, most imposing and enthusiastic ever held in the United States."

At three o'clock, Lincoln arrived at the fairgrounds in a carriage. Everywhere, the speaking stopped, as the crowds converged on Lincoln with such excitement that onlookers feared they would crush the carriage and injure the candidate. Lincoln was finally conveyed safely to a platform, where he waited several minutes for the cheering to subside before saying . . . nothing.

"My fellow citizens," he told the crowd, "I appear among you upon this occasion with no intention of making a speech. It has been my purpose, since I have been placed in my present position, to make no speeches. This assemblage having been drawn together at the place of my residence, it appeared to be the wish of those constituting this vast assembly to see me; and it is certainly my wish to see all of you. I appear upon this ground here at this time only for the purpose of affording myself the best opportunity of seeing you, and enabling you to see me. I confess with gratitude, be it understood, that I did not suppose my appearance among you would create the tumult which I now witness."

That was about it; in his present state, suspended between politician and president, committed to silence, Lincoln was merely a totem, an idol. He could offer his followers nothing but his physical manifestation, which was enough to set off a demonstration louder and more enthusiastic than any partisan speech. The more Douglas spoke, the more he diminished in stature; the less Lincoln said, the more he grew. He asked his listeners to "kindly let me be silent" and leave the partisan addresses to "others of our friends."

The most significant friend was Trumbull, who spoke that evening in a Wigwam erected for the rally, after a torchlight parade and fireworks display. Douglas's seatmate spent two hours attacking Douglas. Listing five examples of Douglas contradicting his former principles, mostly to enable the spread of slavery, he called the Democrat "an imposter and a cheat." The "Douglas party" was the "Northern wing of the Buzzard Party," and the public was sick enough of Douglas's "windings and twisting" "to spew him out of their mouths in November." Popular sovereignty was anarchy. Utah could not legalize polygamy; Kansas could not reintroduce the African slave trade; no government could sanction theft and murder. The territories belonged to all twenty million Americans, not just the first 5,000 settlers. Douglas was also lying when he said the Republicans opposed the admission of new slave states. Lincoln himself had refuted that at Freeport.

Lincoln could not endorse Trumbull's remarks, but he doubtless agreed with them. He had said much the same about Douglas in their Senate debates, but not in such vituperative language. Douglas had been sitting beside Lincoln on the platform, and Lincoln was a man of decorum.

City of Norfolk Courthouse, Norfolk, Virginia, August 25, 1860

"My dear Judge," wrote A. D. Banks of Hampton, in an importuning letter to Douglas. "It is of the first importance that you should visit Virginia. Our friends have become a little dispirited. All the leaders and nearly all the press have caved in. The masses have nothing to rally them. Do come at once."

As Douglas's prospects of victory became more remote, he began campaigning less for himself, and more against disunion. For the first time in his career, Douglas had found a cause he valued more than his own ambition. Where better to take his message than the South, where he could appeal to the remaining Unionists not to truckle or compromise with secessionists? Douglas himself wouldn't. Earlier that summer, Jefferson Davis—who would have preferred the Devil to Douglas on a Democratic ticket—had proposed that all Lincoln's opponents drop out of the race and support a Stop Lincoln candidate, such as Horatio Seymour (even though Seymour had declared he would not run). Bell and Breckinridge were amenable, but Douglas refused, not just because it would have meant making common cause with the Fire-Eaters, but because he didn't think it would work—his Northern supporters would vote for Lincoln rather than a candidate endorsed by the South.

As he had in New England, Douglas found a personal reason to go south. The mother of his first wife had died in June in Rockingham County, North Carolina, and her family asked Douglas to help settle the estate, which included 900 acres of land and slaves bequeathed to Douglas's sons. (Douglas's elder son, Robert, would settle on his inheritance and become a justice of the North Carolina Supreme Court—as a Republican. Robert's son would serve as the state's attorney general.)

When U.S. Attorney Robert Dick of Greensboro learned that Douglas was coming to North Carolina, he urged him to attend a convention of regular Democrats who planned to meet on August 30 to nominate pro-Union candidates. Dick had been a delegate to the conventions in Charleston and Baltimore. When the rest of the North Carolinians walked out, Dick remained to vote for Douglas. Most Southern politicians and newspapers were supporting Breckinridge, but Dick tried to encourage Douglas: "Breckinridge won't get North Carolina—that's certain—and I greatly hope and believe that he will not win a single Southern State except South Carolina."

Douglas and Adele traveled by steamer from Baltimore to Portsmouth, Virginia, where they were welcomed by a gun salute and spent the afternoon greeting supporters at the Ocean House. In the evening, Douglas spoke to a crowd of 6,000 from the top step of the courthouse stairs. His message was more about preserving the Union than his own presidential hopes.

"I did not come here to purchase your votes," he said, "I came here to compare notes, and to see if there is not some common principle, some line of policy around which all Union-loving men, North and South, may rally to preserve the glorious Union against Northern and Southern agitators. There is a larger feeling of self pride, of honest ambition, and of patriotism mingled with my efforts in the cause I have undertaken to carry out than there is a desire or longing to be elected President of the United States. I desire no man to vote for me unless he hopes and desires to see the Union maintained and preserved intact."

In the middle of the two-hour speech, William Lamb, editor of the *Southern Argus*, handed Douglas a clipping from his newspaper, which contained two questions for the candidate, composed by a Breckinridge elector.

"I am not in the habit of answering questions propounded to me in the course of an address," Douglas responded, "but on this occasion, I will comply with the request and respond very frankly and unequivocally to these two questions."

Douglas read from the newspaper: "The first question is, 'If Abraham Lincoln be elected President of the United States, will the Southern states be justified in seceding from the Union?'

"To this I emphatically answer no!" Douglas shouted to enormous applause. "The election of a man to the presidency by the American people, in conformity with the Constitution of the United States, would not justify any attempt at dissolving this glorious confederacy! Now I will read to you the next question, and then answer it.

"Question, 'If they, the Southern states, secede from the Union upon the inauguration of Abraham Lincoln, before he commits an overt act against their constitutional rights, will you advise or vindicate resistance by force to their secession?'"

"Bell men say no!" a voice shouted.

Douglas, though, said yes.

"I answer emphatically that it is the duty of the President of the United States, and all others in authority under him, to enforce the laws of the United States as passed by Congress and as the courts expound them. The President of the United States, whoever he may be, should treat all attempts to break up the Union by resistance to its laws, as Old Hickory treated the nullifiers in 1832."

Americans had a right to overthrow the government "whenever it proves destructive to the ends for which it was established," Douglas said. However, "the mere inauguration of a president of the United States whose political opinions were in my judgment hostile to the Constitution and safety of the Union, without an overt act on his part, without striking such a blow at our Constitution or our rights, is not such a grievance as would justify revolution or secession." Whoever was elected president "must be sustained in the exercise of all his just Constitutional prerogatives and powers," but if he overstepped those powers, he should be hanged just as John Brown was hanged in Virginia, Douglas announced to a storm of applause.

Douglas suggested the same questions be posed to Breckinridge, whose candidacy was guaranteeing Lincoln's election by dividing the Democratic vote. If Southern Democrats put Lincoln in the White House, then asked

Douglas to help them break up the Union because they couldn't abide his presidency, he would have just a few words for them: "No—never on Earth."

Douglas had stood on the steps of a courthouse in a slaveholding city and declared secession unconstitutional. Southern newspapers condemned Douglas's "Norfolk Doctrine." The Jackson *Mississippian* called it "treason." A South Carolina newspaper warned that Douglas's speech should not deter Southerners from "asserting and protecting their rights." Douglas newspapers, such as the *Memphis Daily Appeal* and the *Montgomery Confederation* pointed out that he had also warned Lincoln not to violate the Constitution, and had not suggested military action to coerce seceding states back into the Union. The secessionist press was lost to Douglas. A few days later, in North Carolina, he would repeat his defense of a president's duty to maintain the Union, whoever that president was.

State Capitol, Raleigh, North Carolina, August 30, 1860

Douglas's opponents accused him of holding slippery political principles, which he altered to justify whichever law or policy he thought would bring him closer to the presidency. This was often true. In 1850, he codified the Missouri Compromise. Four years later, he discarded it to pass the Kansas-Nebraska Act. Douglas did believe wholeheartedly in the Union, though, and he also believed that all his political twists and turns were motivated by the desire to preserve it. The political situation had changed rapidly in the 1850s, with the emergence of the abolitionist Republicans and the secessionist Southern Democrats, so Douglas had to change, too, to prevent the extremists from pulling the country apart.

As his campaign pressed deeper into the South, closer to the heart of secession, Douglas made his most personal, emotional appeal yet for the preservation of the Union. He loved his children, he said, but did not desire to see them survive the Union, which could be saved only by defeating the disunionists for every office, from the legislature to the presidency. His adopted state of Illinois, he told the crowd in Raleigh, was the Union in miniature: there, he was a New England Yankee, who had settled along-side Virginians and North Carolinians. As if enlisting the support of the Founders in his argument for the Union, Douglas spoke beside a statue of George Washington.

"You cannot sever this Union unless you cut the heartstrings that bind father to son, daughter to mother, and brother to sister in all our new states and territories," he said to cheers. "Besides the ties of blood and affection that bind us to each of the states, we have commercial intercourse and pecuniary interests that we are not willing to surrender. Do you think that a citizen of Illinois will ever consent to pay duties at the Custom House when he ships his commerce down the Mississippi to supply the people below? You cannot sever this Union without blasting every hope and prospect that a Western man has on this Earth. Then, having so deep a stake in the Union, we are determined to maintain it, and we know, but one mode by which it can be maintained; that is to enforce rigidly and in good faith every clause, every line, every syllable of the Constitution as our Fathers bequeathed it to us, and of protecting every right to it, and then hanging every man who takes up arms against it."

"That is Southern enough for us," a voice cried.

Douglas's speech was not Southern enough for the North Carolina Democratic convention, which instructed the state's electors to vote for Bell or Breckinridge if it looked as though Douglas could not win in the Electoral College. (Breckinridge would win a majority in North Carolina, while Douglas received 2,737 votes, a measly 2.83 percent. The Southern unionists, whose votes he was pursuing, went for Bell.)

State Capitol, Richmond, Virginia, September 1, 1860

Douglas was ridiculed in Richmond, the future Confederate capital, where he stopped on his way back north. He paraded from the St. Charles Hotel to the capitol grounds in an open carriage, drawn by four horses trotting behind a donkey, accompanied by an armory band blaring "See the Conquering Heroes!" In the rear of the procession, the *Richmond Enquirer* mockingly reported, were "nearly two hundred niggers kept at a respectful distance—in consideration of the Senator's avowed preference for 'clams.'"

Another newspaper commented on Douglas's old slouch hat, which made him look like "a weary, way-worn, backwoods traveler." His voice was hoarse, and his speech was interrupted by a heckler.

"I say, let the people of each territory settle the slavery question for themselves," Douglas croaked.

"How about the clam question?" a bystander asked.

"I understand that trick of old. The enemy is sending outsiders here to disturb a Democratic meeting."

"What's the meaning of popular sovereignty?" asked another heckler.

"If that individual hasn't the brains to define the term by himself, I am obliged to tell him I left my dictionary at home," Douglas snapped, his nerves on edge after a week of debating secessionists.

Douglas did receive the endorsement of Governor John Letcher, who believed the division of the Democratic Party was no more necessary in 1860 than it had been in 1856. Less than eight months later, Letcher would appoint United States Army colonel Robert E. Lee to command the Army of Northern Virginia.

Monument Square, Baltimore, Maryland, September 6, 1860

Crossing the Potomac River to Union-friendly Maryland, Douglas told a border state audience that, during his Southern tour, he had discovered "a mature plan" to break up the country. Its signal would be the election of Lincoln. The ringleaders wanted Lincoln elected, to justify secession. Douglas did not believe every Breckinridge man was a disunionist, he said, but he did believe every disunionist was a Breckinridge man, so he wanted Breckinridge to answer "whether or not he will enforce the laws of the land in the event of an attempt to secede or break up this union."

Breckinridge did have an answer for Douglas. In his lone campaign speech, at Henry Clay's Ashland estate, he defended the Dred Scott decision, and attacked the Freeport Doctrine, but denied that he had any intention of breaking up the Union. Any such suggestion was scurrilous campaign rhetoric from a desperate Douglas: "It is quite natural for a gentleman as much interested as he is to think than any man who approves of my principles must be a disunionist."

Great Western Depot, Springfield, Illinois, October 1, 1860

William Seward had recovered enough from his convention defeat to campaign for Lincoln in the Northwest, embarking on a five-week barnstorming tour of Michigan, Wisconsin, Minnesota, Iowa, Missouri, Kansas, Illinois, and Ohio. Julius White, a member of the committee organizing Seward's Chicago speech, encouraged Lincoln to meet him there, to smooth over any remaining hard feelings about the nomination: "He is an old soldier in the cause—has an army of admirers, and the news that our candidate gave him a cordial greeting on our own soil would manifestly produce a feeling of gratification, whenever a friend of Mr. Seward is found." Davis, though, advised Lincoln to stay put in Springfield, as he had done throughout the campaign, but to send "as many of your personal friends to Chicago as can go."

Lincoln abided by Davis's advice, although he was becoming bored by lack of involvement in his own campaign. He considered accepting an invitation to a horse show in Springfield, Massachusetts, because it would allow him to visit his son Robert, just enrolled at Harvard. George G. Fogg, secretary of the Republican National Committee, discouraged the trip. Lincoln's silence made him appear more confident and dignified than Douglas. Any public appearance outside his hometown "would relieve Douglas of the charge of being the only stump candidate for the Presidency." To while away the days until the election, Lincoln composed an imaginary debate between Douglas and Breckinridge:

Breck—We insisted on Congressional protection of Slave property in the national territories; and you broke with us professedly
because of this—

Doug—Exactly so; I insisted upon nonintervention—

Breck—And yet you are forming coalitions, wherever you
can, with Bell, who is for this very Congressional practice of
slavery—for the very thing which you pretend drove you to
separate from us—for Bell, with all his Know-Nothingism, and
anti-democracy of every sort.

Doug—Bell is a good Union-man; and you, and your friends,
are a set of disunionists.

Breck—Bah! You have known us long, and ultimately; why did
you never denounce us as disunionists, till since our refusal to
support you for the Presidency? Why have you never warned the
North against our disunion schemes, till since the Charleston
and Baltimore sessions of the National Convention? Will you
answer, Senator Douglas?

Doug—The condition of my throat will not permit me to carry
this conversation any further—

No one had more experience debating Douglas than Lincoln, but
Lincoln never put Douglas at a loss for words, as Breckinridge did in the
fantastic conversation he created. It must have been a satisfying exercise.
Lincoln would not travel to Chicago to stand beside Seward on a speakers'
platform. He did, however, agree to meet Seward at the Springfield train station, during a stopover on a run from St. Louis to Chicago. Their encounter
lasted twenty minutes. Lincoln boarded the train and was introduced to Seward
by Lyman Trumbull. Charles Francis Adams, grandson and great-grandson of

presidents, son of a congressman, was traveling with Seward. Adams thought that Lincoln was "awkward" and Seward "constrained." Their conference was "exactly as if a couple of ordinary business men had come down to the station to meet some travellers passing through." Seward stepped onto the platform and gave a short speech, assuring Springfieldians that "New York will give a generous, and cheerful, and effective, support to your neighbor, Abraham Lincoln." Seward then continued on to Chicago, where he made a few remarks that night from the balcony of the Tremont House.

The Wigwam, Chicago, Illinois, October 2, 1860

Seward drew a crowd of 10,000 to the site of his convention defeat, many of them Wide Awakes who traveled from all over the Northwest on over-crowded trains. The Republican National Convention had been desperate not to nominate Seward, but during the campaign, he was the party's most popular speaker. Lincoln, who merely opposed the spread of slavery, was not antislavery enough for some abolitionists. In September, a group gathered in Worcester, Massachusetts, to discuss forming an Abolitionist Party, which would draw votes away from the Republicans. Wendell Phillips, who preferred disunion to sharing a nation with the slave states, called Lincoln "The Slavehound of Illinois."

Seward's support was a sign that the radical and moderate wings of the Republican Party were united in defeating three candidates who were either indifferent to the spread of slavery or wanted the federal government to support its spread throughout the country.

"I care not, fellow citizens, what reckless men may say in the heat of debate, or under the influence of passion or prejudice," Seward said inside the Wigwam. "It is a matter of indifference whether slavery shall pervade the whole land, or a part of the land, and freedom the residue—that freedom and slavery may take their chances—who 'don't care whether slavery is voted up or voted down.' There is no man who has an enlightened conscience who is indifferent on the subject of human bondage."

The "don't care" quote was Douglas. Seward thanked "your distinguished senator" for abrogating the Missouri Compromise, because that had "shattered" the existing political parties with the result that their antislavery remnants reassembled as Republicans, who believed in a creed of "free soil, free labor, equal rights, and universal suffrage."

"Mr. Lincoln represents the Republican Party," Seward said. "He represents a party which has determined that not one more slave should be imported from Africa, or transferred from any slave state, domestic or foreign, onto the common soil of the United States."

Bell's Constitutional Unionists wanted to ignore slavery altogether. Breckinridge's Democrats wanted to use the power of the federal government to extend slavery. Douglas's Democrats were not a positive party. They wanted Congress to ignore slavery and leave it up to the territories. That was their idea of compromise, but it wasn't compromise enough for the South. The South had repudiated Douglas, "the ablest man among them," because "they will not be satisfied with a Squatter Sovereignty that gives any territory whatever to a free state."

Only the Republicans were a positive party, said Seward. The Republicans had one faith, one creed, one baptism, and would have three victories. The crowd laughed along with Seward. Three days later, Douglas arrived home in Chicago to deliver a response.

Tremont House, Chicago, Illinois, October 5, 1860

The northwestern leg of Douglas's campaign began with—at last—a visit to his mother. Speaking in Clifton Springs, Douglas said he was glad to relieve the anxiety of the Republicans by letting them know that he had found his mother, "who, God bless her, was in fine health, and in no way annoyed by the comments of the partisan press."

From Clifton Springs, Douglas moved westward to Syracuse, Rochester, and Buffalo, speaking to thousands in each city. New York Democrats were attempting to assemble a fusion ticket, which would divide the state's electoral votes between Douglas and Breckinridge. Douglas refused. Sharing a ticket with Breckinridge would mean giving up the claim that he was the one true Democratic nominee. Running alone would cost him 50,000 votes, but if Lincoln lost New York, the election would be decided by the House of Representatives. The House might elect Breckinridge, or it might deadlock, in which case the Senate's choice of a vice president would become president. Because Southern Democrats dominated the Senate, that would certainly be Breckinridge's running mate, Joseph Lane. Either of those outcomes would have been worse than Lincoln's election.

"By God, sir," Douglas told a congressman, "the election shall never go into the House: before it shall go into the House, I will throw it to Lincoln."

When Douglas appeared in Columbus, the *Ohio Statesman* published a few verses of campaign doggerel in honor of Douglas and his running mate, former Georgia governor Herschel Johnson, who had joined him on the Northwestern swing; it was typical of nineteenth-century newspaper prosody:

> *They look to you as true as true and upright friends*
> *Of all the people—your affection*
> *Is national—the Union depends,*
> *The people know, on your election:*
> *And Democratic patriots*
> *Will frown upon disunion plots*

In Toledo, Douglas crossed paths with Seward, who was heading back to New York after his Wigwam speech. Seward was awoken at midnight by cheering from the platform. Moments later, Douglas barged onto the eastbound train, demanding "Where's Seward?" He was clutching a bottle of whiskey—his normal campaign fuel. (Liquor was not the only medication the exhausted Douglas used to treat campaign weariness. In Cleveland, his voice was such an inaudible croak that he squeezed lemons down his throat during a speech.)

Seward's berth was pointed out to Douglas, who pulled aside the curtain and awoke his fellow senator.

"Come governor, they want to see you," shouted Douglas, who had just addressed a crowd on the platform.

"How are you, Judge?" Seward greeted Douglas groggily. "No, I can't go out. I'm sleepy."

"Well, what of that?" Douglas snapped. "They get me out when I'm sleepy." Seward repeated his demurral.

"Well, if you can't go out, you shan't," Douglas said finally and left the train.

The next morning, Seward told Adams that Douglas's invitation to speak was "his idea of political courtesy, but I didn't mean to let him exhibit me to his followers, just to make a little political capital for himself. So far as Douglas himself is concerned, we've always been on the most friendly terms."

"Douglas's conduct on the Senate floor does not always square with that fact," Adams remarked.

"No," Seward replied, "but Douglas always did what you refer to for political effect. Personally, we have always been on friendly terms."

Douglas and Seward were friends, but also political rivals; Douglas was determined to make a bigger display than Seward in his own hometown. He was met by a reception committee in Michigan City. Arriving in Chicago at 8:00 P.M., he was escorted to the Tremont House by a torchlight procession than included four hundred "Ever Readies," the Democratic counterpart of the Wide Awakes. The procession was swelled with his working-class Irish followers, who, according to the *Press and Tribune*, had been lured away from their "coal-heaving, and hod-carrying and lumber-piling" with the promise of "tin cints an hour" to attend their idol's political wake.

Douglas's response to Seward included his usual demagogic accusations that the Republicans were the party of racial equality. He spoke from the Tremont House balcony, his stubby figure illuminated in gaslight for a crowd that covered five city blocks, surrounded by buildings lit up for this occasion. Addressing a Northwestern audience allowed him to make the same charges of disunionism against Lincoln that he had made against Breckinridge in the South. Seward's "irrepressible conflict" and Lincoln's "House Divided" were both incitements to "undisguised revolution." Their plan to eliminate slavery nationwide would break up the Union, just as surely as the Southern Democrats' plan to open all the territories to slavery would.

"I am no alarmist," Douglas said, but "I believe that this country is in more danger than at any other moment since I have known anything of public life. This nation cannot be maintained unless Northern abolitionism and Southern disunion are buried in a common grave."

After Douglas spoke his final words, fireworks exploded over downtown Chicago. Seward's speech hadn't ended with such a display.

Springfield, Illinois, October 9, 1860

The Republicans awaited the results of the statewide elections in Pennsylvania, Ohio, and Indiana almost as eagerly as they awaited November. If they carried those three Lower North states, they would carry the nation. Pennsylvania and Indiana were particularly important, since Buchanan had won both in 1856.

That evening, telegrams arrived in Springfield, bearing news of Republican victories in all three states. From Simon Cameron in Harrisburg: "Pennsylvania comes greeting with twenty five thousand for Curtin." From Cleveland: "Returns indicate Ohio has gone Republican by thirty thousand majority." From Indianapolis: "Indiana Republican by over fifteen thousand (15000) seven (7) Republican congressmen legislature Republican majority. Glory enough."

Pennsylvania and Indiana elected Republican governors; in all three states, Republicans won a majority of congressional seats. The Republicans claimed the Fillmore vote, the middle ground for which both parties were contending. David Davis was said to have received the returns while trying a criminal case. The three-hundred-pound man was supposedly so excited he kicked over the clerk's desk, turned a double somersault, and declared court adjourned until after the presidential election, shouting deliriously, "Lincoln's election is a fixed fact: I know Douglas is sorry he didn't die when he was little!"

The day after telegrams came letters, declaring Douglas finished and Lincoln elected.

"Your majority over Douglas, will be in Nov. at least double that of Lane," Caleb Smith wrote from Indianapolis. "Our success in Pa. and Ind. Settles the presidential contest, and your election is now as certain as the continuance of your life."

Lincoln himself was confident enough to write to Seward, "[it] now really looks as if the Government is about to fall into our hands. Pennsylvania, Ohio, and Indiana have surpassed all expectations, even the most extravagant."

In Springfield, local Wide Awakes fired salutes, set off fireworks, and marched to Lincoln's house, where they cheered for the candidate, for Pennsylvania, for Ohio and Indiana. Lincoln stood on his doorstep, bowing, but saying nothing, still bound to silence for another month.

Clinton House, Iowa City, Iowa, October 9, 1860

Douglas received news of the Republican victories after delivering a speech in Iowa City's City Square. It was a speech in which he still sounded like a candidate. He told Iowa's farmers that, unlike Lincoln, he would support a Homestead Bill, granting 160 acres of land to any settler. He called Lincoln the candidate of Southern disunionists, because his election would justify secession.

"They are doing everything in their power to enable Lincoln to be elected over myself," Douglas charged.

Shouts from the crowd: "They can't elect him. He can't be elected, never, never."

"No, my friends, he cannot," Douglas said. "I have seen enough to convince me that the American people never intend to entrust their destiny to the keeping of the Republican Party, and November will demonstrate that fact."

It was the last time Douglas would speak of victory from the stump. From his campaign headquarters in Washington, he received a telegram with the results from Pennsylvania, Ohio, and Indiana. As a practical, vote-counting politician, he knew what the numbers portended.

"Mr. Lincoln is the next president," Douglas told his secretary, James B. Sheridan. "We must try to save the Union. I will go south."

CHAPTER 8

THIS GLORIOUS UNION

Market Square, Memphis, Tennessee,
October 24, 1860

D ouglas's hopes for the presidency, the office he had coveted for a decade, were shattered. There was nothing to campaign for now but the Union. It must have galled Douglas to lose the prize to Abraham Lincoln, of all people. Their rivalry went back twenty years, to nights debating politics around the stove in the back room of Joshua Speed's store in Springfield, when Lincoln was a Sangamon County legislator and Douglas registrar of the Springfield Land Office. For most of those years, Douglas had gotten the better of Lincoln, right up through their Senate race. As even Lincoln admitted, he had been a failure at politics, while Douglas's name filled the nation.

Douglas was no idealist, nor was he a man who took political differences personally. He was friendly with Seward, after all. He was a practical politician who understood that, as Edmund Burke wrote, there were no permanent friends or enemies in his profession, only permanent interests.

There could be no more permanent interest than the Union: arguments for popular sovereignty meant nothing compared to arguments for the nation's continuing existence.

By going South, Douglas would not be campaigning for Lincoln, but he would be campaigning for acceptance of a Lincoln presidency, which he now saw as a fait accompli. The Fire-Eaters planned to use Lincoln's election to justify secession. Douglas hoped to persuade Southern audiences that no legally elected president, no matter how hostile to their way of life he may seem, provided license for breaking up the Union. He also hoped to persuade Southerners that Lincoln would be prevented, by the Constitution and a Democratic Congress, from trampling on their rights. Douglas was the greatest orator of his age, so he imagined his rhetoric could reach the hearts of the moderate, Union-loving masses, who were being led toward calamity by Fire-Eating newspaper publishers and politicians.

Of the four candidates in the 1860 presidential election, only Douglas was running a nationwide campaign. There were really two elections going on: one between Lincoln and Douglas in the free states, another between Bell and Breckinridge in the slave states. Among the slave states, Lincoln's name appeared on the ballot only in Maryland, Delaware, Virginia, Kentucky, and Missouri. He would finish last in all except Delaware. Support for Douglas would not exceed 20 percent in any slave state but Missouri—the only state he won.

Why did Douglas spend the last two weeks of the campaign in states he had no chance of winning? For one thing, he took the threat of secession far more seriously than the Republicans. Lincoln had written that "the people of the South have too much good sense, and good temper, to attempt the ruin of the government, rather than see it administered by the men who made it. At least, so I hope and believe." John Botts, a former congressional colleague from Virginia, reassured him that "in no probable event will there be any very formidable effort to break up the Union." George G. Fogg wrote Lincoln that "I do not believe there is any real danger of a secession of a single state."

Ohio journalist Donn Piatt ate supper in Lincoln's home just after the election and warned him that the South was serious about secession. The skeptical Lincoln could not understand that men "would get up in their wrath and fight for an idea," brushing off secession talk as political posturing.

"They won't give up the offices," he told Piatt. "Were it believed that vacant places could be had at the North Pole, the road there would be lined with dead Virginians."

Republicans dismissed the secession threat because they did not want the public to believe that voting for Lincoln would result in civil war. The Republicans were also a Northern party with no Southern adherents. In that provincial era, most Republicans had never visited the South. During the 1858 debates, Douglas called the Republicans a sectional party and declared that, just because he belonged to the stronger section, he would not vote to restrict the weaker section's rights. That was what he saw the Republicans trying to do in 1860. As steward of a Mississippi plantation, and widower of a wife from North Carolina, Douglas had more contact with the South and Southern attitudes than most Yankees. He caucused with Southern Democrats in the Senate and debated Southern senators over their demand for a slave code. He was a presidential candidate despite two attempts to undermine his nomination by Southerners who walked out of conventions in Charleston and Baltimore. When the Southern states threatened to walk out of the Union next, Douglas believed them.

Douglas could not go South immediately after the October elections; he still had a slate of Northwestern appearances to fulfill, in Iowa, Wisconsin, Michigan, Missouri and Illinois. After an October 22 speech in Centralia, Illinois—his final free-state rally—Douglas caught an Illinois Central train for Memphis, accompanied by Adele, his brother-in-law, James Madison Cutts Jr., and his secretary, James Sheridan. Douglas's last-ditch crusade to stop secession was not welcomed by all Southerners. From Virginia, the *Petersburg Bulletin* called him an "itinerant peddler of Yankee notions" who hated the South and whose entire campaign was "directed to the further-ance of Lincoln interests."

"We regard it as somewhat of a bold move on the part of Judge Douglas, to venture on Southern rail in the present excited condition of the public mind," the *Bulletin* editorialized. "We do not believe he will be permitted to finish out his appointments, but before the programme is completed, that he will be indignantly expelled from the limits of the South. And we sincerely hope so."

Memphis was friendlier to Douglas than most Southern cities. As a Mississippi River port, it received traffic from both North and South, so its merchants and bankers had a strong interest in maintaining the Union. The *Memphis Appeal*, the city's largest newspaper, endorsed Douglas, and pro-Douglas Democrats held ratification meetings in Memphis and the Arkansas and Mississippi Deltas, resisting the sentiment for Breckinridge in those states. Tennessee senator Andrew Johnson campaigned for Breckinridge in Memphis but refused to denounce Douglas, encouraging Northerners to vote for him to stop Lincoln.

Douglas arrived in Memphis at 11:00 P.M. on the 23rd, after a day of speeches. In Jackson, Tennessee, he spoke for two hours to a crowd of 10,000; he delivered whistle-stop homilies at Humboldt, Brownsville, Mason's Depot, and Grand Junction. In Bluff City, he was met by forty marshals on horseback, three bands, and a carriage drawn by four bay horses, which transported him from his rail car as cannons boomed and skyrockets and Roman candles colored the darkness. The *Appeal* compared his entrance into Memphis to Garibaldi entering Naples or Napoleon Milan. From the balcony of the Gayoso Hotel, Douglas explained that he had given three speeches in the last twenty-four hours without going to bed but promised to address all the great political topics the next day.

The next day, Douglas spoke for three hours in Market Square, not just to Memphians, but Kentuckians, Mississippians, and Alabamians who had ridden half-fare trains to the market city of the Mid-South. Douglas was addressing all Southerners, trying to reassure them that their rights and their property would be safe in the Union—even a Union presided over by Lincoln.

"I do not come to solicit your suffrages," he began, "but to make an appeal in behalf of the glorious Union by an exposition of those principles which, in my opinion, can only preserve the peace of this country."

Douglas believed in equal rights for all (White) citizens, including the right to bring slaves into the territories. The Constitution's Fugitive Slave Clause applied to persons "held to Service or labor in one State," thus making slaves a matter for the states, "beyond the reach of federal power, beyond the control of Northern abolitionists, where your Lincolns, your Sewards and your Chases cannot touch them."

In 1850, Douglas had stood up for the Great Compromise against "Seward, Chase and Sumner, and Giddings, and the whole abolition crew of the North, together with Jefferson Davis and Hunter and Mason, and the Fire-Eaters of the South." Why, in Chicago, he had stood down abolition mobs of free Blacks and runaway slaves wielding pistols.

"Hit 'em again!" a voice cried.

Douglas was hitting 'em again. Ten years after 1850, the same crowd was trying to destroy his candidacy so it could destroy the Union. Breckinridge men in Maine, Ohio, and Indiana were voting Republican to elect Lincoln. In Norfolk, a Breckinridge man had the brass to ask Douglas whether he'd help break up the Union.

"I reply that if they elect Mr. Lincoln, on their heads rests the responsibility," Douglas blustered. "No man on Earth has exerted his energies so much to defeat Lincoln's election as I have. No man on Earth would regret his election more than I would. I regard him as the head of a party, the whole principles of which are subversive of the Constitution and the Union. I would regard his election as a great public calamity, but not as a cause of breaking up this government. The election of no man on Earth by the people, according to the Constitution, is a cause of breaking up this government."

Even if Lincoln were elected, he would be a "powerless" president, checked by Democratic majorities in the House and Senate. In elections that summer and fall, Arkansas, Missouri, Florida, and South Carolina had voted for nearly all-Democratic House delegations, and more Democrats would be elected in November. If Lincoln got into any mischief, if he violated any man's Constitutional rights, the Democrats should be ready to punish him to the full extent the Constitution allowed. That, not secession, was the proper response to President Lincoln.

"I will never consent to any line of policy that will break up this glorious Union," Douglas concluded. "There is no evil of which any man complains for which disunion would furnish a remedy, but, on the contrary, it would be aggravated by disunion. I hold, further, that there is no evil in this country for which the Constitution and laws will not furnish a remedy."

Davidson County Court House, Nashville, Tennessee, October 26, 1860

In Nashville, Douglas crossed paths with Yancey, who arrived in town just as Douglas was beginning his eleven o'clock speech. A few of the four hundred Fire-Eaters who greeted Yancey at the depot wanted to create a demonstration by pulling his carriage through the streets, but the Great Disunionist refused to upstage the Great Unionist. Yancey would have his own say in the evening, at the state capitol. He did allow his supporters to follow him to the Sewanee Hotel, where he addressed them from the balcony. Yancey had just returned from a tour of New York, Boston, and Philadelphia, trying to persuade the Yankees that Southerners were not trying to break up the Union but only sought to live in a "constitutional union" that respected their right to hold slaves. The free states could do their part to maintain that Union by not forcing Lincoln on the South.

Yancey's carriage was accompanied to the capitol by Breckinridge Guards, Lane Guards, and Union Guards. To a crowd of 10,000, he denounced popular sovereignty and its champion. Congress, he claimed, had protected the right of nonresident slaveholders in the Florida territory. He read a section from the Compromise of 1850 that gave Congress "the power to set aside any obnoxious act of the Territorial legislature."

"Douglas says that the Fire-Eaters denounce the Cincinnati platform," Yancey shouted. "Where and when did I ever denounce it?"

To Yancey's critics, that was an admission that he was a Fire-Eater—and, therefore, a secessionist. Yancey was followed on the platform by former Mississippi governor Henry S. Foote, a Unionist who had condemned the Southern walkout in Charleston and met Douglas at the depot that morning. Speaking from ten o'clock to midnight, Foote called Yancey's address "the most spiritless and ineffectual attempt I ever listened to," and Yancey himself "a more consistent, persistent, obstinate and designing traitor than Catiline," the Roman who attempted to overthrow the Republic. Yancey and his followers were "traitors endeavoring to break up the country," Foote charged. The nooses, he warned, "were already fabricated to swing up all the traitors to their country."

Public Square, Atlanta, Georgia, October 30, 1860

In Atlanta, Douglas was introduced by Alexander Stephens, one of his few remaining supporters among the Southern political class. During the conventions, Stephens defended Douglas and popular sovereignty as protecting Southern rights, but even he now saw that Douglas's campaign was hopeless. Secession fever doomed him in the South: "I am pained and grieved at the folly which thus demanded the sacrifice of such a noble and gallant spirit as I believe Douglas to be," Stephens wrote a friend. "I can see but one possible ground that his nomination may effect, and that is he may get enough electoral votes in the North to defeat Lincoln in the colleges and thus throw [it] to the House when he may be the stepping stone for his party rival (Breckinridge) to rise into office."

Douglas did not discuss his own candidacy. He praised the Georgia Platform of 1850. The Platform endorsed the Compromise, but also warned that Georgia would not submit to any diminution of slaveholders' rights, such as passage of the Wilmot Proviso, banning the slave trade in the District of Columbia, or repeal of the Fugitive Slave Law. Douglas approved of all those demands. As long as they were met, there was no cause for secession. Respecting Southern rights was essential to preserving the Union.

"Why cannot the people of Georgia stand by their own platform?" Douglas asked, receiving responses of "We will!" and "We intend to!" "If there was a public man in Georgia of any party who was not pledged in faith and honor to that Georgia platform, I never heard of him. Why then can we not stand together on these propositions?"

Since he was decrying his personal interest in the presidency, and pleading for the Union, Douglas revealed "what no man before has known, and what once stated will astonish the person alluded to more than anyone else in this assemblage"—during the Baltimore convention, he had written a letter to William Richardson, offering to withdraw his candidacy if the party nominated a Southerner who stood by the Cincinnati platform. His first choice: Alexander Stephens.

"I have always been willing to take myself out of the way in order to restore harmony to my party and secure the ascendancy of Democratic principles," Douglas said to cheers.

Douglas then repeated his answers to the Norfolk Questions, asking why the same had never been posed to Breckinridge. Without mentioning Lincoln's name, he declared that whoever was elected president "must be sustained in the exercise of all his just Constitutional prerogatives and powers." What folly it would be, though, to secede from the happiest, wealthiest, most powerful nation on Earth?

"Are your oppressions so intolerable that you cannot bear up any longer?" Douglas asked. "Were the people of the South ever more prosperous than now?"

"No!" came the response from his listeners. Those voices would soon be a minority in Georgia, and all over the South.

State Capitol, Montgomery, Alabama, November 2, 1860

If it was bold of Douglas to venture into the South, it was boldest of all for him to venture into Alabama. Alabama was Yancey's home state, standing

alongside Mississippi and South Carolina in the front ranks of the secession movement.

From the moment of his arrival, Douglas's visit to Montgomery was
cursed by misadventure. When the candidate's carriage halted in front of
his hotel, it was pelted with rotten eggs and tomatoes. The missiles missed
their targets but landed on members of the reception committee. For three
long hours on the capitol steps, the weary Douglas delivered a stumbling
address—stammering, repeating his points, lapsing into hoarseness. It
was the worst speech of his Southern campaign, and the most pessimistic.
Since Lincoln's election four days hence was a certainty, Douglas assumed
secession was, too. He warned Alabama of its consequences.

"The Republic is more involved in darkness, and surrounded with those
elements of discord which inspire the patriot's head with dread," Douglas
began, retailing rumors of war. "I sincerely cherish the hope that the light
of reason and patriotism will enter the hearts of our countrymen, and guide
their action in such direction as will save this Republic from threatened
disaster."

Douglas repeated that he was running on the same platform that elected
Buchanan and Breckinridge in 1856, and that "gentlemen from Alabama"
had "abandoned the party at Charleston and Baltimore because the party
would not abandon its principles." The moment for making that argument
was long past, though. The party was split. Alabama had gone with the
Breckinridge faction. (Breckinridge would win 54 percent of the state's
vote, to Bell's 31 and Douglas's 15.) Now, Douglas could only lay out the
consequences of following secession from the Democratic Party with secession from the Union. If the slavery question were decided by Congress, as
both Breckinridge and Lincoln insisted, the result would be "a perpetual
conflict between hostile sections," which the South would lose, since "the
stronger will outvote the weaker."

"Those of us who will not join either faction are to be crushed out,"
Douglas lamented.

That was the epitaph for Douglas's presidential campaign and his political career. With his insistence that slavery remain a local issue, Douglas

stood between the intransigent "passions and prejudices" of Abolitionists and Fire-Eaters, both clamoring for the federal government to settle the question in their favor. The Fire-Eaters knew the existing government would not pass a law protecting slavery in the territories, so they planned to use Congress's refusal as a pretext for forming their own.

"They are going to inflame Southern passion, and make such a law the condition upon which they will remain in the Union; and when it is refused, they will ask you to break up the Union because of that refusal," Douglas said.

The South's insistence on a slave code would result in an "irreconcilable conflict" with "all Northern men" under one banner, and all Southern men under another. That was as close as he could come to threatening civil war, without using the actual words.

After the speech, Douglas and Adele boarded a steamer for the journey down the Alabama River to Selma. As Douglas delivered farewell remarks to the crowd on the wharf, the upper railing broke under the weight of the passengers pressing against it, pitching forty people to the lower deck. Douglas hurt his foot in the fall and would be forced to walk on a crutch for a few days. (The following March, after Alabama left the Union, Douglas received a bill for the crutch, with an overdue notice.) Adele was so shaken up she stayed behind in Montgomery, joining her husband a few days later in Mobile.

"This is my first lesson in precipitation and in Yancey's home," Douglas joked to his fellow passengers as soon as he regained his feet.

Mobile County Courthouse, Mobile, Alabama, November 5, 1860

Douglas's best friend in Alabama was John Forsyth, publisher of the *Mobile Register*. After Yancey led Alabama out of the Charleston convention, Forsyth organized the pro-Douglas convention that elected the slate of delegates recognized in Baltimore, thus precipitating the breakup of that convention. Forsyth was at the wharf to greet Douglas when he stepped off the steamer *Duke*, along with former governor John Winston, who had known Douglas since 1848, when Douglas campaigned for Cass in Alabama.

Like most cities of its size, Mobile had more than one newspaper. During his speech, Douglas was challenged on two points by a reporter from the pro-Breckinridge *Daily Mercury*. First, he was asked if the election went to the House of Representatives, and he saw he could not be elected there, would he ask his supporters to vote for Lincoln or Breckinridge? Second, if Lincoln became president, would Douglas accept an appointment to his cabinet?

Douglas saw the questions as an attempt to expose him as a stalking horse for Lincoln. He answered the second question first, after insisting that only a "wretch" could ask it. No, he would not serve in the cabinet of Lincoln, nor of Breckinridge, nor any other "sectional candidate who advocates the doctrine of Congressional intervention. I would not surrender my seat in the Senate to accept any executive appointment under any man who may succeed to the presidency in the present contest."

Douglas then addressed the question of supporting Lincoln in a contingent election: "No event or contingency could possibly happen in which I would advise any friend of mine to vote for Abraham Lincoln or could any event or contingency possibly happen in which I would advise any friend of mine to vote for John C. Breckinridge." Both men stood for Congressional control over slavery in the territories, which Douglas had spent months campaigning against. Douglas would not even support himself if his were one of the three names sent to the House: "I shall not be a candidate there," he said. "I am unwilling to accept the presidential office unless chosen by the popular vote, which would bring with it the moral power to sustain me in the performance of my duties."

Douglas returned to his hotel. He would await the election results in Mobile, in the company of Forsyth. Mobile, on the Gulf of Mexico, was 850 miles from Chicago, on the Great Lakes, but one day, Douglas expected, they would be joined by railroads, the threads that knit together his beloved Union.

State House, Springfield, Illinois, November 6, 1860

At first, Abraham Lincoln did not plan to vote on Election Day, thinking it unseemly to cast a ballot for himself. That morning, though, as he was working in Ozias Hatch's State House office, he was visited by his law partner, Herndon, who reminded him that Republicans needed votes to win control of the legislature and reelect Trumbull. The House and Senate then sitting had elected Douglas. Lincoln conceded the point and, at three o'clock in the afternoon, walked to the county courthouse with Herndon, Ward Hill Lamon, and Elmer Ellsworth, his twenty-three-year-old law clerk, who would, six-and-a-half months later, become the first Union officer killed by Confederate forces. Wagons carried bands through the streets to rouse the populace to the polls. When Lincoln walked up the stairs to the courtroom where the voting was taking place, even the Democrats cheered.

"You ought to vote for Douglas, Uncle Abe," one shouted, "he has done all he could for you."

Lincoln snipped the line for presidential electors off the top of his ballot and dropped it in a glass bowl labeled "Republican." Back at the State House, he received the first encouraging news of the day, a telegram from Simeon Draper, chairman of the New York Republican Party, assuring him that "the city of New York will more than meet your expectations." He also received a telegram from Charleston. Its author hoped that Lincoln would win, because then South Carolina "would soon be free."

As Lincoln held court, in an armchair too commodious for even his gangly frame, a visitor from New York asked whether the South would secede if he were elected.

"They might make a little stir about it before," Lincoln said, still uncomprehending of the passion his candidacy had aroused in the South, "but if they wait until after the inauguration and for some overt act, they will wait all their lives."

Hatch joked to Lincoln that he was lucky women couldn't vote, otherwise he would be defeated by his own portrait. Lincoln was relaxed enough to tell Hatch, "There is a great deal more in that idea than you suppose," then spin a yarn about a Presbyterian Church in McLean County whose elders had elected a new pastor.

"In an evil hour somebody got hold of the man's likeness and exhibited it to the sisters," Lincoln joked. "They did not like the wart he had on his nose, so they turned out in force and voted down the call."

At five o'clock, Lincoln went home for supper with Mary, Bob, Willie, and Tad. By the time he returned to the state house at seven, the Republicans had set up a watch party in the House Chamber, where a crowd awaited the returns. Lincoln, never a man for crowds, repaired to the Springfield telegraph office with Hatch, Auditor of Public Accounts Jesse K. Dubois, Nicolay, and Samuel Weed, a reporter for a St. Louis newspaper. First came the local reports: a 2,500-vote majority in Chicago, reported Norman Judd. Lincoln was particularly pleased to see that he was winning in southern Illinois's Saline County, which had cast a single vote for Fremont in 1856.

"It's a tribute from Egypt to the success of our public school fund," he told his friends.

Illinois seemed secure. As polls closed around the country, reports clacked in from states essential to a Republican victory. Lincoln received a telegram from Indianapolis, promising large Republican gains." From Philadelphia came word that "our majority in the state will be between 50,000 and 70,000." By ten o'clock, Lincoln had still seen no results from New York, where the Democrats had fielded a fusion ticket, engineered by Belmont over Douglas's objections. If New York divided its thirty-five electoral votes among Douglas, Bell, and Breckinridge, Lincoln would not win a majority in the Electoral College, and the choice of a president would be sent to the House of Representatives, where the Republicans did not control enough state delegations to elect Lincoln.

Ten o'clock passed. New York had still not reported.

"The news will come quickly enough if it's good," Lincoln remarked, "and if bad, I'm not in any hurry to hear it."

At ten-thirty a wire arrived from Thurlow Weed. Lincoln read it aloud to his close circle: "We are encouraged at this hour to believe you have carried this state."

"The news is satisfactory so far," Lincoln fretted, "only it's not conclusive."

In New Jersey, the Democratic fusion ticket appeared headed for victory, but Massachusetts went for Lincoln by 50,000 votes. Lincoln was only somewhat encouraged by the news from abolitionist New England.

"That's a clear case of the Dutch taking Holland," he cracked.

James E. Harvey sent good news from Philadelphia: the City of Brotherly Love would "give you a majority of about 5,000 and a plurality of 15,000," thanks to a strong Quaker turnout.

Lincoln took in the news quietly and anxiously, showing a sign of satisfaction only when he learned that his Springfield precinct had voted Republican. Toward midnight, Missouri showed a close race between Douglas and Bell, leading Lincoln to remark that "we should now get a few licks back."

Lincoln was happy with the news that Bell had carried Virginia. "This is the most hopeful return I've heard for the peace of the country," he said. "I hope the majority is so large as to crush out the Fire-Eaters completely."

At twelve-thirty, with New York still in doubt, Lincoln and his friends left the telegraph office to take refreshments at a State House party organized by Republican women who "surrounded, and took possession, and clung to Lincoln when he appeared, kissing him on the cheek." Lincoln accepted the attention with good nature, since it was "a form of coercion not prohibited by the Constitution or Congress."

The party returned to the telegraph office to find news from New York. The city had reported its returns first. With their large Irish-Catholic populations and commercial ties to the South, Manhattan and its surrounding counties had voted Democratic.

"City complete, fusion majority 27,600," Simeon Draper wired. However, western and central New York, Seward's home territory, were strongly antislavery, and broke Republican. "Great gains throughout the state for Republicans," Draper added. "State sure for Republicans."

Lincoln still was not convinced, telling his companions, "Not too fast, my friends. Not too fast. It may not be over yet."

Then a second message from Draper arrived. "Mr. Lincoln," the office manager said excitedly, "here is news that will do you good."

"Read it," Lincoln instructed.

"The fusion majorities in New York and Brooklyn will not exceed 35,000 majority. We tender you our congratulations on a magnificent victory."

For the first time, Lincoln allowed the emotions of Election Night to overtake him, letting out a crow of triumph.

"Well, Uncle Abe, are you satisfied now?" DuBois asked.

"Well, the agony is most over, and you will soon be able to go to bed," Lincoln replied.

Draper's congratulations were read from the window of the telegraph office. The cheering spread through the streets of Springfield. Church bells rang. At four in the morning, a cannon was fired. (The Republican victory included both houses of the Illinois legislature, which would reelect Trumbull.) Lincoln asked for his overcoat, stuffed Draper's telegram in a pocket, and announced, "It's time I go home and tell the news to a little woman who's sitting up for it."

Mobile Register Offices, Mobile, Alabama, November 6, 1860

Douglas received the news of his defeat sitting beside the telegraph in John Forsyth's newspaper office—he had expected to lose, but not as badly as he did. Only in Missouri did he win outright, defeating Bell by 429 votes. In New Jersey, Democratic electors received a majority of votes, but even there a divided party allowed Lincoln to win. The Democratic fusion ticket allotted three electoral votes to Douglas, two to Bell, and two to Breckinridge. Douglas Democrats, indignant about sharing a ballot with Southerners, fielded their own slate of seven electors, which included the three on the fusion ticket. Voters cast ballots for individual electors.

The Douglas electors were the top three vote-getters, but the next four were Lincoln's, giving him a majority of the state's electoral vote.

Nationwide, Lincoln carried 39 percent of the popular vote to Douglas's 29 percent. Douglas, however, won only 12 electoral votes, placing him fourth in the Electoral College. Lincoln won every free state, giving him a majority of 180, Breckinridge swept most of the South for 72, while Bell won the border states of Virginia, Kentucky, and Tennessee, giving him 39.

Once Lincoln's victory was apparent, Forsyth told Douglas he planned to write an editorial calling for a state convention to deliberate on Alabama's response. Douglas, who favored no response but acquiescence to the result, was opposed to the idea. Forsyth argued the best way to stop secession was to appear to go along with the Fire-Eaters, then elect enough Unionists to the convention to control its outcome.

"If you can't prevent the holding of a convention, you can't hope to control it when it's held," Douglas responded.

Forsyth, though, knew that the secession fever aroused by Lincoln's victory made a convention inevitable. He would publish the editorial. Douglas rose and left the office "more hopeless than I had ever seen him," his secretary, Sheridan, wrote.

Lincoln did not turn the tables on Douglas simply because the Democrats were divided. In three of the four states where Democrats ran a fusion ticket—New York, Pennsylvania, Rhode Island—Lincoln won an outright majority. Of the eighteen states Lincoln won—all of them free states—only in California and Oregon would the combined Democratic vote have deprived him of victory, and their seven electoral votes were not enough to deny him the presidency. The Republican campaign combined the support of abolitionists, Old Whigs, Know Nothings, and German immigrants—all groups who considered Lincoln more acceptable than any Democrat. (Douglas had condemned the Know Nothings out of solidarity with his Irish supporters. Because of that, the Irish overlooked the "Dutch plank" in the Republican platform that won the votes of Germans.) Lincoln was especially popular with young first-time voters who filled the ranks of Wide Awake companies. Lincoln the Railsplitter, born in a log cabin in

Kentucky, stood for the free White farmer against the aristocratic Southern Bourbon, and for the growing industrial North against the backward, stagnant, agrarian South.

At the same time, Lincoln was a sectional, minority president, whose election sent a message to the South that the North had the power to vote its way of life out of existence and was now exercising it. His 39 percent of the popular vote was an all-time low for a candidate who also won in the Electoral College. That was a victory Douglas would have scorned, but in a four-way election, it was the only victory possible. Despite his defeat, Douglas could still claim he was the only national candidate. Only Douglas won electoral votes in both a free state (New Jersey) and a slave state (Missouri). Douglas received popular votes in 31 of 33 states, more than any other candidate. (In nine Southern states, Lincoln was not even on the ballot.) While Douglas's support was broader than any candidate's, nowhere was it as deep. In 1860, the electorate was polarized between Northerners who wanted to stop the spread of slavery and Southerners who demanded its expansion. Douglas, who based his campaign on the principle that the federal government should not take either side, was rejected by majorities in both sections. (The Electoral College was particularly unforgiving toward Douglas's candidacy. Under a different system, such as a French-style runoff between the top two vote-getters, he probably would have won. It's hard to see Lincoln adding another 11 percent to his popular vote total. As odious as Douglas was to the South, he was less odious than Lincoln. Douglas accused extreme Fire-Eaters of seeking Lincoln's election to justify secession, but the Southern masses would not have voted to make that a reality.)

Regardless of how Lincoln had won, he had won according to the rules set out in the Constitution. Douglas considered himself a Constitutional patriot and a devoted Unionist, so he saw no justification for questioning or quibbling with the result. No man in the republic had campaigned against Lincoln as long as Douglas. No man had worked harder to prevent him from coming to power, first as a senator, then as president. Now, though, Lincoln was going to be Douglas's president, and Douglas was going to be a member of the loyal opposition supporting Lincoln's right to discharge the duties of his office, as long as he obeyed the Constitution. There was only one thing worse than a Lincoln presidency—a broken Union. That was a message Douglas had preached across the South, and one he would continue to preach now that a Lincoln presidency was coming.

St. Charles Hotel, New Orleans, Louisiana, November 8, 1860

During the campaign, Douglas was invited to New Orleans by the Louisiana Democratic State Executive Committee, which believed that his "coming down would decide in our favour the doubtful states of Louisiana and Alabama, and would necessarily produce the best moral effect on the States of Mississippi, Texas, and Alabama."

The presidential campaign was over, but the campaign against secession was just beginning, so two days after the election, Douglas and Adele boarded a train to New Orleans. They were met at the Pontchartrain Railroad terminus by Pierre Soulé, who had headed the Douglas slate in Baltimore. Already, Southern newspapers were condemning Lincoln's election as an insult to the South's honor. The *Charleston Mercury* hung a Palmetto flag from an upper window of its offices and, that morning, published a leading article reporting that "our citizens thronged the business thoroughfares, expressing their determination to resist Lincoln's election at all hazards." In Charleston, the U.S. district judge, the U.S. attorney, and the collector of ports resigned their offices; in Columbia, the legislature passed a resolution calling for "a Convention of the people of the state," to consider secession.

As a port city that traded with the North, Unionist New Orleans voted for Bell. Douglas won three rural parishes near the mouth of the Mississippi River. He was encouraged by the fact that the combined vote for his candidacy and Bell's exceeded Breckinridge's by more than 100,000 throughout the South. Breckinridge won Louisiana, but the two Unionists polled 27,829 votes to his 22,681. Those results gave Douglas hope that his closing arguments for national unity had been effective, even if they benefited Bell, and that he could still persuade Southerners to accept Lincoln as their president.

At the train depot, Soulé praised Douglas for campaigning against "treason, under the garb of sectional pride." (Six months later, Soulé would be arrested by federal troops for plotting treason against the United States and imprisoned in Massachusetts.) Douglas acknowledged the "vast crowd" that came out to greet him in the rain, calling it proof "that there is yet hope for our glorious union." On the carriage ride to the St. Charles Hotel, accompanied by the Douglas-Johnson Young Men's Club, the defeated candidate was showered with wreaths and bouquets, flung from balconies. New Orleans had greeted him two years earlier, after he defeated Lincoln, and it now greeted him "with a welcome which could not have been excelled even if I had come among you as president-elect."

"You will be in 1864," shouted a voice, as a banner bearing a portrait of Douglas and the legend 1864 was waved above the crowd.

"I have pleasure to believing that this demonstration is not intended as a mere personal compliment to myself," Douglas said. "It is the more gratifying to me because it is the evidence of your devotion to those great principles of self-government and constitutional liberty to which my life is devoted. Let us now bury the excitement and angry passions which have manifested themselves during the contest. Let us lay aside partisan feeling, and act as becomes patriots and lovers of our country. Let us unite to put down sectionalism and abolitionism and every other element of political and national discord. Let no grievances, no embittered feelings, impair the force of our efforts. Let us put ourselves to work to rescue the government of the country from the hands of those whom we think unworthy to administer it. If Abraham Lincoln is president, what harm can he do?"

"None," cried a voice from the crowd.

"There is a majority against him in the Senate, and a majority in the House of Representatives. He is powerless for mischief—all he can do is fill the offices, and there is a majority in the Senate to reject those he nominates if they are not good men. He will be an object of commiseration and pity rather than fear. Then why should we break up the best government that the sun in its circuit around the earth ever shone upon, merely because we have been defeated in a presidential election?"

Douglas, who enjoyed the pleasures of New Orleans, spent several days in the city, attending the opera with Adele on Saturday night. Local business leaders, anxious about secession, asked him for a statement "on the present condition of the affairs of the country." He responded with a letter asserting that "no man regrets the election of Mr. Lincoln more than I do," that "none made more strenuous efforts to defeat him," and that "none differ with him more radically and irreconcilably upon all the great issues involved in this contest." Lincoln and the Republicans, though, did not have the power to change the existing laws protecting slavery. Lincoln's "mischief" would be thwarted by Taney's Supreme Court, and by a congressional coalition of Southerners and Northern Democrats pledged to Douglas's principle of nonintervention toward slavery in the states and territories. Congress could not pass antislavery laws "unless a portion of the Southern Senators and Representatives absent themselves, so as to give an Abolition majority in consequence of their absence." If Southerners wanted to preserve their right to hold slaves, their safest course of action was to remain in the Union, not leave it.

Douglas made his way back home to Chicago on the steamboat *James Battle*, making a brief anti-secession speech from the dock in Vicksburg, stopping at his family's Mississippi plantation, and attempting to rest, put on weight, and regain his vigor and health after the most rigorous campaign any presidential candidate had ever undertaken. Douglas would work even harder to hold the Union together when he resumed his Senate seat in December. As his great ally William Richardson, who had just won a seat in the House of Representatives from the Quincy district, wrote, "We are beaten but not conquered."

CHAPTER 9

THE SECESSION WINTER

Senate Chamber, United States Capitol, Washington, D.C., December 18, 1860

John J. Crittenden was born before the Constitution was ratified and first elected to represent Kentucky in the Senate in 1817, when James Monroe was president. Then, Crittenden had just reached the legal age of thirty years old. Now, at seventy-four, he was the Senate's oldest member, although not its dean, since he had three times left that body. First, he left to practice law. Then, he served as attorney general of the United States, under presidents Harrison and Tyler. Later, he left to serve as governor of Kentucky, then attorney general again, under Fillmore.

For most of his years in politics, Crittenden had been known as "Clay's Lieutenant," laboring in the shadow of the Great Compromiser, his fellow bluegrass Whig. Clay had been dead eight years. His ten-year-old compromise seemed on the verge of death as well. In his annual message to Congress earlier that month, President Buchanan had declared that the "intemperate interference of the Northern people

with the question of slavery in the Southern states has at length produced its desired effects." No state had the right to secede, especially
not over "the election of any one of our fellow-citizens as president," but
neither did Congress have the right to force a state to remain in the Union.

"Our Union rests upon public opinion, and can never be cemented by
the blood of its citizens shed in civil war," the president declared.

Buchanan was a lame duck, though, with less than three months
remaining in his term. Southern honor could not countenance submission
to his successor, who believed Blacks were equal to Whites, at least in
their right to profit from their labor, and who was determined to prevent
slaveholders from carrying their legal property into the territories—a cir-
cumscription that would result in the institution's death, just as Lincoln
intended. On December 13, seven senators and twenty-three representatives
from the cotton states of Texas, Arkansas, Louisiana, Mississippi, Georgia,
South Carolina, and North Carolina released a manifesto declaring their
intention to form an independent confederacy.

"The argument is exhausted," they wrote. "All hope of relief in the
Union, through the agencies of committees, Congressional legislation, or
constitutional amendments, is extinguished . . . the Republicans are resolute
in the purpose to grant nothing that will or ought to satisfy the South."

On the 17th, South Carolina convened a Secession Convention at First
Baptist Church in Columbia. The Palmetto State's senators had resigned a
month earlier, five days after Lincoln's election, so the convention's decision
was not in doubt. Likewise, Treasury Secretary Howell Cobb, a Georgia
Fire-Eater, resigned from Buchanan's cabinet, on the grounds that in a
time of "troubles . . . consequent to the late presidential election," his first
loyalty was "to the honor and safety of my State."

"The evil has now passed beyond control," Cobb wrote Buchanan, "and
must be met by each and all of us under our responsibility to God and our
country."

Buchanan's secretary of state, Lewis Cass of Michigan, also resigned
over the dithering president's reluctance to reinforce Fort Sumter, South
Carolina, which Buchanan feared would provoke the South.

Crittenden was in the winter of his career, preparing to leave public life, when his term expired in March. Snow had settled in his flossy hair, and the points of his high collar—the fashion of another era—were lifted toward the sunken cheeks of his austere face. As a founder of the Constitutional Union Party, Crittenden had been offered its presidential nomination but declined, due to his age and impending retirement. In these final months of his career, he saw an opportunity to craft an even greater compromise than his mentor's—in 1850, Clay had not been faced with the Union's imminent breakup. It was fitting that the task would again fall to a Kentuckian, representative of a border state that prided itself on buffering the passions of the abolitionist North and the secessionist South. Crittenden was himself a slaveholder, but his holdings were those of a country lawyer—a few hundred acres, and a few hands to farm it.

Crittenden came up with a package of proposals he believed would keep the South (except for irreconcilable South Carolina) in the Union, while allowing the North to maintain its honor. The Crittenden Compromise, as it came to be known, would be more comprehensive, and more enduring, than the Compromise of 1850—six constitutional amendments, none of which could be repealed, and four congressional resolutions. On December 18, he rose to present it to the Senate.

Crittenden began his speech, "I have endeavored by the resolutions to meet all these questions and causes of discontent, and by amendments to the Constitution of the United States, so that the settlement, if we can happily agree on any, may be permanent, and leave no cause for further controversy."

These were Crittenden's six amendments:

1. Restore the Missouri Compromise, extending the 36' 30° line to the eastern boundary of California. Slavery would be prohibited in territories north of the line and permitted south. When states were formed from those territories, they could choose to permit slavery or not.

2. Prohibit Congress from abolishing slavery on government property in the slave states.

3. Prohibit Congress from abolishing slavery in the District of Columbia, as long as it existed in Maryland and Virginia.

4. Guarantee the right to transport slaves between states.

5. Pay to masters the full value of fugitive slaves "rescued by force" by abolitionist vigilantes.

6. Prohibit Congress and the states from amending the Constitution to eliminate the three-fifths compromise, overturn the fugitive slave clause, or "abolish or interfere with slavery in any of the States by whose laws it is, or may be, allowed or permitted."

In addition, Crittenden proposed four Congressional regulations:

1. That the Fugitive Slave Law was "in strict pursuance of the plain and mandatory provisions of the Constitution."

2. That "personal liberty laws," which allowed jury trials for fugitive slaves in Northern states, were unconstitutional, and ought to be repealed.

3. The Fugitive Slave Law should be amended so that free state authorities were only required to assist in the recapture of slaves "in cases where there shall be resistance or danger of resistance or rescue."

4. Congress should enforce the ban on the African slave trade, and pass any laws required to suppress it.

Crittenden understood that restoring the Missouri Compromise line would be a "great difficulty" for Republicans, who had just fought and won a presidential campaign on a platform of banning slavery in the territories. But, he entreated, "think whether, for such a comparative trifle as that, the Union of this country is to be sacrificed." The nation had lived "quietly and peacefully" with the line for thirty years. "Can we not do it again? We did it then to preserve the peace of the country." The South could certainly ask no more than that from the North, unless it was "bent on revolution, bent on disunion."

"I do not despair of the Republic," Crittenden told his colleagues, who listened as silently and as respectfully as if he were a togaed Roman transported to the American Senate. "When I see before me senators of so much intelligence and so much patriotism, who have been so honored by their country, sent here as guardians of that national flag, I cannot despair; I cannot despond, I cannot but believe that they will find some means of reconciling and adjusting the rights of all parties, by concession, if necessary, so as to preserve and give more stability to the country and to its institutions."

The elderly solon, though, could not comprehend the passions over slavery that were pulling apart his beloved country. They had not animated public discourse during most of his tenure in the Senate; they were not something he felt in his old age. He still believed that reasonable gentlemen could settle their differences on any issue, even slavery.

In deference to his fellow Kentuckian, Vice President Breckinridge appointed a Committee of Thirteen to consider Crittenden's proposals. From the South, the committee included Robert Toombs of Georgia and Jefferson Davis, who had both signed the December 13 secession manifesto; from the North, William Seward, who had just been invited to join Lincoln's cabinet as secretary of state, and Douglas. In the House, a similarly composed Committee of Thirty-Three was already considering compromise resolutions, including admitting the territory south of the Missouri Compromise line as a state and allowing its residents to decide on slavery—a maneuver to dispense with the Republicans' territorial objections.

Douglas immediately embraced Crittenden's plan, even though it restored the Missouri Compromise, which had been abolished by his own Kansas-Nebraska Act, and even though it dispensed with popular sovereignty, the doctrine that was central to his political identity. Douglas was no ideologue. He sought practical solutions to the problem of national unity and was willing to embrace any idea or ally that advanced the cause of Unionism. That was why he argued that the South should accept Lincoln's election, and why he could jettison popular sovereignty to ally with Crittenden.

"I am ready to act with any party, with any individual of any party, who will come to this question with an eye single to the preservation of the Union," Douglas told the Senate on December 10.

On the Committee of Thirteen, and in the Senate as a whole, Crittenden and Douglas became the strongest voices for compromise. The key to passing a compromise through the Senate, though, was Seward, who was thought to be amenable to restoring the Missouri Compromise line, even though that violated the Republican Party's Chicago platform. New York's commercial interests were clamoring for a solution that averted war. Thurlow Weed, Seward's patron, had editorialized in favor of the line, and of compensation for escaped slaves, in his *Albany Times-Union*. The two men were political twins, so it was assumed Weed would not have published the editorials without Seward's authorization. "Weed is Seward and Seward is Weed, each approves what the other says or does," was the saying in New York political circles.

Seward made no public statements on compromise proposals. When Virginia Unionist James Barbour told Seward that "nothing materially less than the Crittenden compromise would allay [the excitement] in Virginia," Seward reportedly replied that he favored it. To Weed, he wrote "The Republican Party today is as uncompromising as the Secessionists in South Carolina. A month hence each may come to think that moderation is wiser."

However, the ambitious Seward had accepted Lincoln's offer to become secretary of state, his compensation for losing the nomination in Chicago. Because of that, his views on compromise were required to reflect the incoming administration's. Lincoln was inflexibly opposed to restoring the Missouri Compromise line and instructed Illinois representatives on the Committee of Thirty-Three to vote against any measure endorsing it.

"Entertain no proposition for a compromise in regard to the extension of slavery," Lincoln wrote to William Kellogg. "The instant you do, they have us under again; all our labor is lost, and sooner or later must be done over. Douglas is sure to be again trying to bring in his 'Pop. Sov.' Have none of it. The try has to come and better now than later."

To Elihu Washburne, Lincoln wrote "there is no possible compromise" on "a Mo. Line . . . or Pop Sov. Let either be, and immediately filibustering and extending slavery recommences. On that point hold firm as with a chain of steel."

Perhaps, thought Seward, the president-elect, isolated in his provincial prairie town, did not understand the gravity of the situation in Washington. The only way to save the Union was to grant the South some concession that would allow it to back down from its threat of secession with honor intact. In an attempt to change Lincoln's mind, Seward dispatched Weed to Springfield.

Eighth and Jackson Streets, Springfield, Illinois, December 20, 1860

Thurlow Weed's latest *Albany Times-Union* editorial arrived in Springfield on the same day its author did. It endorsed the particulars of Crittenden's plan, specifically the Missouri Compromise line. "What matter of difference between individuals, families, Committees, States, or nations, was ever settled except by 'Compromise?'" it asked, then reminded readers that "when this Union was formed, slavery was the RULE—Freedom the EXCEPTION."

In inviting Weed to Springfield, Lincoln was clear that "I will be inflexible on the territorial question"; any compromise permitting the extension of slavery, even into a territory as inhospitable to plantation agriculture as New Mexico, south of the line, "would lose us everything we gained by the election," by enabling the creation of more slave states.

Weed arrived at Lincoln's house at nine o'clock in the morning, for their second face-to-face meeting since the election. His article was delivered with the evening mail.

"This is a heavy broadside," Lincoln told Weed, after reading it. "You have opened your fire at a critical moment, aiming at friends and foes alike.

It will do some good or much mischief. Will the Republicans of New York sustain you in this view of the question?"

"I acted on my own sense of what was wise for our cause," Weed replied. "I shall be denounced in most Republican journals; enlightened politicians who entertain similar views will hesitate to express them, and it will largely impair, if not wholly destroy my influence in the Republican Party. Notwithstanding those consequences, I shall unflinchingly persevere in the course I have marked out, with a clear and firm conviction that in doing so, aided by a small minority of Republican journals, with here and there a conservative statesman, we shall keep the North united in prosecuting a war which, in preserving the government and Union, will overwhelm and destroy rebellion and slavery."

"Those views had not occurred to me," Lincoln allowed. "I will watch the progress of popular sentiment, but I hope to find your apprehensions unfounded. While there are some loud threats and muttering in the cotton states, I hope that by wisdom and forbearance the danger of serious trouble might be averted, as such changes have been in former times."

(Even as Lincoln and Weed were meeting the South Carolina Secession Convention was assembling at Institute Hall in Charleston. Where the Democratic Party died, so did the Union—the delegates voted unanimously to secede.)

Lincoln and Weed spent most of their two-day visit discussing cabinet appointments, with Weed suggesting at least two "white crows"—men from slave-holding states; he named Unionists from Maryland, Virginia, Tennessee, and North Carolina.

"Would you rely on such men if their states should secede?" Lincoln asked.

"Yes, sir; the men whom I have in mind can always be relied on."

Lincoln would appoint Montgomery Blair of Maryland as postmaster general and Edward Bates of Missouri as attorney general—both men from loyal border states.

Weed was unsuccessful in moving Lincoln an inch toward acceptance of the Crittenden Compromise. Lincoln sent him back to New York with a letter, titled "Resolutions Drawn up for Republican Members of Senate Committee of Thirteen." It endorsed enforcing the Fugitive Slave Law and repealing state laws that conflicted with it, but was silent on the territorial question. He was using Weed as an intermediary to let Seward know he would not compromise on the Missouri line, and neither should the other Republicans on the committee. He also sent a copy of the resolutions to Lyman Trumbull, writing "I think it would be best for Mr. Seward to introduce them, and Mr. Weed will let him know that I think so. Show this to Mr. Hamlin; but beyond him, do not let my name be known in the matter."

No one would influence the Committee of Thirteen more than Lincoln, who was not scheduled to arrive in Washington for another two months.

United States Capitol, Washington, D.C., December 21, 1860

The Committee of Thirteen began its deliberations without Seward, who was still at home in Auburn, New York, planning to meet with Weed once he returned from Springfield. Neither Seward's presence nor Lincoln's letter were required to stiffen Republican resistance to Crittenden. Senator Benjamin Wade, an Ohio abolitionist, argued that Lincoln should have the same right as any other president to put his policies into action. "Little is expected from the action of the Committee," reported the *New-York Tribune*. "The Republicans seem to be more united than ever, declaring that the demands of the Southerners are preposterous, and cannot be thought of for a moment."

The next day, a Saturday, the committee met for six and a half hours, discussing at length Crittenden's proposal to extend the Missouri Compromise line to California. Douglas repeated that he would support the plan "for the preservation of the country."

"If that mode of compromise will not answer," he added, "I am willing to go for any other consistent with honor of justice."

Senator William Bigler, a Pennsylvania Democrat, also backed the line, "because in that way the question of slavery can be taken out of Congress and separated entirely from the popular elections in the North, without which we can never have permanent peace."

The four Republicans present—Wade, James Doolittle of Wisconsin, Jacob Collamer of Vermont, and James Grimes of Iowa—took the position that the question of slavery in the territories had been settled by the presidential election. They could not offer any concession that went against the will of the voters. The Republicans were reluctant to proceed without Seward's guidance, but since the senators had no word of when he would return to Washington, they decided to vote. There were three Southern Democrats on the committee—Davis, Robert Toombs of Georgia, and Robert M. T. Hunter of Virginia. All were willing to vote for the line, or for any proposal that would guarantee the South its constitutional rights, but only if the Republicans agreed as well. So extending the Missouri Compromise line was voted down, 7–5. The Southerners and the Republicans voted no. Douglas, Crittenden, and Bigler were joined in favor by Minnesota Democrat Henry Rice and Kentucky Democrat Lazarus Powell. By the same vote, the committee rejected the five remaining amendments in Crittenden's compromise, then adjourned to try again at ten o'clock the next day.

United States Capitol, Washington, D.C., December 24, 1860

On Christmas Eve, the fourth day of the committee's deliberations, Douglas introduced his own package of amendments. Unsurprisingly, the plan promoted popular sovereignty by prohibiting Congress from legislating on slavery in the territories and requiring that the current status of slavery in each territory should remain unchanged until the population reached 50,000, at which point the settlers could decide for themselves. New territory could only be acquired with the approval of two-thirds of Congress. Douglas also wanted to prohibit Blacks from voting and allow Congress to acquire colonies in Africa or South America for resettling freed slaves.

Seward returned to Washington that day, joining the committee just in time to cast a late vote against one of Crittenden's amendments. On his way, he shared a train between Syracuse and Albany with Weed, who reported on his meeting with Lincoln. Weed laid out Lincoln's three-point plan for the committee but did not give Seward the letter. Seward didn't want it; he was still hoping to broker some sort of compromise between the Republicans and the South. Hard proof of Lincoln's intransigence would interfere with his plans. In New York City, Seward checked into the Astor Hotel, which was that night hosting the annual banquet of the New England Society. Seward was called down from his room to make a speech. He told the diners that this "anomalous condition of our affairs—produced by this disposition of some of the American States to secede from the Union," was simply a family squabble whose passions would soon abate. Why, if France or England or Russia were to invade New York tomorrow, South Carolina would take up arms to defend its sister state. Lincoln's election had set off a secession mania, but "fifty days have now passed, and I believe that every day the sun has set since that time it has set upon mollified passions and prejudices, and if you will only await the time, sixty more suns will shed a brighter light and illuminate a more cheerful atmosphere."

Yankee politicians such as Seward and Lincoln truly believed that the South would soon come to its senses and call off its bluff of secession, whether or not the North made concessions on slavery.

"In the middle states, however, there was great alarm," Henry Adams would write. "They knew their neighbors better." Border state Unionists "urged earnestly and honestly on the Republicans a retreat from the positions of the campaign . . . something, no matter what, with which they could go home and deny the charges of the disunionists."

That Christmas, Douglas was feeling pessimistic about the possibility of compromise, and the nation's future unity.

"The prospects are gloomy," he wrote to Charles Lanphier on Christmas Day, "but I do not yet despair of the Union." Secession was illegal, but Douglas would not consent to war "until all efforts at peaceful adjustment have been made and have failed." The Republicans, he believed, were eager for war, because that would lead to the withdrawal of Southern senators, allowing the remaining Northerners to approve all of Lincoln's appointees.

"I am for the Union, and hence am ready to make any reasonable sacrifice to save it," he told Lanphier. "No adjustment will restore and preserve peace which does not banish the slavery question from Congress's power and place it beyond the reach of Federal Legislation. Mr. Crittenden's proposal to extend the Missouri line accomplishes this object, and hence I can accept it now for the same reason I proposed it in 1848."

The next day, Douglas and Crittenden received a telegram from a group of prominent Georgians, alarmed by Senator Toombs's proclamation that "the Black Republicans" on the committee would not protect "security for your constitutional rights in the Union."

"Is there any hope for Southern rights in the Union?" the Georgians implored the two senators most counted on for compromise. "We are for the Union of our fathers, if Southern rights can be preserved in it. If not, we are for secession . . . You are looked to in this emergency. Give your views by dispatch."

Douglas and Crittenden wired back, "We have hopes that the rights of the South and of every State and Section may be protected within the Union. Don't give up the Ship. Don't despair of the Republic."

Southerners were writing to Douglas, assuring him that Unionist sentiment was still alive in the South, and imploring him to come up with a solution that would satisfy slaveholders. Toward the end of the year, though, he received a dispiriting letter from his friend John Forsyth, the Mobile newspaper publisher. Just the month before, Douglas had received the election returns in Forsyth's office and argued against his plan to write an editorial calling for a statewide convention. Douglas believed the secessionists could not be controlled. Now Forsyth, his strongest Southern ally, was a secessionist himself.

"With your defeat the cause of the Union was lost," Forsyth wrote ruefully. "The feeling in the South is that to remain in the Union is sooner or later to succumb to Abolition rule . . . It seems to me we must part and that we of the South had better meet a long and bloody war than stay to be stripped of our slave property to have turned loose among us 9,000,000 of freed Blacks."

That week, Alabama had joined Florida and Mississippi in electing conventions to consider the state's status within the Union. Alabama "will without doubt adopt an ordinance of secession," Forsyth predicted.

United States Capitol, Washington, D.C., December 26, 1860

When the Committee of Thirteen reassembled after a Christmas Day break, Seward presented three proposals: an unamendable constitutional amendment prohibiting the federal government from interfering with slavery in the states; amending the Fugitive Slave Law to allow a jury trial for escaped slaves; and a recommendation that states "repeal all laws that conflict with the constitution and laws of the United States"—obviously aimed at personal liberty laws. All had Lincoln's approval. The first was adopted almost unanimously, but only Republicans voted for the latter two. Toombs countered with a resolution that all Americans should be allowed to settle in the Territories "with whatever property they may possess, including slaves." All the Republicans voted no, so it failed, according to the rule that any measure must have the support of both parties. Before the committee adjourned, the Southerners repeated their offer to accept a new Missouri Compromise line, which would have resulted in 900,000 square miles of free territory, and 240,000 square miles of slave territory.

While the senators were deliberating, U.S. Army major Robert Anderson spiked the guns at Fort Moultrie, South Carolina, and moved his troops to the more defensible Fort Sumter. This alarmed the commissioners from the newly declared independent state of South Carolina, who had arrived in Washington that day. They thought they'd had a truce: South Carolina would not attack federal property as long as the government maintained the military status quo in Charleston Harbor. Buchanan agreed to meet with them, two days hence.

Eighth and Jackson Streets, Springfield, Illinois, December 28, 1860

Before the last year of peace ended, Lincoln entertained one more visitor who urged him to accept Crittenden's compromise. Duff Green was a sixty-nine-year-old newspaper publisher, railroad man, and retired diplomat. A Kentuckian, he was also a distant relation of the Lincoln family: Mary was the sister of his nephew's wife. Green put a copy of Crittenden's proposal in Lincoln's hands and invited him to travel to Washington to collaborate with Buchanan on "measures necessary to preserve the Union."

The South, Green told Lincoln, could not "consent to remain as members of a government which is to be permanently under the control of a sectional majority, organized as a political sectional party, on the basis of warfare to the institutions of the South." The Republicans in Congress were opposing the Missouri Compromise line to preserve their newly won sectional dominance: "They see if they relinquish that pretence, and permit the question of slavery in the territories to be adjusted, then the South will become a part of the United States, and have its due proportionate influence in the government."

Lincoln agreed that restoring the Missouri Compromise would calm the current secession mania, but the South would inevitably attempt to annex more of Mexico and spread slavery there.

After the meeting, Green told the *New York Herald* that "although Mr. Lincoln did not say so . . . he desires a satisfactory adjustment," and would "rejoice" at the Crittenden Compromise's passage.

Lincoln did not say so because he desired no adjustment whatsoever. He wrote a letter to Green stating that he did not favor new constitutional amendments but would not interfere with the public's right to pass one—not likely, given the Republicans' unanimous opposition to Crittenden. He repeated that each state had the right "to order and control its own domestic institutions." Still reluctant to make any public statements as president-elect, he asked Green not to publish the letter unless it was endorsed by six of the twelve senators from Georgia, Alabama, Mississippi, Louisiana, Florida, and Texas—also unlikely, since they wanted constitutional amendments. He didn't give the letter to Green—he sent it to Trumbull: "Gen. Duff Green is out here endeavoring to draw a letter out of me. I have written one, which herewith I inclose to you, and which I believe could not be used to our disadvantage. Still, if, on consultation with our discreet friends, you conclude that it may do no harm, do not deliver it."

It never was delivered. Like Weed, Green had journeyed to Springfield hoping to wring a compromise out of Lincoln and come away with nothing.

United States Capitol, Washington, D.C., December 28, 1860

Douglas's compromise proposal finally came to a vote by the Committee of Thirteen—and was almost unanimously rejected. Only the author and Crittenden voted in favor. Crittenden floated a new Missouri Compromise plan, which would have admitted all the unorganized land south of the line as the state of New Mexico. That got around the Republicans' objection to slavery in the territories, but slaveholders would be allowed to take their property into the new state. So the Republicans voted no. Henry Rice, the Minnesota Democrat, suggested admitting all territory north of the line as the state of Washington, and all territory south as the state of Jefferson, without any reference to slavery. The Republicans and the Southern Democrats voted against that. After that, the committee gave up. The thirteen senators finally came to an agreement, which was to report to the Senate "that they had been unable to agree on any basis of settlement, and that the minutes of their proceedings be published."

That evening, after the adjournment, Douglas visited the journalist William Henry Hurlbert. He was in "a state of some excitement"—not over the committee's proceedings, but over Fort Sumter. He had heard a story that Captain Abner Doubleday, Anderson's second-in-command, had taken orders from that wretched abolitionist Ben Wade to move the troops to Sumter, in order "to make a pacific settlement of the questions at last impossible." Lincoln, he was certain, had not approved of the move—his fellow Sucker was not as radical as the Republicans in the Senate.

"Mind, I don't for a moment suspect Lincoln had anything to do with this," Douglas told Hurlbert. "Nobody knows Abraham Lincoln better than I do, and he is not capable of such an act. Besides, it is quite incompatible with what I have heard from him. A collision and civil war will be fatal to him and his administration, and he knows it—he knows it. But Wade and that gang are infuriated at Seward's coming into the cabinet, and their object is to make it impossible for Lincoln to bring him into it. I think, as a friend of Seward's, you ought to understand this."

Senate Chamber, United States Capitol, Washington, D.C., January 3, 1861

Shortly after the New Year, the Committee of Thirteen presented the report of its failure to the Senate. Crittenden and Douglas were not giving up on compromise, though. Their colleagues were stubborn politicians, committed to the most extreme sectional and partisan doctrines. They would try to take their case to the people. Crittenden rose in the Senate to present what he admitted was "a measure . . . of extraordinary character": a nationwide referendum on the Crittenden Compromise.

"It is a scruple only, a scruple of as little value as a barleycorn, that stands between us and peace and reconciliation and union," Crittenden declared, referring to the Missouri Compromise line, "and we stand here pausing and hesitating about that little storm which is to be sacrificed. Sir, it may be that we are spell-bound in our party politics, and in opinions which they have generated, and fastened and bound upon us against our will; but I appeal with confidence to that great source from which we derive our power. If we cannot combine the requisite majority here to propose amendments to the Constitution which may be necessary to the settlement of our present difficulties, the people can."

Seward objected that passing constitutional amendments by popular vote was unconstitutional, but Crittenden's resolution had not proposed such an end run around the rules: it only proposed "taking the sense of the people." If it passed, though, Republicans would be under pressure to vote out Crittenden's amendments and send them to the states. Only the most radical, such as Wade and Sumner, would be able to resist the public's demand. A number of moderate Republicans had already come out for compromise. The previous evening, a group of prominent New York businessmen had thrown a dinner for Congressional Republicans at the Willard, the capital's most elegant hotel: seventy attended—half the delegation. William E. Dodge, one of Wall Street's wealthiest Merchant Princes, tried to persuade them to sacrifice the Chicago Platform.

"Shall we . . . stand upon a platform made some time ago in view of facts which then existed, and which have ceased to exist now; or shall we be willing to . . . yield some fair concession, without any sacrifice of principle?" Dodge asked.

Two Republican senators spoke in favor of compromise: Lafayette Foster of Connecticut and Simon Cameron of Pennsylvania—Lincoln's future secretary of war.

The November election results suggested that compromise had a good chance of winning public approval. Lincoln had won 39 percent of the popular vote. Douglas and Bell, the moderate candidates, had combined for 41 percent. Significantly, the two men had carried Missouri, Kentucky, Tennessee, and Virginia. By now, the Cotton States seemed bent on secession: the day before, Georgia had elected delegates to a secession convention, and that day, the state's governor, Joe Brown, seized Fort Pulaski near Savannah. However, if compromise could save the border states for the Union, their Confederacy would be too small, too weak, to support or defend itself.

Douglas rose in the Senate to second Crittenden, delivering a two-and-a-half-hour speech that, as was Douglas's wont, attached equal blame to secessionists and Republicans for the current crisis. Secession could never be permitted. The South should not be allowed to shut off interior states from foreign commerce "within the circle of a Chinese wall," nor to seize "light-houses, navy yards, forts, and arsenals" built with funds from the national treasury. He could understand why the South was in a panic over the impending accession of "the dominant party of the North," which had as its object "the ultimate extinction of slavery in all the states." In the event of a rebellion, though, "the Federal Government is and ought to be clothed with the power and duty to use all the means necessary to coerce obedience to all the laws made in pursuance of the Constitution. Sir, the word government means coercion. There can be no Government without coercion. Coercion is the vital principle upon which all Governments rest."

As bellicose as that sounded, Douglas was not prepared for a "war with our own brethren and kindred." There didn't have to be a war if the Republicans would simply agree to extend the Missouri Compromise line to California. Today's Republicans had "sung poems" to the line and "uttered imprecations enough and curses on my head" when the Kansas-Nebraska Act repealed it; they would now be justified "in claiming a triumph by its reestablishment." Douglas hoped Lincoln would abandon his "dangerous and revolutionary" goal of eradicating slavery, and that once he became president, "he will be fully impressed with the necessity of sinking the politician in the statesman, the partisan in the patriot and regard the obligation which he owes to his country as paramount to those of his party."

Douglas believed the Republicans had decided "that the unity of their party is dearer to them than the Union of the states. The argument is that the Chicago platform having been ratified by the people in a majority of the States must be maintained at all hazards, no matter what the consequence to the country." The American people, though, "have not decided that they preferred the disruption of this Government, and civil war with all its horrors and miseries, to surrendering one iota of the Chicago platform. If you believe that the people are with you on this issue, let the question be submitted to the people on the proposition offered by the Senator from Kentucky." If the Republicans refused, on them would be the "fearful responsibility" of a war "waged by the people of eighteen States against the people and domestic institutions of fifteen other States."

The difficulty for Douglas and Crittenden was passing their plebiscite proposal through a Congress unable to find any common ground on slavery. Douglas's demagoguery toward the Republicans—blaming them for civil war if they didn't go along with his plan—won him no supporters among the opposition. In a letter to Lincoln, Elihu Washburne called Douglas's speech "utterly infamous and damnable," and "the crowning atrocity of his life."

Senate Chamber, United States Capitol, Washington, D.C., January 16, 1861

From all across the country, North and South, petitions poured into Washington, demanding Congress pass Crittenden's compromise. The Senate Journal listed entreaties from "Citizens (12,000) of Baltimore," "a meeting of mechanics and workingmen of Newark, New Jersey," "a mass meeting of working-men of Philadelphia," "the mayor, aldermen, council, and over 22,000 citizens of Boston," "citizens of Pike County, Missouri," and "citizens of Monongalia County, Virginia." In the border states of Delaware, Virginia, and Kentucky, legislatures endorsed the compromise. From Massachusetts, Edward Everett, the Constitutional Union Party's vice presidential nominee, led a delegation that tried to move Senator Charles Sumner toward compromise. Sumner would not be moved, even after a petition bearing 22,000 names from 182 Bay State cities and towns was delivered to the capital. Sumner had written the Duchess of Argyll that "if secession is limited to the cotton states, I shall be willing to let them go."

From New York, a correspondent wrote Douglas that if Crittenden's resolutions "were submitted this day to the people of the North . . . they would be adopted with a unanimity hitherto unprecedented in the history of our country." From Kentucky came a letter reporting that "the feeling here is almost unanimous in favor of the Crittenden resolution and I believe should they be adopted Kentucky will be satisfied to stay in the Union."

Yet Senate Republicans were employing dilatory tactics to prevent action on Crittenden's resolutions. On January 9, Crittenden moved for their adoption. Senator Daniel Clark of New Hampshire countered with a resolution of his own: "That the provisions of the Constitution are ample for the preservation of the Union," and that "new guarantees for particular interests, compromises for particular difficulties, or concessions to unreasonable demands" were unnecessary. Senator Henry Wilson of Massachusetts moved to postpone debate because the Senate printer had not yet produced a copy of Clark's resolution. Bigler, a Pennsylvania Democrat, frantically objected that the 36th Congress would conclude in seven weeks. Unless a bill to hold a plebiscite was passed promptly, "there will be no time to get the sense of the people, and afterwards act upon these proposed amendments."

On the 12th, Seward delivered a much-anticipated speech that gave hope to both Douglas and Crittenden. "Dissolution would not only arrest but extinguish the greatness of our country," Seward declared, while Crittenden bowed his head and wept at his colleague's praise for the Union. "If the constellation is to be broken up, the stars, whether scattered widely apart or grouped in small clusters, will thenceforth shed only feeble, glimmering and lurid lights. Nor will great achievements be possible for the new confederacies."

Seward offered five concessions that he (and presumably Lincoln) was willing to make to preserve the Union. First, a repeal of all state laws that conflicted with the Constitution's fugitive slave clause. Second, an unamendable constitutional amendment preventing Congress from abolishing or interfering with slavery in any state. Third, the admission of the territories as "two new states"—the southern portion, presumably, the slave state of New Mexico. After "the angry excitement of the hour shall have subsided," a convention could be held to consider new constitutional amendments on slavery. Fourth, laws to prevent "mutual invasions of states by citizens of other states," i.e., Virginia and John Brown. Fifth, two Pacific Railroads, a southern running to New Orleans, a northern through St. Louis to Chicago.

The next day's *New York Herald* reported that Seward's proposals had been "denounced by both extremes," but that Douglas "regards it as a great speech." It would not do as an ultimatum, since it did not satisfy Southerners' demands to travel freely with their slaves, "but if it is an entering wedge, or basis of settlement, much good will result of it."

Two years earlier, the 36th Congress had been sworn in with a 38–25 Democratic majority, which was now eroding as a result of secession. South Carolina's senators resigned their seats in December. Mississippi, Florida, and Alabama seceded during the second week of January; their senators had not resigned but were no longer taking part in the body's business. Barnstorming the South during the last days of the presidential campaign, Douglas warned that secession would empower the Republicans. Without Southern votes, Crittenden's compromise was doomed to fail. Which it did when the Kentuckian's resolutions finally came to a vote on the 16th. Crittenden's seatmate, Lazarus Powell, proposed amending the first resolution to allow slavery in any territory "now held or hereafter to be acquired" south of the Missouri Compromise line. Douglas objected. The wording was unnecessary, since the resolution "applies to the country we now have, and when we get any more it will apply to that when we get it." Douglas also knew the amendment would make the compromise a harder sell to the North: Had not Lincoln opposed restoring the line because the South would expand slave territory by seizing more of Mexico? Senator James Mason of Virginia insisted the compromise would be "of no value" to the South without Powell's amendment, so Douglas voted for it, helping it pass 29–24.

The amendment turned out to be a moot point. Before Crittenden's compromise could come to a vote, Clark again moved to substitute his own resolution. The vote was called so quickly that Douglas, who had been summoned to the cloakroom, could not get back to the floor in time to vote nay. One vote would not have made a difference. Clark's amendment passed, 25–23. All the Republicans voted in favor. Seven Democrats abstained: both senators from Texas and Louisiana, Alfred Iverson of Georgia, Robert Johnson of Arkansas, and William Gwin of California. They knew the compromise could not succeed without the support of Lincoln and the Republicans, so they wanted to put their opponents on record as being unwilling to satisfy the South. Douglas raced back to the chamber, insisting his vote be "recorded in opposition to the amendment of the senator from New Hampshire." The Republicans objected. He was too late.

The Senate's rejection of Crittenden's resolutions convinced many Southerners that compromise was dead. The news was telegraphed to the Georgia secession convention, which reacted by voting to secede three days later. Senator Judah P. Benjamin, who had stuck to his seat and did not rise to vote on the Clark Amendment, informed colleagues in Louisiana, "We cannot get a settlement." Louisiana's secession on January 26 particularly galled Douglas, because the Louisiana Purchase had cost the nation $15 million, and because its loss cut off Illinois from the Mississippi River and the Gulf of Mexico. Louisiana had been bought "with the national treasure, for the common benefit of the whole Union in general, and for the safety, convenience, and prosperity of the Northwest in particular," he raged. The Clark Amendment even inflamed secessionist sentiment in moderate Southern states. "The South will not be satisfied with anything less than a recognition of the rights of slaveholders in the Territories, as embodied in the Crittenden Compromise, to wit: the running of the Missouri Compromise line to the Pacific," opined North Carolina's *Weekly Raleigh Register*. That was further than Seward was willing to go, and Seward's "speech is regarded as an exposition of the views and policy of the President elect."

Douglas, as usual, felt betrayed by abolitionists on one side and secessionists on the other. He angrily accused both of acting "in concert" to pass the Clark Amendment. The Republicans voted yes to hasten a civil war that would allow them to crush slavery; the Southerners refused to vote, to prove that compromise with the North was impossible, and justify their argument that the South was no longer safe in the Union.

Still, Douglas continued working for a compromise. The day after the Clark Amendment passed, he held a private meeting with Seward and Senator James Dixon of Connecticut. "I can say with confidence that there is hope of adjustment, and the prospect has never been better," Douglas wrote to Virginia Unionist James Barbour. Meanwhile, Seward dispatched another emissary to Springfield, to learn how much Lincoln would compromise. The president-elect spent most of the 20th and 21st with Representative William Kellogg of Illinois, a member of the House Committee of Thirty-Three. Republican hardliners Salmon P. Chase, Carl Schurz, and Schuyler Colfax were all entreating Lincoln to resist any compromise that would permit slavery's extension. "The moment seems to have arrived which will put manhood to a final test," Schurz wrote to Lincoln. Wavering Republicans were signaling their support for Crittenden, but "you are the man, who by a single stroke of the pen, may counteract the machinations at Washington" and guarantee "the future of liberty." Colfax objected to admitting New Mexico as a slave state, as Seward had hinted, because "with this sovereignty, she may secede the next month as she cannot now."

Lincoln did not disappoint the hardliners. He sent Kellogg back to Washington with his strongest statement yet against the proposals of Crittenden, Douglas, Seward, and all the other compromisers in the capital: "I will suffer death before I will consent or will advise my friends to consent to any concession or compromise which looks like buying the privilege of taking possession of this government to which we have a constitutional right; because, whatever I might think of the merit of the various propositions before Congress, I should regard any concession in the face of menace the destruction of the government itself, and a consent on all hands that our system shall be brought down to a level with the existing disorganized state of affairs in Mexico."

As decisive as that sounded, Douglas hosted a dinner party for Seward, Dixon, Crittenden, and foreign diplomats, at which the mood was confidence that the Union would endure.

"Away with all parties, all platforms, all previous committals, and whatever else will stand in the way of restoration of the American Union," Seward toasted.

Crittenden was moved. He set down his drinking glass so hard it broke.

"Don't forget in the morning what you drank at night," Douglas reminded his colleague.

When the Senate again debated compromise, Douglas took the side of Unionism against Senator Louis T. Wigfall of Texas.

"I see indications every day of a disposition to meet this question now and consider what is necessary to save the Union," Douglas said. "I believe that, as the crisis approaches, as the time of salvation becomes short, all men will become convinced that their duty to themselves, to their country, and to their God, require them to make concessions, in order to save the country."

Wigfall retorted that it was "the merest balderdash, the most unmitigated fudge, for anyone to get up here and tell men who have sense, who have brains, that there is any prospect of two-thirds of this Congress passing any proposition as an amendment to the Constitution, than any man who is White, twenty-one years old, and whose hair is straight, living south of the Mason-Dixon line, will be content with."

Douglas's hopeful message was not intended for Texas, which would secede on March 2. It was intended for Virginia. The Old Dominion, the Cradle of the Constitution, the Mother of Presidents had so far stopped short of secession. Instead, the Virginia legislature called for a peace conference, beginning February 4 in Washington, to which representatives from every state were invited for "a final effort to restore the Union and the Constitution, in the spirit in which they were established by the fathers of the Republic." If Virginia could be saved so, too, could Arkansas, Tennessee, and North Carolina, which would vote in February on calling state conventions. They must be convinced that there was some chance of overcoming Republican obstinacy.

"There is hope of preserving peace and the Union," Douglas wrote to a Petersburg man. "All depends on the action of Virginia and the border States. If they remain in the Union and aid in a fair and just settlement, the Union may be preserved. But if they secede, under the fatal delusion of a reconstruction, I fear that all is lost. Save Virginia and we will save the Union."

Willard's Hall, Washington, D.C., February 4, 1861

President John Tyler called the Peace Convention to order on the same Monday morning that representatives of the six seceded states were meeting in Montgomery, Alabama, to found the Confederate States of America. When Tyler proposed the convention, he suggested inviting only the slave states, so they could present to the North terms on which they would remain in the Union. Wisely, Virginia invited the entire nation, since any compromise the Convention produced would have to be approved by a Congress now dominated by free states.

"The great object of Virginia," Senator James Mason told his colleagues, was to "devise some additional amendment to the Constitution in some form that will guarantee the rights of the minority section, which will be acceptable to all the Southern states, and may even win back those that have separated themselves from the Union."

One hundred and thirty-three delegates, from twenty-one of the thirty-three states, crowded into Willard's Hall, a disused theater that the Willard Hotel had made available free of charge, hoping the conference would drive business to its bar. The Confederate states were not there. Neither were Arkansas and Louisiana, soon to join them. California and Oregon were too distant to send delegates, and the Northwestern states of Michigan, Wisconsin, and Minnesota refused, but the Yankee representatives included some of the North's most celebrated antislavery men: Chase of Ohio, Wilmot of Pennsylvania, William Pitt Fessenden of Maine, and Amos Tuck of New Hampshire. Among the Northern moderates were New York's William E. Dodge, who had organized the dinner at this same hotel to persuade Republican congressmen to support the Crittenden compromise.

The night before the conference opened, Douglas called on John M. Palmer, an anti-Nebraska Democrat-turned-Republican representing Illinois.

"I have beaten you long ago, and you at last have beaten me," Douglas said, referring to Palmer's loss of an 1859 congressional race to Douglas ally John McClernand. "According to your own limitation we are friends again."

The two men talked for half an hour. Douglas upbraided Palmer and the Republicans for not supporting him on the Lecompton Constitution.

"You and your friends did me great injustice in the Lecompton Controversy," Douglas said. "If I had had my way, and Buchanan had not been a traitor, I would have compelled Davis to raise the standard of rebellion during that controversy, and then there would have been Union sentiment enough in the country to put him down in thirty days; but now this continent will tremble under the tread of a million armed men before the rebellion is ended."

The gaunt Tyler, who had reached his threescore and ten, and was consumed by ailments that would take his life in less than a year, took his seat in the president's chair, before a full-length portrait of George Washington. Tyler had been an unpopular, unsuccessful president, but in his opening address, he was not complimentary to Washington and the Founders, either.

"Gentlemen, the eyes of the whole country are turned to this assembly in expectation and hope," Tyler told the delegates. "I trust that you may prove yourselves worthy of the great occasion. Our ancestors probably committed a blunder in not having fixed upon every fifth decade for a call of a general convention to amend and reform the constitution. On the contrary, they have made the difficulties next to insurmountable to accomplish amendments to an instrument which was perfect for millions of people, but not wholly as to thirty millions. Your patriotism will surmount the difficulties, however great, if you but will accomplish one triumph in advance, and that is, a triumph over party. And what is party when compared to the task of rescuing one's country from danger? Do that, and one large loud shout of joy and gladness will resound throughout the land."

Tyler appointed a Committee of Fifteen, composed of one member per state, to come up with a slate of constitutional amendments for the convention to consider. As chair, he chose former treasury secretary James Guthrie, from the great compromising state of Kentucky. After eleven days of deliberation, the committee delivered seven amendments, almost identical to Crittenden's. The Missouri Compromise line would be extended to California. No new territory could be acquired without the consent of four-fifths of the Senate. Congress could never abolish slavery where it existed. The Fugitive Slave Law would be enforced, the Atlantic slave trade banned, the three-fifths compromise preserved, and owners of runaway slaves rescued by mobs compensated. That still was not enough for Virginia. Virginia insisted that slavery be permitted in lands "now held or hereafter acquired" south of the Missouri Compromise line, which could mean Cuba, Mexico, or Central America. If slavery could not expand, it would die.

"We must have new lands," Virginia's James Seddon told Massachusetts governor Thomas Boutwell.

Boutwell did not agree. Few Northerners did. Seward wrote to Lincoln on January 27, warning him that his presidency would be opposed by "a hostile armed Confederacy," which could be dissolved only with "force or conciliation." The North would not tolerate a protracted civil war, so "every thought that we think ought to be conciliatory, forebearing and patient, and so open the way for the rising of a union party in the seceding states which will bring them back into the Union." It was a final plea for flexibility, a hope that Lincoln would be less "reckless" than Wade, Sumner, and the other Republican radicals who found "compromise or concession . . . as a means of averting dissolution . . . intolerable."

Lincoln wrote back that he did not "care much about New-Mexico," which Seward had proposed admitting as a slave state, "if further extension were hedged against." However, he wrote, "I am for no compromise which assists or permits the extension of the institution on soil owned by the nation. And any trick by which the nation is to acquire territory, and then allow some local authority to spread slavery over it, is as obnoxious as any other."

A trick such as calling a Peace Conference in order to deliver an ultimatum to the free states: give us more slave territory or we break up the Union. Rewarding that would lead to anarchy.

While the Peace Conference met, Republicans used their new Senate majority to pass the Morrill Tariff, protecting Northern industries by increasing import duties 70 percent. A higher tariff was part of the Chicago

Platform, and Lincoln had promised to sign one. Southern senators opposed the tariff, but so many had resigned that the votes to stop it were gone. Douglas opposed tariffs on principle—they protected one sector of the economy while damaging another—and worried that taking advantage of the Southern absence to pass a bill benefiting the North would make it more difficult to lure back the Confederate states. Douglas began collecting statistics for a paper on a new economic arrangement between the separated sections, which he called a "Continental Commercial Union or Alliance." It would establish a free trade zone throughout the continent, based on the German Zollverein, which Douglas observed during his 1853 European tour. The Zollverein eliminated customs and duties among the dozens of German-speaking principalities. Douglas was becoming ever more fearful that secession would be permanent, and ever more anxious about a foreign power controlling the Mississippi River, depriving Illinois farmers and industries "of all access to the ocean and all communication with the markets and people of the world beyond the great waters!" A commercial union composed of the United States, British Canada, Mexico, Cuba, Central America, and the Confederacy would allow all North Americans to trade freely, despite "differences of race, language, religion, forms of government and systems of civilization."

The Willard Hotel, Washington, D.C., February 23, 1861

Lincoln arrived in the capital at six in the morning, having slipped through Baltimore in the dead of night to avoid a suspected assassination plot. With his inauguration and his occupancy of the Executive Mansion still nine days away, he checked into a five-room suite in the southwest corner of the Willard, where his family would join him that afternoon. As president-elect, Lincoln's first duty was to call on his predecessor. Accompanied to the White House by Seward, he unwittingly interrupted a cabinet meeting. Buchanan was cordial, asking Lincoln whether he had enjoyed a "satisfactory reception" in Harrisburg, which was near his Wheatland estate, and introducing him to each member of the cabinet. At four o'clock, Lincoln received the Illinois congressional delegation, led by its dean and senior senator, Douglas.

"The meeting was less formal perhaps than would be the case at the interview with any other delegation, from the fact that they were all friends and acquaintances before," reported the *New York Herald*. "The interview between Mr. Lincoln and Mr. Douglas was particularly pleasant."

It was the first time Lincoln and Douglas had seen each other face-to-face since the Alton debate, two and a half years earlier. Then, they had been on opposite sides of the most divisive issue of the day, the extension of slavery. Now, they were on the same side of this day's most divisive issue: both were Union men, who agreed that secession was illegal, that the nation must be preserved, and that Lincoln's impending inauguration was no justification for breaking it up. They disagreed, though, on the severity of the crisis, and the best means of resolving it.

Lincoln's journey from Springfield to Washington had been a twelve-day whistle-stop, with speeches in Indianapolis, Cincinnati, Columbus, Pittsburgh, Cleveland, Buffalo, Albany, New York, Trenton, Philadelphia, and Harrisburg. In Pittsburgh, Lincoln gestured south, toward Virginia, and blithely declared, "notwithstanding the troubles across the river, there really is no crisis . . . excepting such a one as may be gotten up at any time by designing politicians. My advice, then, under such circumstances, is to keep cool. If the great American people will only keep their temper, on both sides of the line, the troubles will come to an end, and the question which now distracts the country will be settled just as surely as all other difficulties of like character which have originated in this government have been adjusted." He asked Clevelanders, "What then is the matter" with the South? "Do they not have their fugitive slaves returned now as ever? Have they not the same constitution that they have lived under for seventy odd years? Why all this excitement? Why all these complaints?"

That evening, at the end of Lincoln's long first day in his capital, he was visited at the Willard by Peace Conference delegates who wanted to learn, in person at last, how much he was willing to compromise. If not at all, they believed, the conference would be in vain. Lincoln played the country politician, extending his lanky arms to his visitors and greeting them with humorous remarks.

"You are a smaller man than I suspected," said Lincoln, the tallest man in the room—as he was in every room—to former senator William Cabell Rives of Virginia. "I mean in person: everyone is acquainted with the greatness of your intellect."

The sixty-seven-year-old Rives told Lincoln he had come out of retirement and left his plantations to answer Governor Letcher's call to save the Union.

"The clouds that hang over it are very dark," Rives said. "I have no longer the courage of my younger days. I can do little—you can do much. Everything now depends on you."

"I cannot agree to that," Lincoln replied. "My course is as plain as turnpike road. It is marked out by the Constitution. I am in no doubt which way to go. Suppose now we all stop discussing and try the experiment of obedience to the Constitution and the laws. Don't you think it would work?"

James Seddon, the future Confederate secretary of war, who had tried to force the convention to accept Virginia's demand for the right to acquire more slave territory, now forced his way into this conversation.

"It is not of your professions we complain," he told Lincoln. "It is of your sins of omission—of your failure to enforce the laws—to suppress your John Browns and your Garrisons, who preach insurrection and make war upon our property!"

"I believe John Brown was hung and Mr. Garrison imprisoned," Lincoln retorted. "You cannot justly charge the North with disobedience to statutes or with failing to enforce them. You have made some which were very offensive, but they have been enforced, notwithstanding."

"You do not enforce the laws," Seddon insisted. "You refuse to execute the statute for the return of fugitive slaves. Your leading men openly declare that they will not assist the marshals to capture or return slaves."

"You are wrong on your facts again," Lincoln said. "Your slaves have been returned, yes, from the shadow of Faneuil Hall in the heart of Boston. Our people do not like the work, I know. They will do what the law commands but they will not volunteer to act as tip-staffs or bean-bailiffs. The instinct is natural to the race. Is it not true of the South? Would you rein in the pursuit of a fugitive slave if you could avoid it? Is such the work of gentlemen?"

"Your press is incendiary!" Seddon exploded. "It advocates insurrection, and advises our slaves to cut their masters' throats! You do not suppress your newspapers. You encourage their violence."

"I beg your pardon, Mr. Seddon. I intend no offense, but I will not suffer such a statement to pass unchallenged, because it is not true. No Northern newspaper, not the most ultra, has advocated a slave insurrection or advised the slaves to cut their masters' throats. A gentleman of your intelligence should not make such assertions. We do maintain the freedom of the press—we deem it necessary to a free government. Are we peculiar in that respect? Is not the same doctrine held in the South?"

Dodge, the Merchant Prince, told Lincoln that on him depended the fortunes of Wall Street: "It is for you, sir, to say whether the whole nation shall be plunged into bankruptcy; whether the grass shall grow in the streets of our commercial cities."

"Then I say it shall not," Lincoln responded jocularly. "If it depends upon me, the grass will not grow anywhere except in the fields and in the meadows."

"Then you will yield to the just demands of the South," Dodge entreated. "You will leave her to control her own institutions. You will admit slave states into the Union on the same conditions as free states. You will not go to war on account of slavery!"

Lincoln told Dodge he would defend the Constitution, "let the grass grow where it may." A New Jersey delegate asked whether the North should make further concessions to avoid a civil war, such as allowing any territory to enter the Union as a slave state, as was provided for in the Committee of Fifteen's first amendment.

"It will be time to consider that question when it arises," Lincoln replied calmly. "Now we have other questions we must decide. In a choice of evils, war may not always be the worst. Still, I would do all in my power to avert it, except to neglect a Constitutional duty. As to slavery, it must be content with what it has. The voice of the civilized world is against it; it is opposed to its growth or extension. Freedom is the natural condition of the human race, in which the Almighty intended men to live. Those who fight the purposes of the Almighty will not succeed. They always have been, they always will be, beaten."

Douglas believed Lincoln's views were those of a small-town politician who did not understand the seriousness of the secession threats or the power of the office he was about to occupy. He told William Henry Hurlbert he thought Montgomery Blair, Lincoln's choice for postmaster general, and his father, Francis, were trying to manipulate Lincoln into a position hostile to the South, and to Seward's efforts at conciliation. The Blairs wanted a civil war that would result in the abolition of slavery and the expulsion of the Blacks. They had been among Lincoln's first visitors in Washington.

"If they can get and keep their grip on Lincoln, this country will never see peace or prosperity again, in your time, or in mine, or in our children's children's time," Douglas said.

Hurlbert asked Douglas how it was possible for anyone to manipulate Lincoln, unless he was "a weak and pliable character."

"No, he is not that sir, but he is eminently a man of the atmosphere which surrounds him," Douglas said. "He has not yet got out Springfield, sir. He has Springfield people with him. He has his wife with him. He does not know that he is President-elect of the United States, sir. He does not see that the shadow he casts is any bigger now than it was last year. It will not take him long to find out when he has got established at the White House. But he has not found it out yet. Besides, he knows that he is a minority president, and it breaks him down."

The Willard Hotel, Washington, D.C., February 27, 1861

Four days after Lincoln's arrival in Washington, Douglas visited his old rival alone, in his suite at the Willard, and begged him to use his influence to prevent the Peace Conference from breaking up without a resolution. If that happened, the border states might secede before Congress had a chance to pass conciliatory amendments. "Only you can save the country now," Douglas told Lincoln. Unless Lincoln did everything possible to preserve the Union, he would bear "the fearful responsibility" of seeing it break up on his watch. It was imperative that he speak to his Republican allies in the conference immediately. Another twenty-four hours and it might be too late.

"You have children as well as I do," Douglas burst out. "In God's name act the patriot and try to save our children a country to live in! I am your political opponent, and I expect to oppose the political measures of your administration, but I assure you that no partisan advantage should be taken, or political capital manufactured, out of an act of patriotism which would preserve the Union of the States. I have now performed my duty, and I ask you to perform yours."

Lincoln assured Douglas that he had been "engrossed" in the proceedings of the Peace Conference, which was voting that day on a final report to send to Congress. Douglas promised his support for the new administration, should the civil war they both dreaded come.

"Should any attempt be made by the advocates of secession and disunion to carry out their treasonable designs, by force or otherwise, I will aid and sustain you in any effort you may deem proper to save our Union—with all our strength and energy we will aid you. This country must be saved—our Union must be preserved. I am with you Mr. President, and God bless you."

Lincoln was moved by Douglas's declaration of loyalty to the country, and to himself. After the half-hour interview ended, he turned to James Pollock, chairman of the Pennsylvania delegation to the Peace Conference, and an old friend from the days when they had boarded together as congressmen.

"We have always been opposed politically, but now when the country needs the help of every true patriot, he forgets party and pledges his aid to me and the Union," Lincoln said. "I did not expect such a pledge—such a promise of co-operation."

The Illinois delegation played a key role in passing the Peace Conference's final report, which was crafted by Kentucky's Guthrie. On the initial vote, the essential first amendment to extend the Missouri Compromise line was defeated, 11–8. Most free states objected because it allowed slavery in the Southern territories. Some slave states—including Virginia—objected because it lacked the clause providing for territory "hereafter acquired." Border state delegates "wept like children," fearful that the Conference's failure would push their people toward secession. Francis Granger of New York moved to reconsider the vote, and it was brought up again on the 27th. Lincoln continued to meet with the Illinoisians. Palmer would recall that he "advised us to deal as liberally as possible with the subject of slavery." On the second vote, Illinois reversed itself. The amendment passed, 9–8. Massachusetts's Boutwell believed "the reconsideration was attributed to the interference of Mr. Lincoln or of his recognized friends."

The Conference endorsed a thirteenth amendment to the Constitution, protecting slavery where it existed. That still wasn't enough for the South. As he adjourned the Conference, Tyler praised its "intelligent, thoughtful [and] patriotic men," expressing his hope that "your labors . . . will bring to our country that quiet and peace which every patriotic heart so earnestly desires." He would have preferred the adoption of proposals "recommended by the Legislature of Virginia"—i.e., the "hereafter acquired" clause—but "still it is my duty to give them my official approval and support."

Tyler's endorsement of the Conference's labors lasted as long as it took him to cross the Potomac back into his native state. The very next day, he stood on the steps of the Exchange Hotel in Richmond, where he told his fellow Virginians "that he was now confident no arrangement could be made, that every hour's delay was perilous, and that nothing remained but to act promptly and boldly in the exercise of the State sovereignty."

(As Douglas feared, one of Virginia's complaints was the passage of the Morrill Act in the absence of Southern senators. That was regarded as taxation without representation—an established justification for revolution.)

Senate Chamber, United States Capitol,
Washington, D.C., March 2, 1861

The Peace Conference's proposals were in the hands of the 36th Congress, which had five days left to run. Douglas and Crittenden knew this was not enough time to shepherd through seven constitutional amendments. However, on February 28, the House had passed an amendment sponsored by Representative Thomas Corwin, an Ohio Republican. It banned the banning of slavery—the intention of the Peace Conference's third proposal. The so-called Corwin Amendment read: "No amendment shall be made to the Constitution which will authorize or give to Congress the power to abolish or interfere, within any State, with the domestic institutions thereof, including that of persons held to labor or service by the laws of said State."

Douglas introduced the amendment to the Senate on March 1. It was taken up a day later, with barely forty-eight hours left on the congressional calendar. The amendment was consistent with the Republican Party's Chicago Platform, which had endorsed "the right of each state to order and control its own domestic institutions." Still, Douglas received resistance from both Republicans and Southerners. Senator James Mason of Virginia objected to voting on the Corwin Amendment while ignoring the Peace Conference's other proposals.

"I am for both," Douglas said, "but this one is within our reach. We can close this much in five minutes."

Douglas added that he was glad that the senator from Virginia had become such a warm advocate of the Peace Conference's report, since, like former president Tyler, he had "denounce[d] it as unworthy of the consideration of Southern men or of this country."

The Republicans tried to run out the clock with procedural quibbles. Overcoming them required all the legislative legerdemain Douglas had acquired during his eighteen years in Washington. Senator Clark, of New Hampshire, raised the point of order that the amendment had not gone through three readings on three consecutive days. Douglas moved to repeal that rule, as it applied to constitutional amendments.

"We all know that the object is to get a vote on the third reading of motions to amend the Constitution," Douglas said. "We all know there is an attempt on the part of a portion of those on the other side of the Chamber to defeat that third reading today."

Then Senator George Pugh, an Ohio Democrat, moved to strike the words "authorize or" from the amendment, since they were a redundancy that violated the rules of proper English. The vote was a 19–19 tie, which Vice President Breckinridge broke by voting aye. That put Douglas in a panic. It was Saturday evening. The House would not convene again until ten o'clock Monday morning—two hours before Lincoln's inauguration, not enough time to consider a corrected amendment. Crittenden was also incredulous that a constitutional amendment could be defeated over a grammatical point too petty for the most pedantic English master.

"Why should we put this resolution at hazard by an amendment to correct some misprision of language?" asked the baffled solon.

Pugh moved to reconsider, and Senator Thomas Clingman of North Carolina changed his vote. The amendment was "a mere tub thrown to a whale . . . to make the public suppose we were doing something," Clingman said, but "gentlemen who are here think it a matter of very great consequence that this resolution should be passed."

Senator Mason then threw in his own filibuster; he introduced the Peace Conference resolutions, with the Virginians' "hereafter acquired" clause, as "an amendment to the proposition of the senator from Kentucky."

At midnight, the Senate adjourned until seven o'clock on Sunday night, when it would hold a last-ditch debate on the only constitutional measure with any chance of passing. The Corwin Amendment might not hold the Union together, but at least the senators could go home and report that some compromise had emerged from the deadlocked capital.

The galleries were packed to sweaty overcapacity, every inch of seating covered with women in floral dresses and black-suited men shoving and jostling for a view of the floor. President-elect Lincoln, who was less than twenty-four hours from becoming President Lincoln, arrived to hear Crittenden deliver the last speech of a Senate career begun forty-four years earlier. Lincoln's appearance may have implied support for the Corwin Amendment: he would endorse it in his Inaugural Address the next day.

Crittenden first introduced his successor, none other than Vice President Breckinridge, who had been elected by the Kentucky legislature, and would serve until December, when he was expelled for accepting a commission as a Confederate general. (Crittenden's retirement would be short-lived: later that year, he won a special election to the House of Representatives, on a Unionist ticket.)

"A few months ago, we were a united, and, I may say a happy people," Crittenden began. "Now, our Union is dismembered."

At this point, a man fainted in the overheated galleries, which were cleared of spectators standing in the aisles.

"Mr. President, it is an admitted fact that our Union, to some extent, has already been dismembered; and that further dismemberment is impending and threatened," Crittenden continued. "We are about to adjourn. We have done nothing. Even the Senate of the United States, beholding this great ruin around them, beholding dismemberment and resolution going on, and civil war threatened as a result, have been able to do nothing."

Crittenden again pleaded with Republicans to mollify Southern honor by permitting slavery in the New Mexico Territory, where only a couple dozen slaves lived, and which could never become a slave state, because slavery could not be "properly employed there."

Crittenden addressed the Republicans, "You have now grown greater than those who adopt this system of labor. You have just now triumphed in a great national controversy. The Republican Party are coming into power with a President to execute their will, and with a majority here to proclaim the will of the whole nation. Now give us some security that you will not abuse that power."

To prepare for a long night of debate, senators uncorked bottles of bourbon and set up cots beside their desks. Even Lincoln's friends were fractured in their support of the amendment. Lyman Trumbull announced that he would never amend the Constitution to make "perpetual slavery anywhere, no sir; no human being shall ever be made a slave by my vote."

But Senator Edward Baker of Oregon, a former Illinois congressman, and the namesake of Lincoln's second son, argued that the amendment was the only way to prevent Kentucky, Virginia, Tennessee, and North Carolina from seceding and strengthening the Confederacy. Permitting slavery to persist in New Mexico was "compromising, it is conceding," but "I do believe now it is necessary to preserve the Union by yielding, conceding, compromising, a little more than I did a year ago."

When Baker finished speaking, at close to midnight, Douglas praised "the patriotic speech of the Senator from Oregon," as a "contrast with the more political speeches which we had been compelled on this Sabbath Day to listen to."

Throughout the wee hours of March 4—Inauguration Day—opponents of compromise offered resolutions to smother the Corwin Amendment. Pugh moved to substitute the Crittenden resolutions. Even Crittenden voted against that, knowing they had no chance to pass. Douglas agreed with Pugh that the resolutions would have "saved all the States except South Carolina." He was in favor of them, even though "they were not in accordance with my cherished views." At this point, though, he said, "I do not think these facts furnish any reason why we should not take the resolution of the House of Representatives, being all we can now get." Senator Kinsley Bingham of Michigan tried to revive the Clark Resolution, which held that the Constitution needed no new amendments. It was voted down 25–13. Senator Robert Ward Johnson of Arkansas proposed to substitute the Peace Convention plan. That lost, 34–3. Douglas argued against every substitute, until finally, at four o'clock in the morning, there was nothing left to vote on but the Corwin Amendment itself. The amendment passed, 24–12—the exact two-thirds majority required to send it to the states. All the no votes were cast by Republicans. The senators from North Carolina and Texas abstained, as did James S. Green of Missouri, but the rest of the Democrats joined eight Republicans in voting aye. (Among Lincoln's future cabinet members, Simon Cameron voted aye, while Seward abstained.) That was as far as any Republican was willing to go. Douglas insisted on a "separate and distinct vote" on the Crittenden Resolutions, but with no

Republican support, the Senate adjourned, leaving its members just a few hours to get some sleep before the inauguration. The Senate had done something, but not enough to prevent more states from leaving the Union. The proposed Thirteenth Amendment was ratified by only five states. The actual Thirteenth Amendment, ratified in 1865, had the exact opposite effect, abolishing slavery throughout the United States.

East Portico, United States Capitol, Washington, D.C., March 4, 1861

On the day of his inauguration, Lincoln rose before sunrise in his rooms at the Willard and asked his son Robert to read aloud his address one last time. Lincoln had begun writing the speech in January, in Springfield, at a tall cubbyhole desk in a back room of a store owned by his brother-in-law, Clark Smith, where he could hide from office seekers. The speech had gone through multiple drafts, and been read by multiple political allies, but was still not finished: later that morning, Seward visited the Willard to confer with Lincoln on a passage about forcing "obnoxious strangers" on rebellious states to collect duties and imposts.

Inauguration Day dawned grayly, with low-hanging clouds spattering raindrops on the capital's unpaved streets—not quite enough to tamp down the dust, which was blown into the faces of the crowd by a bracing northwest wind. The fifes and drums of the militia, organized by General Winfield Scott to protect the president-elect from potential violence, drowned out the robins at that hour. Beginning at eight o'clock, the street outside the Willard was thronged with men and women waiting for Lincoln's emergence, some clutching carpet bags, because they had found no lodgings the night before. Throughout the morning, there was no sign of Lincoln, only his many visitors, including future cabinet members Seward, Edward Bates, Gideon Welles, and Simon Cameron, as well as Illinois friends David Davis, Lyman Trumbull, and Tom Marshall, a state senator from Charleston.

The inaugural procession began forming at nine, led by marshals in black hats, black frock coats, black pantaloons, and blue scarves, riding horses whose blue saddle cloths were trimmed in gilt. President Buchanan, occupied by signing bills until the hour his term expired, left the White House shortly before noon in an open brett for the three-block ride to the Willard. He alighted outside the ladies' entrance and went inside to greet his successor, supposedly with the words, "Sir, if you are as happy in entering the White House as I shall feel on returning to Wheatland, you are a happy man indeed."

"Mr. President," Lincoln is said to have replied, "I cannot say that I shall enter it with much pleasure, but I assure you that I shall do what I can to maintain the high standards set by my illustrious predecessors who have occupied it."

The outgoing and incoming presidents emerged to cheers from a crowd pressing against the police lines, and the fanfare of a military band blaring "Hail, Columbia." The barouche in which they rode was so tightly surrounded by mounted marshals and Army cavalry that "a shot could not have possibly been aimed at [Lincoln] so dense was the military enclosure." Troops gathered in platoons along Pennsylvania Avenue, dispatch riders waited on every corner to relay messages to General Scott, and snipers crouched on rooftops.

Lincoln arrived at the Capitol at 1:15, accompanied by Senators Solomon Foot and Edward Baker, looking "pale and wan, fatigued and anxious." The president-elect walked through the Senate chamber to the President's Room, where he brushed the dust of Washington's streets off his black broadcloth suit.

The wooden inaugural platform stood halfway up the Capitol's northeast steps, surrounded by seating for dignitaries. The Capitol's modern dome was still under construction—a job that would remain unfinished until after the impending war. Two tiers of columns were still surmounted by scaffolding, so the most distinguished architectural feature overlooking the inauguration was the Genius of America, a triangular sandstone and marble frieze depicting three togaed figures: a woman lifting the scales of justice, a man leaning on an anchor, and a woman beside an eagle, holding a spear and a shield lettered USA. Mrs. Lincoln emerged from the Capitol first, then frail Chief Justice Taney, supported by the clerk of the Supreme Court, who held in his other hand his personal Bible, on which Lincoln would take the oath of office.

Lincoln and Buchanan sat down directly in front of the platform. They were followed by members of the Senate, including Douglas, who had slept just a few hours since the Senate's adjournment early that morning. Douglas settled himself at the south end of the front row, in a seat that backed up to a wooden board facing the platform. When everyone was seated, Senator Baker stepped forward and announced, "Fellow Citizens, I introduce to you Abraham Lincoln, the President-elect of the United States of America." Although Buchanan's term had expired at noon, Lincoln would not take the oath of office until after delivering his address.

Lincoln rested his stovepipe hat on his lap, unsure where to store it while he read his speech. As Baker introduced him, he moved to place it beneath his seat. At that moment, Douglas stepped forward, hands outstretched. With the words, "Permit me, sir," he relieved Lincoln of the hat, which he held throughout the inaugural address. (A waggish newspaperman who witnessed the scene cracked, "Mr. Douglas could not be president himself, but he held the hat of the man who was.")

Lincoln donned a pair of steel spectacles and unfurled his speech, pinning it to the lectern with an ebony-tipped gold cane. For nearly ten months, since his nomination in Chicago, he had made almost no public statements, referring those who inquired about his views on slavery and secession to previous speeches, letters, or his party's platform. There had never been a more anxiously awaited inaugural speech. If Lincoln believed he could in half an hour end the secession fever incited by his election, he again misunderstood the South. Most of the speech was directed not to his supporters, the 25,000 fanned out beyond the Capitol steps, but to the secessionists, especially those in the eight slave states that had not yet left the Union.

"Apprehension seems to exist among the people of the Southern states that by the accession of a Republican administration their property and their peace and personal security are to be endangered," Lincoln began. "I have no purpose, directly or indirectly, to interfere with the institution of slavery where it exists. I believe I have no lawful right to do so, and I have no inclination to do so."

Lincoln read the Constitution's fugitive slave clause and endorsed a law to enforce it. Having, he hoped, reassured the South that its way of life was secure in a United States governed by President Abraham Lincoln, he made it clear that secession was anarchy, and that the very nature of the Union meant it could not be dissolved except with the consent of all its members: "No state upon its own mere motion can lawfully get out of the Union; that resolves and ordinances to that effect are legally void, and that acts of violence within any State or States against the authority of the United States are insurrectionary or revolutionary." As president, he would, without "bloodshed or violence," collect imports and deliver the mails, although, as he had discussed with Seward that morning, he would not impose "obnoxious strangers" to perform those duties in hostile regions of the country.

"One section of our country believes slavery is right and ought to be extended, while the other believes it is wrong and ought not to be extended," Lincoln said. "This is the only substantial dispute."

Lincoln spoke as though the right to bring slaves into territories was a quibble the South could ignore for the sake of national unity, so long as he protected slavery in the states and enforced the Fugitive Slave Law. (Secession, he warned, meant Southerners would never get back slaves who escaped to free states.) Republican resistance to slavery in the territories had been the only substantial dispute in the Crittenden Compromise and the Peace Conference, but it had been substantial enough to scuttle both and drive the Gulf states toward secession.

"Physically speaking, we cannot separate," Lincoln said of the North and South. "We cannot remove our respective sections from each other nor build an impassable wall between them. A husband and wife may be divorced and go out of the presence and beyond the reach of each other, but the different parts of our country cannot do this. They can not but remain face to face, and intercourse, either amicable or hostile, must continue between them."

As another gesture of conciliation toward the South, Lincoln asserted that he had no objection to the Corwin Amendment, which had passed the Senate hours earlier, being made "express and irrevocable."

The "momentous issue of civil war," Lincoln said, was not in his hands, but those of "my dissatisfied fellow countrymen." His government would not assail them. His purpose was to "preserve, protect, and defend" the Constitution, in the words of the oath he was about to swear. Only Southern aggression could bring about a conflict.

"We are not enemies, but friends," Lincoln closed, in a famous passage polished just that day. "We must not be enemies, though passion may have strained it must not break our bonds of affection. The mystic chords of memory, stretching from every battlefield and patriot grave to every living heart and hearthstone all over the broad land, will yet swell the chorus of the Union, when again touched, as surely as they will be, by the better angels of our nature."

Douglas listened intently to Lincoln's address, exclaiming at certain points, "Good," "That's fair," "No backing out there," "No coercion," and "Good again." (Buchanan displayed his relief at transferring his responsibilities to Lincoln by paying no attention to his successor's remarks.) Earlier that day, Douglas had told William Henry Hurlbert that he had seen parts of Lincoln's speech, that the illegality of secession was a point all constitutional Democrats could "brace themselves against," and that "he meant to put himself as prominently forward in the ceremonies as he properly could, to leave no doubt in anyone's mind of his determination to stand by the Administration in the performance of its first great duty to maintain the Union."

After the speech, Lincoln was administered the oath of office by Taney. He shook hands with the chief justice, then with Buchanan, Chase, and Douglas, receiving the congratulations of three of the four members of the "Stephen and Franklin and Roger and James" cabal he once accused of plotting the Dred Scott decision. Douglas told reporters on the scene that Lincoln's speech was sufficiently conservative.

"He does not mean coercion," Douglas said to one correspondent, "he says nothing about retaking the forts, or federal property—he's all right."

To another, he sounded more skeptical of Lincoln's purposes: "Well, I hardly know what he means. Every point in the address is susceptible of a double construction; but I do not think he means coercion."

The parade from the Capitol to the White House included a float labeled CONSTITUTION drawn by six white horses, whose saddlecloths read UNION in red lettering. Aboard it stood thirty-five girls, wearing white dresses and carrying laurel wreaths. Two represented the Goddess of Liberty; the rest carried a coat of arms from each state—even those that had seceded.

At the inaugural ball, Douglas escorted Mrs. Lincoln into the gaslit hall, adorned with shields and flags, and, at half past midnight, danced the quadrille with her.

Senate Chamber, United States Capitol, Washington, D.C., March 6, 1861

In the South, Lincoln's inaugural address was received as an incitement to war, due to his determination to protect federal installations in the seceded states.

"Civil war must now come," the *Richmond Enquirer* editorialized the morning after. "Sectional war, declared by Mr. Lincoln, waits only the signal gun from the insulted Southern Confederacy, to light its horrid fires all along the borders of Virginia."

Wrote a correspondent from New Orleans, "The assertion that the ordinances of the seceded states are void, and their acts insurrectionary, coupled with the determination to hold, occupy, and possess the government property, and to collect revenue, are received as an open declaration of war."

Two days after the inauguration, Senator Thomas Clingman of North Carolina, one of the few remaining Southern senators, took to the Senate floor to amplify his section's cry that Lincoln was a warmonger.

"The President declares expressly in the inaugural, that he intends to treat those states as though they were still members of the Union," said Clingman, who would soon wear the star of a Confederate brigadier general. "In plain, unmistakable language, he declares that it is his purpose to hold, occupy, and possess the forts and arsenals in those states. Surely, I need not argue to any senator that this must lead to a collision of arms."

Douglas immediately rose to defend the president. Lincoln's speech was "a peace offering rather than a war message," he told Clingman. Nothing in it committed the administration to recapturing forts, collecting revenue, or enforcing federal laws in the seceded states, "no matter what may be the circumstances that surround him."

Lincoln believed that, under the Constitution, the Union remained intact, regardless of the actions of a few states, but he was committed to a peaceful settlement of differences with the secessionists. That was Douglas's interpretation of the inaugural address.

"If maintaining possession of Fort Sumter would facilitate peace, he stands pledged to maintain its possession; if, on the contrary, the abandonment of Fort Sumter and the withdrawal of the troops would facilitate a peaceful solution, he is pledged to abandon the fort and withdraw the troops," Douglas insisted, unaware that Navy Secretary Gideon Welles had that day proposed relieving the fort, which was down to its last six weeks of provisions.

Douglas seized on Lincoln's statement that he recognized "the rightful authority of the people" to amend the constitution as proof that Lincoln would accept any policy that preserved peace. Of course, said Douglas—to demonstrate that he had not changed his ideals in spite of his newfound fondness for Lincoln—the solution to the current crisis was a constitutional amendment prohibiting Congress from regulating slavery in the territories. He was sure Lincoln would not resist such an amendment.

"We are authorized to infer that if the people do originate such amendments to the Constitution as will settle the slavery question—even if the settlement be repugnant to the principles of the Republican Party, in violation of the Chicago Platform, and against the right of Congress to prohibit slavery in the territories, Mr. Lincoln and his party would accept it."

Later that night, Douglas was heard to say, "Some people think Mr. Lincoln's inaugural does not jibe with the Chicago Platform. Well, what of it? I don't say it does or it does not; but if it does not it shows that Mr. Lincoln has the nerve to say what is right, platform or no platform. I defend the Inaugural if it is as I understand it, namely, an emanation from the brain and heart of a patriot, and as I mean, if I know myself, to act the part of a patriot."

Douglas strongly supported the appointment of Crittenden to the Supreme Court to replace John Archibald Campbell of Alabama, whose state had seceded. The "moral effect" of demonstrating that "Mr. Lincoln does not mean to have merely a partisan administration" would strengthen Unionist sentiment in Virginia, Tennessee, Maryland, and Arkansas. (Lincoln drew up papers to appoint Crittenden, but Campbell withdrew his resignation, only to resubmit it after Fort Sumter, by which time Lincoln had changed his mind about Crittenden.) Douglas and Crittenden continued to bolster Southern Unionists. They received a message from members of the Virginia Convention, which was debating secession: "Is there any hope for us? Can we remain in the Union?"

"Yes, there is hope," Douglas and Crittenden wired back. "Stand firm and all will yet be right."

Douglas's apparent alliance with his oldest political rival confused some of his allies. "I was somewhat surprised to find that you endorse Mr. Lincoln's inaugural in the whole," wrote a friend from Philadelphia. "There are some things I cannot reconcile myself to, but perhaps you can enlighten me on."

Douglas was playing a double game: trying to reassure the border states that Lincoln had only peaceful intentions toward the South, and trying to maneuver Lincoln into a more moderate position than the hard-liners in his cabinet. J. Anderson of New York seemed to understand Douglas's motives when he wrote, "I believe, and appreciate, your high purpose . . . I shall endeavor to hope that whatever the President did mean—if indeed he had a positive meaning at all—that your criticism may aid him in believing that he did mean peace and avoidance of war."

Senate Chamber, United States Capitol, Washington, D.C., March 7, 1861

Douglas introduced a resolution to ask the administration how many men were garrisoning federal outposts on the seceded states, whether reinforcements were required to hold them, and "whether the government has the power and means, under existing laws, to supply such reinforcements within each time as the exigencies and necessities of the case may demand." He informed the Senate that Fort Sumter had only thirty days of provisions left, and that resupplying it would require an army that could not be raised in such a short time. His resolution was intended to force Lincoln toward a policy of peace, by exposing the impracticality of defending Sumter. There were only three possible outcomes to the secession crisis, he said: restoring the Union "by such amendments to the Constitution as will insure the domestic tranquility, safety, and equality of all the States"; a peaceful separation; or war. Douglas favored the first: over the past year, every compromise he had proposed had been rejected, either by Fire-Eaters or Republicans, but he still insisted that the Cotton States could be lured back into the Union by his non-intervention amendment. The South would see an attempt to resupply Sumter as coercion, strengthening the hand of secessionists in the border states, especially Virginia, where Unionists controlled the Richmond Convention, but were ready to bolt at the first sign of aggression from Lincoln. Douglas believed the radical Republicans were trying to manipulate Lincoln into a war to destroy slavery.

"Mr. Lincoln does not meditate war," Douglas said. "What man in America, with a heart in his bosom, who knows all the facts connected with Fort Sumter, can hesitate in saying that duty, honor, patriotism, humanity, require that Anderson and his gallant band should be instantly withdrawn?"

The Republicans reduced Douglas's resolution to a simple listing of the forts in Confederate territory, without any enumeration of how many troops they contained, or how many would be required to hold them. Senator Henry Wilson of Massachusetts, who Douglas considered a member of the Republican war party, called his speech "mischievous," "wicked," and "unpatriotic—another unwelcome attempt to speak for Lincoln, as well as an effort to force the administration to publicize its military policy."

On March 27, the Republicans killed Douglas's Fort Sumter resolution and passed their own, composed by Trumbull. It stated that "the true way to preserve the Union is to enforce the laws of the Union; that resistance to their enforcement whether under the name of anti-coercion or any other name, is encouragement to disunion; and that it is the duty of the President to use all the means in his power to hold and protect the public property of the United States."

That was a rebuke to Douglas, who had been pleading against coercion, and a message to Lincoln that his party supported resupplying Sumter. Two days earlier, Douglas's frustration at his election loss, and the country's seemingly unstoppable slide toward war, had boiled over during a debate with Daniel Clark, the New Hampshire senator whose amendment killed the Crittenden compromise. Douglas praised Lincoln for—he imagined—pledging not to collect revenue, blockade ports, or use military force in the South without the consent of Congress.

"Nothing is to be done that leads to war," Douglas said. "That is a very good policy, a much wiser and better policy than I had expected or hoped for from a Republican administration. I do not know that I should have made as great efforts to defeat them if I thought they would have acted with as much wisdom and patience."

"You did not defeat them," Clark reminded Douglas.

"No, nor would I have made as great efforts to defeat them."

"You did no harm," Clark said, to laughter from his side of the chamber.

"If I did not defeat you, it was not my fault. I used my best effort to do it."

"You could not quite come it."

"I could not quite come it, and you see the consequences," Douglas raged. "Seven states are out of the Union, civil war is impending over you, commerce is interrupted, confidence destroyed, the country going to pieces, just because I was unable to defeat you. No man in America believes these consequences would have resulted if I had been successful in my efforts to defeat you. You can boast that you have defeated me, but you have defeated your country with me. You can boast that you have triumphed over me, but you have triumphed over the unity of these states. Your triumph has brought disunion, and God only knows what consequences may grow out of it."

CHAPTER 10

PATRIOTS OR TRAITORS

Treasury Building, Washington, D.C., April 10, 1861

Douglas and his wife were riding in a carriage down Pennsylvania Avenue when the senator spotted Navy Secretary Gideon Welles on the sidewalk outside the treasury building. Douglas ordered the driver to halt then jumped out of the cab to buttonhole Welles. Fort Sumter was on his mind.

"The Rebels are determined on war," he told Welles earnestly. "They are about to make an attack on Sumter. Immediate and decisive measures should be taken. It's a mistake that there has not already been more action. The dilatory proceedings of this government will bring on a terrible civil war. The whole South is united and in earnest. I have differed with this administration on important questions, and I will never be in accord with some of its members on fundamental principles and measures, but I have no fellowship with traitors or disunionists. I am for the Union and will stand by the administration and all others in its defense, regardless of party."

Welles suggested the two men drop in on Seward at the Northeast Executive Building, which contained the State Department's offices. It was nearby, at 15th Street NW and Pennsylvania Avenue. Douglas looked astonished, but agreed, leaving Adele behind in the carriage.

"Then you have faith in Seward?" he asked Welles. "Have you made yourself acquainted with what has been going on here all winter? Seward has had an understanding with these men. If he has influence with them, why don't he use it?"

"Seward is a member of the Administration," Welles said. "Nothing can be done without the knowledge of himself and his associates. To meet him frankly and give him confidence is probably the best course under the circumstances."

"Perhaps it is," Douglas conceded. "I can now see no alternative. Lincoln is honest and means well. He will do well if counseled right. You and I are old Democrats, and I have confidence in you, though we have differed of late. I was glad when I learned you were to be one of the Cabinet and have told Lincoln he could safely trust you. Seward has too much influence with him."

In fact, Douglas's position on Fort Sumter was closer to Seward's than Lincoln's. Seward had argued for abandoning the fort. He believed it had no strategic value, and that attempting to reinforce or resupply it would provoke an armed response that would push the border states into the Confederacy, defeating any chance of bringing the secessionists peacefully back into the Union. By the time Douglas encountered Welles on Pennsylvania Avenue, Lincoln had dispatched a fleet from New York Harbor, bearing provisions to Fort Sumter. As the fleet sailed, the president sent a message to South Carolina governor Francis Pickens, informing him that "an attempt will be made to supply Fort Sumter with provisions only; and that, if such an attempt not be resisted, no effort to throw in men, arms or ammunition will be made without further notice, or in case of an attack on the fort."

Pickens forwarded Lincoln's message to the Confederate government in Montgomery, which regarded the president's promise to use force if the fleet was turned away as an ultimatum. Confederate secretary of war L. P. Walker ordered General P. G. T. Beauregard, the commanding officer in Charleston, to demand Fort Sumter's evacuation, and "reduce" the fort if Major Anderson refused. War was now inevitable. Neither Lincoln nor Jefferson Davis could back down without destroying the prestige of their new, untested administrations. If Lincoln abandoned Sumter, he would legitimize secession by conceding that his government had no authority in a state he still insisted was part of the Union. If Davis tolerated a federal fortress in Charleston Harbor, how could he portray the Confederacy as an independent nation to England and France, whose recognition he hoped to gain?

Seward was the most dovish member of Lincoln's cabinet. The secretary of state thought evacuating Sumter would buy time for the "blind unreasoning popular excitement" in the South to give way to a new "devotion to the Union." He favored asserting federal authority by resupplying Fort Pickens, off Pensacola, Florida, which the Navy could provision from the Gulf of Mexico without coming into conflict with Confederate forces. Seward had even given hope to Unionists for the Richmond Convention by hinting that Sumter would be surrendered. It was an interesting role reversal, since Lincoln had won the Republican nomination by playing the moderate to Seward's radical. Lincoln reminded Seward that at his inauguration, "I said 'The power confided to me will be used to hold, occupy and possess the property and places belonging to the government, and to collect the duties and imposts.' This had your distinct approval at the time; and, taken in connection with the order I immediately gave General Scott, directing him to employ every means in his power to strengthen and hold the forts, comprises the exact domestic policy you urge, with the single exception, that it does not propose to abandon Fort Sumter."

By the time Seward received Welles and Douglas in his office, he was reconciled to Lincoln's Fort Sumter policy. Taking a pinch of snuff, instead of his usual cigar, he listened to Douglas and promised to relay his concerns to the president.

"I know there are wild and reckless men in Charleston and we shall have difficulty with them, but I know of no way to prevent an assault if they are resolved to make one," the secretary of state said.

After the meeting, Douglas told Welles that he had been watching the course of events for months but had been unable to do anything to control it.

"I have found myself in the confidence of neither party," he said ruefully. "I tried to rally the Democracy, but the party was broken up. Slidell, Cobb, Breckinridge, and others were determined to break up the Union, too. I could do nothing with them; others like you took the opposite course and got mixed up with old Whigs, and I had as little influence with you. Buchanan was feeble and incompetent. The great point with him and his Cabinet was to drift over to the fourth of March."

Douglas considered himself a man without a party and without influence, but in the last two months of his life, he would put partisanship aside and make his greatest contribution to the nation—a final effort to defeat the secessionists he had spent his career trying to appease.

The White House, Washington, D.C., April 14, 1861

The Civil War began at 4:30 on the morning of April 12, when Beauregard's batteries opened fire on Fort Sumter. The next evening, when news of the fort's surrender was telegraphed to Washington, an entire nation felt itself under attack—especially Douglas. For more than a decade, he had done everything he could to conciliate the South, granting the slave states almost every concession they demanded to remain in the Union. He had shepherded the Compromise of 1850 through Congress, written the Kansas-Nebraska Act, defended the Dred Scott decision, and supported the Crittenden Compromise and the Corwin Amendment. It had not been enough. First, the South destroyed Douglas's presidential campaign because he refused to support a law protecting slavery in the territories. Now, it was attempting to destroy the United States of America over the same principle. The Union, he now understood, could no longer be preserved by placating the South; it could be preserved only by defeating the South.

George Ashmun, a former Whig congressman who had chaired the 1860 Republican National Convention, was on friendly terms with Douglas and realized that the leading Northern Democrat's support could be vital to the war effort. In the free states, a faction of Democrats who would become known as Copperheads were opposed to Mr. Lincoln's war. They favored allowing the South to secede peacefully. Most had voted for Douglas. Late that afternoon, Ashmun called on Douglas at his Minnesota Avenue mansion. After an hour's discussion of "the whole nature of his relations to Mr. Lincoln's administration and his duty to the country," Ashmun asked Douglas to accompany him to the White House, "and make a declaration of his purpose to sustain [Lincoln] in the needful measures . . . which the law demanded."

At first, Douglas was reluctant, telling Ashmun, "Mr. Lincoln has dealt hardly with me, in removing some of my friends from office, and I don't know if he wants my advice or aid."

Ashmun persisted; this moment of national peril was no time for squabbles over patronage.

"The question now presented rises to a higher dignity than could belong to any possible party question," he told Douglas. "It is now in your power to render such a service to your country as would not only give you a title to its lasting gratitude, but would at the same time show that in the hour of your country's need, you could trample all party considerations and resentments underfoot."

Adele came into the room. At her urging, Douglas agreed to see Lincoln.

Douglas and Ashmun arrived at the White House at the dark end of the early spring dusk. Lincoln was alone, and happy to see them. From a desk drawer, he withdrew a wartime proclamation he had just composed and read it aloud. The proclamation called for 75,000 militiamen "to re-possess the forts, places, and property which have been seized from the Union" and summoned Congress back into session on the Fourth of July.

"Mr. President, I cordially concur in every word of that document," Douglas said, "except that instead of the call for seventy-five thousand men, I would make it two hundred thousand. You do not know the dishonest purposes of these men as well as I do."

Douglas walked over to a map hanging on a wall at the end of the room and indicated strategic points that should be strengthened against possible Confederate attack: Fort Monroe and Harpers Ferry in Virginia (which would vote to secede three days later); Cairo, Illinois, at the meeting of the Ohio and Mississippi rivers; and Washington. Douglas told Lincoln it might be difficult to move troops overland through Baltimore, where secessionist sentiment was still strong. He suggested an alternate route through Perryville, Havre de Grace, and Annapolis.

As they left the White House after the two-hour conference, Ashmun suggested that Douglas write an account of his strategy session with Lincoln and send it to the newspapers.

"You have done justice to your own reputation and to the president, and the country must know it," Ashmun said. "The proclamation will go by telegraph all over the country in the morning, and the account of this interview must go with it. I shall send it, either in my own language or yours. I prefer that you should give your own version."

"Drive to your room at Willard's and I will give it shape," Douglas agreed. At the hotel, Douglas composed this dispatch for the Associated Press: "Mr. Douglas called on the President this evening, and had an interesting conversation on the present condition of the country. The substance of the conversation was that while Mr. Douglas was unalterably opposed to the administration on all its political issues, he was prepared to sustain the President in the exercise of all his constitutional functions to preserve the Union, and maintain the government and defend the federal capital. A firm policy and prompt action were necessary. The capital of our country was in danger and must be defended at all hazards, and at any expense of men or money. He spoke of the present and future without reference to the past."

At the telegraph office, Douglas ran into a friend, who asked how the president should respond to the shelling of Fort Sumter.

"If I were president," Douglas said, "I'd convert or hang all the traitors within forty-eight hours." Then he added, "I have known Mr. Lincoln a longer time than you have, or the country has; he will come out all right, and we will all stand by him."

John W. Forney, the clerk of the House of Representatives, asked Douglas a similar question when they met on Pennsylvania Avenue: "What is now to be done? My dear friend, what are we to do?"

"We must fight for our country and forget all differences," Douglas told Forney. "There can be but two parties—the party of patriots or traitors. We belong to the first."

Over the next week, Douglas attended several more strategy sessions with Lincoln and Winfield Scott, the elderly, rotund Mexican War hero who was, for the moment, commanding the Union forces. A rumor went about that Lincoln was considering appointing Douglas a brigadier general. Lincoln responded that he doubted Douglas would accept a commission, but "I can imagine few men better qualified."

Douglas was a politician, not a soldier, and he was more useful to the war effort as a politician. Missouri, the only state he had carried in the presidential election, was divided in its loyalties. The new governor, Claiborne Fox Jackson, had campaigned as a Douglas Democrat but was now attempting to lead his state into the Confederacy. Douglas received telegrams from St. Louis, where Union sentiment was strongest, asking whether it was true that he supported the administration's war on the South.

"Do you endorse Lincoln's war policy?" one asked. "Missouri will not."

"I deprecate war," Douglas replied, in a response that was published in the newspapers, "but if it must come I am with my country and for my country, under all circumstances, and in every contingency. Individual policy must be subordinated to public safety."

Secession had personal, as well as political, consequences for Douglas. Early that month, he wrote to James McHatton, overseer of his family's Mississippi plantation, asking whether he could "arrange to send me two thousand dollars—or even one thousand, to relieve my immediate necessities?" McHatton, as much a Confederate as any of his neighbors, wrote back that Mississippi was now in a foreign country and "every house in N.O. will stop payment." The *Memphis Avalanche* suggested seizing the Douglas family's plantation and selling it "for the purpose of defending the South in a war which he and Lincoln have involved the country."

To the South, Douglas was now as much an enemy as Lincoln.

State House, Springfield, Illinois, April 25, 1861

The day after the attack on Fort Sumter, a dozen men gathered in a saloon in Marion, Illinois, the seat of Williamson County, to discuss drafting an ordinance of secession from the Union. Marion, in the heart of Egypt, lay at the same latitude as Richmond and was nearly as Southern in its heritage, its outlook, and its politics. While there was no slavery in Egypt, there was little enthusiasm for a war against the South, the land of most Egyptians' ancestors.

"A large share of Southern Illinois is peopled with men from or descended from citizens of the slave states, and they naturally sympathize with the South," the *Chicago Times's* Springfield correspondent reported. "The opinion is freely expressed that an army of ten thousand men from Northern Illinois, marching against the South, could not reach the Ohio River. Hundreds are ready to fight in defense of the South."

This was a strategic concern, since Douglas had impressed upon Lincoln the importance of reinforcing Cairo, which lay across the Ohio River from Kentucky and the Mississippi from Missouri and was key to controlling traffic on both rivers. On Monday, April 15, the would-be secessionists gathered in front of the county courthouse where, with one dissenting vote, they passed a series of resolutions demanding "a division of the state," as a result of which they would "attach ourselves to the Southern Confederacy." (Thirty-four local men would enlist in Company 6, the "Illinois Company" of the 15th Tennessee Regiment Volunteer Infantry.)

There were also doubts about the loyalty of Egypt's congressman, John A. Logan, a Douglas ally. In the run-up to Sumter, Logan had been a strong voice in favor of compromise and against coercion. His father-in-law, John W. Cunningham, helped draft Williamson County's secession resolutions. Logan told Cunningham the resolutions were "treasonous," but "that he would suffer his tongue to cleave the roof of his mouth, and his right arm to wither . . . before he would take up arms against his Southern brethren, unless it was to sustain the Government." Logan, who introduced Illinois's Black Law to the legislature in 1853—it was known as "Logan's Black Law"—swore that "if war was presented solely for the purpose of freeing Negroes, he would not only ground his arms but would turn and shoot them North."

On the same day the secessionists gathered in Marion, Governor Richard Yates called an April 23 special session of the legislature, for the purpose of raising a militia to defend the Union. (From Shawneetown, on the Ohio River, John Olney wrote Yates to assure him of Egypt's loyalty: The people of Saline County were "all for the Union and the enforcement of the laws." There were two secessionists in Hardin County, but "they must dry up or leave.")

From Springfield, Charles Lanphier wired Douglas that there were "grave reasons" he should attend the special session. Douglas shared Lanphier's message with Lincoln. He offered to remain in Washington if Lincoln needed him there. Both agreed he could better serve the war effort in Illinois, where he could, in Douglas's words, "come home to arouse the people in favor of the Union." The old adversaries shook hands and parted. It would be Douglas's last trip to the adopted state they shared, but only he would see Springfield again.

Douglas and Adele left Washington on the 21st, aboard a Baltimore and Ohio train. The railroad's tracks crossed through Virginia, which was now part of the Confederacy. Virginia militia stopped and searched the train. Discovering that Douglas was a passenger, they threatened to detain the Yankee senator.

"A sojourn at Harpers Ferry might not be disagreeable," Douglas told the soldiers, "but if I am kept prisoner, a force will soon arrive from the west larger than any that has ever been in Virginia before."

Douglas was permitted to pass through Virginia, but his train was detained so long he missed his connection in Bellaire, Ohio, across the river from Wheeling, and was forced to spend the night there. When the townspeople learned Douglas was staying at LaBelle House, they gathered outside the hotel to cheer the Union, cheer the flag, and demand a speech. Douglas told the Ohioans, close neighbors to Virginia, that the nation could never be subdivided into "little, petty confederacies" demanding duties wherever "a bushel of wheat" crossed a state line.

"I have a most exhausted strength, and voice, and life, in the last two years, in my efforts to point out the dangers upon which we were rushing," he said. "And we have no time now to stop to inquire as to the causes of those mischiefs, nor as to the merits or foibles of sects or parties. Unite, as a band of brothers, and rescue your governments and its capital and your country from the enemy who have been the authors of your calamity!"

The crowd cheered wildly, crying, "We will!" and "That's what we are going to do!" Douglas caught the five o'clock train to Columbus. He did not deliver a formal speech in the state capital. Rather, he appeared half dressed in the window of his room at the American House, addressing a sober crowd that did not greet him with torches or music, as they might at a partisan gathering. This crowd was composed of Breckinridge men who had abandoned their candidate now that he was making common cause with the Confederacy, and Republicans who wanted to see whether such an influential Democrat had really gone over to Lincoln. The Union must be preserved and the insurrection crushed, Douglas told them, pledging his hearty support to Mr. Lincoln's administration in achieving those goals.

"There was no uncertainty in his tone," wrote future Union general and Ohio governor Jacob Dolson Cox, who was in attendance that night. Not only an abolitionist, but an Oberlin graduate, Cox was grateful to hear such sentiments from a politician whose principles he must have despised: "I do not think we greatly cheered him—it was rather a deep Amen that went up from the crowd. We went home breathing freer in the assurance we now felt that, for a time at least, no organized opposition to the federal government and its policy of coercion would be formidable in the North."

Douglas arrived in Springfield on the morning of the 25th, on the same train as a company of volunteers from Vandalia, which he addressed at the station. He immediately sought out Orville Hickman Browning, a friend of Lincoln's and an old political opponent of Douglas's—they had run against each other for Congress in 1842, when Douglas was first elected. Douglas thought they could work together to produce "harmony and concert" between Republicans and Democrats. The two men then met with Governor Yates, Senator Trumbull, and former lieutenant governor Gustave Koerner, who assigned them to come up with a bill for raising troops that would be acceptable to both parties. The Democrats had been resistant. After meeting with the chairman of the House Committee on Militia, Browning "drew one up which is satisfactory to all parties in regard to the excess of volunteers now here over and above what were demanded by the President," and which was passed that day. (In just over two months, Yates would appoint Browning to replace Douglas in the Senate.)

The House and Senate passed a joint resolution inviting Douglas to address both bodies at seven o'clock that evening, in the House chamber. The chamber was outfitted with desks for seventy-five representatives but was crowded with far more men that night. The address, which is known to history as the "Protect the Flag" speech, was the greatest of Douglas's career. Considering the moment, the sentiments, and the years of discord between Douglas and the man to whom he pledged his loyalty, it may be regarded as the greatest argument any politician has ever delivered on setting aside partisanship in a time of national crisis.

In the previous year's elections, Republicans had won control of both houses of the legislature, including a 40–35 majority in the House, so Douglas was introduced by Republican Speaker Shelby Moore Cullom (who would one day hold his Senate seat). He addressed himself mostly to his fellow Democrats, though. The Douglas who stood before the legislature was a different Douglas than those veteran Illinois politicians were used to seeing. As he admitted to the crowd in Ohio, two years of trying to prevent his party, then his country, from falling apart had exhausted him. His eyes were sunken, his face furrowed, his voice raspy. No one who heard his words, though, would ever forget their strength.

"For the first time since the adoption of the Federal Constitution," he began, standing at the burnished speaker's rostrum, before a portrait of Washington, "a widespread conspiracy exists to destroy the best government the sun of heaven ever shed its rays upon. Hostile armies are now marching upon the federal capital, with a view of planting a revolutionary flag upon its dome; seizing the national archives; taking captive the president elected by the votes of the people, and holding him in the hands of secessionists and disunionists."

Douglas had "prayed and implored" for compromise, "spared no effort" for a peaceful solution, but now that peace had failed and war was declared, "there is but one course left for the patriot, and that is to rally under that flag which has waved over the Capitol from the days of Washington." The South had no grievances that could justify rebellion. The Fugitive Slave Law was enforced. The Republicans in Congress had organized the Colorado, Dakota, and Nevada territories without any restrictions on slavery! Yet simply because "a certain political party has succeeded in a presidential election," the slave states thought their liberties unsafe in the Union. Refusing to abide by the results of an election would make the United States as chaotic and unstable as Mexico, whose every president was overthrown before serving out his term.

"You all know that I am a very good partisan fighter in partisan times," Douglas said. "And I trust you will find me equally as good a patriot when the country is in danger."

Now that the country was facing the greatest threat in its eighty-five-year history, it was the duty of every man in the room, Republican and Democrat, "to lay aside, for the time being, your party creeds and platforms; to dispense with your party organizations and partisan appeals; to forget that you were ever divided, until you have rescued the government and the country from their assailants. When this paramount duty shall have been performed, it will be proper for each of us to resume our respective political positions, according to our convictions of public duty. Give me a country first, that my children may live in peace; then we will have a theatre for our party organizations to operate upon."

Douglas appealed directly to his "Democratic friends" who were reluctant to support a Republican president: "Do not allow the mortification, growing out of defeat in a partisan struggle, and the elevation of a party to power that we firmly believed to be dangerous to the country—do not let that convert you from patriots to traitors in your own land . . . The greater the unanimity the less blood will be shed. The more prompt and energetic the movement and the more imposing the numbers, the shorter will be the struggle."

Some Democrats looked startled and angered by that statement, but Republicans were thrilled. Horace White, a *Chicago Press and Tribune* reporter who was in the State House that night, described Douglas's speech as "a blast of thunder . . . that hushed the breath of treason in every corner of the state."

Logan was also present for Douglas's speech. According to Usher F. Linder, a friend of both men, he considered it such an unforgivable attack on the Democratic Party that he refused to shake Douglas's hand when they encountered each other on the street. Another account says that Douglas told Logan, "The time has now arrived when a man must be either for or against his country. Indeed so strongly do I feel this, and that further dalliance with the question is useless, that I shall myself take steps to join the army and fight for the maintenance of the Union."

Logan returned to southern Illinois still not committed to the war, still hoping, along with many of his constituents, that his section of the state could moderate the conflict between "fanatics North and South." Logan's law partner was a Peace Democrat. Egypt would take the side of the Union, though. By early May, 4,000 federal troops occupied Cairo. By the end of that month, the first local regiments had mobilized. Logan was waiting to see whether public opinion in his district tended to peace or war. When he saw it was war, he enlisted in a Michigan regiment that would fight at Bull Run, then resigned his seat in Congress to organize the 31st Illinois Volunteer Regiment, which he led with distinction as a major general. Logan's devotion to Unionism was so complete that after the war, he joined the Republican Party and served two terms as a United States senator. Frank

E. Stevens, Douglas's biographer, credits the "Protect the Flag" speech for the conversion of Egypt: "There was just one object [the people in southern Illinois] adored more than the Fire-Eaters of their ancestors and that was Douglas. Like wildfire his speech spread through Egypt and over into the border states, and without a draft, Egypt furnished more than its quota of men to the Union armies."

In the words of Gustave Koerner, who also witnessed the speech, "Douglas's influence was of large advantage to our cause, as he was really the idol of the Northern Democracy. The counter-efforts that were made for some time by John A. Logan and Dan Voorhees, who denounced Douglas as having betrayed his party, fell dead, and Logan soon found it advisable, in order not to kill himself forever, to join the volunteer army."

In late April, though, the loyalty of Logan and Egypt was still in doubt. Douglas wrote Lincoln from Springfield that he had "found the state of feeling here and in some parts of the state much less satisfactory than when I arrived. There will be no outbreak however and in a few days I hope for entire unanimity in the support of the government and the Union."

Douglas so virulently desired the Confederacy's destruction because he felt double-crossed by the South. As he admitted in his speech, he had "lean[ed] too far" toward the South's interests, against those of his own section. No compromise had been enough. Before leaving Springfield, he told Browning of a plot among Buchanan, Jefferson Davis, Robert Toombs, and Secretary of War John B. Floyd of Virginia. If Breckinridge had carried all the slave states, plus Oregon and California, they planned to give him control of the army and navy and inaugurate him as president, in spite of Lincoln's electoral majority. This he knew for a fact. Days later, in Chicago, Douglas delivered his most bitter attack yet against the South.

National Hall, Chicago, Illinois, May 1, 1861

After passing the Kansas-Nebraska Act, Douglas was burned in effigy in his hometown. On his final trip home, he received "an ovation . . . of which any man might have been proud." Thousands awaited his train at the Chicago, Alton and St. Louis Railroad Depot. When Douglas and Adele disembarked, the crowd cheered at the top of every lung, gathering itself into a parade that escorted the senator to the National Hall (the Wigwam's new, nonpartisan name), serenaded by brass bands. Chicago had voted for Lincoln, but on this day, Douglas was the city's idol.

Douglas deplored the war, he told the crowd, and had done all he could to prevent it. He had not only granted to the South "what was theirs of right, but I have gone to the very extreme of magnanimity." Now that North and South were at war, he understood that nothing could have satisfied the secessionists. The Fire-Eaters had been plotting "an enormous conspiracy" to dissolve the Union for more than a year, since before the Democratic Convention, which they broke up to ensure Lincoln's election.

"The slavery question is a mere excuse," Douglas raged. "The election of Lincoln is a mere pretext. They use the Slavery Question as a means to aid the accomplishment of their ends. They desired the election of a Northern candidate by a sectional vote in order to show that the two sections cannot live together."

Douglas repeated his words to John Forney in Washington—"there can be no neutrals in this war, only patriots or traitors"—and thanked God Illinois was not divided along party lines, as the South had hoped.

"There is but one way to defeat this," Douglas said. "In Illinois it is being so defeated by closing up the ranks. War will thus be prevented on our own soil. While there was a hope of peace I was ready for any reasonable sacrifice or compromise to maintain it. But when the question comes of war in the cotton fields of the South or the cornfields of Illinois, I say the further off the better."

Douglas stepped off the stage to nine cheers—the last he would ever hear. The welcoming committee escorted him back to the Tremont House, where he and Adele stayed in Chicago. That night, he complained of feeling unwell but thought a two-month rest before the War Congress convened on July 4 would allow him to regain his strength. The previous twelve months had been a time of enormous physical and emotional strain, as Douglas forced his constitution to its limits by campaigning nationwide for the presidency, then for compromise in Washington. He dealt with the stress by increasing his already heavy drinking and cigar smoking, dissipating his body's ability to fight off illness. What at first felt like a cold blossomed into a fever. By May 10, Douglas's arms were so weakened by what he believed was a severe attack of rheumatism that he was forced to dictate a letter to Virgil Hickox, chairman of the Democratic State Central Committee. Hickox wanted him to explain the discrepancy between his efforts at compromise and his support for Lincoln—a concern for Democrats who thought he had gone over to the Republicans.

"We should never forget that a man cannot be a true Democrat unless he is a loyal patriot," Douglas responded.

Soon, Douglas was not even lucid enough to dictate a letter. On the 19th, he was well enough to step outdoors, which encouraged Adele to believe he was recovering. The next day, she called in doctors after Douglas exhibited alarming symptoms. Besides the rheumatism, he was afflicted with typhoid, an ulcerated sore throat, torpor of the liver, and constipation of the bowels. As he lay on his deathbed, Douglas's mind was still consumed with war and politics.

"Why do we stand still?" he cried. "Let us press on! Let us to Alexandria quickly!"

As one of his doctors administered a blister, Douglas ordered him, "Stop! There are twenty against me. The measure is defeated."

Tremont House, Chicago, Illinois, June 3, 1861

Throughout Douglas's illness, Chicago newspapers posted daily front-page updates on his condition. On June 1, the *Press and Tribune* reported that the senator was comfortable, but likely in his last hours. A bloody flux had set in, and he was declining rapidly. Hundreds gathered outside the Tremont House, seeking news of the senator's health. On Sunday the 2nd, the family had some hope of his recovery. Adele called in the Roman Catholic bishop of Chicago, James Duggan, who asked Douglas if he had been baptized.

"Never," Douglas replied.

"Do you desire to have mass said after the ordinances of the Holy Catholic Church?" the bishop asked.

"No, sir," replied Douglas, a freethinker to the end. "When I die, I will communicate with you freely."

At four o'clock Monday morning, Douglas took a sudden turn for the worse. Four doctors were summoned. Douglas asked them to change his position in bed, so he could look out onto the street. Dr. Rhodes lifted him to a sitting posture, but Douglas closed his eyes and murmured, "Death!—Death!—Death!"

"Do you have a message for your mother, or your sister Sarah, or your boys Robby and Stevie?" Dr. Rhodes asked.

When Douglas did not reply, Adele put her arm around his neck and whispered, "My dear, do you know Cousin Dan?"

"Yes," he mumbled.

"Your boys, Robby and Stevie, and your mother and sister Sarah—have you any message for them?"

"Tell them to obey the laws and support the Constitution of the United States"—his last patriotic message to the world and the words later carved on his sarcophagus.

Dr. Rhodes moved Douglas back onto his side. As Adele held her husband's right hand and wept, Rhodes observed, "I am afraid he does not lie comfortable."

"He is—very comfortable," Douglas said.

The great orator spoke no more. Adele asked, "Husband, do you know me? Will you kiss me?" Douglas lifted his eyes to his wife, and, with his last bit of strength, forced a smile. That morning, the forty-eight-year-old senator died.

Adele, always more comfortable in Washington than Illinois, wanted Douglas's body transported there for burial and asked that no religious services be performed until it arrived. Governor Yates immediately formed a committee of prominent politicians to petition Adele to bury Douglas in Chicago. The widow agreed. Douglas's casket was taken to Bryan Hall, at Clark and Lake Streets, and placed under a canopy topped with a bronze eagle, on which was pinned an American flag. The funeral would not be held until the 7th, to give Douglas's sons—twelve-year-old Robert and eleven-year-old Stephen Jr.—time to return to Chicago from their Catholic school in Georgetown. Over two days, 50,000 Chicagoans filed past the bier, which was surrounded by Chicago Light Guard in blue pantaloons and shako hats. Disturbed by the news that Douglas's burial service would be performed by Bishop Duggan, 1,800 Freemasons held a Masonic funeral for their prominent brother on the 6th, presided over by a Methodist minister from Evanston.

The next morning, the two-mile long funeral procession formed outside Bryan Hall to accompany Douglas's body to a waiting grave at Oakenwald, his South Side estate. Mayor Julian Rumsey ordered all businesses closed, so Michigan Avenue was lined with mourners, who witnessed the sixteen military companies following the hearse. Since Douglas had not belonged to any religious sect, Duggan did not perform a mass but delivered a simple eulogy. A band struck up a lively air, and the mourners dispersed.

Douglas was no less mourned in Washington. On the day after his death, Secretary of War Cameron ordered all regimental colors draped in mourning and issued a proclamation to be read to the troops, calling Douglas "a man who nobly discarded party for country," and his death "a national calamity." President Lincoln ordered the White House covered in black crepe. On the day of Douglas's funeral, he closed all executive departments and received no visitors. Lincoln understood the debt he owed to the man with whom he had so long struggled for power, and the gap that Douglas would leave as the leader of a loyal opposition in Congress. As the nation's most prominent War Democrat, Douglas's actions since Fort Sumter had rallied members of his party throughout the North behind Lincoln's leadership, helping to unify the nation against the Confederate rebellion. As Gustave Koerner would write, had Douglas "died two months sooner, his name would not have shone as bright in the remembrance of the American people as it does now." History remembers Lincoln and Douglas as antagonists, but they ended their relationship as allies, bonded, finally, by their shared belief in the Union.

NOTES

AL: Abraham Lincoln papers, Library of Congress
ALPLM: Abraham Lincoln Presidential Library and Museum
CW: Roy Basler, ed., *Collected Works of Abraham Lincoln* (New Brunswick, N.J.: Rutgers University Press, 1953).
Letters of SAD: Robert W. Johannsen, ed., *The Letters of Stephen A. Douglas* (Urbana: University of Illinois Press, 1961).
SAD Papers: Stephen A. Douglas papers, University of Chicago

CHAPTER 1
p. 1   Since the U.S. Senate's adjournment: Damon Wells, *Stephen Douglas: The Last Years, 1857–1861* (Austin: University of Texas Press, 1971), 3–6.
p. 2   "I believe this government cannot endure": "A House Divided," Speech at Springfield, Illinois, June 16, 1858, *CWII*, 462–470.
p. 3   "I shall have my hands full": John W. Forney, *Anecdotes of Public Men*, Vol. 2; (New York: Harper & Bros., 1881), 179–180.
p. 3   Douglas's return to Chicago: *Chicago Press and Tribune*, July 10, 1858.
p. 5   "There were about half a dozen locomotives": John H. Stover, *History of the Illinois Central Railroad* (New York: Macmillan, 1975), 75.
p. 6   "an attempt to import Southern aristocracy": Robert W. Johannsen, *Stephen A. Douglas* (Urbana: University of Illinois Press, 1973), 450.
p. 6   Charles Walker, a local attorney: *Chicago Press and Tribune*, July 10, 1858.
p. 7   "When I found an effort being made." Ibid.
p. 9   In his speech to the Republican convention: "A House Divided," Speech at Springfield, Illinois, June 16, 1858, *CWII*, 462–470.
p. 9   "a thing shadowy and fleeting": Dunbar Rowland, ed., *Jefferson Davis, Constitutionalist: His Letters, Papers and Speeches*, Vol. 3 (Jackson: Mississippi Department of Archives and History, 1923), 572.

p. 9   "Mr. Lincoln asserts": *Chicago Press and Tribune*, July 10, 1858.

p. 11   "a concluding speech on him": AL to William Fithian, Sept. 3, 1858, *CWIII*, 84.

p. 11   Despite the marching bands: *Chicago Press and Tribune*, July 12, 1858.

p. 12   "squatter sovereignty": Ibid.

p. 13   "I am not pro-slavery": George Murray McConnel, "Recollections of Stephen
          A. Douglas," *Transactions of the Illinois State Historical Society for 1900*, 48.

p. 13   Douglas was the de facto master: Johannsen, *Stephen A. Douglas*, 211.

p. 14   "I have become a *Western* man": SAD to Julius N. Granger, Dec. 15, 1833,
          Letters of SAD, 3.

p. 16   "the least man I ever saw": Frank E. Stevens, "Life of Stephen Arnold
          Douglas," *Journal of the Illinois State Historical Society*, 16, 290.

p. 16   Douglas proposed they air their differences: David Zarefsky, *Lincoln, Douglas,
          and Slavery: In the Crucible of Public Debate* (Chicago: The University of
          Chicago Press, 1990), 36–37; Frank Everett Stevens, "Life of Stephen Arnold
          Douglas," *Journal of the Illinois State Historical Society*, 16, nos. 3–4 (October
          1923–January 1924): 323–328.

p. 16   "The Democratic giant is here": AL to John T. Stuart, Dec. 23, 1839, *CWI*, 160.

p. 16   "is in favor of allowing free Negroes": Paul Simon, *Lincoln's Preparation for
          Greatness: The Illinois Legislative Years* (Urbana: University of Illinois Press,
          1971), 136.

p. 17   "Douglas has got to be a great man": Sidney Blumenthal, *All the Powers of
          the Earth: The Political Life of Abraham Lincoln, Vol. 3, 1856–1860* (New York:
          Simon & Schuster, 2019), 192.

p. 17   "Twenty-two years ago": "Fragment on Stephen A. Douglas," Dec. 1856,
          CWII, 382–383.

p. 17   "intensely jealous": Ward Hill Lamon, *The Life of Abraham Lincoln: From
          His Birth to His Inauguration as President*, (Boston: James R. Osgood & Co.,
          1872), 341.

p. 18   "If Illinoisans understood": Allen R. Guelzo, *Lincoln and Douglas: The Debates
          That Defined America* (New York: Simon & Schuster, 2008), 48.

p. 18   "I think Greeley is not doing me right": Harold Holzer, *Lincoln and the Power
          of the Press: The War for Public Opinion* (New York: Simon & Schuster, 2014),
          171.

p. 18   "is from this time forward": Robert W. Johannsen, *The Frontier, the Union, and
          Stephen A. Douglas*, (Urbana: University of Illinois Press, 1989), 229.

CHAPTER 2

p. 19   The Douglas Limited departed Great Central Station: Stevens, "Life of
          Stephen Arnold Douglas," 549–551.

p. 21   "I do not believe that the signers of the Declaration of Independence":
          "Speech Delivered at Bloomington, Ill., by Senator S. A. Douglas," Northern
          Illinois University Digital Library.

p. 22   "This meeting was called by the friends of Judge Douglas": Stevens, "Life of
          Stephen Arnold Douglas," 550.

p. 23   The 1820 Census found 917 slaves: Arthur C. Boggess, *The Settlement of Illinois, 1778–1830* (Chicago: Chicago Historical Society, 1908), 187.

p. 23   "[A] poor man in a slave state": "Spartacus," *Illinois Intelligencer*, June 25, 1824.

p. 23   The referendum to lift all restrictions on slavery in Illinois failed: *History of Sangamon County, Illinois* (Chicago: Inter-State Publishing Company, 1881), 268.

p. 23   The following census: SangamonLink, "Population Changes, 1830–2010," https://sangamoncountyhistory.org/wp/?p=4948.

p. 23   In 1829, seven Yale Theological Seminary students: Charles Henry Rammelkamp, *Illinois College: A Centennial History, 1829–1929* (New Haven, Conn.: Yale University Press, 1928), 23.

p. 24   "believing that the College": William Henry Herndon and Jesse William Weik, *Herndon's Lincoln* (Chicago: Belford, Clarke & Company, 1889), 178–179.

p. 24   Elijah Lovejoy, the son and grandson of Congregationalist ministers: Paul Simon, *Freedom's Champion: Elijah Lovejoy* (Carbondale: Southern Illinois University Press), 31.

p. 25   "There is no grievance": "The Perpetuation of Our Political Institutions: Address before the Young Men's Lyceum of Springfield, Illinois," Jan. 27, 1838, *Journal of the Abraham Lincoln Association*, 6, no. 1 (1984): 6–14.

p. 25   Lincoln voted in favor of an amendment: Paul Simon, *Lincoln's Preparation for Greatness: The Illinois Legislative Years* (Norman: University of Oklahoma Press, 1965), 130.

p. 25   "admitting all whites to the right of suffrage": *Sangamo Journal*, June 13, 1836.

p. 26   "They believe that the institution of slavery": *CWI*, 75.

p. 26   "dangerous" for an Illinois politician: Thomas Ford, *A History of Illinois* (Chicago: S. C. Griggs & Co., 1854), 34.

p. 27   "I think annexation an evil": AL to Williamson Durley, *CWI*, 347–348.

p. 27   He found one in the Colonization Society: Eric Foner, "Lincoln and Colonization," in *Our Lincoln: New Perspectives on Lincoln and His World*, Eric Foner, ed. (New York: W. W. Norton & Co., 2008), 139–140.

p. 28   "the elements of a just and liberal adjustment": *Sangamo Journal*, August 2, 1850.

p. 28   "Cast into life where slavery was already widely spread": "Honors to Henry Clay," July 6, 1852, *CWII*, 121–133.

p. 28   "all parties, save a few abolitionists": Patricia Lee Luthe, "The Compromise of 1850 as Seen in Selected Illinois Newspapers" (M.A. thesis, Illinois State University, 1968), 71.

p. 29   "We had hoped to gain a short respite": *Illinois State Journal*, Jan. 15, 1854.

p. 29   "There has never been, in my opinion": David Davis to Julius Rockwell, July 15, 1854, David Davis Papers, ALPLM.

p. 29   "I was losing interest in politics": AL to Joshua Speed, Aug. 24, 1855, *CWII*, 321–324.

p. 30   "it was thereby discovered": Ibid.

p. 30   "directly at war with the genius": Richard Yates, speech before the United States House of Representatives, Feb. 28, 1855, cited in *The Congressional Globe*, Vol. 31, Parts 1–2.

p. 31   "was done without the consent of the people": "Speech at Bloomington, Illinois, Sept. 12, 1854," *CWII*, 230–233.

p. 31   "I have not been in public life as Judge Douglas has": "Speech at Springfield, Illinois, Oct. 4, 1854," *CWII*, 240–247.

p. 33   "the right and duty of the General Government": Graham A. Peck, "How Moderate Were the Moderates? Reconsidering the Origins of the Republican Party in Illinois," *Journal of Illinois History* 17 (Autumn 2014): 173.

p. 33   "I have been perplexed": AL to Ichabod Codding, Nov. 27, 1854. *CWII*, 288.

p. 34   "a dangerous extreme": *Illinois State Journal*, Sept. 26, 1855.

p. 34   "Stand WITH the abolitionist": "Speech at Peoria, Ill., Oct. 16, 1854," *CWII*, 248–284.

p. 34   "We recognize the legal rights of the slave states": *Peoria Weekly Republican*, Feb. 29, 1855.

p. 35   "Will meet you. Radicals and all.": Reinhard H. Luthin, "Abraham Lincoln Becomes a Republican," *Political Science Quarterly*, 59, no. 3 (Sept. 1944): 420–438.

p. 36   "We won't go out of the Union, and you shan't!": *Alton Weekly Courier*, June 5, 1856.

p. 36   "power should be exerted": Peck, "How Moderate Were the Moderates?"

p. 37   "No man at this day occupies a more conspicuous position": *Illinois State Register*, July 17, 1858.

p. 37   Springfield and its hinterlands: Stevens, "Life of Stephen Arnold Douglas," 550–551.

p. 37   "What is his remedy for this imaginary wrong": "Speech Delivered at Springfield, Illinois, by Sen. S. A. Douglas," Northern Illinois University Digital Library.

p. 39   "in less than five years, you would need a search warrant": Ibid.

p. 40   "However many of them": *Illinois State Journal*, August 1857.

p. 40   "There is a point beyond which the slave power": *Quincy Daily Whig*, April 14, 1857.

p. 40   "The Symbols of Bleeding Sumner": William E. Gienapp, *The Origins of the Republican Party, 1852–1856* (New York: Oxford University Press, 1987), 347.

p. 41   "Senator Douglas is of world-wide renown": "Speech at Springfield, Illinois, July 17, 1858," *CWII*, 505–522.

p. 42   "Do not spend too much time in the North": Thomas Harris to SAD, SAD Papers, UC.

p. 43   Lincoln was making the same calculations: "1858 Campaign Strategy," *CWII*, 477–482.

p. 43   "by some persons unknown": *Chicago Times*, July 19, 1858.

p. 44   "There are two very good circuses": *Chicago Times*, July 1858.

p. 44   "Messrs. Lincoln and Douglas will speak together": *New-York Tribune*, July 12, 1858.

p. 44   "canvass the State together": *Chicago Press and Tribune*, July 22, 1858.

p. 45   "My Dear Sir: will it be agreeable": *CWII*, 523.

p. 45   "What do you come to me with such a thing as this for?": *An Oral History of Abraham Lincoln: John G. Nicolay's Interviews and Essays*, Michael Burlingame, ed. (Carbondale: Southern Illinois University Press, 2006) 44–45.

p. 45   "Between you and me": Stevens, "Life of Stephen Arnold Douglas," 553.

p. 46   "the usual, almost universal western style": *Chicago Press and Tribune*, August 2, 1858.

p. 46   "I will, in order to accommodate you": Stevens, "Life of Stephen Arnold Douglas," 554.

p. 47   "There are but few present": "Speech at Clinton, Illinois," *CWII*, 525–527.

p. 47   "Come to, Lincoln, return to Bement": Stevens, "Life of Stephen Arnold Douglas," 556–557.

p. 48   "I did not know that such proposal": AL to SAD, July 29, 1858, *CWII*, 529–531.

CHAPTER 3

p. 49   "the crowd had a holiday air": C. C. Tisler and Aleita G. Tisler, *Lincoln Was Here (For Another Go at Douglas)*, (Jackson, Tenn.: McCowat-Mercer Press, Inc., 1958), 36.

p. 50   By the time Lincoln arrived: William Osman, "Recollections of the Lincoln-Douglas Debate," LaSalle County Historical Society; *Ottawa Daily Times*, June 18, 1908.

p. 50   Douglas received a more rustic greeting: *Ottawa Free Trader*, Aug. 21, 1858; *Ottawa Daily Times*, June 18, 1908.

p. 50   Trapped by the crowds: "The Lincoln-Douglas Debates," LaSalle County Historical Society.

p. 51   "in Louisiana and Massachusetts alike": Paul M. Angle, ed, *The Complete Lincoln-Douglas Debates of 1858* (Chicago: University of Chicago Press, 1958), 103–144.

p. 51   Douglas began his opening speech: *The Complete Lincoln-Douglas Debates*, 287.

p. 53   "Douglas had a deep bass voice": Tisler and Tisler, *Lincoln Was Here*, 25–26.

p. 54   "I have no purpose directly or indirectly": *The Complete Lincoln-Douglas Debates*, 114–130.

p. 56   "Douglas and I": AL to Joseph O. Cunningham, *CWIII*, 37.

p. 56   "the only representative of the shorthand art": "The Accuracy of Newspaper Accounts of the 1858 Lincoln-Douglas Debates" in Walter Barlow Stevens, *A Reporter's Lincoln*, Michael Burlingame ed. (Lincoln: University of Nebraska Press, 1998), 229.

p. 57   "the Republicans have a candidate for Senate": Ibid., 230.

p. 57   "Perhaps no local contest": *New-York Tribune*, Aug. 26, 1858.

p. 58   "an examination of Clay's principles": *Chicago Press and Tribune*, Aug. 28, 1858.

p. 58   Lincoln agreed to meet with Judd: "Conversation with Hon. N. B. Judd, Washington, Feb. 28 '76," in *An Oral History of Abraham Lincoln: John G.*

Nicolay's Interviews and Essays, Michael Burlingame, ed. (Carbondale: Southern Illinois University Press, 1996), 45–46.

p. 58   "Put a few ugly questions at Douglas": Joseph Medill to AL, Aug. 27, 1858, AL Papers.

p. 59   "wouldn't budge an inch,": Burlingame, *An Oral History of Abraham Lincoln*, 45–46.

p. 60   "all prairiedom has broken loose": *New York Evening Post*, Sept. 2, 1858.

p. 60   The crowd followed Lincoln: *Freeport Debate Centennial* (Freeport, Ill.: Lincoln-Douglas Debate Society, 1958), 31–40; *Freeport's Lincoln* (Freeport, Ill.: W. T. Rawleigh, 1930), 133–189.

p. 60   "the skeleton of some greyhound": *Freeport Weekly Bulletin*, Sept. 2, 1858.

p. 60   "dressed like a cavalier": *Freeport's Lincoln* (Freeport, IL: W. T. Rawleigh, 1930), 85.

p. 61   "Hold on, Lincoln, you can't speak yet": Stevens, *A Reporter's Lincoln*, Michael Burlingame, ed. (Lincoln, Neb.: Bison Books, 1998), 50.

p. 61   "Question 1": *The Complete Lincoln-Douglas Debates*, 140–141.

p. 63   "THE RESOLUTIONS WERE FRAUDS AND FORGERIES": *Chicago Press and Tribune*, Aug. 23, 1858.

p. 63   Douglas had heard about the resolutions: SAD to Charles Lanphier, *Letters of SAD*, 426–427.

p. 64   "Question 1": *The Complete Lincoln-Douglas Debates*, 143–144.

p. 65   "I answer emphatically": Ibid., 152.

p. 65   "Judge Douglas avowed the doctrine": *Nashville Patriot*, Sept. 15, 1858.

p. 66   "The last time I came here to make a speech": *The Complete Lincoln-Douglas Debates*, 156.

p. 68   "Douglas pretends to be horrified at amalgamation": Speech at Carlinville, Ill., Aug. 31, 1858.

p. 68   "They say you have turned your coat": *The Complete Lincoln-Douglas Debates*, 179–180.

p. 68   Two days before the debate: George W. Smith, *When Lincoln Came to Egypt* (Herrin, Ill.: Crossfire Press, 1993), 114–117.

p. 68   "For God's sake, Linder": SAD to Usher F. Linder, August 1858, *Letters of SAD*, 427.

p. 69   Douglas's supporters greeted the steamboat's landing: Darrel Dexter, *A Trot Down to Egypt: The Lincoln-Douglas Debates in Jonesboro, Illinois* (Jonesboro Lincoln-Douglas Debate Sesquicentennial Committee, 2008), 39–42.

p. 70   The Wednesday afternoon crowd at Jonesboro: Ibid., 47–48, 57–59.

p. 70   "A little further south they became bleached": *The Complete Lincoln-Douglas Debates*, 193–204.

p. 71   "If the slaveholding citizens": Ibid., 220.

p. 71   "It is a fundamental article in the Democratic creed": Ibid., 229.

p. 72   "As much as I admired Lincoln": John McLean, *One Hundred Years in Illinois* (Chicago: Peterson Linotyping Company, 1919), 118–119.

p. 72   Twenty-five-year-old Tillman Manus: Smith, *When Lincoln Came to Egypt*, 130.

p. 73   "denouncing Douglas in the strongest possible terms": Dexter, *A Trot Down to Egypt*, 62.

p. 73   "If you do this, the thing is settled": William Herndon to Lyman Trumbull, June 23, 1858, Lyman Trumbull Papers, Library of Congress.

p. 73   "Stephen A. Douglas had deserted the Democracy": *Chicago Press and Tribune*, Sept. 18, 1858.

p. 73   "REASONS FOR OPPOSING DOUGLAS": *Jonesboro Gazette*, Oct. 23, 1858.

p. 74   Both candidates spent the night in Mattoon: Charles H. Coleman, *Abraham Lincoln and Coles County, Illinois* (New Brunswick, N.J.: Scarecrow Press, 1955), 173–179.

p. 75   "Say to him that if we could meet now": AL to John Johnston, April 12, 1851, *CWII*.

p. 76   Once the candidates reached the fairgrounds: Coleman, *Abraham Lincoln and Coles County*, 180.

p. 76   "While I was at the hotel today": *The Complete Lincoln-Douglas Debates*, 235.

p. 77   "there was a preconceived arrangement": Speech of Hon. Lyman Trumbull on the Great Issues of the Day, Delivered in Chicago, Aug. 7, 1858, in *Chicago Press and Tribune*, Aug. 9, 1858.

p. 78   "The point upon Judge Douglas is this": *The Complete Lincoln-Douglas Debates*, 247.

p. 78   "He has devoted his entire time": Ibid., 252.

p. 78   "The general rule made the law silent": Ibid., 251.

p. 79   During his rejoinder: Ibid., 271–272.

p. 79   "I flatter myself that thus far my wife": Don E. Fehrenbacher and Virginia Fehrenbacher, eds., *Recollected Words of Abraham Lincoln* (Redwood City, Calif.: Stanford University Press, 1996), 143.

p. 80   "bloated as I ever saw him": William Herndon to Theodore Parker, Oct. 4, 1858, Herndon-Parker Mss., University of Iowa Library, Iowa City, Iowa.

p. 80   "I will postpone to 3 o'clock": *The Complete Lincoln-Douglas Debates*, 276–280.

p. 80   "Mr. Lincoln, you must be having a weary time": *Julian M. Sturtevant, An Autobiography*, (New York: F. J. Revell Company, 1896), 292.

p. 81   Douglas had visited Galesburg: "The Blanchard-Douglas Debate," *Lincoln-Douglas Debate Centennial, 1858–1958* (Galesburg, Ill.: Knox College, 1958).

p. 81   The debate took place: Earnest Calkins, "Galesburg's Big Day," *Lincoln-Douglas Debate Centennial, 1858–1958*, 6–8; *Rock Island Argus*, Oct. 7, 1958; "The Big Day: A Galesburg Swede Views the Lincoln-Douglas Debate, *Knox Alumnus*, Winter 1990; "Reminiscences of the Lincoln-Douglas Debate," Knox College Library; Herman E. Muelder, "Why Galesburg and Knox College Were on Lincoln's Side," *Lincoln-Douglas Debate Centennial, 1858–1958*, 10–12.

p. 83   "While I hold that under our Constitution," Ibid., 295.

p. 85   "Judge Douglas, and whoever like him," Ibid., 311.

p. 85   On his way to Quincy: *Herndon's Informants: Letters, Interviews, and Statements About Abraham Lincoln*, Douglas L. Wilson, Rodney O. Davis, eds., (Urbana: University of Illinois Press, 1997), 387.

p. 88   The Quincy debate was a homecoming: Carl Landrum, "The Start of Douglas' Political Career," *Quincy Whig-Herald*, Aug. 21, 1994.

p. 87   Quincy welcomed back its temporary son: Carl Landrum, "Setting the Lincoln-Douglas Debate Scene," *Quincy Whig-Herald*, May 15, 1994.

p. 87   He then spent half an hour in the carpet store: David Wilcox, *Quincy and Adams County History and Representative Men* (Chicago: Lewis Publishing Company, 1919), 467–470.

p. 87   Lincoln was on a morning train: *The Reminiscences of Carl Schurz*,Vol. 2, *1852–1863* (New York: McClure Company, 1907), 89–91.

p. 88   "no purpose to introduce political and social equality": *The Complete Lincoln-Douglas Debates*, 327–328.

p. 89   "Judge Douglas had the privilege of replying to me at Galesburg": Ibid. 328–329.

p. 89   "I will say now that there is a sentiment": Ibid. 333–334.

p. 89   Douglas looked Lincoln up and down: "Meeting of Survivors," Oct. 12, 1908, Historical Society of Quincy and Adams County.

p. 89   Schurz thought that Douglas looked rather natty: *The Reminiscences of Carl Schurz*, 94.

p. 90   only a "quibble": *The Complete Lincoln-Douglas Debates*, 335–336.

p. 90   "I do not choose to occupy the time": Ibid., 344.

p. 91   Lincoln "would prohibit slavery everywhere": Ibid., 343.

p. 91   "Judge Douglas could not let it stand": Ibid., 354.

p. 91   "If you withhold that necessary legislation": Ibid., 356.

p. 92   As he stepped off the platform: Carl Landrum, "After Debate, Lincoln Took a Beer," *Quincy Whig-Herald*, Oct. 9, 1994.

p. 92   Back at his room in Quincy House: Allen Thorndike Rice, *Reminiscences of Abraham Lincoln by Distinguished Men of His Time* (New York: North American Publishing Company, 1886), 441–443.

p. 93   The meeting, however, probably never took place: Neil Zurcher, *Strange Tales from Ohio: True Stories of Remarkable People, Places and Events in Ohio History* (Cleveland: Gray & Company, 2008), 44–47.

p. 93   The Lincoln banners in the streets: *Daily Courier* (Alton, Ill.), Oct. 16, 1858.

p. 94   "Let us go up and see Mary": *Memoirs of Gustave Koerner, 1809–1896* (Cedar Rapids, Iowa: Torch Press, 1909), 66–69.

p. 95   "it was not the act and deed of the people of Kansas": *The Complete Lincoln-Douglas Debates*, 368.

p. 95   "In this state, every postmaster": Ibid., 370.

p. 96   "We in Illinois tried slavery": Ibid., 375.

p. 96   he quoted Henry Clay: Ibid., 381–383.

p. 97   "How many times have we had danger": Ibid., 388.

p. 97   "an outlet for free White people": Ibid., 390.

p. 97 "I care more for the great principle": Ibid., 400.

p. 98 "about fifteen Celtic gentlemen": AL to Norman Judd, Oct. 20, 1858, *CWIII*, 329–330.

p. 98 "Doubtless Mr. Lincoln entertains": *Jacksonville Sentinel*, Oct. 22, 1858.

p. 98 "I am not, nor have ever been": AL to Edward Lusk, Oct. 30, 1858, *CWIII*, 333.

p. 98 "How can anyone who abhors oppression of negroes": AL to Joshua Speed, Aug. 24, 1855, *CWII*, 321–324.

p.99 "I love you & want you to be a U.S. Senator": Frederick Trevor Hill, *Lincoln, the Lawyer* (New York: Century Co., 1906), 264.

p. 99 "gone over completely to the abolitionists": Stevens, *A Reporter's Lincoln*, 259.

p. 99 "he did not know any of his friends": Fehrenbacher and Fehrenbacher, *Recollected Words of Abraham Lincoln*, 140.

p. 99 "the substance of a conversation between us in relation to Judge Douglas": John J. Crittenden to T. Lyle Dickey, Aug. 1, 1858, in *The Life of John J. Crittenden*, Vol. 2, Ann Mary Butler Crittenden Coleman, ed. (Philadelphia: J. B. Lippincott & Co., 1871) 164–166.

p. 99 "I am prompted . . . by a story being whispered about": AL to John J. Crittenden, July 7, 1858, *CWII*, 484–485.

p. 99 "have always belonged to different parties": John J. Crittenden to AL, July 29, 1858, AL Papers.

p. 100 "the people of Illinois little knew how much they really owed": Coleman, *The Life of John J. Crittenden*, 165.

p. 100 "control 20,000 American or old line Whig votes in center & south": Thomas Harris to SAD, July 7, 1858, SAD Papers, UC.

p. 100 "My friends, today closes the discussion of this canvass": Fragment: Last Speech of the Campaign at Springfield, Illinois, Oct. 30, 1858, *CWIII*, 334–335.

p. 101 "who make themselves whole by whipping": *Chicago Press and Tribune*, Oct. 30, 1858.

p. 101 Slidell had spent two days in Chicago: A. L. Diket, "John Slidell and the 'Chicago Incident' of 1858," *Journal of Louisiana History*, 5, no. 4 (Autumn 1964): 369–386.

p. 101 Allegedly, he also spread rumors: James W. Sheahan, *Life of Stephen A. Douglas* (New York: Harper & Brothers, 1860) 439–442.

p. 101 "a more honorable man": *Washington Union*, Dec. 18, 1858.

p. 101 the Democrats won 40 of the 75 seats: 1858 Election Results, Illinois State Archives, Springfield.

p. 102 "An apportionment law ridiculously adopted": *Chicago Press and Tribune*, Nov. 6, 1858.

p. 102 "the Pharisaical old Whigs": David Davis to AL, Nov. 7, 1858, AL Papers.

p. 102 "Irish colonization": David Davis to George Davis, Nov. 7, 1858, David Davis Papers, ALPLM.

p. 103 "My foot slipped out from under me": *Inside Lincoln's White House: The Complete Civil War Diary of John Hay*, Michael Burlingame, John R. Turner Ettinger, eds. (Carbondale: Southern Illinois University Press, 1999), 244.

p. 103   "The emotions of defeat": AL to John J. Crittenden, Nov. 4, 1858, *CWIII*, 335–336.

p. 103   "Wentworth's Chicago paper": *Springfield* (Mo.) *Mirror*, Nov. 27, 1858.

p. 103   "that I can assure you as a Democrat": James B. Ficklin to SAD, Nov. 5, 1858, SAD Papers, UC.

CHAPTER 4

p. 105   "I have the honor to invite you": George Manypenny to SAD, July 27, 1859, Douglas Papers, University of Chicago.

p. 107   Brown rose in favor: Congressional Globe, 35th Congress, 2nd Session, 1243.

p. 108   "I never would vote for a slave code": Ibid., 1244.

p. 108   If "the Convention shall interpolate": Douglas to J. B. Dorr, June 22, 1859, The Letters of Stephen A. Douglas, 446–447.

p. 109   even Douglas's future biographer: Robert W. Johannsen, "Stephen A. Douglas, 'Harper's Magazine' and Popular Sovereignty," *Mississippi Valley Historical Review*, 45, no. 4 (March 1959): 606–631.

p. 111   when Douglas "proposed to furnish us with a paper": Harper and Brothers to O. Jennings Wise, Sept. 21, 1859.

p. 111   Brown wrote to Douglas: Albert Gallatin Brown to SAD, Sept. 10, 1859, SAD.

p. 111   Senator Alfred Iverson wrote: *New York Times*, Oct. 3, 1859.

p. 111   The proslavery *Louisville Courier* declared Douglas's offering: quoted in *New York-Tribune*, Sept. 6, 1859.

p. 112   Five thousand people were waiting: *Ohio Statesman*, Sept. 8, 1859.

p. 114   "The telegraph gives the speaker": *New York Times*, Sept. 9, 1859.

p. 115   Met at the Cincinnati: *Cincinnati Daily Enquirer*, Sept. 10, 1859.

p. 117   Black had written: Black to J. W. Davidson, August 1, 1858, House Reports, 36th Congressional 1st Session, No. 648, 323–324.

p. 117   To Black, there was no difference: House Reports, 36/1, no. 648, 323–324.

p. 119   "It was smart quarterbacking": Earl W. Wiley, "Behind Lincoln's Visit to Ohio in 1859," *Ohio History Journal*, 60, no. 1 (January 1951): 28–47.

p. 119   "Now, we desire to head off the little gentleman": William T. Bascom to AL, Sept. 1, 1859, AL.

p. 119   "I shall try to speak at Columbus and Cincinnati": AL to Peter Zinn, Sept. 6, 1859, *CWIII*, 400.

p. 119   The Oberlin-Wellington Rescue Case: Oberlin-Wellington Rescue, *Encyclopedia of Cleveland History*, Case Western Reserve University.

p. 120   "Two things done by the Ohio Republican convention": AL to Samuel Galloway, July 28, 1859, *CWIII*, 394–395.

p. 120   Lincoln's friend Samuel Galloway: Samuel Galloway to AL, Sept. 23, 1858, AL Papers.

p. 120   Lincoln wrote back: AL to Salmon P. Chase, June 20, 1859, *CWIII*, 386.

p. 121   Lincoln agreed that Chase: AL to Samuel Galloway, July 28, 1859, *CWIII*, 394–395.

p. 121   Lincoln's meeting in Columbus: Earl W. Wiley, "Behind Lincoln's Visit to Ohio in 1859," *Ohio State Archaeological and Historical Quarterly*, Jan. 1951, 28–47.

p. 121   "Douglas never lets the logic of principle": *CWIII*, 398.

p. 122   "In pursuance of their base design": *Ohio Statesman*, Sept. 13, 1859.

p. 122   "tall, sad, earnest, grave": Osman C. Hooper, *History of the City of Columbus, Ohio: From the Founding of Franklinton in 1797, through the World War Period, to the Year 1920* (Columbus: Memorial Publishing Company, 1920), 44.

p. 122   "beggarly account of empty boxes": *Ohio Statesman*, Sept. 17, 1859.

p. 124   Stopping in Dayton: *Dayton Daily Empire*, Sept. 19, 1859.

p. 125   Among that meager gathering: Whitelaw Reid, *Ohio in the War: Her Statesmen, Her Generals, and Soldiers*, Vol. 1 (Cincinnati: Moore, Wilstach & Baldwin, 1868), 727.

p. 127   "On the whole Lincoln's appearance": *Autobiography, Memories and Experiences of Moncure Daniel Conway*, Vol. 1 (Boston: Houghton Mifflin & Co., 1905), 317–318.

p. 129   Lincoln's Cincinnati speech: Daniel J. Ryan, *Lincoln and Ohio* (Old Hundreth Press, 2008), 65.

p. 130   Two days after the vote: William T. Bascom to AL: Oct. 13, 1859, AL Papers.

p. 130   Galloway wrote that: Samuel Galloway to AL: Oct. 13, 1859, AL Papers.

p. 130   In early December: Ohio Republican Central Committee: Dec. 7, 1859, AL Papers.

p. 131   "difficulties interposed by the fears": Samuel Galloway to AL, Jan. 24, 1860, AL Papers.

p. 131   Published in March 1860: David C. Means, "Abraham Lincoln Goes to Press: A Documentary Memorandum," *Quarterly Journal of Current Acquisitions*, 4, no. 9 (August 1953): 182–191.

p. 131   "Those facts lead us to believe": *Cincinnati Enquirer*, Oct. 16, 1859.

p. 131   Abner Backus . . . informed Douglas: Abner Backus to SAD, Oct. 23, 1859, SAD Papers, UC.

CHAPTER 5

p. 134   The Wisconsin delegation snowshoed: Paul Starobin, *Madness Rules the Hour: Charleston, 1860 and the Mania for War* (New York: PublicAffairs, 2017), 41–45.

p. 134   "the convention might appoint as many": Charles Lanphier to SAD, Jan. 1, 1860, *Letters of SAD*, 482.

p. 134   The Douglas campaign set up its headquarters: Murat Halstead, *Three Against Lincoln* (Baton Rouge: Louisiana State University Press, 1960), 7–8.

p. 135   "We are now on the eve of events": *Charleston Mercury*, April 23, 1860.

p. 136   Yancey, whose powerful pleas: Eric H. Walther, *William Lowndes Yancey and the Coming of the Civil War* (Chapel Hill: University of North Carolina Press, 2006), 238.

p. 137   "The disruptionists came here": John Forsyth to SAD, SAD Papers, UC.

p. 137   In response to Harpers Ferry: "The Introduction of a Resolution Relative to the
          Invasion of States, Delivered in the Senate of the United States, Jan. 23, 1860."

p. 138   "the integrity of the Democratic Party:" *Congressional Globe*, 36th Congress,
          1st Session, 2156.

p. 138   Buchanan, who told California Senator Milton S. Latham: "The Day Journal
          of Milton S. Latham," *California Historical Society Quarterly*, 11, no. 1 (1932):
          2–28.

p. 138   Leery of Charleston's secessionist sympathies: Robert W. Johannsen,
          "Douglas at Charleston" in *Politics and the Crisis of 1860*, Norman A.
          Graebner, ed., (Urbana: University of Illinois, 1961) 61–79.

p. 139   "I am surprised at the bitterness": Murray McConnel to SAD, April 23, 1860,
          SAD Papers, UC.

p. 139   "My opinion still is": Halstead, *Three Against Lincoln*, 12.

p. 139   In a private parlor: Ibid., 11.

p. 140   "are those who labor to overthrow": "Proceedings of the National Democratic
          Convention, Charleston, S.C., April 23, 1860" (Cleveland: Plain Dealer Press
          Office, 1860), 8.

p. 141   "Give me an endorsement": *A Fire-Eater Remembers: The Confederate Memoir of
          Robert Barnwell Rhett* (Columbia: University of South Carolina Press, 2000), 11.

p. 141   As the *New York Herald* reported: *New York Herald*, April 25, 1860.

p. 142   they found allies in the California: David A. Williams, "California
          Democrats of 1860: Division, Disruption, Defeat," *Southern California
          Quarterly*, 55, no. 3, 239–352.

p. 142   "The gentleman forgets to tell the ladies": *New York Daily Herald*, April 30,
          1860.

p. 143   Yancey himself had argued: Walther, *William Lowndes Yancey and the Coming
          of the Civil War*, 219.

p. 143   "it is the duty of the Federal Government": "Proceedings of the National
          Democratic Convention," 15.

p. 143   "I appeal to my friend from Rhode Island": Ibid., 18.

p. 144   the majority report: Ibid., 19.

p. 144   the minority report: Ibid., 20.

p. 145   "life and death" for the South: *Charleston Courier*, April 28, 1860.

p. 145   The majority platform, Avery pointed out: *New York Daily Herald*, April 28,
          1860.

p. 146   "We hold the Constitution up against": *Charleston Daily Courier*, April 30, 1860.

p. 147   Yancey's incitement to secession: Halstead, *Three Against Lincoln*, 55.

p. 148   "pause before consummating this action": "Proceedings of the National
          Democratic Convention," 30.

p. 148   "That gentleman had asked": *Charleston Courier*, May 2, 1860.

p. 149   "That the Congress of the United States has no power": "Proceedings of the
          National Democratic Convention," 33.

p. 150   "Fourth of July feeling": Halstead, *Three Against Lincoln*, 87.

p. 150   Rhett's newspaper: *Charleston Mercury*, May 11, 1860.

p. 150   The Ohio delegation had run out: Halstead, *Three Against Lincoln*, 67.
p. 150   "The president will be nominated": Ibid., 68.
p. 150   The morning session began: "Proceedings of the National Democratic Convention," 41.
p. 151   "I will stay here until the last feather": Halstead, *Three Against Lincoln*, 89.
p. 151   "and her sister state of Kentucky": "Proceedings of the National Democratic Convention," 42–43.
p. 152   On Wednesday morning: *Charleston Courier*, May 2, 1860.
p. 152   "When the first ballot was cast": Ibid., 46.
p. 154   "The friends of Douglas now concede": *New York Herald*, May 3, 1860.
p. 154   "I will not believe that the noble work": *Charleston Courier*, May 4, 1860.
p. 155   "We have, Mr. President, in our possession": Ibid.
p. 155   Only the faro bank men: Starobin, *Madness Rules the Hour*, 67.
p. 157   The day after the Charleston conventions broke up: "The Day Journal of Milton S. Latham," 18.

CHAPTER 6
p. 159   "Oh, Fell, what's the use": Sherman Day Wakefield, *How Lincoln Became President* (New York: Wilson, Erickson Inc., 1936), 96–97.
p. 160   To Mark Delahay: AL to Mark Delahay, May 14, 1859, *CWIII*, 378–379.
p. 160   He wrote to Schuyler Colfax: Ibid., 390–391.
p. 161   "We in New York are guilty": *Works of William H. Seward*, Vol. 3 (New York: Houghton Mifflin and Company, 1884), 291–293.
p. 161   Seward's maiden speech: "California, Union and Freedom. Speech of William H. Seward, of New York, in the Senate, March 11, 1850," Appendix to the *Congressional Globe*, 31st Congress, 1st Session, 260–269.
p. 161   Seward "would not be the nominee": Josiah Lucas to AL, Jan. 24, 1860, AL Papers.
p. 162   "Old John Brown has just been executed": Speech at Leavenworth, Kansas, *CWIII*, 497–502.
p. 162   "At twenty-one I came to Illinois": *CWIII*, 511–512.
p. 163   Fell told Lincoln: Wakefield, *How Lincoln Became President*, 95.
p. 163   "An inspection of the Constitution will show": *CWIII*, 522–550.
p. 164   "the taste is in my mouth": AL to Lyman Trumbull, *CWIV*, 45–46.
p. 164   "Lincoln . . . is the most available candidate": Nathan M. Knapp to Ozias M. Hatch, Ozias M. Hatch Papers, Abraham Lincoln Presidential Library.
p. 165   A few days before the convention: Mark A. Plummer, *Lincoln's Rail Splitter: Governor Richard J. Oglesby* (Urbana: University of Illinois Press, 2001), 42–43; James T. Hickey, "Oglesby's Fence Rail Dealings and the 1860 Decatur Convention," *Journal of the Illinois State Historical Society*, 54, no. 1 (Spring 1961): 5–24.
p. 166   Between delegates and spectators: "Two Days in Decatur: Changing the Face of America" (Decatur, Ill.: Millikin University), 3–4.

p. 166   "An old Democrat of Macon County": Plummer, *Lincoln's Rail Splitter*, 42–43.

p. 166   "I am not in a position": AL to Norman Judd, Feb. 9, 1860, *CWIII*, 517.

p. 167   Orville Hickman Browning of Quincy believed: *Diary of Orville Hickman Browning*, Vol. 1 (Springfield: Trustees of the Illinois State Historical Library, 1925), 407.

p. 167   "The pillars supporting the roof": *Chicago Press and Tribune*, May 14, 1860.

p. 168   "There are now at least a thousand men": Halstead, *Three Against Lincoln*, 143–147.

p. 168   Pennsylvania's David Wilmot: "Proceedings of the National Republican Convention, Held at Chicago, May 16th, 17th & 18th, 1860" (Chicago: Press and Tribune Office, 1860), 2.

p. 169   John Hoge Ewing of Pennsylvania rose to defend: "Proceedings of the National Republican Convention," 13–19.

p. 169   Davis assigned: Michael Burlingame, *Abraham Lincoln: A Life*, Vol. 1 (Baltimore: Johns Hopkins University Press, 2008), 609.

p. 170   Even Kansas's tiny six-man territorial delegation: Addison G. Procter, "Lincoln and the Convention of 1860: An Address before the Chicago Historical Society, April 4, 1918," Chicago Historical Society, 1918, 6–13.

p. 171   The morning of the convention's second day: Halstead, *Three Against Lincoln*, 149, 164.

p. 171   Norman Judd dispatched telegraphs: R. Craig Sautter and Edward M. Burke, *Inside the Wigwam: Chicago Presidential Conventions, 1860–1996* (Chicago: Wild Onion Books, 1996), 11.

p. 171   "I was not aware that [the Democrats]": "Proceedings of the National Republican Convention," 21.

p. 172   The convention, though, voted down Giddings's amendment: Halstead, *Three Against Lincoln*, 153–154.

p. 172   So was Section 8: "Proceedings of the National Republican Convention," 22.

p. 173   the New Yorkers were so confident: Halstead, *Three Against Lincoln*, 159–160.

p. 173   "The friends of Seward are firm": Ida M. Tarbell, "The Story of Lincoln's Nomination in 1860," *McClure's*, November 1896, 43–56.

p. 173   At 11:40 P.M. on Thursday: Halstead, *Three Against Lincoln*, 161.

p. 174   In the wee hours: Douglas H. Maynard, "Dudley of New Jersey and the Nomination of Lincoln," *The Pennsylvania Magazine of History and Biography*, 82, no. 1 (Jan. 1958): 100–108.

p. 174   "Damn Lincoln!": Henry C. Whitney, *Lincoln the Citizen* (New York: Baker & Taylor Company, 1908), 289.

p. 174   "My assurance to them": Leonard Swett to AL, May 20, 1860, AL Papers.

p. 175   "Indiana is all right": Jesse K. Dubois and William Herndon to AL, May 14, 1860, AL Papers.

p. 175   "Unless Seward has strength sufficient": Mark Delahay to AL, May 16, 1860, AL Papers.

p. 175   "Am very hopeful": David Davis to AL, May 17, 1860, AL Papers.

p. 175   "I am governor of Indiana": Procter, "Lincoln and the Convention of 1860," 12–13.

p. 176   When the time came for balloting: Tarbell, "The Story of Lincoln's Nomination in 1860," 54.

p. 176   "I desire," Judd declared, "to put in nomination": "Proceedings of the National Republican Convention," 30.

p. 176   The men on the floor flung their black hats: Tarbell, "The Story of Lincoln's Nomination in 1860," 55.

p. 177   "all the hogs in Cincinnati": Halstead, *Three Against Lincoln*, 165.

p. 177   Once the din subsided: "Proceedings of the National Republican Convention," 30–31; Halstead, *Three Against Lincoln*, 166–172.

p. 178   "The Republican Party is today": "Proceedings of the National Republican Convention," 33.

p. 179   After seeing the results of the second ballot: Whitney, *Lincoln the Citizen*, 292.

p. 179   "I do not think there were a dozen": Schuyler Colfax to AL, May 18, 1860, AL Papers.

p. 180   "You have beaten him once": Luther Wright to SAD, May 18, 1860, SAD Papers, UC.

p. 180   "I think it finishes his prospects": Lyman Trumbull to AL, May 18, 1860, AL Papers.

CHAPTER 7

p. 182   "We repudiate the late Montgomery convention": Forsyth to SAD, May 9, 1860, SAD Papers, UC.

p. 182   "a demagogue, a broken-down politician": J. Jones to SAD, June 9, 1860, SAD Papers, UC.

p. 183   "All of us who will not endorse": John W. Duncan to SAD, June 8, 1860, SAD Papers, UC.

p. 183   "I believe that the principle": "Non-Interference by Congress with Slavery in the Territories, Speech of Senator Douglas, of Illinois, Delivered in the United States Senate, May 15 & 16, 1860." https://www.google.com/books /edition/Non_interference_by_Congress_with_Slaver/18ANAQAAMAAJ ?hl=en&gbpv=0.

p. 184   "Does the senator consider it": *Congressional Globe*, 36th Congress, 1st Session, 2143–2156.

p. 184   "The proposition of the honorable senator from Illinois": Ibid., 2826–2833.

p. 184   "The Old Line Whigs": H. W. Starr to SAD, May 25, 1860, SAD Papers, UC.

p. 185   "unless regularly accredited": August Belmont to SAD, May 18, 1860, SAD Papers, UC.

p. 185   "the *New York Herald* predicted": *New York Herald*, June 19, 1860.

p. 186   When the Baltimore convention was gaveled to order: "Democratic National Convention, 1860, at Charleston and Baltimore. Proceedings at Baltimore, June 18–23," 96.

p. 186   "What did they do at Richmond?": Ibid., 103.

p. 186   "Everyone was 'scratching' for the door": Letter to SAD from Coleman's Eutaw House, Baltimore, June 21, 1860.

p. 187   The majority report: "Proceedings at Baltimore," 114–116.

p. 187   "A duel between the parties": *New York Herald*, June 20, 1860, SAD Papers, UC.

p. 187   The minority report favored: Ibid., 116–120.

p. 187   "I am neither for the Union *per se*": Halstead, *Three Against Lincoln*, 221–222.

p. 188   "I am of the opinion": Felix McCloskey to SAD, June 13, 1860, SAD Papers, UC.

p. 188   "Vote in New York delegation": S. S. Hayes to SAD, June 21, 1860, SAD Papers, UC.

p. 188   "If my enemies are determined": SAD to Dean Richmond, June 22, 1860, *Letters of SAD*, 493.

p. 189   "settled this as all other contested questions": Halstead, *Three Against Lincoln*, 232.

p. 189   The convention tried to move on: "Proceedings at Baltimore," 145–152.

p. 192   the convention's nearly the unanimous choice: Ibid., 163–166.

p. 193   "Is there any objection to withdrawing the resolution": Halstead, *Three Against Lincoln*, 252.

p. 193   "The Convention assembled elsewhere": Ibid., 265–277.

p. 195   "smite the Manhattan rock": Irving Katz, *August Belmont: A Political Biography* (New York: Columbia University Press, 1968), 74.

p. 195   "a most *urgent personal* appeal": Ibid., 76–78.

p. 196   "some assurance of success": August Belmont to SAD, July 28, 1860, SAD Papers, UC.

p. 197   "If my political opinions are not known": *New York Times*, July 3, 1860.

p. 197   "disgust the people": SAD to Nathaniel Paschall, *Letters of SAD*, 497.

p. 197   "We must make the war boldly": SAD to Charles Lanphier, Ibid., 497–498.

p. 198   "I was expecting to pass through this city": *Hartford Courant*, July 17, 1860.

p. 199   "The history of Massachusetts": *Boston Post*, July 18, 1860.

p. 200   "the men who fought against British tyranny": *Boston Evening Transcript*, July 20, 1860.

p. 200   "This distinguished gentleman": *Brandon Gazette*, Aug. 2, 1860.

p. 202   "The New Hampshire boy who removes west": *Boston Post*, Aug. 3, 1860.

p. 204   Douglas ended his New England journey: *Fall River Daily Evening News*, Aug. 3, 1860.

p. 204   "No other man in the Union": Emerson D. Fite, *The Presidential Campaign of 1860* (New York: Macmillan, 1911), 207.

p. 204   "In any other equally prominent politician": *New York Times*, Aug. 10, 1860.

p. 204   Henry C. Whitney, a friend of Lincoln's: Whitney, *Lincoln the Citizen*, 292.

p. 205   "He is about five feet nothing in height": *Buffalo Weekly Express*, Sept. 4, 1860.

p. 205   "I am sure that I express the wish": William Cullen Bryant to AL, June 16, 1860, AL Papers.

p. 206   "at Quincy or elsewhere": AL to Abraham Jonas, July 21, 1860, *CWIV*, 85–86.

p. 206   "no ticket could have been nominated": Schuyler Colfax to AL, June 25, 1860, AL Papers.

p. 206   "This State is confessedly ours": Alexander McClure to AL, July 2, 1860, AL
          Papers.

p. 206   Richard W. Thompson, a leader of the Constitutional Union Party: Richard
          W. Thompson to AL, June 12, 1860, AL Papers.

p. 207   "Tell him my motto is 'fairness to all'": AL to John Nicolay, June 16, 1860,
          CWIV, 83.

p. 207   Lincoln broke his practice: AL to James E. Harvey, Oct. 2, 1860, *CWIV*, 125.

p. 207   "the Republican demonstration": *Chicago Press and Tribune*, Aug. 9, 1860.

p. 208   "My fellow citizens": "Remarks at a Republican Rally, Springfield, Illinois,"
          Aug. 8, 1860, *CWIV*, 91–92.

p. 208   The most significant friend was Trumbull: *Illinois State Journal*, Aug. 13, 1860.

p. 209   "My dear judge": A. D. Banks to SAD, Aug. 2, 1860, SAD Papers, UC.

p. 209   Earlier that summer, Jefferson Davis: Robert W. Johannsen, *Stephen A.
          Douglas* (Urbana: University of Illinois Press, 1973), 792.

p. 210   "Breckinridge won't get North Carolina": Robert Dick to SAD, Aug. 2, 1860,
          SAD Papers, UC.

p. 210   Douglas and Adele traveled by steamer: *New York Herald*, Aug. 27, 1860.

p. 212   Southern newspapers condemned: Donald E. Reynolds, *Editors Make War:
          Southern Newspapers in the Secession Crisis* (Nashville, Tenn.: Vanderbilt
          University Press, 1970), 135–136.

p. 213   "You cannot sever this Union": *The Weekly Standard*, Sept. 5, 1860.

p. 213   Douglas was ridiculed in Richmond: *Richmond Enquirer*, Sept. 4, 1860.

p. 214   "a mature plan": *The Daily Exchange*, Sept. 7, 1860.

p. 215   "It is quite natural for a gentleman": *Baltimore Sun*, Sept. 7, 1860.

p. 215   "He is an old soldier in the cause": Julius White to AL, Sept. 20, 1860, AL
          Papers.

p. 215   "as many as your personal friends": David Davis to AL, Sept. 24, 1860, AL
          Papers.

p. 215   "would relieve Douglas of the charge": George G. Fogg to AL, Aug. 14, 1860,
          AL Papers.

p. 215   To while away the days: "Dialogue between Stephen A. Douglas and John C.
          Breckinridge," Sept. 29, 1860, *CWIV*, 123–124.

p. 217   In September, a group gathered: Tilden G. Edelstein, *Strange Enthusiasm:
          A Life of Thomas Wentworth Higginson* (New Haven, Conn.: Yale University
          Press, 1968), 239.

p. 217   Adams thought that Lincoln was "awkward": *Charles Francis Adams, 1835–1915,
          An Autobiography* (Boston and New York: Houghton Mifflin Company, 1916),
          64–65.

p. 217   "I care not, fellow citizens": *Chicago Press and Tribune*, Oct. 3, 1860.

p. 218   "who, God bless her": *Baltimore Sun*, Sept. 18, 1860.

p. 218   New York Democrats were attempting: *Syracuse Daily Courier and Union*,
          July 18, 1860.

p. 219   "By God, sir": Michael S. Green, *Lincoln and the Election of 1860* (Carbondale:
          Southern Illinois University Press, 2011), 93.

p. 219   Douglas crossed paths with Seward: *Charles Francis Adams, 1835–1915, An Autobiography*, 65–66.

p. 220   Douglas's response to Seward: *Chicago Press and Tribune*, Oct. 6, 1860.

p. 221   From Simon Cameron in Harrisburg: AL Papers.

p. 221   David Davis was said to have received: Ward Hill Lamon to AL, Oct. 10, 1860, AL Papers.

p. 222   "Your majority over Douglas": Caleb Smith to AL, Oct. 10, 1860.

p. 222   "[it] now really looks": AL to William Seward, Oct. 12, 1860, *CWIV*, 126–127.

p. 222   In Springfield, local Wide Awakes: *Illinois State Journal*, Oct. 12, 1860.

p. 222   Douglas received news of the Republican victories: Rita Makenna Carey, *The First Campaigner: Stephen A. Douglas* (New York: Vantage Press, 1964), 83.

CHAPTER 8

p. 224   "the people of the South have too much good sense": AL to John B. Fry, Aug. 15, 1860, *CWIV*, 95.

p. 224   "in no probable event": George G. Fogg to AL, Oct. 26, 1860, AL Papers.

p. 225   Ohio journalist Donn Piatt: Donn Piatt, *Men Who Served the Union* (New York: Belford Clarke & Company, 1883), 29–30.

p. 225   "itinerant peddler of Yankee notions": *Petersburg Bulletin*, quoted in *Council Bluffs Nonpareil*, Nov. 3, 1860.

p. 226   Douglas arrived in Memphis: *Memphis Appeal*, Oct. 24, 1860.

p. 228   Yancey had just returned: Walther, *William Lowndes Yancey and the Coming of the Civil War*, 261–266.

p. 229   "Douglas says that the Fire-Eaters": *Tennessean*, Oct. 27, 1860.

p. 229   "I am pained and grieved at the folly": Alexander Stephens to J. Henly Smith, July 2, 1860, quoted in *The Correspondence of Robert Toombs, Alexander H. Stephens and Howell Cobb*, Ulrich L. Phillips, ed. (Washington: American Historical Association, 1913), 483–486.

p. 231   From the moment of his arrival: *Daily Enquirer*, Nov. 5, 1860.

p. 231   "The Republic is more involved in darkness": David R. Barbee and Milledge L. Bonham Jr., "The Montgomery Address of Stephen A. Douglas," *The Journal of Southern History*, 5, no. 4 (Nov. 1939): 527–552.

p. 232   Douglas and Adele boarded a steamer: *Mobile Register*, Nov. 6, 1860.

p. 232   Forsyth organized the pro-Douglas convention: Lionel Crocker, "Campaign of Stephen A. Douglas in the South, 1860," in *Anti-Slavery and Disunion, 1858–1861*, J. Jeffrey Auer, ed., (New York: Harper and Row, 1963), 276.

p. 233   Douglas was challenged on two points: Ollinger Crenshaw, *The Slave States in the Presidential Election of 1860* (Baltimore: Johns Hopkins University Press, 1945), 85–86.

p. 234   At first, Abraham Lincoln did not plan to vote: Burlingame, *Abraham Lincoln: A Life*, 676–669.

p. 234   Hatch joked to Lincoln: Samuel Weed, "Hearing the Returns with Mr. Lincoln," *New York Times*, Feb. 14, 1932.

p. 235   Illinois seemed secure: *Illinois State Journal*, Nov. 8, 1860.

p. 235 "The news will come quickly enough": Weed, "Hearing the Returns with
        Mr. Lincoln."
p. 237 Church bells rang: *New York Herald*, Nov. 11, 1860.
p. 238 Once Lincoln's victory was apparent: Henry Wilson, *History of the Rise and
        Fall of the Slave Power in America*, Vol. 2 (Boston: J. R. Osgood and Company,
        1872), 700.
p. 240 "coming down would decide": Louis Dufan to SAD, Oct. 9, 1860, SAD
        Papers, UC.
p. 240 "our citizens thronged the business thoroughfares": *Charleston Mercury*,
        Nov. 8, 1860.
p. 240 "a Convention of the people of the State": *Daily Delta* (New Orleans, La.),
        Nov. 8, 1860.
p. 241 At the train depot: *New Orleans Bee*, Nov. 9, 1860.
p. 242 "No man regrets the election of Mr. Lincoln": "To Ninety-six New Orleans
        Citizens," Nov. 13, 1860, *Letters of SAD*, 499–500.
p. 242 "We are beaten but not conquered": William Richardson to SAD, Nov. 27,
        1860, SAD Papers, UC.

CHAPTER 9

p. 244 "Our Union rests upon public opinion": James Buchanan, Fourth Annual
        Message to Congress, Dec. 3, 1860. https://www.presidency.ucsb.edu
        /documents/fourth-annual-message-congress-the-state-the-union.
p. 244 "The evil has now passed beyond control": *New York Times*, Dec. 14, 1860.
p. 245 "I have endeavored by the resolutions": *Congressional Globe*, Senate, 36th
        Congress, 2nd Session, 112–114; Albert D. Kirwan, *John J. Crittenden: The
        Struggle for the Union* (Lexington: University of Kentucky Press, 1962),
        375–376.
p. 248 "I am ready to act with any party": *Congressional Globe*, Senate, 36th Congress,
        2nd Session, 28.
p. 248 "The Republican Party today is as uncompromising": Frederic Bancroft, *The
        Life of William H. Seward*, Vol. II (New York: Harper & Brothers, 1900), 32n.
p. 248 "Entertain no proposition for a compromise": AL to William Kellogg,
        Dec. 11, 1860, *CWIV*, 150.
p. 249 "when this Union was formed": *Albany Times-Union*, Dec. 17, 1860.
p. 249 "I will be inflexible on the territorial question": AL to Thurlow Weed,
        Dec. 17, 1860, *CWIV*, 154.
p. 249 "This is a heavy broadside": *Life of Thurlow Weed Including His Autobiography
        and a Memoir*, Vol. 2 (Boston: Houghton Mifflin & Company, 1884),
        605–614.
p. 251 "I think it would be best": AL to Lyman Trumbull, Dec. 21, 1860, *CWIV*, 158.
p. 251 "Little is expected from the action of the Committee": *New-York Tribune*,
        Dec. 22, 1860.
p. 251 "If that mode of compromise will not answer": *New-York Tribune*, Dec. 24,
        1860.

p. 252   Douglas introduced his own package of amendments: *New York Daily Herald*, Dec. 27, 1860.

p. 253   "The prospects are gloomy": SAD to Charles Lanphier, Dec. 25, 1860: *Letters of SAD*, 504.

p. 253   "anomalous condition of our affairs": *New York Times*, Dec. 24, 1860.

p. 253   "In the middle states, however, there was great alarm": Henry Adams, *The Great Secession Winter of 1860–61 and Other Essays*, George Hochfield, ed. (New York: Sagamore Press, 1958), 3.

p. 254   "Is there any hope for Southern rights?": Georgians to Crittenden and Douglas, Dec. 12, 1860, SAD Papers, UC.

p. 254   "We have hopes that the rights of the South": To [William Ezzard, et al.], Dec. 29, 1860, *Letters of SAD*, 506.

p. 254   "With your defeat the cause of the Union was lost": John Forsyth to SAD, Dec. 28, 1860, SAD Papers, UC.

p. 255   Seward presented three proposals: *New-York Tribune*, Dec. 28, 1860.

p. 256   "invited him to travel to Washington": Duff Green, *Facts and Suggestions, Biographical, Historical, Financial and Political: Addressed to the People of the United States* (New York: Richardson & Co., 1866), 225–231.

p. 256   Lincoln did not say so: AL to Duff Green, Dec. 28, 1860: *CWIV*, 162–163.

p. 257   "Gen. Duff Green is out here": AL to Lyman Trumbull, Dec. 28, 1860, *CWIV*, 163.

p. 257   Douglas's compromise proposal: *New York Herald*, Dec. 29, 1860.

p. 258   "Mind, I don't for a moment suspect Lincoln": "The Diary of a Public Man," *North American Review*, Aug. 1879, 130–131.

p. 258   "It is a scruple only": *Congressional Globe*, Senate, 36th Congress, 2nd Session, 237.

p. 259   The previous evening: David M. Potter, *Lincoln and His Party in the Secession Crisis* (New Haven, Conn.: Yale University Press, 1942), 125–126.

p. 259   Douglas rose in the Senate to second Crittenden: Speech of Hon. Stephen Douglas, of Illinois, in the Senate, Jan. 3, 1861. https://www.loc.gov /item/19003109/.

p. 261   "utterly infamous and damnable": Elihu Washburne to AL, Jan. 7, 1861, AL Papers.

p. 261   From all across the country: *Senate Journal*, 36th Congress, 2nd Session, 494–497: Kirwan, *John J. Crittenden*, 403–404.

p. 261   "if secession is limited to the cotton states": Charles Sumner to the Duchess of Argyll, Dec. 14, 1860, *Selected Letters of Charles Sumner*, Vol. 2: *1859–1874*, Beverly Wilson, ed. (Boston: Northeastern University Press, 1990), 233.

p. 261   "were submitted this day to the people of the North": C. C. Rockwell to SAD, Jan. 17, 1861, SAD Papers, UC.

p. 261   "the feeling here is almost unanimous": H. Pound to SAD, Jan. 28, 1861, SAD Papers, UC.

p. 262   "That the provisions of the Constitution": *Congressional Globe*, Senate, 36th Congress, 2nd Session, 289–290.

p. 262   "Dissolution would not only arrest but extinguish": Ibid., 290.

p. 263   "denounced by both extremes": *New York Herald*, Jan. 13, 1861.

p. 263   when the Kentuckian's resolutions finally came to a vote: *Congressional Globe*,
          Senate, 36th Congress, 2nd Session, 402–410.

p. 264   "we cannot get a settlement":

p. 264   "with the national treasure": Johannsen, *Stephen A. Douglas*, 826.

p. 264   "The South will not be satisfied": *Weekly Raleigh Register*, Jan. 23, 1861.

p. 264   "in concert": *Congressional Globe*, Senate, 36th Congress, 2nd Session, 661.

p. 264   "I can say with confidence": SAD to James Barbour, Jan. 27, 1861, in *Illinois
          State Register*, Feb. 2, 1861.

p. 265   "The moment seems to have arrived": Carl Schurz to AL, Jan. 30, 1861, AL
          Papers.

p. 265   "with this sovereignty": Schuyler Colfax to AL, Feb. 1, 1861, AL Papers.

p. 265   "I will suffer death": "Remarks Concerning Concessions to Secession,"
          Jan. 19–21, 1861, *CWIV*, 175–176.

p. 265   "Away with all parties": Johannsen, *Stephen A. Douglas*, 827–828.

p. 266   "I see indications every day": *Congressional Globe*, Senate, 36th Congress, 2nd
          Session, 669.

p. 266   "a final effort to restore the Union": *New Orleans Daily Picayune*, Feb. 8, 1861.

p. 266   "There is hope of preserving peace and the Union": letter published in
          Staunton (Va.) *Spectator*, Feb. 12, 1861, SAD.

p. 267   "The great object of Virginia": *Congressional Globe*, Senate, 36th Congress, 2nd
          Session, 590.

p. 267   One hundred and thirty-three delegates: Samuel Eliot Morison, "The
          Peace Convention of 1861," Proceedings of the Massachusetts Historical
          Society, Third Series, Vol. 73 (1961), 58–80; William W. Hoppin, "The
          Peace Conference of 1861 at Washington, D.C.," read before the Rhode
          Island Historical Society and the New Haven Colonial Historical Society
          (Providence, R.I.: Standard Printing Company, 1903).

p. 267   "I have beaten you long ago": *Personal Recollections of John M. Palmer*
          (Cincinnati: Robert Clarke Company, 1901) 89–90.

p. 268   "Gentlemen, the eyes of the whole country": Hoppin, "The Peace Conference
          of 1861," 8–9.

p. 269   "now held or hereafter acquired": Morison, "The Peace Convention of 1861," 67.

p. 269   "we must have new lands": Ibid., 68.

p. 269   "a hostile armed Confederacy": William Seward to AL, Jan. 27, 1861, AL
          Papers.

p. 269   "care much about New-Mexico": AL to William Seward, *CWIV*, 183.

p. 270   Douglas began collecting statistics: Stephen A. Douglas, *Continental
          Commercial Union or Alliance* (Washington, D.C.: Thomas McGill & Co.,
          1869).

p. 271   "The meeting was less formal": *New York Herald*, Feb. 24, 1861.

p. 271   "notwithstanding the troubles across the river": Speech in Pittsburgh, Feb. 15,
          1861, *CWIV*, 210–215.

p. 271   "What then is the matter?": Speech at Cleveland, Ohio, Feb. 15, 1861, *CWIV*, 215–216.

p. 272   "You are a smaller man than I suspected": L. E. Chittenden, *Recollections of President Lincoln and His Administration* (New York: Harper & Brothers, 1891), 68–78.

p. 274   "If they can get and keep their grip on Lincoln": "The Diary of a Public Man," xx.

p. 275   "You have children as well as I do": *Daily Missouri Republican*, March 4, 1861.

p. 275   "Should any attempt be made": James Pollock, "Douglas the Loyal," *Journal of the Illinois State Historical Society*, 23 (April 1930): 163–170.

p. 276   "wept like children": Morison, "The Peace Convention of 1861," 75.

p. 276   "advised us to deal as liberally as possible": *Personal Recollections of John M. Palmer*, 90.

p. 276   "the reconsideration was attributed": George Boutwell, *Reminiscences of Sixty Years in Public Affairs*, Vol. 1 (New York: McClure, Phillips & Co., 1902), 274.

p. 276   "intelligent, thoughtful [and] patriotic men": L. E. Chittenden, *A Report of the Debates and Proceedings in the Secret Sessions of the Conference Convention for Proposing Amendments to the Constitution of the United States, Held at Washington, D.C., in February, A.D. 1861* (New York: D. Appleton & Company 1864), 451–452.

p. 276   "that he was now confident": Lyon G. Tyler, *The Letters and Times of the Tylers*, Vol. 2 (Richmond, Va.: Whittet and Shepperson), 616.

p. 277   "Corwin Amendment": *Congressional Globe*, House of Representatives, 36th Congress, 2nd Session, 1263.

p. 277   "I am for both": *Congressional Globe*, Senate, 36th Congress, 2nd Session, 1362.

p. 278   "We all know that the object": Ibid., 1360.

p. 278   "authorize or": Ibid., 1364.

p. 278   "Why should we put this resolution at hazard?": Ibid, 1365.

p. 278   The galleries were packed: *New York Herald*, March 5, 1861.

p. 279   "A few months ago": *Congressional Globe*, Senate, 36th Congress, 2nd Session, 1375–1380.

p. 279   "perpetual slavery anywhere": Ibid., 1380–1381.

p. 280   "compromising, it is conceding": Ibid., 1383–1386.

p. 280   "the patriotic speech of the senator from Oregon": Ibid., 1386.

p. 280   "saved all the states except South Carolina": Ibid., 1391.

p. 280   Senator Kinsley Bingham of Michigan tried to revive: Ibid., 1401.

p. 280   Senator Robert Ward Johnson proposed to substitute: Ibid., 1402.

p. 280   there was nothing left to vote on but the Corwin Amendment: Ibid., 1403.

p. 281   On the day of his inauguration: *New York Times*, March 5, 1861; *Lincoln Day by Day: A Chronology, 1861–1865*, Earl Schenck Miers, ed. (Dayton, Ohio: Morningside, 1991), 24–26.

p. 281   Throughout the morning, there was no sign of Lincoln: *New York Herald*, March 5, 1861.

p. 282 The inaugural procession began forming at nine: Allen C. Clark, *Abraham Lincoln in the National Capital* (Washington, D.C., 1925), 11–16.

p. 282 "Sir, if you are as happy in entering the White House": Philip S. Klein, *President James Buchanan: A Biography* (Newtown, Conn.: American Political Biography Press, 1962), 402.

p. 282 "a shot could not have possibly been aimed at [Lincoln]": *New York Herald*, March 5, 1861.

p. 282 "pale and wan, fatigued and anxious": Ibid.

p. 283 "Fellow Citizens, I introduce to you Abraham Lincoln": Ibid.

p. 283 Lincoln rested his stovepipe hat: Allan Nevins, "He Did Hold Lincoln's Hat," *American Heritage*, Feb. 1959, 98–99; Rufus Rockwell Wilson, *Intimate Memories of Lincoln* (Elmira, N.Y., Primavera Press, 1945), 364–366.

p. 283 "Mr. Douglas could not be president himself": *New York Herald*, March 5, 1861.

p. 283 "Apprehension seems to exist": First Inaugural Address, March 4, 1861, *CWIV*, 249–271.

p. 285 Douglas listened intently: *New York Times*, March 5, 1861; Clark, *Abraham Lincoln in the Nation's Capital*, 15.

p. 285 "He does not mean coercion": *New York Herald*, March 5, 1861.

p. 286 "Civil war must now come": *Richmond Enquirer*, March 5, 1861.

p. 286 Two days after the inauguration: *Congressional Globe*, Senate, 36th Congress, 2nd Session, 1436–1438.

p. 287 "a peace offering rather than a war message": Ibid., 1439.

p. 287 "Some people think Mr. Lincoln's inaugural": *New York Times*, March 7, 1861.

p. 288 Douglas strongly supported the appointment of Crittenden: *Hartford Courant*, March 8, 1861.

p. 288 "Is there any hope for us?": *Cincinnati Daily Press*, March 8, 1861.

p. 288 "I was somewhat surprised to find": "A Friend" to SAD, March 11, 1861, SAD Papers, UC.

p. 288 "I believe, and appreciate, your high purpose": L. J. Anderson to SAD, March 8, 1861, SAD Papers, UC.

p. 289 "Mr. Lincoln does not meditate war": "Remarks of Hon. Stephen A. Douglas, In the Senate of the United States, March 6, 1861." Congressional Globe, Senate, 37th Congress, 4th Session, 1458–9.

p. 289 The Republicans killed Douglas's Fort Sumter resolution: Ibid., 1519.

p. 290 "That is a very good policy": Ibid., 1502–1503.

p. 291 "The Rebels are determined on war": *Diary of Gideon Welles*, Vol. 2, 32–35.

p. 292 "an attempt will be made to supply Fort Sumter": Charles H. Ramsdell, "Lincoln and Fort Sumter," *The Journal of Southern History*, 3, no. 3 (Aug. 1937): 259–288.

p. 293 "blind unreasoning popular excitement": Walter Stahr, *Seward: Lincoln's Indispensable Man* (New York: Simon & Schuster, 2013), 261.

p. 293 "The power confided to me": AL to William Seward, April 1, 1861, *CWIV*, 316.

p. 294   "I have found myself in the confidence of neither party": *Diary of Gideon Welles*, 34–35.

p. 295   Late that afternoon, Ashmun called on Douglas: F. Lauriston Bullard, "Abraham Lincoln and George Ashmun," *The New England Quarterly*, 19, no. 2 (June 1946): 184–211.

p. 295   "to re-possess the forts, places, and property": *CWIV*, 331–332.

p. 296   "Mr. President, I cordially concur": Bullard, "Abraham Lincoln and George Ashmun."

p. 296   "Mr. Douglas called on the President": *North Star* (Danville, Vt.), April 20, 1861.

p. 297   "If I were president": "Reminiscences of Stephen A. Douglas," Usher F. Linder, *Reminiscences of the Early Bench and Bar of Illinois* (Chicago: The Chicago Legal News Company, 1879), 212.

p. 297   "I deprecate war": *Holmes County Republican* (Millersburg, Ohio), May 16, 1861.

p. 297   Secession had personal, as well as political, consequences: Johannsen, *Stephen A. Douglas*, 861.

p. 298   "A large share of Southern Illinois": *Salem Advocate*, Jan. 31, 1861.

p. 298   "a division of the state": Milo Erwin, *The History of Williamson County, Illinois, from the Earliest Times, Down to the Present, 1876* (Herrin, Ill.: Herrin News, 1876), 258–265.

p. 299   "that he would suffer his tongue to cleave": James Pickett Jones, *Black Jack: John A. Logan and Southern Illinois in the Civil War Era* (Tallahassee: Florida State University, 1967), 79.

p. 299   "all for the Union and the enforcement of the laws": John Olney to Richard Yates, undated, Yates Family Papers, ALPLM.

p. 299   "grave reasons": George Fort Milton, *Eve of Conflict: Stephen A. Douglas and the Needless War* (Cambridge, Mass.: Riverside Press, 1934), 564.

p. 299   "come home to arouse the people in favor of the Union": William Henry Herndon and Jesse William Weik, *Herndon's Life of Lincoln: The History and Personal Recollections of Abraham Lincoln*, Paul M. Angle, ed. (New York: Fawcett Publications, 1961), 434n.

p. 299   The railroad's tracks crossed through Virginia: Milton, *Eve of Conflict*, 564.

p. 299   "A sojourn at Harpers Ferry": Johannsen, *Stephen A. Douglas*, 863.

p. 300   "little, petty confederacies": *Detroit Free Press*, April 26, 1861.

p. 300   "There was no uncertainty in his tone": Jacob Dolson Cox, *Military Reminiscences of the Civil War*, Vol. 1 (New York: C. Scribner's Sons, 1900), 5–6.

p. 301   "drew one up which is satisfactory to all parties": *Diary of Orville Hickman Browning*, Vol. 1 (Springfield, Ill: Trustees of the Illinois State Historical Library, 1933), 465–466.

p. 302   "For the first time since the adoption of the Federal Constitution": Speech of Senator Douglas, Before the Legislature of Illinois, April 25, 1861 (pamphlet). https://www.senate.gov/artandhistory/history/resources/pdf/DouglasSpeech_Apr251861.pdf.

p. 303 Some Democrats look startled and angered: "Recollections of Judge Franklin Blades," *Abraham Lincoln by Some Men Who Knew Him* (Bloomington, Ill.: Pantagraph Printing and Stationery Co., 1910), 137.

p. 303 According to Usher F. Linder: Jones, *Black Jack: John A. Logan and Southern Illinois in the Civil War Era*, 80.

p. 303 "The time has now arrived": I. M. Short, *Abraham Lincoln: Early Days in Illinois. Reminiscences of Persons Who Became Eminent in American History* (Kansas City, Mo.: Simpson Publishing Company, 1927), 273.

p. 303 "fanatics North and South": John A. Logan to I. H. Haynee, Jan. 18, 1861, Logan Papers, Library of Congress.

p. 303 "hushed the breath of treason": Short, *Abraham Lincoln: Early Days in Illinois*, 275.

p. 304 "There was just one object": Ibid.

p. 304 "Douglas's influence was of large advantage": *Memoirs of Gustave Koerner*, 134.

p. 304 "found the state of feeling here": SAD to AL, April 29, 1861, Letters of SAD, 511.

p. 304 "an ovation . . . of which any man might have been proud": *Chicago Press and Tribune*, May 2, 1861.

p. 306 "We should never forget": SAD to Virgil Hickox, May 10, 1861, *Letters of SAD*, 511–513.

p. 306 "Why do we stand still?": *New York Herald*, June 7, 1861.

p. 307 "Do you have a message for your mother?": *Atlantic Monthly*, Aug. 1861.

p. 307 Douglas's casket was taken to Bryan Hall: Wayne C. Temple, *Stephen A. Douglas, Freemason* (Bloomington, Ill.: Masonic Book Club, 1982).

p. 308 "a man who nobly discarded party": *Philadelphia Inquirer*, June 4, 1861.

p. 308 President Lincoln ordered the White House: *Lincoln Day by Day, 1861–1865*, 46–47.

p. 308 "died two months sooner": *Memoirs of Gustave Koerner*, 149.

INDEX